A HANDBOOK OF
PRACTICAL
BUSINESS
FINANCE

A HANDBOOK OF

PRACTICAL BUSINESS FINANCE

RAY FITZGERALD

SECOND EDITION

KOGAN
PAGE

First published in 1987 by The Irish Management Institute, Dublin
First published in Great Britain in 1990 by Kogan Page
Second edition published in 1992

Kogan Page Limited
120 Pentonville Road
London N1 9JN

© Ray Fitzgerald, 1990, 1992

British Library Cataloguing in Publication Data

A CIP catalogue record for this book is available from the British Library.

ISBN 0 7494 0800 6

Typeset by Advanced Filmsetters (Glasgow) Ltd.
Printed and bound in Great Britain by
Biddles Ltd., Guildford and King's Lynn

Contents

CONTENTS

Preface

Most people from a non-accounting background need a practical guide to finance to help them contribute effectively to planning control and decision making. This book was written to help such managers.

I have built a range of qualities into the book which, I believe, reflects the needs of a wide range of UK business people. These include:

1. Simple definitions and illustrations of all major financial terminology.

2. Detailed illustrations of the preparation, interpretation and action(s) prompted by different types of financial reports and analyses.

   The content is specifically designed to relate to principles, practice and legislation in the United Kingdom. As such, I believe it will be easy to apply the material learned in this book to the manager's own business. This is often difficult if using one of the excellent texts that are designed to service the needs of business people in a variety of international markets.

3. Bookkeeping issues are kept to the absolute minimum. Many excellent texts spend much time on the recording of business transactions. I believe that the vast majority of non-accounting managers wish to, and can, avoid involvement in bookkeeping. It only diverts time and energy from the more important tasks of formulating and implementing financial policy.

4. Coverage of a wide range of financial topics. In attempting to meet twin objectives of examining the crucial things that the business person needs to understand, and avoiding the risk that readers could be put off by the volume of information and illustrations, I have tried to steer a middle course. I hope that I succeeded in covering all the important and topical issues. In some cases I have suggested alternative sources of information for those who wish to examine a particular topic in greater detail now that the foundations are solidly laid.

I hope that a large number of business people will find these qualities attractive. In particular, I hope that they will study the whole book carefully, so as to be familiar with all the important terminology and be capable of identifying alternatives in various situations, and keep it on their office bookshelf. It is intended as a practical guide to financial decision making. It will need to be referred to, frequently, when carrying out key financial tasks, such as:

- correct interpretation of financial and management accounts;
- proper formulation of financial budgets;
- the use of costing in the decision-making process;
- the evaluation of capital investment opportunities;
- the raising of finance from economic sources and the avoidance of uneconomic ones;
- the management of foreign currency exposures as non-sterling transactions increase, etc.

I hope you will make this book a constant ally in years to come. This is particularly true, if your business is too small to justify the full-time employment of a skilled financial manager.

Good reading and financial decision making.

Ray Fitzgerald
December 1991

Acknowledgements

It took a great deal of help, tolerance and understanding on the part of a variety of people and organisations to bring this book to market. I would particularly single out the following: my wife and three sons who strongly supported my endeavours and accepted some inattention to family duties during the various stages; my employer who encouraged me to devote much time to bringing it to the technical quality that is so vital in a book of this type; the various specialists who assessed the text for technical accuracy and appropriateness of illustrations – Maitiu Breathnach and Robert Galligan of Price Waterhouse who checked the audit and tax areas, Derek Saunders of Ashridge Management College who checked the capital investment and ratio analysis material, Keith O'Byrne of Kredietbank who checked the foreign exchange issues, and Michael Phelan of CDEME (Ireland) Ltd who checked the merger and acquisition data; my publishers, printers and literary agent who helped me through the various complications involved in getting this book into the market place.

To all the above and the many colleagues and businesses whose ideas and practice I adopted in the text, I wish to express my warmest appreciation for their help and support along the way.

Chapter 1

Introduction

There are many books on finance for non-accounting managers available in the UK. Most of them focus on rules and concepts. The balance tends to be 70% concepts and 30% examples/applications. This book is different. The emphasis is on application. The principles that affect each topic area are developed. Then illustrations and advice, which dominate the text, are used to ensure that the reader will be able to apply the ideas as they are learned.

Financial management is not difficult. The one key rule is to make sure enough cash is coming in to cover your outgoings and to put a bit by for a rainy day. What makes it seem difficult is the use of jargon developed by experts to make it appear so. My major objective in writing this book is to help non-experts to understand the meaning of financial jargon, the techniques which the jargon describes, and the opportunities such techniques offer to improve financial performance.

The book is designed for people from non-accounting backgrounds who recognise that financial decision making is not the sole province of accountants. It is a task in which everyone responsible for creating or spending significant amounts of cash must participate. The book has been written for readers, from non-accounting backgrounds, who wish to make a worthwhile contribution to financial decision making. It will be particularly relevant to managers in organisations that:

1 Do not make enough sales to justify the cost of a professional finance manager. A non-expert must try to fit the accounting obligations into a diverse schedule in which other priorities may be regarded as more important.
2 Like to make fast creative financial decisions and are disenchanted with their conservative finance manager. When one or two attractive opportunities have been missed, due to agonising over proposals, a company may be tempted to by-pass the accounting function in making important corporate finance decisions.
3 Have a finance manager who views his or her role is just to keep the books and records accurately, and is not sufficiently active in the development of the organisation's financial capability.

INTRODUCTION

In these cases senior managers, responsible for significant movements of cash, must have the knowledge and skill to ensure that financial proposals will improve the profitability and stability of the business.

Crucial Errors in Finance

A number of major errors can leave an organisation exposed to the danger of a receivership or liquidation. I hope that the following brief summary of these errors will inspire you to study the causes and the ways of avoiding the consequences as explained in detail in subsequent chapters.

1 Borrowing too much.
2 Borrowing from expensive sources when cheaper ones are available. Small companies often pay very high interest rates on their borrowings, which their present and future profit potential cannot adequately service. It is sad but true that borrowing is cheaper and easier to arrange in large, established, profitable businesses, and dearer and more difficult to arrange in recently established, smaller or less profitable businesses. Many of the most attractive funding forms are totally closed to small business borrowers.
3 Committing a business to repay borrowings more quickly than the future cash availability will permit. (Would you raise a £500,000 overdraft to acquire an apartment in London's Dockland?)
4 Spending too lavishly. This can include:
   ● Making or buying products or services that your customers do not want;
   ● Palatial offices, equipment, vehicles and so on that the business cannot afford. (This is often a smokescreen used by businesses in trouble. Shrewd bankers see through it. Management would be wiser to aim for a modest survival than a lavish route into liquidation.); and
   ● Inattention to cost control. Examples include: poor productivity, excessive waste, pilferage, breakage, rework etc., and assumptions like 'if we spend 5% more than last year on XXXXXXX we will be doing well!'
5 Not keeping the product range and manufacturing technology up to date.
6 Failure to ensure an adequate contribution from the owners of the business towards the cost of identifying and launching new products or services. Owners contribute in two ways. They can be asked: (a) not to withdraw too much profit (some must be

retained to share in financing expansion or modernisation); and (b) to give more capital to the business (this is called a rights issue – shareholders are given the right to buy new shares in proportion to their existing holdings). These requests may fall on deaf ears if the past profits (the only justification for their existing investment) have been disappointing, or the future prospects are discouraging.

7   Overdependence on one customer. The business can be squeezed for excessive credit or discounts and if the customer collapses the consequent bad debt may wipe it out.

8   Poor control of high-risk business development. Examples include inappropriate takeovers, currency or commodity speculation, and ill conceived capital investments.

These faults are easy to list. They are not easily identified in a business enterprise. If they are identified a strategy will have to be developed to eliminate or mitigate them. Such a strategy will emerge as you work your way through the pages of this book.

The Content and Sequence of the Book

The first section of the book is designed to give readers a thorough understanding of the purpose and content of financial statements and the ways of putting correct £ values on the items in the statements.
Chapter 2: The Balance Sheet.
The concept of balance; the classification of items; the valuation process; layouts in frequent use.
Chapter 3: The Profit and Loss Account.
The concept of profit or loss; measurement of income and expenditure; layouts in frequent use.
Chapter 4: Cash Flow Statements.
Identification of cash flows, interpretation of cash flows, abuse of short-term inflows.
Chapter 5: Cash Forecasting.
Forecasting cash movements in and out of a business; negotiating borrowings to cover cash requirements.

Section two deals with testing financial statements for strengths and weaknesses and developing plans to build on the strengths and minimise the impact of the weaknesses. It is akin to a medical examination which helps a manager to write a prescription for financial health in a business.
Chapter 6: Ratio Analysis.
Testing the acceptability of relationships between figures in financial

15

statements; comparison of ratios over time to assess progress; contrasting ratios with those of similar businesses.

Chapter 7: Working Capital.

Assessment of the funds required to create future sales and cash collections (the working capital requirement); ratios that test the management of working capital; techniques that help to optimise the working capital investment.

Section three examines how to plan and control the finances of a business.

Chapter 8: Budgeting.

The purpose(s) of budgeting; the timetable for budgeting; the sequence and process used in developing challenging but attainable budgets; testing plans for acceptability against ratio and funds flow criteria.

Chapter 9: Financial Control.

Comparison of budget against actual performance; the steps required to capitalise on favourable variances and minimise unfavourable ones. Revision of estimates of future profit and cash requirements.

Chapter 10: Total Costing Systems.

Allocation of the cost of running a business to the products or services it creates and sells; comparison of cost against market price; steps that can be taken where costings are out of line with market prices; activity based costing; transfer pricing.

Chapter 11: Contribution Costing.

Classification of costs (fixed and variable); development of break-even and profit targets in single- and multi-product businesses; appropriate cost structures for boom and recession.

Section four deals with corporate finance techniques designed to develop the organisation.

Chapter 12: Capital Investment Decisions.

Compound interest and discount interest; forecasting cash flows; testing the cash flows against payback, return on investment, net present value and internal rate of return criteria; the cost of capital; capital rationing; risk and uncertainty.

Chapter 13: Foreign Currency Transactions.

Buying, selling, borrowing and investing in foreign currencies; managing exchange risk; conversion of foreign currency transactions into sterling for financial and management accounts.

Chapter 14: Mergers and Takeovers.

Valuation of a business (vendor and purchaser perspective); advantages, disadvantages and risks involved in takeovers; mergers and acquisitions; types of takeover likely to succeed and fail.

Chapter 15: Any Other Business.
Managing corporation tax; group accounts; finance leases; operating leases; matters of life and death for a business.

Matters Not Included in the Book

1   Detailed analysis of the methodology of bookkeeping. Most business managers don't need to understand and involve themselves in recording transactions. Those who wish to get involved in bookkeeping will find that there are many suitable textbooks and courses available. We start with the output from bookkeeping. This is when senior managers become involved in financial planning, control and decision making.
2   Conceptual frameworks that form part of some academic treatments of finance but are rarely used in practice. I concentrate on methodologies that are tried and tested and extensively used in UK industry.
3   Financial manipulation aimed at prolonging the life of a dying business and fraudulent treatment of lenders and customers.
4   Financial statements other than those of limited companies and public limited companies. Business promoters are advised to seek the protection of limited liability where permitted.

Using the Book

The book is designed to provide a comprehensive understanding of practical finance. Three major points about using the book effectively are:

1   You cannot expect to retain all the relevant information from one quick reading. Deep concentration is required to derive full value from the content. A number of short reading sessions spread over several weeks is recommended. Many chapters will provide additional insights at a second reading.
2   It is unlikely that you can remember and apply all the concepts as you work through the book. I hope you will find a space for the book on your office bookshelf and revisit it frequently, to remind yourself of the relevant practice, as important issues arise.
3   To get the best out of the book a reader must trace his or her way through the illustrations very carefully, not simply read them like a novel. If an illustration is difficult to understand or apply in your company, ask a friend or colleague, with a sound financial knowledge, for a little help.

INTRODUCTION

The world of corporate finance is changing rapidly. Even since the copy for the hardback edition of this book was submitted in September 1989 significant changes have taken place. These include: (a) a new accounting standard on segmental reporting and a revised one for government grants; (b) seven Exposure Drafts that are in the process of obtaining or reviewing commentators' opinions prior to modification and/or issue as accounting standards; (c) an increased rate of VAT and a reduced rate of corporation tax; and (d) the blossoming of a savage economic recession which has killed or severely wounded huge numbers of UK businesses including many 'household' names.

Many further changes can be predicted. Hopefully the arrival of a more stable business climate will be an early arrival. Other predictions, that hardly require a crystal ball, include changes in taxation as part of EC harmonisation, adjustments to accounting regulations as variations compared to other countries are ironed out, movement towards a more structured European trading currency and mega-mergers as a result of the increasing emphasis on a single Europe. There is, too, an increasing demand that accountants should help to make accounts more meaningful and to provide clearer insights into what is really happening in the business that is being reported.

The list is terrifying. Some vital issues of the 1990s will inevitably not be addressed in this book. Some illustrations will become dated and irrelevant. We cannot afford to wait until the situation stabilises. It never will. However, 90% of the content will, I hope, be as relevant in five years' time as it is now. The effective manager will understand and apply this 90%. He or she will also monitor changes in business thinking and legislation that affect planning control and decision making as they emerge.

I wish you good reading and good fortune in applying the ideas which I hope will help you to survive and thrive in the battleground of business.

Chapter 2

The Balance Sheet

The balance sheet of a business enterprise is probably its most important financial statement. It discloses what a business owns (assets) and how the ownership of the assets is financed (liabilities and shareholders' funds) at a particular date. The term balance sheet is appropriate. The assets must always be matched by an equal amount of funding (provided by the owners and lenders of various kinds).

This framework needs to be clearly understood. There are several serious misconceptions about the content of a balance sheet. First, a balance sheet values the assets on a going concern basis. It does not attempt to show their disposal value. For example, John Bermingham recently started a manufacturing business. He bought a machine for £25,000. John expects the machine to produce goods for profitable sale over the next five years. In preparing his balance sheet after one year in business, John might value the machine at £20,000. He would argue that four-fifths of its useful life (and ongoing value to the business) remained. The fact that the machine might realise £10,000 if sold is not relevant. John has no intention of selling it. He uses a going concern valuation. Note that if the business was in serious financial difficulties John could not justify this value. The machine would probably have to be sold, to repay a secured lender. A going concern value would not be appropriate.

The second misconception concerns the fact that the value of some of the assets in a balance sheet varies significantly at different times in the year. This can result in major changes in the size of the total assets and the level of borrowings to support them. Consider a business, the major asset of which is a crop which, when harvested at the end of September, yields 12,000 tonnes, costing £10 each. This crop is expected to be sold at the rate of 1000 tonnes per month. The balance sheet at various stages during the year would show:

THE BALANCE SHEET

	30 September	31 December	31 March	30 June
Stock	120,000	90,000	60,000	30,000
Financed by:				
Owners' funds	30,000	30,000	30,000	30,000
Bank overdraft	90,000	60,000	30,000	–
	120,000	90,000	60,000	30,000

If the business published its balance sheet as at 30 June, it would show a low stock investment and no bank overdraft. If it published the figures as at 30 September, it would show four times as great a stock figure and a large bank overdraft (three times as great as the owners' funds).

Two major points emerge from this example. First, a company in this type of business would be unwise to publish its balance sheet as at 30 September. Bank borrowings are too high at that time. People, not fully aware of the seasonal nature of the stockholding, would categorise the business as high risk. By publishing as at 30 June, the business appears more stable and superficial analysts would classify it as secure. The sensible business will set a balance sheet date when the assets are low. Secondly, an outsider examining the 30 June balance sheet would be wise to pose the question: 'How typical is the asset and borrowing pattern as disclosed?' An analyst who understood the seasonal pattern should be able to conclude that the stock was probably four times greater the previous September and that this would have necessitated high borrowings. This could be partly verified by checking the interest charge in the profit and loss account. This is an intelligent interpretation of the results. The management and the balance sheet will not draw attention to the size of high-season borrowings.

Once these reservations about the usefulness of a balance sheet are properly understood, we can proceed to examine its components.

The Assets

The assets in a balance sheet are classified in two major groupings: fixed assets and current assets.

A new definition of fixed assets emerged in the Companies Act 1985, Schedule 4, Paragraph 75: 'Assets of a company shall be taken to be fixed assets if they are intended for use on a continuing basis in the company's activities. Any assets not intended for such use shall be taken to be current assets.'

Tangible Fixed Assets

Some fixed assets are tangible assets which we acquire intending to keep and use in the business for a long time. The machine that John Bermingham bought is a tangible fixed asset.

John spent £25,000 on the machine. He will not charge the full amount against the income of his first year in business. To do so would result in low profits in years where he buys a machine and high ones in other years. John will carry the machine in his balance sheet and charge depreciation as a running expense. This has the effect of spreading the loss of value involved in using it in the business over its useful life. The result is more stable profitability and a balance sheet that reflects the ongoing earnings potential.

The types of tangible fixed assets frequently encountered in a balance sheet are: land, plant and machinery, fixtures and fittings, freehold and leasehold buildings, vehicles and office equipment. All of these items except land (other than land from which minerals are extracted resulting in a permanent reduction in value) will decline in value due to their use in the business. They should be subjected to depreciation charges to reflect this decline. In framing the depreciation charges, management will have to consider the following issues:

1 How long will an asset be capable of being used in the business?
2 Is it likely that the asset will become obsolete before its useful life has ended?
3 What are the probable proceeds from disposal when the asset ceases to be used?

When these questions are answered, a suitable depreciation policy will emerge. Let us consider John's machine. John purchased it for £25,000. He believes he will be able to use it for five years, that it will not become obsolete before this period ends and that the disposal value will be £5,000. The depreciation could be calculated on a straight line basis (the most frequent approach):

$$\frac{\text{cost} - \text{disposal value}}{\text{working life}} = \frac{£25,000 - £5,000}{5} = £4,000$$

The balance sheet (in £'000) on the date of purchase and in subsequent years would include:

	Day 1	Year 1	Year 2	Year 3	Year 4	Year 5
Machine at cost	25	25	25	25	25	25
Aggregate depreciation		4	8	12	16	20
Book value	25	21	17	13	9	5

Only in five years' time will the book value attempt to approximate the market worth of the machine. The tax authorities will not recognise the accounting depreciation as a deductible expense in computing the tax liability. They allow a writing down allowance instead.

The £4000 depreciation will be treated as a running expense each year. This apparent overstatement of the running cost is aimed at conserving cash for replacement. If this cash were not conserved, John might be misled into withdrawing money from the business which he will subsequently need to replace the worn out machine. Depreciation is charged to avoid this danger.

It should be noted that charging depreciation does not of itself guarantee a replacement fund. First, rising replacement costs could mean that the sum of the depreciation funds and the proceeds from disposal will not be sufficient to finance a new machine and, secondly, the creation of a depreciation pool does not stop an imprudent proprietor from using these funds for other purposes. To protect the substance of his business John will have to ensure that adequate funds are available for replacing the machine when it is worn out. The key issue for John is that he must either conserve cash or systematically reduce borrowings to a level from which they will be permitted to increase when he needs to buy a replacement machine. This point is often misunderstood by business managers. If they cannot obtain adequate funds for replacement they may be forced to rely on worn out or technologically obsolete assets. Then running costs become uncompetitive. The business will be on the slippery slope towards liquidation.

Discussion of other fixed assets (intangibles and long-term investments) is covered later in the chapter.

Current Assets

Current assets include cash and other items which can reasonably be expected to turn into cash within one year of the balance sheet date. The major items found in current assets are material stocks, work in progress, finished stocks, trade debtors, staff loans, prepayments, cash balances, bank balances and short-term investments. To illustrate the main items, we will look at the plans for the first 18 weeks in the life of John's business:

Week	Unit Material Purchases	Unit Production Completed	Unit Work in Progress	Unit Sales
1	1,000	60	20	40
2	100	80	20	40
3–6	100	110	20	55
7–10	120	120	20	90
11–15	150	135	20	140
16–18	180	150	30	175

	£
Material cost per unit	10
Production cost per unit	2
Selling price per unit	14

Where items are in process, at the end of a week £1 per unit of the production cost will have been spent. A further £1 per unit will be spent in completing them the following week. Customers are expected to pay in the seventh week after sale.

Assuming that John commenced business with £30,000, his current asset position after nine weeks, if things go as planned will be:

	£
Raw material stock	9,000
Work in progress	220
Finished stock	4,440
Trade debtors	6,090
Cash	11,390
	31,140

John now has £1,140 additional current assets. This is because he made a profit of £2 on each of the 570 items he sold in the first nine weeks of operations. The various figures are arrived at as described below.

Material Stock

Week	Units Purchased	Units Issued	Closing Material Stock	Unit Cost £	Stock Value £
1	1,000	80[a]	920	10	9,200
2	100	80	940	10	9,400
3	100	110	930	10	9,300
4	100	110	920	10	9,200
5	100	110	910	10	9,100
6	100	110	900	10	9,000
7	120	120	900	10	9,000
8	120	120	900	10	9,000
9	120	120	900	10	9,000
	1,860	960			

[a] 60 were produced and the work in progress was 20 units. The issues must have been 80 units in week 1.

Work in progress: 20 items are in progress each week. They are valued at the full material cost of £10 and 50% of the production cost (manufacture half completed). The material stock is valued at £10 per unit. The 20 items in progress are valued at £11 per unit. (The rules on stock valuation will be discussed in detail in Chapter 3.)

Finished Stock

Week	Units Produced	Units Sold	Closing Units	Unit Cost £	Stock Value £
1	60[a]	40	20	12	240
2	80	40	60	12	720
3	110	55	115	12	1,380
4	110	55	170	12	2,040
5	110	55	225	12	2,700
6	110	55	280	12	3,360
7	120	90	310	12	3,720
8	120	90	340	12	4,080
9	120	90	370	12	4,440
	940	570			

[a] 80 were issued to production. The work in progress was 20 units. 60 units were completed in week 1.

The finished stock is valued at £12 per unit. £10 of this is the material cost and £2 is the production cost.

Sales and Debtors

Week	Units Sold	Unit Price £	Sales Revenue £	Cash Collected £	Debtors £
1	40	14	560	–	560
2	40	14	560	–	1,120
3	55	14	770	–	1,890
4	55	14	770	–	2,660
5	55	14	770	–	3,430
6	55	14	770	–	4,200
7	90	14	1,260	560	4,900
8	90	14	1,260	560	5,600
9	90	14	1,260	770	6,090
	570		7,980	1,890	

No cash is collected until week seven. The amount owed by customers, called trade debtors, rises to £4200 during the first six weeks. The collections in subsequent weeks, being six weeks behind the rising sales, increase the trade debtors to £6,090 at the end of week nine.

Cash

Week	Opening Cash £	Payments Suppliers £	Payments Production £	Customer Collections £	Closing Cash £
1	30,000	(10,000)	(140)	–	19,860
2	19,860	(1,000)	(160)	–	18,700
3	18,700	(1,000)	(220)	–	17,480
4	17,480	(1,000)	(220)	–	16,260
5	16,260	(1,000)	(220)	–	15,040
6	15,040	(1,000)	(220)	–	13,820
7	13,820	(1,200)	(240)	560	12,940
8	12,940	(1,200)	(240)	560	12,060
9	12,060	(1,200)	(240)	770	11,390
		(18,600)	(1,900)	1,890	

This table shows the frightening speed at which cash is consumed in John Bermingham's business. The main reason is that he has to pay for

25

his materials and his production expenses, while his receipts from customers are delayed by six weeks. If the business continues to grow John could be in danger of running out of cash.

You should now try to prepare similar tables for weeks 10 to 18 and John's current asset position after 18 weeks. This will help you to understand the effect of these key items on the balance sheet of a business. The results are reproduced in the next section so that you can check your workings.

Current assets, John Bermingham week 18

	£
Raw materials stocks	10,550
Work in progress	330
Finished goods	3,600
Trade debtors	13,230
Cash	6,060
	33,770

Once again the basis for these totals is described below.

Material Stock

Week	Units Purchased	Units Issued	Closing Material Stock	Unit Cost	Stock Value
10	120	120	900	10	9,000
11	150	135	915	10	9,150
12	150	135	930	10	9,300
13	150	135	945	10	9,450
14	150	135	960	10	9,600
15	150	135	975	10	9,750
16	180	160[a]	995	10	9,950
17	180	150	1,025	10	10,250
18	180	150	1,055[b]	10	10,550
	1,410	1,255			

[a] 150 units were produced and the work in progress increased to 30 units. The issues must have been 160 units in week 16.
[b] John expects to start week 10 with 900 items in stock. Purchases exceed sales by 155 in the next 9 weeks. His unit closing stock must be 1,055.

Work in progress: The work in progress rose to 30 items in week 16.

26

They are valued at the full material cost of £10 and 50% of the production cost (manufacture half completed); 30 items at £11 each = £330.

Finished Stock

Week	Units Produced	Units Sold	Closing Units	Unit Cost £	Stock Value £
10	120	90	400	12	4,800
11	135	140	395	12	4,740
12	135	140	390	12	4,680
13	135	140	385	12	4,620
14	135	140	380	12	4,560
15	135	140	375	12	4,500
16	150[a]	175	350	12	4,200
17	150	175	325	12	3,900
18	150	175	300[b]	12	3,600
	1,245	1,315			

[a] 160 units were issued to production. The work in progress increased to 30 units. 150 units were completed in week 16.
[b] John expects to start week 10 with 370 items in stock. Sales exceed production by 70 in the next 9 weeks. His unit closing stock must be 300.

Sales and Debtors

Week	Units Sold	Unit Price £	Sales Revenue £	Cash Collected £	Debtors £
10	90	14	1,260	770	6,580
11	140	14	1,960	770	7,770
12	140	14	1,960	770	8,960
13	140	14	1,960	1,260	9,660
14	140	14	1,960	1,260	10,360
15	140	14	1,960	1,260	11,060
16	175	14	2,450	1,260	12,250
17	175	14	2,450	1,960	12,740
18	175	14	2,450	1,960	13,230[a]
	1,315		18,410	11,270	

[a] At the end of week 9 customers owed £6,090. Sales for the next nine weeks exceeded collections by £7,140. John is now owed £13,230 by his customers.

Cash

Week	Opening Cash	Payments		Customer Collections	Closing Cash
		Suppliers	Production		
10	11,390	(1,200)	(240)	770	10,720
11	10,720	(1,500)	(270)	770	9,720
12	9,720	(1,500)	(270)	770	8,720
13	8,720	(1,500)	(270)	1,260	8,210
14	8,210	(1,500)	(270)	1,260	7,700
15	7,700	(1,500)	(270)	1,260	7,190
16	7,190	(1,800)	(310)	1,260	6,340
17	6,340	(1,800)	(300)	1,960	6,200
18	6,200	(1,800)	(300)	1,960	6,060

A further £5,330 of John's cash balance was used in this nine week period. He is in serious danger of running out of cash.

The decline in cash will be examined in detail in Chapter 7 when we look at working capital management. John faces a further problem. He needs to buy the machine and other fixed assets to achieve the production and sales. The estimated cash costs for the other items total £40,000 (premises £30,000 and motor vehicle £10,000). John will also have to pay an insurance premium of £520 for one year, in advance. In accounting, prepayments of this kind are charged against profits at the rate of £20 per week. The unexpired balance is treated as a current asset in the balance sheet.

These assets, combined with the cost of the machine and the investment in current assets will require more than John's available capital. He will need to arrange extra finance if the business is to survive and develop.

Financing the Assets

CREDIT FROM SUPPLIERS

John should try to arrange credit from suppliers to help finance the stocks. If six weeks' credit could be obtained, it would slow down the cash decline. He would start paying his supplier £10,000 in week seven rather than week one. At the end of 18 weeks he would not yet have paid for supplies bought in weeks 13 to 18. The cash situation would improve as follows:

	£	£
Original closing cash		6,060
Unpaid amounts: Week		
13	1,500	
14	1,500	
15	1,500	
16	1,800	
17	1,800	
18	1,800	9,900
Revised closing cash		15,960

The £9,900 not yet paid to suppliers would be shown in his balance sheet as an amount due and payable in under one year. Unpaid suppliers are called trade creditors.

MORTGAGES

A building society or bank might be prepared to arrange a mortgage or other loan to cover part of the premises cost. An 80% loan would provide £24,000 of the cost.

GOVERNMENT GRANTS

If John starts his business in a 'development area', he will be able to obtain a grant of 15% towards the cost of new buildings and plant. SSAP 4 requires that, in the balance sheet, such grants are recorded as deferred income rather than as a reduction from the cost of the related asset. This is necessary to comply with paragraphs 17 and 26 of schedule 4 to the Companies Act 1985. The main requirements of SSAP 4 are:

A Fixed assets should be shown at purchase price or production cost.
B Depreciation based on this cost must be deducted to provide the book value.
C Grants which contribute towards specific expenditure on fixed assets must be released to profit and loss over the expected lives of the related assets.
D Deferred credits in respect of grants must be included under the heading 'Accruals and deferred income' and identified separately in a note to the balance sheet.
E The total amount credited to profit and loss account in respect of grants should be disclosed in a note to the profit and loss account.

29

F   Potential liabilities to repay grants in specified circumstances should, if necessary, be disclosed in accordance with SSAP 18 (Accounting for contingencies).

Grant Illustration

A company has just purchased a machine at a cost of £100,000. It obtained a capital grant of 15%. The grant agreement specified that it would be repayable in full if the asset was disposed of within five years and that the amount repayable on disposal would decline at a rate of 20% per annum thereafter. The machine will have a ten year life and zero disposal value.

Balance Sheet Disclosure

Year	Fixed Asset at Cost	Aggregate Depreciation	Book Value	Deferred Credit	Contingent Grant Liability
0	100,000	–	100,000	15,000	15,000
1	100,000	10,000	90,000	13,500	15,000
2	100,000	20,000	80,000	12,000	15,000
3	100,000	30,000	70,000	10,500	15,000
4	100,000	40,000	60,000	9,000	15,000
5	100,000	50,000	50,000	7,500	15,000
6	100,000	60,000	40,000	6,000	12,000
7	100,000	70,000	30,000	4,500	9,000
8	100,000	80,000	20,000	3,000	6,000
9	100,000	90,000	10,000	1,500	3,000
10	100,000	100,000	–	–	–
Rule	A	B		D	F

The company provides £10,000 per annum for depreciation but offsets £1,500 of this by reducing the amount of deferred credit each year. The contingent liability will be disclosed in the notes to the accounts (rule F). The depreciated liability will be shown as a deferred credit in the funding section of the balance sheet (rule D).

   This treatment would not be used if it was felt that a 'going concern' approach could not be justified. The liability would be real rather than potential.

BANK TERM LOANS AND OVERDRAFTS

John might also apply for a bank loan to help with the funding. Let us assume that £16,000 is required from a bank. The bank will look for the following:

1 A presentation about John's business to persuade them that it is a good risk. This will cover the management, the technology, the competition and the prospects for financial stability and profitability.
2 Security to protect them against loss if the business fails. Security is normally sought by way of a first claim on assets in liquidation and personal guarantees from the owners.
3 A good indication of when the funding will no longer be required. It is vital to realise that bank overdraft funding is repayable at the call of the lender. John will not be able to repay on demand so he should seek a long-term loan.

HIRE PURCHASE

If a bank loan is not available, John might obtain hire purchase finance for the car and/or machinery. The interest rate on hire purchase loans is high and John should avoid it if cheaper funds are available.

ACCRUALS

Not all the expenses of a business are paid for as value is received. Items such as telephone bills, bank interest etc. are charged in arrears. This legitimate delay in settlement will conserve John's cash. Nevertheless the amounts are owed by the organisation and the liability must be accrued in the balance sheet. It is due and payable in under one year and will be charged as an expense in measuring profit or loss.

Classification of Liabilities

Liabilities are amounts that a business owes. Some liabilities are short term in nature (e.g., bank overdrafts, trade creditors and accruals) – others are longer term (e.g., debentures and term loans). In accounting, any liability that is due and payable in under one year must be classified as such in the balance sheet. Many companies continue to use the name current liabilities to describe these items. They indicate a short-term pressure on the cash resources of a business. Sums due beyond one year must also be classified as such.

Provision must be made for other liabilities (notable among which is deferred taxation). This will be discussed later in the chapter.

The Companies Act 1985 permits two balance sheet layouts:

Balance Sheet, John Bermingham as at Week 18 (Layout One)

	£	£
Fixed assets		
Building	30,000	
Plant[1]	25,000	
Vehicle[1]	10,000	65,000
Current assets		
Stocks	14,480	
Debtors	13,230	
Insurance prepaid[3]	340	
Cash[2]	440	28,490
		93,490
Financed by:		
Creditors due within one year		
Trade creditors		9,900
Creditors due beyond one year		
Mortgage	24,000	
Term loan	16,000	
Government grant[1]	10,000	50,000
Shareholders' funds		
Share capital	30,000	
Retained profit[3]	3,590	33,590
		93,490

[1] Depreciation ignored.
[2] Too little to cover unexpected problems. The amount is made up as follows:

	Plus	Minus
Capital introduced	30,000	
Mortgage introduced	24,000	
Term loan introduced	16,000	
Grants received	10,000	
Collection from customers[a]	13,160	
Paid for materials[b]		22,800
Paid for conversion[c]		4,400
Insurance		520
Fixed assets		65,000
Cash remaining	–	440
	93,160	93,160

[a] Sales £26,390 less debtors £13,230 = £13,160 collected.
[b] Purchases £32,700 less creditors £9,900 = £22,800 paid.
[c] Production units 2185 at £2 each.   £4,370
　　Work in progress 30 at £1.   £　30
　　　　　　　　　　　　　　　　£4,400

[3] John sold 1885 items. He made a profit of £2 on each. His profit would have been £3,770, but he should charge 18 weeks insurance against this at £10 per week. This leaves a profit of £3,590. Note that the insurance for the next 34 weeks remains prepaid in his current assets.

Balance Sheet, John Bermingham as at Week 18 (Layout Two)

	£	£	£
Fixed assets			
Building	30,000		
Plant	25,000		
Vehicle	10,000		65,000
Current assets			
Stocks	14,480		
Debtors	13,230		
Insurance prepaid	340		
Cash	440	28,490	
Creditors due within one year			
Trade creditors		9,900	18,590
			83,590
Financed by:			
Creditors due beyond one year			
Mortgage		24,000	
Term loan		16,000	
Government grant		10,000	50,000
Shareholders' funds			
Share capital		30,000	
Retained profit		3,590	33,590
			83,590

Layout one shows the total assets and how they are financed. Layout two shows the net assets (after deducting short-term liabilities) and how they are financed. Most organisations use layout two but I prefer layout one. It highlights the total assets of a business and it also corresponds with disclosure in the USA.

Comments on Other Liabilities

The amounts due and payable in under one year will often include the following headings: accruals (light, bank interest, phone, etc.); bank overdrafts; unpaid PAYE and VAT; customer deposits; corporation tax; dividends proposed but not paid; and a portion of term loans, hire purchase loans, mortgages and debentures and finance leases.

The amounts due and payable in beyond one year often include the following: mortgages; term loans; hire purchase finance; grants; loan stocks; finance leases; and debentures. The amounts due and payable in beyond one year, excluding interest (it has not been earned by the lender), will be included in each case.

In the provisions for liabilities and charges, we may find deferred tax and provisions for extraordinary items.

DEDUCTIONS/CHARGES

A business should deduct PAYE, social security and National Insurance contributions from its employees. Similarly, most businesses are obliged to charge VAT to their customers. Payroll deductions must be remitted in the following month. VAT is usually payable, for each quarter, in the month following the end of the quarter. A business will have the use of these funds, until they become payable. After deduction, but before settlement, such items are amounts due and payable in under one year. Failure to remit them to the Revenue Commissioners by the due date will expose an organisation to substantial interest charges.

CUSTOMER DEPOSITS

In some cases a business may require advance payments from its customers. If value has not been given to the customers at the balance sheet date, then the customers are owed money (or value). They are treated as creditors and shown separately as amounts due and payable in under one year.

CORPORATION TAX

If a corporate entity makes a profit, it will normally be liable to corporation tax. The tax becomes due for payment nine months after the end of the financial year. It is deducted from the profits and is placed in amounts due and payable in under one year. Not all expenses charged against profits are allowed as deductions for corporation tax purposes. (Readers who wish to examine this issue in detail are directed towards *Corporation Tax* by HCD Rankin and DM Catterall, published by Macmillan Education Ltd.)

PROPOSED DIVIDENDS

The owners of a profitable business expect a cash reward for their investment. This reward is made by way of dividend. A successful business will usually set aside some profit after tax for payment to shareholders. It is deducted from the profit and loss account and is included in amounts due and payable in under one year. It will normally be approved by shareholders at the annual general meeting and be paid to them soon afterwards.

TERM LOANS

A term loan commits an organisation to periodic repayments of capital and interest. The capital element is a liability and must be shown in the balance sheet. Interest accrued but not necessarily payable at the moment is also a liability. The treatment is shown in the following illustration.

On 1 July, 1989 a company negotiated a term loan of £100,000 from its bankers. The loan was repayable in five equal annual instalments including interest at 16%. Compound interest tables (discussed briefly in Chapter 12) will indicate a repayment of £30,541 per annum.

Term Loan Repayment Schedule

	Opening Loan (A)	Interest (A×16%=B)	Loan and Interest (A+B=C)	Repaid (D)	Closing Loan (C−D=E)
1 July, 1989	100,000	16,000	116,000	30,541	85,459[1]
1 July, 1990	85,459	13,673	99,132	30,541	68,591
1 July, 1991	68,591	10,975	79,566	30,541	49,025
1 July, 1992	49,025	7,844	56,869	30,541	26,328
1 July, 1993	26,328	4,213	30,541	30,541	–

[1] 30 June, 1990.

We can divide the annual repayments into capital and interest components:

	Total Repayment	Interest Component	Capital Component
30 June, 1990	30,541	16,000	14,541
30 June, 1991	30,541	13,673	16,868
30 June, 1992	30,541	10,975	19,566
30 June, 1993	30,541	7,844	22,697
30 June, 1994	30,541	4,213	26,328
	152,705	52,705	100,000

In the balance sheet as at 31 December the amounts due and payable in under and beyond one year are as follows:

| | Capital | | | Interest Accrued Under 1 Year |
	Under 1 Year	Beyond 1 Year	Total	
31 December, 1989	14,541	85,459	100,000	8,000
31 December, 1990	16,868	68,591	85,459	6,837
31 December, 1991	19,566	49,025	68,591	5,488
31 December, 1992	22,697	26,328	49,025	3,922
31 December, 1993	26,328	–	26,328	2,107

The figures in the total column of this statement are the same as in the first column of the repayment schedule. The figures for beyond one year are the same as the last column. The balance sheet is as at 31 December and a half year of interest is due. It is not payable until 30 June next. It is a cost of running the business for the six months since interest was last paid and must be accrued in amounts due and payable in under one year.

HIRE PURCHASE

If John Bermingham hire purchased the vehicle and committed his business to pay a 25% deposit and 12 quarterly repayments (including interest at a flat rate of 12% per annum), and VAT at 17.5% on the interest element, then the repayment obligations would be:

Cost of vehicle		10,000.00
Less deposit		2,500.00
		7,500.00
Interest[a]	2,700.00	
VAT[b]	472.50	3,172.50
Total instalments		10,672.50

Quarterly instalment (£10,672.50÷12) =   £889.30

[a] £7,500×12% for 3 years = £2,700.
[b] £2,700×17.5% = £472.50.

A simple way to calculate the capital repayment obligations is to use the 'rule of 78'. It works as follows:

Q	Gross Allocated	Gross Interest	Total Repaid	Capital Repaid	Capital Due	Under 1 Year	Beyond 1 Year
1	12/78	488[c]	889	401	7,099	2,012	5,087
2	11/78	447	889	442	6,657	2,175	4,482
3	10/78	407	890	483	6,174	2,337	3,837
4	9/78	366	889	523	5,651	2,500	3,151
5	8/78	325	889	564	5,087	2,663	2,424
6	7/78	285	890	605	4,482	2,825	1,657
7	6/78	244	889	645	3,837	2,988	849
8	5/78	203	889	686	3,151	3,151	–
9	4/78	163	890	727	2,424	2,424	–
10	3/78	122	889	767	1,657	1,657	–
11	2/78	81	889	808	849	849	–
12	1/78	41[d]	890	849	–	–	–
		3,172	10,672	7,500			

The capital repayments would be included in the balance sheet as per the last two columns. The interest is charged against the profit and loss account (after deducting VAT, which would be offset against the amount charged to customers). The allocation of interest, using the rule of 78 is:

[c] $£3,172.50 \times 12 \div 78 = £488$.
[d] $£3,172.50 \times 1 \div 78 = £41$ etc.

DEBENTURES

A type of loan with special provisions whereby the trustees for the debenture holders can, in default of repayments of capital or interest, or the undermining of the security of lenders (as defined in the covenants contained in the loan agreement), appoint a receiver to manage the company so as to protect their interest. Long-term loans from financial institutions are often of debenture type. There are many similarities with mortgages. Variations include: fixed or floating interest rates; undated (no capital repayments); involving regular capital repayments; and total repayment at a defined future date.

Where capital repayments are involved in a debenture or mortgage, the liabilities are calculated and classified in the same way as with a term loan.

OTHER LIABILITIES

A variety of complicated items are frequently found in the balance sheet of large businesses. The major items (preference shares, loan stocks, deferred tax, finance leases and intangible assets) are dealt with in the appendix to this chapter.

Shareholders' Funds

This category of funding can be divided into five sections: ordinary share capital; revenue reserve; capital reserve; share premium; and capital redemption reserve.

Ordinary Share Capital

This is the nominal value of all shares issued by a business. They are usually £1 shares although nominal values of 50p or 10p are sometimes used. This will probably be the price at which an original share issue was made. The balance sheet value is not meant to reflect the market price of the shares. If the company is successful, the market value will rise above the nominal value. If it performs badly, the price may fall below the nominal value. The balance sheet reflects the nominal capital amount of the value received as a result of the share issue. The balance sheet, or supporting notes, will disclose both the authorised share capital, defined in the memorandum of association (the rule book of the company) and the issued share capital.

Say a company issued 1,000,000 £1 ordinary shares for cash at par. £1 will remain as the nominal value of the shares. A decision to subdivide the shares (for example, to give 2 shares of 50p each in exchange for 1 existing share of £1) simply changes the denomination, but not the amount of funds which the business can utilise. Equally a decision to consolidate the shares (for example, to give 1 share of £1 in exchange for 10 existing shares of 10p) changes the denomination, but not the amount of funds in the business. The issue of further shares at a later date would change the quantity of shares but not their nominal value.

Revenue Reserve

This is the sum of all undistributed profits (less losses) since the business started. By not taking the profits as dividends the shareholders contribute towards expansion. In John's balance sheet, earlier in the chapter, retained profit of £3,590 finances part of the assets. If John had withdrawn this profit for his own use his business could only have financed assets of £89,900. In the early life of a business, capital is frequently inadequate. Large borrowings are obtained to finance assets. If the business is successful and profits are retained, they can quickly increase the shareholders' funds to an acceptable level. Revenue reserves are often converted into share capital. This is done, through a bonus or capitalisation issue of free shares. The effect of a bonus issue is twofold:

1   It reduces the share price, but not the value of the underlying

shareholders' investment. This makes the shares more marketable. Many people would ask their stockbroker to buy 1,000 shares at £1 each, but would be reluctant to order 50 shares at £20 each, even though both orders would cost £1,000 plus expenses.

2 It increases lenders' confidence in their security. Lenders are wary of large revenue reserves. If they are used to pay dividends, the security of the lenders declines. They rightly regard share capital as more permanent and secure.

Capital Reserve

A capital reserve is a 'profit' which by law or good business practice will not be distributed to shareholders by way of dividend, through the profit and loss account. The sum of all such profits less losses since the business started is shown in capital reserve. The major way that a capital reserve arises is through an unrealised profit on revaluation of assets. Note that this could be an operating profit in a property business. In any other type of organisation, it would be a revaluation reserve and be included in capital reserves. The rules relating to revaluation of assets are contained in ED 51. Key provisions are:

1 The directors must determine for each category of fixed asset whether it is accounting policy to carry that class at cost or valuation.
2 A fixed asset should not be included in the balance sheet at a valuation undertaken more than five years previously.
3 Any surplus recognised in the valuation must be credited to revaluation reserve. Deficits recognised on valuation must be charged against the reserve.
4 Where there is a permanent diminution in the value of a fixed asset it should be recognised in the profit and loss account for the period in which it occurs.

ED 51 also includes detailed disclosure provisions designed to facilitate comparison between entities that carry assets at valuations and those that do not. These rules may need to be revised before becoming standard. They relate more to the 'integrity' of the historic cost system than to pragmatic assessment of business performance.

Suppose that Beta Ltd bought a property in January 1985 for £250,000. It was valued in the balance sheet at this amount, less depreciation (2% per annum straight line) in subsequent years. In January 1990 Beta Ltd obtained an independent professional valuation at £405,000. This is how the balance sheet would appear at the end of 1990 with and without the valuation:

Balance Sheet Extract

		Without Revaluation		With Revaluation
Cost	250,000			
Valuation			405,000	
Less aggregate depreciation	30,000	220,000	9,000	396,000
Cash		30,000		30,000
		250,000		426,000
Represented by:				
Share capital		250,000		250,000
Profit and loss reserve		–		(4,000)
Revaluation reserve		–		180,000[1]
		250,000		426,000

[1] Book value January 1990 $(£250,000-£25,000) = 225,000$
Valuation January 1990   405,000

Revaluation surplus   180,000

Profit and Loss Extract 1991

		Without Revaluation		With Revaluation
Cash income		5,000		5,000
Less depreciation	5,000		9,000[2]	
transfer to profit and loss reserve	–	5,000	4,000	5,000
Retained profit		–		–

[2] Depreciation calculations:
Historic cost £250,000 over 50 years = £5,000 per annum
Valuation £405,000 over 45 years = £9,000 per annum

The 'profit' on revaluation is not available for distribution. If the property was sold, any profit realised is exposed to capital gains tax. SSAP 15 requires the company to estimate the potential liability and make a deferred tax provision.

Share Premium

A share premium is the surplus over the nominal value of its shares which a company has been able to command on their issue. For example, a company started life with 100,000 shares of £1 each. It subsequently wished to raise further share capital for expansion and it was advised to offer each shareholder the right to buy one new share at £1.60 for each share held. If all the shareholders accepted the offer the company would raise £160,000. £100,000 would be the nominal value of the new shares. The remaining £60,000 would be a share premium. The costs of the issue (say £16,000) would be deducted from the share premium because the company really raised £144,000.

Capital Redemption Reserve

Where a public company buys back shares and does not replace their par value with the proceeds of a fresh issue, Section 170 of the Companies Act 1985 requires the transfer of an amount equivalent to their nominal value from the revenue reserves to a capital redemption reserve. This law is designed to protect other lenders against diminution of their security. In the case of redeemable preference shares it is wise to start providing for such transfer from the outset. On 1 January, 1990, Growth PLC issued £1 million of redeemable preference shares dated 1994. The company should replace these shareholders' funds from revenue reserves at £200,000 per annum, unless it intends to redeem them from the proceeds of a subsequent issue.

Valuation of Assets

As a general principle, the assets of a business will be valued at cost, unless they are worth less than this. We will now explore the valuation of various types of assets.

41

Valuing Assets

Asset	Basis of Valuation
Land	Land is usually valued at cost. It can be revalued, upwards on a professional valuer's certificate. It would be wrong to carry land at cost if it had declined in value. This frequently happens where the purchase price reflected some mineral worth that was subsequently extracted.
Freehold buildings	Freehold buildings are often valued at cost less depreciation. This can be a misleading representation of their real value. It is regarded as good practice to obtain a revaluation at least once every five years and to include this revised figure instead of cost. Freehold buildings are regarded as having a defined life. Depreciation must be provided.
Leasehold buildings	Leasehold buildings are also often valued at cost. They may also appreciate and can be uplifted on the basis of a professional valuation. Their life is clearly definable and depreciation must be provided.
Plant and machinery Vehicles Furniture and fittings Office equipment	All these items are prudently valued at cost less appropriate depreciation.
Stocks	SSAP 9 requires stock to be valued at the lower of cost or net realisable value. Some problems arise in the interpretation and application of this rule but the matter is most appropriately handled when reviewing the measurement of profit (see Chapter 3).
Debtors	The records of the company should disclose all amounts owed to the business. It is necessary to deduct amounts regarded as uncollectable. This could arise because of disputes or business failures.
Cash	Clearly, the easiest to value. You count it.
Bank balances	Not quite as easy as it seems. A bank statement reflects cashed cheques and lodgements. A balance sheet shows the amount according to the company's records not the bank's. If our books are properly kept we will know our balance and be able to explain any variations from the bank statement.

A Closer Look at Depreciation

Depreciation is the process by which a loss in value of fixed assets arising from their use in the business is recognised. The following illustrations will help explain the process.

Example 1

We have just obtained a 35-year lease on a building, paying a premium of £70,000 for the leasehold interest. The lease will decline in value as we move closer to its end. It would be foolish not to recognise this declining value. Depreciation is provided as follows:

$$\frac{\text{Cost of asset} - \text{disposal value}}{\text{life of asset}} = \text{annual depreciation}$$

In this case the disposal value is zero. The annual depreciation is £70,000 ÷ 35 = £2,000 per annum. The leasehold would be valued in the balance sheet as follows:

	Balance Sheets (£'000) Years After Acquisition					
	1	*2*	*5*	*15*	*25*	*35*
Leasehold interest at cost	70	70	70	70	70	70
Aggregate depreciation	2	4	10	30	50	70
Book value	68	66	60	40	20	–

The disposal value of the leasehold interest might be far greater than the book value. If 10 years later a professional valuation of £100,000 was obtained, it could be incorporated in the balance sheet. If this was done, subsequent depreciation would be £100,000 ÷ 25 = £4,000 per annum.

Example 2

Steady Ltd. bought a motor vehicle for £12,000. This company depreciates vehicles on a straight line basis over 4 years and assumes a disposal value which is 10% of cost. The depreciation provision is:

$$\frac{\text{Cost} - \text{disposal value}}{\text{life}} = \text{annual depreciation} = \frac{12,000 - 1,200}{4} = £2,700 \text{ per annum}$$

The balance sheet through the life of the vehicle shows:

	Day 1 £	Year 1 £	Year 2 £	Year 3 £	Year 4 £
Vehicle at cost	12,000	12,000	12,000	12,000	12,000
Aggregate depreciation	–	2,700	5,400	8,100	10,800
Book value	12,000	9,300	6,600	3,900	1,200

43

The figures are different for a competitor who uses a 40% disposal value and a 3-year life. They depreciate at £2,400 per annum and show:

	Day 1 £	Year 1 £	Year 2 £	Year 3 £
Vehicle at cost	12,000	12,000	12,000	12,000
Aggregate depreciation	–	2,400	4,800	7,200
Book value	12,000	9,600	7,200	4,800

If the vehicle was sold 3 years later for £4,000, we would make a profit of £100 on disposal, our competitor would make a loss of £800 on disposal. If the vehicle was sold for £5,000 in Year 3 the profit on disposal would be £1,100 and £200 respectively.

Example 3

We have just purchased a micro-computer for £5,000. We are advised that, with careful maintenance, it will last for 10 years. We would be foolish to depreciate it over this period. It seems abundantly clear that new developments will render the equipment obsolete more quickly. A three-year life, based on technological considerations rather than working capability, is sensible.

The calculation of depreciation provisions in these examples was done on a straight line basis. Other methods are sometimes used. They are more complicated and, in my opinion, less satisfactory.

THE PURPOSE OF DEPRECIATION

In conventional accounting, depreciation is designed to spread the loss of value from using an asset over its expected working life. This objective is met by:

1 Deducting the aggregate depreciation from the cost; and
2 Charging the annual depreciation as a running expense of the business. This *non-cash* charge is a source of extreme suspicion to those who do not properly understand it.

Let us consider a person who starts a taxi business. He buys a vehicle for £10,000 and runs it extensively for 3 years. He then sells it for £100. If he spent all the cash he earned during the three years, then part of his spending was really his initial capital. He will have no cash left with which to buy a replacement vehicle. To protect his capital, he must save £9,900. This can be done by setting a spending ceiling which is £3,300 lower than his earnings each year. Of course, with prices rising, he will still not save enough to enable him to replace the taxi. In conventional accounting he must recgonise the need to keep some of his profit to finance the increased cost of replacement. Inflation accounting would create higher depreciation charges, and, indeed, it was designed to earmark funds for replacement. In the absence of inflation-adjusted accounts, it is necessary for a business to retain profits so as to cover the increased cost of replacement.

What a Balance Sheet Does Not Tell You

A balance sheet will not show all the potential liabilities of a business. Some may only mature in unexpected circumstances – for example, contingent liabilities. Where a possible future loss may arise (e.g. as a result of a legal action), SSAP 18 requires that it be disclosed by way of note to the accounts. Similar examples include redundancy costs, losses on disposal of assets and liquidator's fees in a close down.

There is a more sinister way of excluding relevant information from financial statements. This is referred to as 'off-balance sheet finance'. It involves the creation of an artificial, but legal, structure designed to permit netting of assets and liabilities with a view to concealing debt. The most popular approach is to transfer legal title to a third party while the 'real' owner continues to bear the risks and enjoy the benefits related to such items. In March 1988 the Accounting Standards Committee issued ED 42. It was designed to tackle cases where devices were used to obscure the presentation of a 'true and fair view'. The response from the accounting profession was favourable, but indicated that more guidance was needed on the recognition of devices. In May 1990 the Accounting Standards Committee replaced ED 42 with the more detailed ED 49. This exposure draft, 'Reflecting the Substance of Transactions in Assets and Liabilities', is designed to help readers of financial statements to interpret them correctly. The key, and highly controversial, principle of ED 49 is that substance should take precedence over legal form. It proposes that where a complex transaction is entered into for the specific purpose of removing items from a balance sheet, such items should be restored to the balance sheet with the intention of providing 'a true and fair view'.

Examples of devices with a specific intent to remove items from a balance sheet include:

1 Finance leases. These have been specifically reinstated in the balance sheet courtesy of SSAP 21. This is dealt with in the appendix to this chapter and illustrated in Chapter 15.
2 Consignment stock. This is stock to which legal title does not transfer at point of delivery. The vital issue is to determine which balance sheet should include stock. The answer is that of the entity that bears the risks and rewards consistent with ownership. In principle this is the consignor, in practice it is often the consignee.
3 Sale and repurchase agreements. For example, disposal of trading stock to a third party, accompanied by an option to repurchase it for the same amount plus interest. Is such a transaction a bonafide sale or has it the characteristics of a secured loan? The answer is frequently a secured loan that must be reinstated.
4 Debt factoring. This involves the replacement of a group of debtors with one debtor, the factor. A problem only arises where factoring results in a speed up of cash collection. Has the enhanced cash flow the characteristics of a loan or of a reduction in trade debtors?
5 Quasi subsidiaries. This usually involves the creation of an entity which has all the attributes of a subsidiary except legal form. Assets and liabilities are transferred from the originator to its quasi subsidiary. Prior to the introduction of the exposure drafts the transferred items could have been netted and shown as an investment in the group accounts. ED 49 requires the asset and liability to be shown if the risks and rewards flow to the originator.
6 Loan transfers. These arise where a borrower lends part or all of the loan to a third party. Only when onerous tests (defined on page 48 of the ED) are satisfied can the asset be netted against the liability.

ED 49 has had a stormy reception from the legal profession. They argue that objectivity is best served by sticking to the letter of the law rather than following the 'substance over form' rule. A major battle between the professions is ongoing. The following is an example of off-balance sheet transactions:

The Tricky PLC Balance Sheet

	Pre-manoeuvres	Pre-ED	Post-ED
Buildings	2,000,000	–	2,000,000[1]
Less depreciation	200,000	–	200,000
Book value	1,800,000	–	1,800,000[1]
Investment	–	200,000[1]	–
Trading stock	500,000	–	500,000[2]
Short-term debt	–	–	(500,000)[2]
Cash	–	500,000[2]	500,000
	2,300,000	700,000	2,300,000
Financed by:			
Share capital	600,000	600,000	600,000
Reserves	300,000	100,000[1]	100,000
Minority interest	–	–	200,000[1]
Long-term debt	1,400,000	–	1,400,000[1]
	2,300,000	700,000	2,300,000

[1] The building and term loan were transferred to a friendly company. Tricky PLC holds 50% of the shares. It does not control the composition of the board of directors. This is the legal position. In reality Tricky PLC can buy back the building for £1.8M at any time. It must make the repayments on the term loan. Prior to the EDs the book value of the building and the term-loan obligations would have been removed from the balance sheet and replaced with an investment (50% of the net assets of the friendly company). Tricky PLC has apparently given away 50% of the net assets (£200,000); this 'loss' is deducted from reserves. The building and term loan are reinstated. A minority interest of £200,000 is included in the Tricky PLC balance sheet.

[2] Tricky PLC sold the trading stock to a third party. The stock remains on the premises of Tricky and they will sell it. As sales are made Tricky PLC pays the cost plus interest to a finance house. Tricky carries the risk or reaps the reward. Prior to the exposure drafts the stock would have been replaced with cash. The stock is reinstated but matched by a loan of a similar amount.

Prior to the exposure drafts the result of these manoeuvres would have been to convert a company that was substantially in debt into a cash-positive one. If ED 49 becomes law the 'true' situation on a 'substance over form' basis will emerge. In the meantime it has the status of good practice.

Summary

The balance sheet of a business shows its assets and how they are financed, at a particular point in time, on a going concern basis. If prepared one week earlier or later, it could disclose a very different picture, notably because of changes in the current assets and their corresponding financing. The content is broken into five broad categories. It makes no attempt to disclose the disposal value of the assets.

Some intricate issues encountered in balance sheets are covered in the appendix to this chapter. If you are eager to push on with the basics of finance, you may choose to pass on to Chapter 3 and return to this appendix later or when you encounter strange items in a balance sheet.

Appendix to Chapter 2

Other Balance Sheet Items

This appendix deals with some more complex items that may affect the balance sheet of a business. These are: preference shares (various types); loan stocks; deferred tax; finance leases; operating leases; investments in other businesses; intangible assets; and group accounts.

Preference Shares

Preference shares are a kind of half-way house between lending money to a business and providing ordinary share capital to it. They confer on the holders preferential rights: (a) to obtain a dividend before the ordinary shareholders (this is useful to them if there are only sufficient profits to justify the payment of preference dividend); and (b) to priority repayment of capital in a liquidation (this is attractive where some funds are available for shareholders but not enough for all). Preference shares have not been popular in recent years. Nevertheless, the balance sheets of many companies contain such shares issued in the past.

Types of preference share include:

(a) Cumulative preference shares. (If profits are insufficient to pay the dividend, it will become payable in a subsequent year assuming adequate profits are earned to cover the arrears and the current dividend.);

(b) Redeemable preference shares. (The company can buy them in at defined future date(s). This repurchase potential tends to protect the capital value when interest rates rise.);

(c) Participating preference shares. (As well as providing a preferential fixed dividend such shares entitle the holders to additional payment when the dividends on ordinary shares exceed a defined percentage.);

(d) Convertible preference shares. (These shares can be converted into ordinary shares on defined future dates at specified exchange rates. They can be attractive to both the company and the shareholders, where the funds are invested long term and profits from the investment are likely to grow significantly.)

Several of the above features can be combined, e.g. Cumulative Convertible preference shares.

Loan Stocks

Loan stocks are long-term funding, with priority over preference and ordinary shares for payment of interest and return of capital. Variations are similar to preference shares:

1 Fixed interest (e.g. 16%).
2 Variable interest (e.g. revised six monthly relative to London Interbank Offered Rate. For instance, LIBOR plus 2%).
3 Secured or unsecured.
4 Redeemable or irredeemable.
5 Convertible or non-convertible.

In view of the detailed treatment of preference shares, it is not necessary to illustrate conditions 1 to 5 above.

Deferred Tax

Expenditure charged against income in a profit and loss account is not always allowed as a deduction for corporation tax purposes. Where the allowance occurs in a different pattern rather than being disallowed it is called a timing difference. Such timing differences require a deferred tax provision to be made. Consider the following illustration:

Clock Ltd has just started in business. Its only fixed asset is plant purchased at a cost of £1M. This plant will have a life of five years and zero disposal value. Clock Ltd expects to earn a profit of £500,000 (before depreciation and tax) in each of the next five years. The following will be the after tax results if deferred tax is; (a) ignored, and (b) included:

Deferred Tax Ignored

Year	1	2	3	4	5	Total
Profit before tax[1]	300,000	300,000	300,000	300,000	300,000	1,500,000
Corporation tax[2]	82,500	103,125	118,594	130,195	60,586	495,000
Profit after tax	217,500	196,875	181,406	169,805	239,414	1,005,000

Deferred Tax Included

Year	1	2	3	4	5	Total
Profit before tax[1]	300,000	300,000	300,000	300,000	300,000	1,500,000
Corporation tax[2]	82,500	103,125	118,594	130,195	60,586	495,000
Deferred tax[3]	16,500	−4,125	−19,594	−31,195	38,414	−
	99,000	99,000	99,000	99,000	99,000	495,000
Profit after tax	201,000	201,000	201,000	201,000	201,000	1,005,000

[1] The accounting profit is £500,000 less depreciation £200,000.
[2] The corporation tax provisions will be:

Year	Profit before Depreciation	Writing Down Allowance[4]	Taxable Profit	Corporation Tax at 33%
1	500,000	250,000	250,000	82,500
2	500,000	187,500	312,500	103,125
3	500,000	140,625	359,375	118,594
4	500,000	105,469	394,531	130,195
5	500,000	316,406	183,594	60,586

The corporation tax liabilities will be due for payment nine months after the end of each financial year.
[3] The deferred tax adjustment (the difference between the depreciation charges and the writing down allowances), assuming a constant tax rate of 33% will be:

Year	Depreciation	WDA[4]	Difference	Deferred 33%
1	200,000	250,000	−50,000	−16,500
2	200,000	187,500	12,500	4,125
3	200,000	140,625	59,375	19,594
4	200,000	105,469	94,531	31,195
5	200,000	316,406	−116,406	−38,414
	1,000,000	1,000,000	−	−

[4] The writing down allowances is 25% of the written down value for tax purposes entering each year:

Year	Cost or Balance Forward	WDA 25%	Balance Forward
1	1,000,000	250,000	750,000
2	750,000	187,500	562,500
3	562,500	140,625	421,875
4	421,875	105,469	316,406[5]

[5] A balancing allowance of 316,406 will be obtained in year five, when the machine is scrapped.

Without a deferred tax provision an erratic profit performance emerges. The deferred tax adjustment recognises that the difference relates to timing and yields an even profit pattern.

The basic approach involves providing for corporation tax on the basis of the accounting profit rather than the taxable profit where the difference is one of timing. These are the reasons for the deferred tax adjustments:

1 In year one the writing down allowance exceeds the accounting depreciation. Providing for tax on the basis of the accounting profit earmarks funds for the payment of tax in subsequent years when the position reverses.
2 In year two the accounting depreciation exceeds the writing down allowance. The excess of the corporation tax bill over the year two provision will be met by withdrawal of part of the excess provision in year one.
3 In year three the accounting depreciation exceeds the writing down allowance. There is an insufficient balance of deferred tax remaining fully to compensate for the excess of the corporation tax bill over the year three provision. The shortfall will be recovered in year five as we will see below. The shortfall is a type of long-term debtor and is treated as an asset.
4 In year four the accounting depreciation exceeds the writing down allowance. The long-term debtor increases. In year five the excess of the balancing allowance over the accounting depreciation restores equilibrium.

The following are the balance sheet effects:

Year	Impact on Profit	Provision	Asset
1	$-50{,}000 \times 33\% = -16{,}500$	16,500	
2	$12{,}500 \times 33\% = 4{,}125$	12,375	
3	$59{,}375 \times 33\% = 19{,}594$		7,219
4	$94{,}531 \times 33\% = 31{,}195$		38,414
5	$-116{,}406 \times 33\% = -38{,}414$	–	–

Complicated issues can arise in the case of asset revaluations, advance corporation tax and unutilised losses. A tax advisor should be consulted in such cases. Deferred tax arises in the case of finance leases. An example is given in Chapter 15. SSAP 15 requires companies to account for deferred tax, using the liability method, i.e. it is calculated at the rate of tax that is expected to apply when the timing differences reverse. In the above illustration, I assumed a constant corporation tax rate of 33%. If the corporation tax was predicted to decline to 30%; (a) in year two, and (b) in year three, the deferred tax would change as follows:

Corporation Tax Rate Falls to 30% in Year Two

Year	1	2	3	4	5	Total
Profit before tax[1]	300,000	300,000	300,000	300,000	300,000	1,500,000
Corporation tax[2]	82,500	93,750	107,813	118,359	55,078	457,500
Deferred tax[3]	15,000	−3,750	−17,813	28,359	34,922	–
	97,500	90,000	90,000	90,000	90,000	457,000
Profit after tax	202,500	210,000	210,000	210,000	210,000	1,042,500
Balance sheet						
Provision	15,000	11,250				
Asset			6,563	34,922		

Corporation Tax Rate Falls to 30% in Year Three

Year	1	2	3	4	5	Total
Profit before tax[1]	300,000	300,000	300,000	300,000	300,000	1,500,000
Corporation tax[2]	82,500	103,125	107,813	118,359	55,078	466,875
Deferred tax[3]	15,375	−4,125	−17,813	−28,539	34,922	−
	97,875	99,000	90,000	90,000	90,000	466,875
Profit after tax	202,125	201,000	210,000	210,000	210,000	1,033,125
Balance sheet						
Provision	15,375	11,250				
Asset			6,563	34,922		

SSAP 15 also states that deferred tax should not be accounted for to the extent that it is probable that an asset or liability will not crystallise. This could arise in a case where the capital investment programme was likely to create writing down allowances that exceed accounting depreciation for a number of years into the future.

Finance Leases

The rules of accounting relating to finance leases are explained in Chapter 15. Two examples are also given in that chapter. For the present it is sufficient to state that the Accounting Standards Committee decided that: any lease in which the repayment obligations, after netting out the interest charges, represented 90% or more of the fair value of the leased asset, was really akin to bank borrowings. SSAP 21 requires that:

1 The interest should be eliminated from the future lease obligations and the balance disclosed as short-, medium- and long-term debt. The computation is similar to that illustrated earlier in this chapter for term loans;
2 A leased fixed asset should be installed in the balance sheet (included in tangible fixed assets but shown separately), to match the indebtedness thus created; and
3 Prior to the introduction of SSAP 21 in 1984 the lease instalments were charged as an expense in the profit and loss account. This charge is now replaced by the depreciation and finance charges that such instalments are designed to recoup.

Operating Leases

If, after netting out the finance charge less than 90% of the capital cost is repaid through the life of the lease, then it is an operating lease. The asset and debt are not included in the balance sheet and the expense to be charged against profits is the lease instalments for the accounting period. The repayment obligations must be disclosed in the notes to the accounts. The treatment of operating leases is explained in more detail in Chapter 15.

Investments in Other Businesses

Where a business has surplus funds it may decide to invest them in other businesses. The investments may be short term in nature and be classified as current assets, or strategic in nature and classified as fixed assets. There are some difficulties with the balance sheet valuation of substantial investments in other businesses. Such investments arise in three situations.

First, where the investment is in a subsidiary. A subsidiary is defined by section 736 of the Companies Act 1985 as:

'(a) A company in which another body corporate either;
    (i) is a member and controls the composition of the board of directors, or
    (ii) holds more than half in nominal value of its equity share capital, or
(b) A company which is a subsidiary of a holding company's subsidiary.'

The investment is valued at cost in the balance sheet of the investing company. Group accounts are also required. The investment is replaced by the underlying assets in the group accounts. An example of how this is done is given in Chapter 15. Delicate issues arise in relation to goodwill, minority interests, third party transactions etc. These are examined briefly in later sections of this appendix and in Chapter 15.

The second type of investment is an investment in an associate. An associate is defined in paragraphs 13–16 in SSAP 1.

13 A company not being a subsidiary of the investing group or company in which:
    (a) the interest of the investing group or company is effectively that of a partner in a joint venture or consortium and the investing group or company is in a position to exercise a significant influence over the company in which the investment is made; or

(b)   the interest of the investing group or company is for the long term and is substantial and, having regard to the disposition of the other shareholdings, the investing group or company is in a position to exercise a significant influence over the company in which the investment is made.

Significant influence over a company essentially involves participation in the financial and operating policy decisions of that company (including dividend policy) but not necessarily control of those policies. Representation on the board of directors is indicative of such participation, but will neither necessarily give conclusive evidence of it nor be the only method by which the investing company may participate in policy decisions.

14   Where the interest of the investing group or company is not effectively that of a partner in a joint venture or consortium but amounts to 20% or more of the equity voting rights of a company, it should be presumed that the investing group or company has the ability to exercise significant influence over that company unless it can clearly be demonstrated otherwise, e.g. there may exist one or more other large shareholdings which prevent the exercise of such influence.

15   Where the interest of the investing group or company is not effectively that of a partner in a joint venture or consortium and amounts to less than 20% of the equity voting rights of a company, it should be presumed that the investing group or company does not have the ability to exercise significant influence unless it can clearly be demonstrated otherwise. Unless there are exceptional circumstances, this demonstration should include a statement from the company in which the investment is made that it accepts that the investing group or company is in a position to exercise significant influence over it.

16   Where different companies in a group hold shares in a company, the investment in that company should be taken as the aggregate of the holdings of the investing company together with the whole of those of its subsidiaries but excluding those of its associates in determining whether significant influence is presumed to exist.

The investment will be shown in the accounts of the investing company at cost. Group accounts are also required. The investment is shown in these at cost plus an appropriate proportion of the undistributed profits less losses, earned since the shares were acquired.

The third type of investment, one that does not confer subsidiary or associate status, will be valued in line with the draft rules contained in ED 55. There are three types:

(a) A fixed asset investment. (This is an investment where the intention to hold the investment for the long term can be clearly demonstrated or there are restrictions on the investor's ability to dispose of it.) Fixed-asset investments should be valued at cost, less any provision for a permanent diminution in value. However, ED 51 permits them to be carried at revalued amounts subject to the proviso that where they are so carried they should be revalued annually.

(b) A current asset investment which is not readily marketable. These should be valued at the lower of their original cost and net realisable value. ED 55 also allows them to be valued at current cost, where this can be determined. Where valuation is at current cost any surplus must be taken to revaluation reserve (not taken in as investment income).

(c) A readily marketable current asset investment. (An active, open and accessible market must exist and a market value must be quoted openly.) Such investments must be included in the balance sheet at market value. This is called 'marking to market'. In general the 'bid' price will be the valuation basis. However the ED also permits the use of 'offer' and mid-market price (provided that the basis adopted is consistently applied. A problem can arise where the investment is of a size or nature that the market is not capable of absorbing it without having a material effect on its quoted price. In such cases the value should be adjusted to reflect the proceeds that could be predicted to be raised from its disposal in the ordinary course of business. The effect of profits and losses on revaluation or disposal is discussed in Chapter 3.

Intangible Assets

The term intangible assets is derived from the Latin and means you cannot touch (feel) them. Intangible assets generally reflect the potential to provide future profits. The model layouts permitted by the Companies Act 1985 require the disclosure of intangible assets as a section of fixed assets.

GOODWILL

Goodwill is one of the most controversial issues in accounting. ED 47 explains it as follows: the value of a business will rarely be equal to the sum of all its identifiable assets and liabilities valued separately. A business as a whole is valued on a going-concern basis as a group of assets that are working together to produce future economic benefits and not as a collection of individual assets and liabilities. The amount of goodwill may be calculated for accounting purposes as the difference between the price paid or payable for a business and the sum of the values of its identifiable assets and liabilities.

Such goodwill can be positive or negative. Acquisitive PLC is interested in the takeover of a company whose net assets are valued at £10M and has 5 million shares in issue. Acquisitive PLC offers £1.80 cash per share, thereby valuing the company at £9M. If a bid succeeds there will be £1M of negative goodwill. The net assets for inclusion in the group balance sheet are greater than the purchase consideration. If the bid fails and Acquisitive PLC decides to increase the offer to £2.30 per share and this offer is accepted then the value of goodwill is £1.5M. In this case the purchase consideration exceeds the value of the assets acquired.

Why might a company offer £11.5M for the net assets of another business when that business has net assets of only £10M? ED 47 explains that that company may enjoy advantages that are not attributable to the identifiable assets and liabilities. Such advantages include: (a) customer awareness; (b) reputation for quality; (c) marketing and distribution skills; (d) technical know-how; (e) established business connections; (f) management ability; (g) level of workforce training, etc. These factors could lead to increased economic benefits above those that would be expected using the same basket of identifiable assets and liabilities without these advantages. The existence of negative goodwill would imply disadvantages.

The major problem with goodwill is that it can only be known with reasonable certainty at the point when a business and the goodwill inherent in it are sold.

The key rules contained in ED 47 are as follows:

1 Purchased goodwill only arises in the case of acquisition accounting. (The difference between an acquisition and a merger is discussed in Chapter 14.)
2 The purchased goodwill is based on the difference between the fair value (not necessarily the balance sheet value) of the assets acquired and the purchase consideration.
3 Purchased goodwill should be recognised as an intangible fixed asset and recorded in the balance sheet.
4 No amount should be included for non-purchased goodwill. (It may exist but cannot be objectively valued.)
5 The amount attributed to purchased goodwill should not include any value for identifiable intangible assets. Such value should be included under the appropriate intangible asset heading.
6 Purchased goodwill should be amortised over its useful economic

life, which should be estimated at the date of acquisition. The useful life should be changed if it is seen to be incorrect at a later date.

7   The useful life should not exceed 20 years. A period of up to 40 years is permitted where it can be demonstrated to be more appropriate.

8   Goodwill should be reviewed annually to determine whether the carrying value is excessive. Each acquisition should be reviewed separately. Any permanent diminution should be written down immediately through the profit and loss account. Purchased goodwill should not be revalued upwards.

9   Negative goodwill should be credited systematically to the profit and loss account. The average life of the fixed assets acquired may provide a suitable period over which to take the credit.

Purchased Goodwill Illustration

To illustrate the approach to accounting for purchased goodwill we will assume that the offer of £2.30 per share made by Acquisitive PLC was accepted by all shareholders. The assets and liabilities to be included in the group balance sheet are as follows:

£'000	Pre-acquisition		For Consolidation	
Goodwill				600[3]
Premises at cost	4,000		5,000	
Less depreciation	400	3,600	–	5,000[1]
Plant at cost	2,000		2,000	
Less depreciation	600	1,400	900	1,100[2]
Other assets		9,800		9,800
Liabilities		(4,800)		(5,000)
Net assets		10,000		11,500

[1] A valuation of £5M for the premises was obtained shortly after the acquisition. This was included to reflect the fair value of the asset acquired (rule 2).

[2] The plant is three years old and was depreciated at a rate of 10% per annum straight line. The Acquisitive PLC depreciation policy is 15% per annum straight line. The book value is adjusted to reflect fair value in line with group accounting policy (rule 2).

[3] The adjusted value of the assets acquired is £10.9M. Comparison with the purchase consideration of £11.5M gives rise to a goodwill valuation of £600,000.

If Acquisitive PLC decided to ascribe a life of ten years to the purchased goodwill, the balance sheet value would be reduced by £60,000 per annum. This amount would be charged against the profit or loss on ordinary activities (pre-tax).

If the review of goodwill relating to this acquisition three years later suggested that a life of six years was appropriate, due to a decline in the scale of advantages promising economic benefits, the value would be adjusted as follows:

£'000	Pre-review	Post-review
Goodwill at cost	600	600
Less depreciation	180	300
Balance sheet value	420	300

The effect of this would be to increase the amortisation charge in the third year by £180,000 (to catch up on two years shortfall at £40,000 per annum and provide £100,000 of amortisation for year three). The charge thereafter would be £100,000 per annum until the goodwill is eliminated or the economic life further revised downwards.

BRAND NAMES

Prior to the introduction of ED 47 in February 1990, it was good practice to write off purchased goodwill against reserves (SSAP 22 1985 version). This had the effect of reducing the net asset value and the shareholders' funds of many organisations that were involved in mergers and acquisitions. Coupled with the popular view that Nestlé were allowed to acquire Rowntree Macintosh for a consideration which was lower than its 'real' worth, this opened the way for a flood of inclusions of brand names in balance sheets. Perhaps the most significant was the inclusion of £678M in the balance sheet of Rank Hovis McDougall (representing more than 50% of its stock market capitalisation). At the time industries saw the inclusion of brand names as a way to strengthen their balance sheets. In May 1990 the Accounting Standards Committee issued ED 52, Accounting for intangible fixed assets. This ED specifies that a fixed asset should only be recognised on an enterprise's balance sheet when: (a) it is probable that any future economic benefits associated with the asset will flow to the enterprise; and (b) the asset has a cost, and where carried at a valuation, a value that can be measured reliably.

Since the historic cost of brands is often a meaningless measure of their worth and reliable measurement is, at best, a highly subjective assessment of value, ED 52 effectively rules out the inclusion of brands as a separate intangible asset. It recognises that the value (usually thought of in terms of future earnings potential) has all the major characteristics of accounting goodwill. It requires that brands be subsumed into goodwill and accounted for accordingly. It allows companies to indicate the amount of purchased goodwill carried in the balance sheet which they consider is attributable to brand names.

PATENTS

A patent is a legal protection against imitation by competitors. A business should try to protect itself against such imitation. Competitors with better marketing or distribution might otherwise capture your profitable future business. Patents can be difficult to register. However, registration or purchase of a patent can protect profit potential. ED 52 requires that patents be: (a) amortised over their useful economic life (generally not exceeding 20 years); (b) reviewed annually to determine whether the amortisation period remains appropriate or whether any permanent diminutions in value have occurred.

TRADE MARKS

A trade mark is a protection against imitation of a product name. A good product name offers an expectation of future profit. The cost of trade mark registration or acquisition can be treated as an intangible fixed asset. ED 52 requires that trade marks be amortised and annually reviewed in the same way as patents above.

LICENCES AND FRANCHISES

A company may not have the capability to manufacture and/or market a product which it has developed and patented. In this case, it may license or franchise other companies to manufacture or sell the product. A household name, e.g. Coca-Cola or McDonalds, would be able to charge a substantial up-front fee for the licence or franchise. An acquirer is paying a premium in the hope of future profits. The premium can be included in the balance sheet as an intangible asset. ED 52 requires that licences and franchises be amortised and annually reviewed in the same way as patents above.

RESEARCH AND DEVELOPMENT

The rules of accounting for research and development are defined in SSAP 13. The key paragraphs are 24–26:

24 Expenditure on pure and applied research (other than that referred to in paragraph 21) should be written off in the year of expenditure through the profit and loss account.

25 Development expenditure should be written off in the year of expenditure except in the following circumstances when it may be deferred to future periods:
   (a) there is a clearly defined project, and
   (b) the related expenditure is separately identifiable, and
   (c) the outcome of such a project has been assessed with reasonable certainty as to:
      (i) its technical feasibility, and
      (ii) its ultimate commercial viability considered in the light of factors such as likely market conditions (including competing products), public opinion, consumer and environmental legislation, and
   (d) the aggregate of the deferred development costs, any further development costs, and related production, selling and administration costs is reasonably expected to be exceeded by related future sales or other revenues, and
   (e) adequate resources exist, or are reasonably expected to be available, to enable the project to be completed and to provide any consequential increases in working capital.

26 In the foregoing circumstances development expenditure may be deferred to the extent that its recovery can reasonably be regarded as assured.

PRELIMINARY EXPENSES

When a company is formed, certain legal expenses are incurred in developing an appropriate set of rules (the Memorandum and Articles of Association). Stamp duty must be paid on the authorised share capital. Since the company will not have any income at this stage, there is no place to offset the preliminary expenses. They can be carried forward as an intangible asset. Preliminary expenses have no ongoing value to a business. They should be written off as soon as profits start to be earned.

DISCLOSURE OF INTANGIBLES IN THE BALANCE SHEET

The model layouts permitted by the Companies Act 1985 require the disclosure of intangible assets as a section of fixed assets.

PENSION FUNDS

The publicity that surrounded the penion funds of the Maxwell companies served to highlight the important principles of pension funding:

1 The assets are not owned by the employer organisation;
2 The value of the fund investments should not be inextricably tied to the fortunes of the employer organisation;
3 Any outstanding contributions to a scheme should be accrued; and
4 Regular actuarial assessments of solvency should be carried out and reported to fund members and in the case of a deficiency the action, if any, being taken to deal with it in the current and future accounting periods should be specified in the financial accounts.

Disclosure requirements for published accounts are documented in SSAP 24.

Group Accounts

Group or consolidated accounts are required when an investing company has one or more subsidiary or related companies. The rules for consolidation of subsidiaries are explained in Chapter 15. The following is a summarised illustration of the way in which the results of a related company are consolidated. Tree PLC bought 40% of the shares of Branch Ltd at par. In the year after the investment, Branch Ltd made a profit of £400,000 after tax. No dividends were declared or paid by Branch Ltd.

Balance Sheets (£'000)

	Tree PLC	Group
Other net assets	5,000	5,000
Investment in Branch Ltd	1,600	1,760[1]
	6,600	6,760
Share capital	4,000	4,000
Reserves	2,600	2,760[1]
	6,600	6,760

[1] 40% of the profit after tax is added to the value of the investment and the revenue reserves.

If Branch Ltd had paid a dividend of £200,000 on its share capital the results would be adjusted as follows:

Balance Sheets (£'000)

	Tree PLC	Group
Other net assets	5,080	5,080[1]
Investment in Branch Ltd	1,600	1,680[2]
	6,680	6,760
Share capital	4,000	4,000
Reserves	2,680[1]	2,760[1]
	6,680	6,760

[1] A dividend of £80,000 was received. This increased the net assets and reserves of Tree PLC.
[2] 40% of the profit retained is added to the value of the investment and the revenue reserves.

We will briefly revisit this example in Chapter 3 once the profit and loss aspect of financial statements have been examined.

Chapter 3

The Profit or Loss From Running a Business

The concept of profit or loss is straightforward enough. A profit is created when income exceeds expenditure. A loss is derived when the expenditure is greater than the income. However, some problems arise in defining what is income or expenditure for the purpose of computing profit or loss.

Calculating Income for Profitability Measurement

Income for a business enterprise can be derived from a range of sources. The most commonly encountered forms are:

1   Sales of products or services.
2   Rent charged to tenants/users of our assets.
3   Dividends on investments.
4   Earnings of related companies.
5   Interest earned on deposits.
6   Commissions.
7   Royalties.
8   Gains derived from currency movements.
9   Settlement discounts from suppliers.

Each type of income is examined in the next sections.

Sales of Products or Services

In defining income from this source we need to resolve certain questions:

(a)   If we charge value added tax when selling a product or service, should this be included in our income?
Answer: No, it should not. Value added tax is simply an add on to the 'real' charge to our customers which the government

obliges business to make. It will be passed on to the government after deducting allowable value added tax which we have incurred. We must make our profit from the net of VAT element of our income (SSAP 5, Paragraph 8).

(b) If we pay excise duties on our materials and (obviously) include these duties in the price charged to our customers, is the proportion of the sales price which represents the duties included in income?

Answer: Surprisingly, yes. While VAT charged to or by us is excluded from income and expenditure, excise duties are not.

(c) If we sold goods on credit and have not been paid for them by the end of the accounting period, will these items be included in income?

Answer: Yes, they should. In spite of the propaganda used to stimulate cash collection ('a sale is not a sale until it is paid for'), credit sales not yet collected are treated as income.

(d) If we sell goods subject to a retention of title clause until settlement is received, can these sales be regarded as income?

Answer: Yes. Sales covered by a retention of title clause are income.

(e) If we sold goods which have not been paid for at the end of the accounting period, and we believe there are grounds for thinking the debt is not collectable, should these sales be included in income?

Answer: Yes. The sale is *bona fide* income. If the debt is doubtful or uncollectable, allowance should be made in computing our expenditure and balance sheet value.

(f) If we sold goods which are the subject of a dispute about quality, and we expect they will have to be taken back for full credit, should these sales be included in our income?

Answer: No. It would be unwise to include these as income. The facts seem to indicate that the profit element will not be realised. Indeed, if we are liable for the cost of carrying them back to our stores, we should allow for this in computing our expenditure.

(g) If we sold goods subject to a trade discount of 15% and a settlement discount of 2% for prompt payment, is our sales income (i) 100%, (ii) 85%, or (iii) 83.3%?

Answer: Sales income is 85%. The trade discount reflects the true price obtained from the customer and is an income deduction. The offer of a settlement discount is designed to speed up our cash receipt. As such it is a financing cost. It is shown as a cost, rather than as an income deduction.

COMPREHENSIVE DEFINITION OF INCOME

The value of goods or services sold to our customers, whether paid for or not, excluding value added tax but including excise duties, after allowing for probable returns but ignoring potential bad debts (which will be picked up under the expenditure category), after deducting trade discounts but not settlement discounts.

Here is a self-test to help you understand the definition of sales income. A business enterprise is currently selling its product at the following prices:

	£
Bought in materials	20
Excise duties	3
Conversion costs	5
Overhead allocation	4
Total cost	32
Add profit margin	8
	40
Add value added tax (17.5%)	7
Selling price	47

The following information relates to sales for a week:

1   20 items were sold.
2   A trade discount of 10% was allowed on two of them.
3   11 of the items sold at full price have been paid for. Five of these customers took a discount of 2% on settlement to which they were entitled.
4   One item sold at full price is defective and will be returned to us for full credit.
5   One item sold at full price is now regarded as uncollectable.

You are asked to calculate:

(a)   The income for the week;
(b)   The total debtors at the end of the week;
(c)   The VAT liability;
(d)   Any expenditure indicated by the above information.

Total Income

	Sales		VAT	Total Invoiced
	Units	£	£	£
Full price	18	720.00	126.00	846.00
Discount price	2	72.00	12.60	84.60
	20	792.00	138.60	930.60
Less credit note not yet issued	1	40.00	7.00	47.00
	19	752.00	131.60	883.60

Note: the sales income is £752.

Total Debtors

	£	£
Total amount invoiced		930.60
Less 11 items settled		
Proceeds[1]	512.30	
Credit note due	47.00	
Discount allowed (5 at £47×2%)	4.70	
Bad debt	47.00	611.00
Total debtors[2]		319.60

[1] $(6 \times £47) + (5 \times £47 \times 98\%)$.
[2] $(5 \times £47) + (2 \times £42.30)$.

VAT Liability

	£
Amount invoiced	131.60
Less VAT element of uncollectable item	7.00[1]
Due to Revenue Commissioners	124.60

[1] When the defective goods are returned, we will be able to reduce our VAT payable by a further £7.

As regards running expenses, these will be: (a) bad debt £47 less VAT £7 = £40.00; and (b) settlement discount five items at £47×2% = £4.70.

THE PROFIT OR LOSS FROM RUNNING A BUSINESS

The returnable item will be included in stock which will reduce the cost of sales. More about that when we look at expenditure.

Rent Charged to Tenants/Users of Assets

The calculation of this income is illustrated as follows:

1 We are preparing a profit and loss account for the year ended 30 June, 1990.
2 A tenant rents a room from us on a calendar year basis.
3 The tenant paid the rent for 1989 on 3 January of that year (£500) and on 5 January 1990 for that year (£600). How much is our rental income?

Answer

	£
0.5×£500	250
0.5×£600	300
Rental income	550

Half of the 1989 rent had been received in advance at 30 June, 1989. This would have been carried in the balance sheet at that date as unearned income. It will be earned in the financial year to 30 June, 1990. Similarly, half of the 1990 rent will be treated as received in advance and carried in the balance sheet at 30 June, 1990 as unearned income.

If the rent for 1990 had not been paid, £300 would still be recorded as income unless there were strong grounds for regarding it as uncollectable.

Income from Investments

Income from investments in other businesses, that do not confer subsidiary or related status, is restricted to dividends received. When a company in which we are shareholders has issued a profit and loss account dated before the end of our financial year, containing a proposed dividend, we cannot recognise this as income. Its annual general meeting might decide to eliminate or reduce the proposed dividend. We do not anticipate the income as we have no legal recourse in the event of non-payment. ED 55 also requires the inclusion in income from investments of:
(a) increases or decreases in value of readily marketable securities; and

(b) losses associated with permanent diminution or on disposal of investments. Income from investments in related companies will be recognised in the accounts of the holding company in line with these rules. Profits from holding investments are not usually chargeable to corporation tax. Equally, losses from holding investments are not allowed as a tax deduction. The tax charge or allowance arises at disposal.

Earnings of Related Companies in Group Accounts

In the group profit and loss account we show as income: (a) our proportion of the pre-tax profits, less (b) our proportion of the tax liability. This follows the rule of significant influence in SSAP 1. To illustrate:

Profit and Loss Account Tree Group Ltd (£'000)

£'000	Tree PLC	Branch Ltd	Group
Sales	10,000	4,000	10,000
Operating profit	1,000	615	1,000
Income of associate			246[1]
			1,246
Corporation tax	350	215	436[2]
Profit retained	650	400	810

[1] £615,000×40%.
[2] £350,000+(£215,000×40%).

£160,000 will be added to the carrying value of the investment and the reserves in the group balance sheet. Only the group figures are published. The individual company's accounts are shown here so that you can see how the group figures are arrived at.

Interest Earned on Deposits

The computation of interest income is as follows:

1 Establish the interest received in the year;
2 Deduct any proportion of this which relates to previous years. It has already been brought into income and debtors;
3 Add interest which is due from the bank at the end of the year.

THE PROFIT OR LOSS FROM RUNNING A BUSINESS

To illustrate the interest calculation, assume that a financial year of Surplus Ltd ends on 31 December, 1989. It had £50,000 on deposit (a) at 12% p.a. from 1 October, 1988 to 30 June, 1989 and (b) at 13% p.a. from 1 July, 1989 to 31 March, 1990. The bank calculates and pays interest half-yearly at 31 March and 30 September. The interest is calculated in quarterly and half-yearly fractions of the annual rate to simplify the illustration:

Interest Calculation

	£
At 1 April, 1989 £50,000×6%	3,000
At 1 October, 1989 £50,000×3.0%	1,500
£50,000×3.25%	1,625
	6,125
Less receivable 1 January, 1989	1,500
	4,625
Add receivable 31 December 1989	1,625
Income for the year	6,250

Where the amount on deposit or the interest rate fluctuates, the company seeks a certificate of interest earned for inclusion in its income at 31 December, 1989.

Commissions

Commissions are the main source of income for some businesses, e.g., auctioneers, stockbrokers, insurance brokers, etc. Commissions received and receivable are included in income. The amounts not yet collected are shown as debtors in the balance sheet (subject to allowance for possible bad debts).

Royalties

Royalties can be an important source of income for businesses who license or franchise their technology to other companies. A typical licence agreement could include a payment of 5% of the income derived by the licensee in selling the licensed product. The royalties are brought into income whether received or receivable. Amounts not collected are carried as debtors in the balance sheet.

Gains from Currency Movements

There are three ways in which a company can create income from currency movements. We will discuss these separately as the accounting treatment is not always the same.

SALE OF GOODS ON CREDIT FOLLOWED BY STERLING WEAKNESS

A UK company sold goods to a foreign customer denominated in the currency of the customer country. Sterling weakens between the date of sale and the cash settlement. The amount collected realises more sterling than originally expected and the gain arising from the foreign currency movement is treated as income. When the accounting year-end intervenes between date of sale and settlement, it is necessary to establish the loss or gain in two sections. The following example illustrates this.

Assume a Scottish company sells goods to a US customer on 3 July, 1989 for $377,146 payable on 3 October, 1989. The financial year of the Scottish company ends on 31 August, 1989. We will assume rates of exchange as follows: 3 July £1 = $1.58; 31 August £1 = $1.54; and 3 October £1 = $1.55. Recognition of income is as follows:

1 *3 July:* $377,146÷1.58 = £238,700. This is recorded as the sales income and as a debtor.
2 *31 August:* $377,146÷1.54 = £244,900. Because the dollar has strengthened we now expect to make an additional profit of £6,200 from this sale (£244,900 – £238,700). This is brought in as extra income receivable at 31 August.
3 *3 October:* $377,146÷1.55 = £243,320. Because the dollar weakened, since 31 August £1,580 of the expected profit will not now be earned. This is brought into account as an exchange loss in the next financial year.

PURCHASE OF GOODS ON CREDIT FOLLOWED BY STERLING STRENGTH

A Welsh company bought goods from a Spanish supplier priced in pesetas. Sterling strengthens between the date of purchase and the date of settlement. It will cost less sterling than expected to buy the pesetas for settlement. The decline in cost is an exchange gain. As with the sale situation, the end of a financial year coming between purchase and settlement can give rise to two separate recognitions of profit or loss.

Assume that: (a) On 3 July, 1989 a Welsh company bought goods from a Spanish supplier for 749,034 pesetas. (b) The financial year of the Welsh company ends on 31 July, 1989. (c) Rates of exchange are assumed as follows: 3 July, 1989 £1 = Peseta 198; 31 July, 1989 £1 = Peseta 194; and 3 October, 1989 (settlement) £1 = Peseta 195. The cost of acquisition and currency movements are recorded as follows:

1   *3 July:* 749,034÷198 = £3,783. This is recorded as a cost and as a trade creditor.
2   *31 July:* 749,034÷194 = £3,861. Weakness of sterling has increased the cost and the creditor amount. An exchange loss of £78 will be recognised at 31 July.
3   *3 October:* 749,034÷195 = £3,841.20. Appreciation of sterling has recovered £19.80 of the loss recognised at 31 July. This will be a currency gain in the following year.

ASSETS OF SUBSIDIARIES AND ASSOCIATES IN FOREIGN CURRENCIES

A third area for creating currency gains arises where a UK company has an overseas subsidiary. This item will be dealt with in Chapter 14.

Settlement Discounts from Suppliers

Suppliers sometimes give discounts for prompt payment. Such settlement discounts are treated as income rather than as deductions from the relevant expenditure. Only discounts actually taken should be treated as income. Some businesses try to take discounts even when paying late. If these are misrepresented as income, problems can arise when auditors obtain supplier statements which have disallowed the discount and thus do not correspond with the customer records.

Trade discounts from suppliers lower the cost of acquiring goods and services.

Expenditure

Many problems arise in calculating expenditure for profit and loss computation purposes. Among the major ones are:

1   How do you compute the material, labour and overhead cost of sales?
2   How do you cope with unpaid and prepaid expenses?
3   What impact (if any) does depreciation on tangible and intangible assets have on profitability?
4   What happens when depreciating assets are grant aided?
5   Are the following appropriately charged as expenditure?
    ●   Bank loan repayments
    ●   Interest charges

A HANDBOOK OF PRACTICAL BUSINESS FINANCE

- Owners' drawings
- Dividends
- Taxation

6 What impact does a loss in a subsidiary or an associate have on expenditure?

7 How should extraordinary and exceptional items be treated?

Cost of Sales

Some important issues arise in computing the cost of sales. The following examples show how the issues are handled.

EXAMPLE 1

A company bought 2,000 items for resale. They cost £11.75 each including VAT. During an accounting period it sold 1,500 of these items at £14.10 each including VAT. If there were no other expenses, did it make a profit or loss?

The real cost per item is £10 net of the VAT. The balance of £1.75 per item will be deducted from the VAT charged to customers in computing or payment to the Revenue Commissioners. The real sales price is £12 excluding £2.10 VAT. Based on this the instinctive answer to this question is; income = £18,000, expenditure = £20,000, so loss = £2,000. It is probably wrong. The major issue is the 500 unsold items. We will look at four different situations:

1 They all remain in stock in first class saleable quality.
2 They all remain in stock but, because of deterioration, are believed to have a reduced saleable value of £8 each.
3 Some have been broken beyond repair and some stolen (in total 150 items missing or unsaleable).
4 The stock is there but potential losses will arise. Prices have fallen to £9 each. To sell each item £2.50 each will have to be spent on delivery and commission.

The profit and loss account will be different in each case:

THE PROFIT OR LOSS FROM RUNNING A BUSINESS

		Case 1		Case 2
Sales		18,000		18,000
Purchases	20,000		20,000	
Less stock	5,000[a]		4,000[b]	
Cost of sales		15,000		16,000
Profit		3,000		2,000

		Case 3		Case 4
Sales		18,000		18,000
Purchases	20,000		20,000	
Less stock	3,500[c]		3,250[d]	
Cost of sales		16,500		16,750
Profit		1,500		1,250

[a] The 500 items valued at £10 each are deducted from the purchases in calculating the cost of sales. They are an asset and will be carried in the balance sheet at £5,000.

[b] It is difficult to make a case that the stock is worth £5,000. The prudent valuation is £8 per unit giving a total stock of £4,000. This is deducted in computing cost of sales and carried as an asset in the balance sheet.

[c] There must be only 350 items in stock. The value is £3,500. This is deducted in computing the cost of sales and carried as an asset in the balance sheet.

[d] SSAP 9 requires that stock must be valued at the lower of cost or net realisable value. The net realisable value is £6.50 (£9–£2.50). This is lower than cost. The stock value is £3,250. It is deducted in computing the cost of sales and carried as an asset in the balance sheet.

EXAMPLE 2

Problems also arise when stock is purchased at different prices. We will assume that there are no difficulties with deterioration, shortages, net realisable values and so on, as covered in Example 1.

The following data have been extracted from the stock control records of a business:

	Units In	Units Out	Units Balance	Cost Per Unit
Stock 1 January			900	£5
Sales 1 January		120	780	
2 January		80	700	
3 January		100	600	
Delivery 3 January				
(at close of business)	1,000		1,600	£6
Sales 4 Janaury		140	1,460	
5 January		170	1,290	
6 January		130	1,160	

We will value the stock at 6 January for cost of sales adjustment and inclusion in the balance sheet. There are four basic approaches to the valuation of this stock.

1   First in first out (FIFO). In line with what ought to be the physical movement.
2   Base stock. A conservative method of valuing stock when prices are rising. The system involves carrying stock at the price of the first order. In this example we will use £5 (the cost of the opening stock). In practice the base stock could have been purchased, many years ago, at a much lower price.
3   Last in first out (LIFO). A variation on base stock, also aimed at conservative stock valuation when prices are rising. The stock is judged to theoretically move in reverse of FIFO, even though the oldest units may be the first ones supplied to customers.
4   Weighted average. When a new delivery arrives at a different price from the current stock a new average price is computed.

THE PROFIT OR LOSS FROM RUNNING A BUSINESS

Computation of Stock Values and Cost of Sales

	FIFO	Base Stock	LIFO	Weighted Average
Opening stock[a]	4,500	4,500	4,500	4,500
Purchases	6,000	6,000	6,000	6,000
Cost of potential sales[b]	10,500	10,500	10,500	10,500
Closing stock	6,800[c]	5,800[d]	6,360[e]	6,525[f]
Cost of sales	3,700	4,700	4,140	3,975

[a] This stock was not included in cost of sales for the previous accounting period. It must be included in this period. The value is 900 at £5 each.

[b] The accumulation of what we started with and what we bought. The heading 'Cost of potential sales' is not usually found in financial statements. It is a very descriptive heading which I invented.

[c] Stock valuation FIFO: 160 old stock at £5, plus 1,000 new stock at £6 equals (£800 + £6,000) £6,800.

[d] Stock valuation base stock: 1160 at £5 each = £5,800. Even though the new stock cost £6 each, it is valued at £5. The lower stock valuation compared with FIFO increases the cost of sales and leaves a smaller profit.

[e] Stock valuation LIFO: 560 new stock at £6, plus 600 old stock at £5 equals (£3,360 + £3,000) £6,360. The value lies between the extremes of FIFO and base stock. 300 units of the original stock were sold prior to the new delivery. That left 600 in stock. 440 units of the new delivery were sold. That left 560 in stock.

[f] Weighted average

	Units	Per Unit	Value
Opening stock	900	5	4,500
Cost of sales pre-delivery	300	5	1,500[h]
Stock at delivery	600	5	3,000
Delivery	1,000	6	6,000
Stock after delivery	1,600	5.625[g]	9,000
Cost of sales post-delivery	440	5.625	2,475[h]
Closing stock	1,160	5.625	6,525

[g] Stock valuation on a weighted average basis is £9,000 ÷ 1,600 units = £5.625.

[h] Cost of sales is £1,500 + £2,475 = £3,975.

None of these valuations offends the broad concept of cost. Before we examine their relative merits it is probably a good idea to test your understanding of the concepts while exploring the impact of falling prices.

Self Test: Stock Valuations and Falling Prices

	Units	Per Unit	Value
Stock 1 February	1,000	5	5,000
Sales pre new delivery	700		
New delivery	900	4	3,600
Sales post new delivery	600		

You are asked to calculate the stock valuation (FIFO, base stock, LIFO and weighted average) and the resulting cost of sales figures.

Solution to Stock Valuations and Falling Prices

	FIFO	Base Stock	LIFO	Weighted Average
Opening stock	5,000	5,000	5,000	5,000
Purchases	3,600	3,600	3,600	3,600
Cost of potential sales	8,600	8,600	8,600	8,600
Closing stock	2,400[a]	3,000[b]	2,700[c]	2,550[d]
Cost of sales	6,200	5,600	5,900	6,050

[a] 600×£4 each.
[b] 600×£5 each.
[c] 300×£4 each and 300×£5 each.

[d] Stock pre-delivery	300×£5	1,500
Delivery	900×£4	3,600
	1,200×£4.25	5,100

Closing stock: 600×£4.25 = £2,550

The base stock valuation is now highest and the cost of sales lowest. The FIFO valuation now gives the lowest stock valuation and the highest cost of sales. In all these cases the stock valuation might have to be restricted to the net realisable value (SSAP 9).

The following are the important issues in relation to stock valuation:

1   The basis of stock valuation should be consistent from year to year. It would be undesirable for a company to shift from one method to another so as to show the period results in the most favourable light. If a change in the valuation method is made the auditors' report should contain a commentary such as 'If the stock valuation method had not been changed, the company would have reported a stock value £XXX (higher or lower) and a profit before tax of £XXX.'

2   The accounting policy on stock valuation must be stated. This is required by SSAP 2.
3   Most UK businesses use first in first out to value trading stocks:
    (a)   It most fairly represents their physical movement; and
    (b)   the Revenue Commissioners do not usually accept base stock and LIFO methods.
    Maintenance stocks are frequently valued at weighted average. It is considered the most appropriate method in the case of slow moving parts. Consider the following example:
    A part for a machine was purchased in 1987 at a cost of £50,000. It has not been used. In January 1989, a similar part was purchased for £84,000 so there were now two in stock. In April 1989 the first one was issued to replace a broken item in the machine. In assessing the cost of the repair, should you charge out £50,000 (FIFO) or £84,000 (LIFO and, presumably, replacement cost)? It is generally felt that with a large variety of spares which are only occasionally needed, £67,000 (weighted average) is the most appropriate stock valuation and charge out rate.
4   If the parent company is a foreign multinational and we are preparing accounts for the UK subsidiary, we may use LIFO or base stock valuation methods so as to comply with group accounting policies. In this case a restatement of profits for corporation tax purposes will be required by the Revenue Commissioners.

VALUATION OF WORK IN PROGRESS

The valuation of work in progress is more detailed. In addition to the raw material content (valued using the principles outlined in Examples 1 and 2), it is necessary to consider the value added by completing part of the manufacturing process.

This is a simple example: A company starts to manufacture a new product on a Monday. The product takes two days to complete and the company operates a five-day week. During the first week of operations, two items are fully completed and one item is half way through the process.

Costs for the week were as follows:

	£
Materials (3 items)	300
Labour	55
Power	35
Administration	25
	415

The costs of the business each day are charged to that day's manufacturing activity.

The work in progress is valued as follows:

		£
Material content (300/3)		100
Labour[a]	(55/5)	11
Power[a]	(35/5)	7
		118

[a] Divide by 5. Only on Friday (one-fifth of the week) was work done on the third product.

The administration cost should not be included. Its connection with the work in progress is tenuous. In this case we examined a very simple situation with one stock unit half-processed. In a complicated factory there may be work at various stages, making it necessary to examine job cards to establish the labour and overhead content.

VALUATION OF FINISHED GOODS

In valuing finished goods we will also have to address the issue of value added in the production process. If the item finished on Thursday had not been sold it would be valued as follows:

	£
Material	100
Labour (2 days)	22
Power (2 days)	14
	136

The costs for the week are now represented as:

	£
Cost of sales: 1×£136	136
Finished stock: 1×£136	136
Work in progress: 1×£118	118
Administration costs not included in stock	25
	415

Apart from the issue of tenuous links between administration costs and partly or fully processed products, there are complications where production rises and falls with market demand. Consider a further illustration based totally on finished goods valuation:

	Week 1		Week 2	
Production units	Cost per Unit p.	Total 2,000 £	Cost per Unit p.	Total 1,000 £
Material	15.0	300	15.0	150
Labour	10.0	200	10.0	100
Energy	7.5	150	7.5	75
Rent of factory	5.0	100	10.0	100
Adminstration	2.5	50	5.0	50
	40.0	800	47.5	475

The rent is £100 per week and the administrator is paid £50 per week regardless of output.

If 200 items remained in stock each weekend, a total cost stock valuation would give:

Week 1 = 200÷2,000×£800 = £80   Week 2 = 200÷1,000×£475 = £95

It is difficult to justify a stock value of £80 in total, or 40p per unit, in a week when orders are high and £95 in total, or 47.5p per unit, in a subsequent week when demand is low. If we consistently value the stock on the basis of costs which rise and fall with the volume of output, this problem will be eliminated:

	Week 1	Week 2
(A) Output related costs	650	325
(B) Proportion of output remaining in stock	200÷2,000 = 10%	200÷1,000 = 20%
Stock value (A×B)	650×10% = £65	325×20% = £65

An alternative is to determine the average output per week and the costs associated with this average output. If we assume that the two weeks in the illustration will provide a sensible average, we get:

	Week 1		Week 2		Average	
	Cost per Unit	Total	Cost per Unit	Total	Cost per Unit	Total
Production units	2,000		1,000		1,500	
	p	£	p	£	p	£
Material	15.0	300	15.0	150	15.0	225
Labour	10.0	200	10.0	100	10.0	150
Energy	7.5	150	7.5	75	7.5	112.5
Rent of factory	5.0	100	10.0	100	6.7	100
Administration	2.5	50	5.0	50	3.3	50
	40.0	800	47.5	475	42.5	637.5

The stock would be valued at 42.5p per unit in both weeks if this average was used. If the administration cost was excluded (a prudent approach), the value would be 39.2p per unit.

I would prefer to exclude the rent cost from the stock valuation, although SSAP 9 would permit its inclusion. We can have problems with the net realisable value of finished stocks.

Unpaid and Prepaid Expenses

One of the problems in assessing profitability is to charge the expenditure relevant to the financial year, whether paid for in the previous year, the current year, or remaining unpaid at the end of the year. Areas for consideration are:

1 Purchases of materials. If these have been acquired but not paid for, you must include them as expenditure (subject to appropriate stock adjustment in computing the cost of sales) and carry them in the balance sheet as creditors. The VAT element can be netted against that charged to customers. Only the cost net of VAT is treated as a charge against cost of sales and in the stock valuation.

2 If goods have been paid for in advance, but not taken into possession in the financial year, the cost will not go into purchases or stocks. It will be disclosed in current assets as a supplier advance.

3 Many services obtained by businesses are charged for in arrears. For example, the telephone bill for the quarter from January to March is likely to be charged to us in April. It would be very unwise to overlook this potential bill in computing our running expenses to the end of March. We take it into account as an accrual

(due and payable in under one year), and build it in as a running expense. Similarly, some expenditure items such as rent and insurance are charged in advance. If they are paid for a period beyond the end of the financial year, the prepayment is removed from the expense cost and included in the current assets.

Depreciation and Profitability

The loss of value caused by using fixed assets through the financial year must be charged as a depreciation expense. Reducing the distributable profit keeps the funds in the business. Two major problems can arise:

1 The funds may be spent to acquire additional assets or to repay borrowings. In either case they will not be available to cover the cost of replacement when the asset wears out or becomes obsolete.
2 Even if the funds have not been used to acquire additional assets, or to repay borrowings, they will probably be insufficient to finance replacement because prices have risen.

A major debate, in the accounting profession, about the purpose of depreciation remains unresolved. Should the profit and loss account (a) reflect the loss of value caused by using a fixed asset in the business, or (b) be sufficient and available to provide funds for replacement? The Accounting Standards Committee have made valiant attempts to develop a workable framework for replacement cost depreciation. No framework that they have proposed has attracted majority support from the accounting profession. The current position is:

1 Replacement cost depreciation is not too important because inflation rates are relatively low.
2 There are major conceptual obstructions to the development of a standard accounting policy on replacement cost depreciation.
3 Depreciation should be based on loss of value.
4 Appreciating assets should be revalued at least every five years. Subsequent to revaluations, depreciation will be based on the revised value.
5 Financial accounts cannot be charged with the responsibility for creation of a pool of funds for replacement.
6 Management must be conscious of the need to retain profits in order to build an adequate replacement cost fund (and meet other commitments). If they fail to do so, the financial accounts should not be blamed.

Grant Aided Assets

Where a capital grant has been received towards the cost of a fixed asset, the charge against profit and loss account to reflect the loss of value which the company will experience is based on the net of grant cost. This is logical but it can create difficulties at replacement. A capital grant is not usually available towards asset replacement.

Bank Loan Repayments

Bank loan repayments are not a legitimate charge against profits. The company is really restructuring its balance sheet by reducing the scale of borrowed funds. This can be done in a variety of ways: by disposing of assets; using up the cash which the retained profits and depreciation funds have created; or replacing these loans with funds from other sources.

Interest Charges, Drawings, Dividends

Interest on bank borrowings is a legitimate charge against profits. It is important to distinguish between money spent on the legally enforceable interest on loans, and money spent on the more discretionary rewards that dividends (and owners' drawings in a non-limited company situation) represent. These items are a distribution of profit rather than a cost in determining profit. The distinction is also important because the tax on profits is different from that on distributions. When a limited company pays a dividend the profits from which it is paid will already have been exposed to corporation tax. A shareholder who receives a dividend is liable to personal tax on this income. An imputation system was introduced in 1971 and this is how it works. Assume High Yield Ltd has one million £1 ordinary shares in issue. It has earned a profit after tax of £150,000 and intends to pay a dividend of 10% on the share capital or £100,000.

High Yield Ltd will deduct tax at 25% (the current basic rate) in paying the dividend. A holder of 1,000 shares will receive £75. If the holder is

- liable to tax at 25% no further tax liability will arise;
- liable to tax at 40% he or she will be charged a further £15 in due course; and
- not liable to tax (i.e. small income, pension fund etc.) the £25 imputed can be reclaimed.

The £25,000 deducted in paying the dividends must be paid to the Revenue Commissioners as advance corporation tax. The Revenue treat the ACT as a payment on account of the normal corporation tax liability. The ACT legislation was introduced because companies sometimes had little or no corporation tax liability (due, for example, to capital allowances) and in these circumstances the Revenue quite rightly objected to having to refund tax to exempt investors when they would not receive at least a corresponding amount from the company by way of corporation tax. If the corporation tax assessment of High Yield Ltd was £55,000, then £25,000 of this would be paid to the Revenue Commissioners as ACT and the balance of £30,000 would become payable on the due date for 'mainstream corporation tax'.

Losses in Associated Companies

If associates incur losses the investing company's proportion will be deducted from group profits (as a separate item) and the ongoing value of the investment will be reduced by a corresponding amount in the group accounts. This parallels the treatment of profits of associates.

Exceptional and Extraordinary Items and Prior Year Adjustments

SSAP 6 defines an 'all-inclusive' concept of profit. This includes extraordinary items and prior year adjustments as well as the profit or loss on extraordinary activities.

Exceptional Items: (definition from SSAP 6 paragraph 29)
Material items which derive from events or transactions that fall within the ordinary activities of a company, and which need to be disclosed separately by virtue of their size or incidence if the financial statements are to give a true and fair view. They include:

(a) Restructuring and Reorganisation costs (for accounting periods ending on or after 23 November 1991). The urgent issues task force of the ASB have ruled that these are usually part of the ordinary activities of a business and should be treated as an exceptional item, except where the company incurring them can prove that they are extraordinary);
(b) Abnormal charges for bad debts, stock write-offs etc.;
(c) Settlement of consequential loss insurance claims;
(d) Amounts transferred to employee share schemes;
(e) Profits or losses on disposal of fixed assets.

Exceptional items must be shown separately as part of the computation of profits or losses derived from ordinary activities.

Extraordinary Items: (definition from SSAP 6 paragraph 30)
Material items which derive from events or transactions that fall
outside the ordinary activities of a company and which are therefore
expected not to recur frequently or regularly. Examples include:

(a) The sale of an investment not acquired with the intention of
     resale;
(b) Writing off intangibles because of unusual events or develop-
     ments during the period;
(c) Expropriation of assets;
(d) A change in the basis of taxation, or a significant change in
     government fiscal policy.

In order to present fairly the results from the ordinary activities
extraordinary items must be shown following the ordinary results. The
tax and minority share of such extraordinary items must be shown
separately.

PRIOR YEAR ADJUSTMENTS DEALT WITH THROUGH PROFIT AND LOSS

These arise from corrections and adjustments which are the natural
result of estimates inherent in accounting and, more particularly, in
the periodic preparation of financial statements. Estimating future
events will require reappraisal as new events occur, more experience is
acquired, or new information is obtained. Care must be taken to
ascertain that the change is a reappraisal rather than a real change in
accounting policy.

PRIOR YEAR ADJUSTMENTS NOT INCLUDED IN THE PROFIT AND LOSS
ACCOUNT

These fall into two categories. First, restatements of previous years are
regarded as the most appropriate method for dealing with changes in
accounting policies. (The most likely source of such changes arises
when a new statement of standard accounting practice makes figures
for previous years unreliable as a basis for comparison with the revised
accounting approach in the current year.) Secondly, accounts containing significant errors, which would have been withdrawn if the
errors had been discovered in sufficient time, are most appropriately
treated by restating the prior years resulting in the opening balance of
retained profits being adjusted.

THE PROFIT OR LOSS FROM RUNNING A BUSINESS

Illustrative Layout of Disclosure (Reproduced from SSAP 6)

	£'000	
	1986	*1985*
Turnover	183,000	158,000
Cost of sales	106,140	86,900
Gross profit	76,860	71,100
Distribution and administrative expense	57,160	52,500
Profit before exceptional item	19,700	18,600
Exceptional item[1]	8,600	–
Profit on ordinary activities before tax	11,100	18,600
Tax on profit on ordinary activities	4,500	7,400
Profit on ordinary activities after tax	6,600	11,200
Minority interest	400	370
Profit attributable to members of the holding company	6,200	10,830
Extraordinary loss after taxation[2]	595	1,020
Profit for the financial year	5,605	9,810
Dividends	4,410	4,200
Retained profit for the year	1,195	5,610
[1] Loss on closure X division	2,700	
Provision for loss on long-term contract	5,900	
	8,600	
[2] Expropriation of assets	2,700	
Elimination of intangible		1,020
Less profit on sale of head office	1,030	–
Extraordinary loss	1,670	1,020
Tax relief on extraordinary loss	670	–
	1,000	1,020
Minority share of closure costs	405	–
Extraordinary loss after tax	595	1,020

Later in the book we will meet the concept of earnings per share. This calculation should be based on the profit after tax but before extraordinary items. This rule of accounting is required under SSAP 3.

Profit and Loss Account Structure

The figures disclosed are required by Schedule 4 of the Companies Act 1985. Some comments on the headings and supporting notes are appropriate.

TURNOVER

Where a company carries out two or more classes of business that, in the opinion of the directors, differ substantially from each other, the turnover for each class must be stated and described. Where a company has supplied two or more markets that, in the opinion of the directors, differ substantially from each other, the amount of the turnover in each market must be disclosed. There are two exceptions: (1) Amounts which are not material can be included in a larger class; and (2) If in the directors' opinion disclosure would be seriously prejudicial to the company's interest, the breakdown need not be disclosed. The fact of non-disclosure must be stated in such cases.

DETAILS OF COSTS

These include:

1 Staff costs, distinguishing between wages and salaries, company proportion of social security and other pension costs.
2 Average number of persons employed by the company in the financial year.
3 Depreciation and diminution in the value of tangible and intangible fixed assets.
4 Auditors' remuneration (including expenses).
5 Directors' remuneration:
    ● Emoluments. This includes fees, salaries, bonuses, commissions, taxable expense allowances, benefits in kind and company superannuation contributions.
    ● Directors' or past directors' pensions.
    ● Compensation to directors or past directors in respect of loss of office.
    ● Emoluments of the chairperson.
    ● Emoluments of the highest paid director, if he or she was not the chairperson.
    ● The number of directors whose emoluments were between nil and £5,000 and in each band of £5,000 above this.
    ● The number of directors who have waived emoluments and the aggregate value of such emoluments waived.
6 The number of employees whose emoluments exceed £30,000 in bands of £5,000 above this amount (excluding employees who worked wholly or mainly outside UK).
7 Payments for hire of plant and machinery.

PROFIT BY CLASS

Where the turnover is stated by class, the profit or loss attributable to that class must be stated.

SMALL AND MEDIUM-SIZED COMPANIES

A small company, as defined in the Companies Act 1985, is not required to file a profit and loss account. A medium-sized company, as defined in the Companies Act 1985, may begin its profit and loss account with gross profit.

Segmental Reporting

SSAP 25 is designed to provide the information required by paragraph 55(1) of the Companies Act 1985. It requires disclosure of information to help users of financial statements to interpret performance and assess future prospects where an entity operates in several business areas and/or geographic markets. It is designed to develop accounting legislation to cover analysis of sales, assets and profits by: class of business, and geographical market.

SSAP 25 follows the principles of the EC Fourth Directive. It also requires some disclosure of assets. All entities are encouraged to provide segmental information. However, where, in the opinion of the directors, disclosure would be seriously prejudicial to the interests of the reporting entity, segmental information need not be disclosed but the fact that it has not been disclosed must be stated.

The key segmental information is defined in paragraph 8 as follows:

Significant classes of business which:
Earn a return on investment that is out of line with the remainder of the business; or
Are subject to different degrees of risk; or
Have experienced different rates of growth; or
Have different potentials for future development.

Significance is defined in paragraph 9 as:
Third party turnover in excess of 10% of total; or
Profit or loss in excess of combined profit or loss for all segments; or
Net assets in excess of 10% of total net assets of the entity.

Illustrative segmental reports provided in SSAP 25 are now reproduced to show the type of disclosure required.

Illustrative segmental report
(This Appendix is for general guidance and does not form part of the Statement of Standard Accounting Practice.)

CLASSES OF BUSINESS	Industry A 1990 £000	Industry A 1989 £000	Industry B 1990 £000	Industry B 1989 £000	Other industries 1990 £000	Other industries 1989 £000	Group 1990 £000	Group 1989 £000
TURNOVER								
Total sales	33,000	30,000	42,000	38,000	26,000	23,000	101,000	91,000
Inter segment sales	(4,000)	—	—	—	(12,000)	(14,000)	(16,000)	(14,000)
Sales to third parties	29,000	30,000	42,000	38,000	14,000	9,000	85,000	77,000
PROFIT BEFORE TAXATION								
Segment profit	3,000	2,500	4,500	4,000	1,800	1,500	9,300	8,000
Common costs							300	300
Operating profit							9,000	7,700
Net interest							(400)	(500)
							8,600	7,200
Group share of the profits before taxation of associated undertakings	1,000	1,000	1,400	1,200	—	—	2,400	2,200
Group profit before taxation							11,000	9,400
NET ASSETS								
Segment net assets	17,600	15,000	24,000	25,000	19,400	19,000	61,000	59,000
Unallocated assets							3,000	3,000
							64,000	62,000
Group share of the net assets of associated undertakings	10,200	8,000	8,800	9,000	—	—	19,000	17,000
Total net assets							83,000	79,000

THE PROFIT OR LOSS FROM RUNNING A BUSINESS

GEOGRAPHICAL SEGMENTS	United Kingdom		North America		Fast East		Other		Group	
	1990 £000	1989 £000	1990 £000	1989 £000	1990 £000	1989 £000	1990 £000	1989 £000	1990 £000	1989 £000
TURNOVER										
Turnover by destination										
Sales to third parties	34,000	31,000	16,000	14,500	25,000	23,000	10,000	8,500	85,000	77,000
Turnover by origin										
Total sales	38,000	34,000	29,000	27,500	23,000	23,000	12,000	10,500	102,000	95,000
Inter-segment sales	—	—	(8,000)	(9,000)	(9,000)	(9,000)	—	—	(17,000)	(18,000)
Sales to third parties	38,000	34,000	21,000	18,500	14,000	14,000	12,000	10,500	85,000	77,000
PROFIT BEFORE TAXATION										
Segment profit	4,000	2,900	2,500	2,300	1,800	1,900	1,000	900	9,300	8,000
Common costs									300	300
Operating profit									9,000	7,700
Net interest									(400)	(500)
									8,600	7,200
Group share of the profits before taxation of associated undertakings	950	1,000	1,450	1,200	—	—	—	—	2,400	2,200
Group profit before taxation									11,000	9,400
NET ASSETS										
Segment net assets	16,000	15,000	25,000	26,000	16,000	15,000	4,000	3,000	61,000	59,000
Unallocated assets									3,000	3,000
									64,000	62,000
Group share of the net assets of associated undertakings	8,500	7,000	10,500	10,000	—	—	—	—	19,000	17,000
Total net assets									83,000	79,000

Unallocated assets consist of assets at the Group's head office in London amounting to £2.4 million (1989 £2.5 million) and at the Group's regional office in Hong Kong amounting to £0.6 million (1989 £0.5 million)

Chapter 4

Cash Flow Statements

Critics of accrual accounting, as represented in the profit and loss account and balance sheet of an organisation, rightly argue (a) that such statements fail to identify movements of cash into and out of an enterprise; and (b) do not facilitate assessment of changes in liquidity.

Source and application of funds statements were used for many years to explain such cash movements. They were an integral part of financial reporting required by SSAP 10. In October 1991, following (a) years of criticism of the structure and lack of helpfulness of SSAP 10; and (b) the exposure of its forerunner ED 54, the Accounting Standards Board issued FRS 1 'Cash Flow Statements'. This standard replaces SSAP 10. The major objectives of FRS 1 are to standardise cash flow reports and to increase their usefulness for forecasting and decision making.

Cash flows occur and are recorded in the books of account as an enterprise receives money and pays it to providers of goods, services and assets. These cash flows form the basis of the cash flow statement and also drive the other major financial reports. If a cash flow statement is to be of practical use to investors they should be able to reconcile the cash flows with the related profit and loss account and balance sheet data.

Rules For Identification of Cash Flows

OUTFLOWS

1 A movement which increases the assets in a business causes a cash outflow. A problem arises with depreciation. This will be explained later.
2 A movement which decreases the liabilities of a business or its shareholders' funds causes a cash outflow.
3 Paying running expenses causes cash outflows. In the indirect method these outflows are netted against the inflows from sales. Only the loss that arises when expenditure exceeds the income is disclosed in the indirect method cash flow statement.

4   The payment of corporation tax and dividends are cash outflows. They require special treatment as explained later.

INFLOWS

5   A movement which reduces the assets in a business creates a cash inflow.
6   A movement which increases the liabilities reduces the amount of cash outflow. It is disclosed as an inflow in the indirect method cash flow statement.
7   In a profitable business the operating profit (income less running expenses) is a net cash inflow.
8   Since depreciation is a non-cash cost, it must be added to the operating profit to correct the understatement of the inflow.
9   New capital issues and government grants are cash inflows.

The cash flow statement categorises the flows into six different groupings:

1   Operating activities. This group includes the actual cash flows relating to: (a) customer collections; (b) other income; (c) supplier payments; and (d) other operating expenses.
2   Returns on investments and servicing of finance. This group includes dividends and interest actually received or paid.
3   Corporation tax paid.
4   Investing activities. This group includes all cash inflows and outflows that relate to long-term development of the business. Additions to and disposals of all types of fixed assets are the components of this group.
5   Financing activities. This group includes share issues and repurchases, loan receipts and repayments etc.
6   Increase or decrease in cash or cash equivalents. This group is the net total of the five preceding groups. This figure is then added to the opening cash and cash equivalents so as to reconcile them with the closing cash and cash equivalents.

The statement shows whether the overall business was cash positive or negative during the period thus providing important insights into changing liquidity.

FRS 1 allows presentation in two distinct forms:

1   The indirect method. This layout is designed to explain the effect of movements in balance sheet items into their cash flow components. A snag is that it is difficult to see how the reported flows relate to the actual cash receipts and payments.
2   The direct method. This layout requires the cash flow statement to mirror the actual cash receipts and payments. A snag is that it is

difficult to see how the reported flows relate to the corresponding profit and loss account and balance sheet data.

Both methods have attractive features. However, the existence of two distinctly different methods makes interfirm comparison difficult. Cash flow statements test whether liquidity is improving, remaining static or deteriorating. The formats required by FRS 1 help to reveal changes in liquidity but can conceal problems, as we will see later.

The indirect method cash flow statement is derived from the balance sheet of Iffy PLC as follows:

Balance Sheets Iffy PLC

	£'000			
	1989	1990	Inflow[1]	Outflow[1]
Fixed Assets				
Premises	1,440	1,410	30[a]	
Plant	400	450	130[b]	180[b]
	1,840	1,860		
Current assets				
Stock in trade	200	250		50[c]
Trade debtors	360	300	60[d]	
Prepayments	20	30		10[e]
Cash	50	80		30[f]
	630	660		
Payables under one year				
Bank loans	300	450	150[g]	
Trade creditors	360	330		30[h]
Accruals	50	100	50[i]	
Corporation tax	20	50		20[j]
Proposed dividend	20	30		50[k]
	(750)	(960)		
Net assets	1,720	1,560		
Financed by:				
Share capital	600	600		
Profit and loss account	320	360	150[l]	
Shareholders' funds	920	960		
Long-term load	800	600		200[n]
	1,720	1,560	570	570

[1] These amounts provide the information for inclusion in the cash flow statement. They would not appear on the face of the balance sheet. Footnotes a to n below explain the conversion of balance sheet data into cash flow information.

Balance Sheets Iffy PLC

	£'000			
	1990	1991	Inflow[1]	Outflow[1]
Fixed Assets				
Premises	1,410	1,960	40[a]	
Plant	450	510	130[b]	300[b]
			110[b]	
Financial	–	400		400[m]
	1,860	2,870		
Current assets				
Stock in trade	250	220	30[c]	
Trade debtors	300	460		160[d]
Prepayments	30	50		20[e]
Cash	80	100		20[f]
	660	830		
Payables under one year				
Bank loans	450	950	500[g]	
Trade creditors	330	500	170[h]	
Accruals	100	120	20[i]	
Corporation tax	50	80		50[j]
Proposed dividend	30	30		70[k]
	(960)	(1,680)		
Net assets	1,560	2,020		
Financed by:				
Share capital	600	600		
Revaluation reserve		590		
Profit and loss account	360	430	220[l]	
Shareholders' funds	960	1,620		
Long-term loan	600	400		200[n]
	1,560	2,020	1,220	1,220

[1] These amounts provide the information for inclusion in the cash flow statement. They would not appear on the face of the balance sheet. Footnotes a to n below explain the conversion of balance sheet data into cash flow information.

Profit and Loss Accounts Iffy PLC

	1990	1990	1990	1991
		£'000		
Sales		2,000		2,400
Opening stock	200		250	
Purchases	1,000		1,200	
	1,200		1,450	
Closing stock	250		220	
Cost of sales		950		1,230
Gross margin		1,050		1,170
Payroll	350		360	
Depreciation	160		150	
Other operating costs	370	880	400	910
Profit before interest and tax		170		260
Interest		20		40
Profit before tax		150		220
Corporation tax		50		80[j]
Profit after tax		100		140
Interim dividend paid	30		40	
Proposed final dividend	30	60	30	70[k]
Profit retained		40		70

[a] Premises	1989	1990	1991
	1,440	1,410	1,960

Rule 5 inflow	30
Rule 1 outflow	(550)

Changes in the balance sheet value of the premises seem to imply a disposal in 1990 and a purchase in 1991. This is not correct. The premises were bought in 1988 for £1.5M. They are being depreciated at 2% per annum. An independent valuation of £2M received early in 1991 was included in the 1991 balance sheet, the revaluation surplus being credited to shareholders' funds. The 1991 depreciation charge was increased to £40,000 to reflect the higher valuation. These changes in valuation had no impact on the cash flows of Iffy PLC. The correct cash inflows are 1990 £30,000 and 1991 £40,000 (rule 8). The £590,000 surplus on revaluation is cancelled against the revaluation reserve.

b Plant

	1989	1990	1991
	400	450	510

Rule 1 outflow   (50)   (60)

Changes in the book value of plant and machinery explained in the notes to the balance sheet were:

	Cost	Depreciation	Book Value
1 January 1990	600	200[1]	400
Additions	180	130[2]	50
31 December 1990	780	330	450
Additions	300	150[3]	150
Disposals	(180)	(90)	(90)[4]
31 December 1991	900	390	510

Depreciation policy six years straight line.

[1] Two years' depreciation on a cost of 600 = 200.

[2] One year's depreciation on a cost of 780 = 130.

[3] One year's depreciation on a cost of 900 = 150.

[4] This plant was bought in 1988 for £180,000. Three years depreciation has been charged reducing the book value to £90,000. The sale proceeds were £130,000.

The correct cash flows based on these notes are:

1 Purchase of plant 1990 = £180,000, 1991 = £300,000. Rule 1 outflow.

2 Sale of plant £130,000 in 1991. Rule 5 inflow.

   Depreciation on plant 1990 = £130,000, 1991 = £110,000 (£150,000 less profit on disposal £40,000). Rule 8 inflow.

c Stock

	1989	1990	1991
	200	250	220

Rule 1 outflow   (50)

Rule 5 inflow   30

Inclusion of the stocks in the cost of sales distorts the cash flows. In 1990 the increase in stock consumed cash resources. In 1991 the decline in stocks released cash resources. Payment for the stocks is affected by the creditor adjustment at footnote h.

d Trade debtors

	1989	1990	1991
	360	300	460

Rule 5 inflow   60

Rule 1 outflow   (160)

The reduction in debtors in 1990 means that the sales as an input to the operating cash flow understate the amount of cash received from customers. The increase in debtors in 1991 means that sales overstate the cash received from customers.

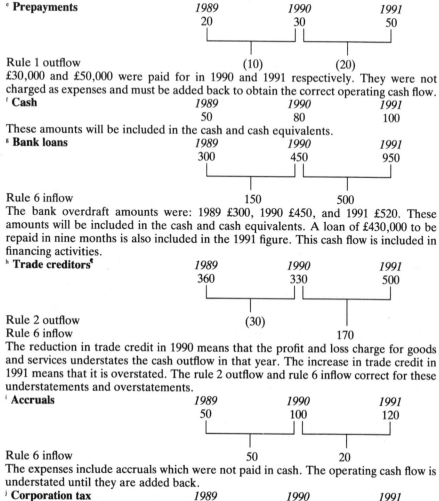

ᵉ Prepayments

	1989	1990	1991
	20	30	50

Rule 1 outflow (10) (20)

£30,000 and £50,000 were paid for in 1990 and 1991 respectively. They were not charged as expenses and must be added back to obtain the correct operating cash flow.

ᶠ Cash

	1989	1990	1991
	50	80	100

These amounts will be included in the cash and cash equivalents.

ᵍ Bank loans

	1989	1990	1991
	300	450	950

Rule 6 inflow 150 500

The bank overdraft amounts were: 1989 £300, 1990 £450, and 1991 £520. These amounts will be included in the cash and cash equivalents. A loan of £430,000 to be repaid in nine months is also included in the 1991 figure. This cash flow is included in financing activities.

ʰ Trade creditors

	1989	1990	1991
	360	330	500

Rule 2 outflow (30)
Rule 6 inflow 170

The reduction in trade credit in 1990 means that the profit and loss charge for goods and services understates the cash outflow in that year. The increase in trade credit in 1991 means that it is overstated. The rule 2 outflow and rule 6 inflow correct for these understatements and overstatements.

ⁱ Accruals

	1989	1990	1991
	50	100	120

Rule 6 inflow 50 20

The expenses include accruals which were not paid in cash. The operating cash flow is understated until they are added back.

ʲ Corporation tax

	1989	1990	1991
	20	50	80

Rule 6 inflow 30 30

Direct comparison of the balance sheet liabilities is misleading. The correct cash outflows (rule 4) are computed by reference to the profit and loss account provisions:

	1990	1991
Opening liability	20	50
Provision (P and L)	50	80
	70	130
Less closing liability	50	80
Corporation tax paid	20	50 = outflows

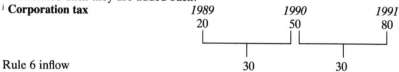

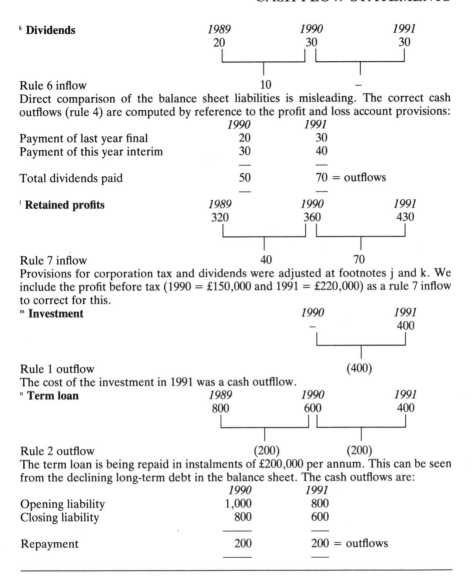

ᵏ Dividends

	1989	1990	1991
	20	30	30

Rule 6 inflow   10   –

Direct comparison of the balance sheet liabilities is misleading. The correct cash outflows (rule 4) are computed by reference to the profit and loss account provisions:

	1990	1991
Payment of last year final	20	30
Payment of this year interim	30	40
Total dividends paid	50	70 = outflows

ˡ Retained profits

	1989	1990	1991
	320	360	430

Rule 7 inflow   40   70

Provisions for corporation tax and dividends were adjusted at footnotes j and k. We include the profit before tax (1990 = £150,000 and 1991 = £220,000) as a rule 7 inflow to correct for this.

ᵐ Investment

	1990	1991
	–	400

Rule 1 outflow   (400)

The cost of the investment in 1991 was a cash outfllow.

ⁿ Term loan

	1989	1990	1991
	800	600	400

Rule 2 outflow   (200)   (200)

The term loan is being repaid in instalments of £200,000 per annum. This can be seen from the declining long-term debt in the balance sheet. The cash outflows are:

	1990	1991
Opening liability	1,000	800
Closing liability	800	600
Repayment	200	200 = outflows

99

Cash Flow Statement Iffy PLC for Year Ended 31 December 1990

INDIRECT METHOD		*1990* *£'000*
Net cash inflow from operating activities		350[1]
Returns on investment and servicing of finance		
Interest paid	(20)	o
Dividend paid	(50)	k
Net cash outflow to returns on investment and servicing of finance		(70)
Taxation		
Corporation tax paid		(20)[j]
Investing activities		
Purchase of fixed assets	(180)	b
Net cash outflow to investing activities		(180)
Net cash inflow before financing		80
Financing activities		
Term loan repayment	(200)	n
Net cash outflow to financing activities		(200)
Increase (decrease) in cash and cash equivalents		(120)[2]

[1] Reconciliation of operating profit to net cash inflow from operating activities

Profit before interest and tax	170
Depreciation	160[a+b]
Change in debtors	60[d]
Change in creditors	(30)[h]
Change in stocks	(50)[c]
Prepayments	(10)[e]
Accruals	50[j]
	350

[2] Analysis of change in cash and cash equivalents during year

	Cash	Overdrafts	Total
Opening	50	(300)	(250)
Closing	80	(450)	(370)
Change	(30)	(150)	(120)

o The interest charge in the profit and loss account was paid in cash in both years.

Cash Flow Statement Iffy PLC for Year Ended 31 December 1991

INDIRECT METHOD		1991 £'000
Net cash inflow from operating activities		450[1]
Returns on investment and servicing of finance		
Interest paid	(40)	o
Dividend paid	(70)	k
Net cash outflow to returns on investment and servicing of finance		(110)
Taxation		
Corporation tax paid		(50)[j]
Investing activities		
Purchase of shares in New Ltd	(400)	m
Purchase of fixed assets	(300)	b
Proceeds of sale of fixed assets	130	
Net cash outflow to investing activities		(570)
Net cash inflow before financing		(280)
Financing activities		
Increase in borrowings short term	430	g
Term loan repayment	(200)	n
Net cash outflow to financing activities		230
Increase (decrease) in cash and cash equivalents		(50)[2]

[1] Reconciliation of operating profit to net cash inflow from operating activities

Profit before interest and tax	260
Depreciation	150[a+b]
Change in debtors	(160)[d]
Change in creditors	170[h]
Change in stocks	30[c]
Prepayments	(20)[e]
Accruals	20[i]
	450

[2] Analysis of change in cash and cash equivalents during year

	Cash	Overdrafts	Total
Opening	80	(450)	(370)
Closing	100	(520)	(420)
Change	20	(70)	(50)

FRS 1 defines cash and cash equivalents very precisely. There are three components:

1   The actual cash on hand and in current accounts.
2   Deposits and other highly liquid investments that can be converted into cash at short notice and are not subject to any significant risk of changes in value owing to changes in interest rates.
3   Short-term bank borrowings.

FRS 1 provides clear guidance on amounts to be included at items 2 and 3 above by specifying a three month maturity threshold. Thus a deposit for a fixed term of one month or a bank loan due for repayment two months after the balance sheet date would be included in cash and cash equivalents whereas a deposit with a maturity date six months after the balance sheet date would be included in investing activities and a bank loan repayable six months after the balance sheet date would be included in financing activities. Some commentators have criticised this ruling but it has two significantly attractive qualities: (a) it is unambiguous, and (b) the 'real' value of loans or deposits of longer than three months can be significantly influenced by interest rates.

The Direct Method

The following is the cash flow statement for Iffy PLC using the direct method. Footnotes explain how the cash flows reconcile with the accrual based statements.

Cash Flow Statement Iffy PLC for Year Ended 31 December 1990

DIRECT METHOD	1990 £'000	
Operating activities		
Cash received from customers	2,051	a
Cash payments to suppliers	(1,026)	b
Other cash payments	(330)	c
Cash paid to and on behalf of employees	(345)	d
Cash flow from operating activities		350
Returns on investment and servicing of finance		
Interest paid	(20)	e
Dividend paid	(50)	e
Net cash outflow to returns on investment and servicing of finance		(70)
Taxation		
Corporation tax paid		(20)[e]
Investing activities		
Purchase of fixed assets	(180)	e
Net cash outflow to investing activities		(180)
Net cash inflow before financing		80
Financing activities		
Term loan repayment	(200)	e
Net cash outflow to financing activities		(200)
Increase (decrease) in cash and cash equivalents		(120)[2]

The footnotes reconciling the cash flow from operating activities with the profit from operations and the cash and cash equivalents in the opening and closing balance sheet would be the same as in the indirect method.

Cash Flow Statement Iffy PLC for Year Ended 31 December 1991

DIRECT METHOD	1991 £'000	
Operating activities		
Cash received from customers	2,264	a
Cash payments to suppliers	(1,055)	b
Other cash payments	(405)	c
Cash paid to and on behalf of employees	(354)	d
Cash flow from operating activities	450	
Returns on investment and servicing of finance		
Interest paid	(40)	e
Dividend paid	(70)	e
Net cash outflow to returns on investment and servicing of finance	(110)	
Taxation		
Corporation tax paid	(50)e	
Investing activities		
Purchase of shares in New Ltd	(400)	e
Purchase of fixed assets	(300)	e
Receipts from seal of tangible fixed assets	130	e
Net cash outflow to investing activities	(570)	
Net cash outflow before financing	(280)	
Financing activities		
Increase in borrowings short term	430	
Term loan repayment	(200)	e
Net cash outflow to financing activities	230	
Increase (decrease) in cash and cash equivalents	(50)[2]	

The footnotes reconciling the cash flow from operating activities with the profit from operations and the cash and cash equivalents in the opening and closing balance sheet would be the same as in the indirect method.

[a] **Sales**   1990 = 2,000   1991 = 2,400
This line in the profit and loss account, if taken in isolation, might imply cash inflows of £2M and £2.4M. Adjustments are required to convert them into customer collections:
1   the company was obliged to charge VAT at 17.5% on the sales (all UK). The VAT is excluded from the sales figures but brought in cash;
2   customers bought on credit; and

3   paragraph 34 of FRS 1 requires that cash collections be shown net of VAT because the VAT element is a temporary timing difference pending settlement of the liability to the tax authorities.

Cash records tell us the collections in each year. This is how they link with the sales and trade debtors:

	1990	1991
Opening debtors	360	300
Sales (including VAT)	2,350	2,820
	2,710	3,120
Closing debtors	300	460
Cash collected	2,410	2,660
Less VAT 17.5%	359	396
Cash collected net of VAT	2,051	2,264

(See also footnote c.)

ᵇ Purchases   1990 = 1,000   1991 = 1,200

This line in the profit and loss account, if taken in isolation, might imply cash outflows of £1M and £1.2M. Adjustments are required to convert them into supplier payments:
1   suppliers charged VAT at 17.5% on their sales. This VAT is not included in the purchases figures (it will be deducted in computing the amount payable on sales). The VAT element of the supplier payments were cash outflows;
2   Iffy PLC took credit from suppliers. Some 1990 purchases were not paid for until 1991. Payment records tell us the amounts paid to suppliers; and
3   paragraph 34 of FRS 1 requires that supplier payments be shown net of VAT (timing difference). Note: supplier payments are shown gross where VAT is not recoverable.

This is how the cash flow to suppliers is computed:

	1990	1991
Opening creditors	360	330
Purchases (including VAT)	1,175	1,410
	1,535	1,740
Closing creditors	330	500
Supplier payments	1,205	1,240
Less VAT	179	185
Supplier payments net of VAT	1,026	1,055

(See also footnote c.)

ᶜ Other expenses   1990 = 370   1991 = 400

This line in the profit and loss account implies cash outflows of 370 and 400 for the two years. The correct cash outflows require adjustment for accruals prepayments and value added tax:

	1990	1991
Opening accrual	18	37[g]
Opening prepayment	(20)	(30)
VAT paid	149	206[f]
Profit and loss charge	370	400
	——	——
	517	613
Closing prepayment	30	50
Closing accrual	(37)	(47)[g]
	——	——
Cash outflow	510	616
VAT customers	(359)	(396)[a]
VAT suppliers	179	185
	——	——
Per cash flow statement	330	405
	——	——

[d] **Payroll cost**   1990 = 350   1991 = 360
The implied cash outflows are incorrect due to unpaid salaries and wages at year end.

	1990	1991
Opening accrual	25	30[g]
Charge for year	350	360
	——	——
	375	390
Closing accrual	30	36[g]
	——	——
Payroll outflow	345	354
	——	——

[e] The other cash flows are computed and reported in exactly the same way as was explained in the indirect method.
[f] The VAT payments are taken from the cash outflow records. They link with the profit and loss and balance sheet as follows:

	1990	1991
Opening liability	7	33[g]
Customer charges	350	420[a]
	——	——
	357	453
Less supplier charges	175	210[b]
	——	——
	182	243
Less closing liability	33	37[g]
	——	——
VAT paid	149	206
	——	——

Note: Depreciation is excluded (non-cash).
[g] Accruals figure in the balance sheets were as follows:

	1989	1990	1991
Other expenses[e]	18	37	47
Payroll [d]	25	30	36
VAT [f]	7	33	37
	——	——	——
	50	100	120
	——	——	——

Paragraph 34 of the standard requires the disclosure of cash flows net of any attributable Value Added Tax or other sales tax unless the tax is irrecoverable by the reporting entity. This rule is derived from the fact that the gross cash collections, which include VAT, are a temporary receipt which will soon be passed to the Revenue Commissioners. The treatment as a temporary timing difference seems to me to place undue emphasis on purity of accounting at the expense of sensible disclosure. I would prefer it if the operating activities mirrored the actual cash flow as follows:

	1990	1991
Operating Activities		
Customer collections (inc. VAT)	2,410	2,660[a]
Supplier payments (inc. VAT)	(1,205)	(1,240)[b]
Other cash payments	(361)	(410)[h]
Value Added Tax	(149)	(206)[f]
Cash paid to and on behalf of employees	(345)	(354)[d]
Cash flow from operating activities	350	450

[h]	1990	1991
Opening accrual	18	37[g]
Opening prepayment	(20)	(30)
Profit and loss charge	370	400
Closing prepayment	30	50
Closing accrual	(37)	(47)[g]
Per cash flow statement	361	410

The Accounting Standards Board appear to have been seduced by the timing argument which will lead to unnecessary confusion. The actual cash receipts are certainly £2.41M in 1990. How can disclosure as £2.051M be justified? Equally the supplier payments are actually £1.205M in 1990. To show them as £1.026M is misleading. I hope that as the pressure for consistent and logical disclosure increases nationally and internationally the proposed treatment of VAT will be adjusted as above.

Managers that are used to source and application of funds statements will probably prefer the indirect method. Disclosure and logic of the approach are similar to SSAP 10. The core issue in the indirect method is that in a fast-growing business operating profit tends to exceed cash creation. Inclusion of the impact of cash flows relating to stocks, debtors, prepayments, creditors and accruals in the operating activities section helps to recognise their impact on liquidity. Managers new to cash flows will probably favour the direct method. It relates more clearly to the underlying cash transactions.

Two major reasons the ASB advanced for the issue of FRS 1 were:

1 The need to increase comparability and therefore usefulness of such statements.
2 The wish to stop enterprise from focusing on working capital changes in reporting sources and applications of funds.

The direct and indirect method are technically excellent and reasonably easy to understand. However, allowing both methods will make interfirm comparison difficult where major competitors do not use the same cash flow reporting framework.

Iffy PLC is well named. Correct analysis of the cash flows reveals a potential liquidity crisis. The following cash flow matrix shows the pressure on liquidity.

1990 Cash Flow Matrix

	Inflows		Outflows	
Long	Operating[1]	260	Investing	180
			Financing	200
				380
Short	Liquidity	120		
		380		380

[1] Operating flow £350,000, minus interest £20,000, dividend £50,000 and tax paid £20,000.

This matrix shows that £120,000 of the long-term outflows were financed by declining liquidity. If the decline in liquidity was a deliberate run down of excess cash it would not be a source of concern. If, on the other hand, it resulted in an increase in the bank overdraft (repayable on demand) Iffy PLC might not be able to repay it and could be in severe financial difficulties.

1991 Cash Flow Matrix Version One

	Inflows		Outflows	
Long	Operating[1]	290	Investing	570
	Financing	230		
		520		
Short	Liquidity	50		
		570		570

A matrix prepared direct from the cash flow statement shows long-term outflows of £0.57M of which £50,000 was financed by declining liquidity. If the bank overdraft were recalled it could force Iffy PLC to

108

dispose of its new strategic investment and they would probably obtain a very poor price.

The matrix seriously distorts the true decline in liquidity. The loan of £430,000 is repayable in nine months and will impose huge pressure on liquidity. The matrix would be more correctly stated as follows:

1991 Cash Flow Matrix Version Two

	Inflows		*Outflows*	
Long	Operating	290	Investing	570
			Financing	200
				770
Short	Liquidity	480		
		770		770

Iffy PLC has used £480,000 from short-term sources to finance the long-term outflows. The most serious part of this liquidity decline could have been avoided if Iffy PLC had, more sensibly, arranged a long-term loan to fund the investment. This version of the matrix provides the clearest picture of the scale of overdependence on short-term funds.

We can derive a vital principle of good business practice from our review of Iffy PLC cash flows. A company should not use short-term funds to finance assets or long-term investments. Breaching this simple rule has led to the downfall of many businesses and losses to their financiers. Iffy PLC is sailing rapidly into dangerous waters.

Financial Institutions an Exception

There is only one exception to the rule that using short-term cash inflows to finance long-term investment is dangerous. This approach is normal practice for financial institutions, e.g. building societies. They accept call deposits and lend these funds to home owners for periods of up to 25 years. A building society or bank can reduce the demand for loans and increase the amount of deposits by raising interest rates. Similarly they can reduce the scale of deposits and increase the demand for loans by reducing interest rates. Providing there is public confidence in these institutions they can continue to borrow short and lend long. The regulatory mechanism works by monitoring cash inflows and outflows. If

1 Supply and demand for funds are in balance, hold interest rates;
2 Demand for funds exceeds supply, increase interest rates to reduce demand and increase supply (this was the major cause of the collapse of the UK property market starting in 1989);
3 Supply of deposits exceeds loan applications, reduce interest rates to discourage deposits and increase demand for loans. The current trend towards lower interest rates should increase confidence in property investment, stimulating more loan applications and lead to improved property prices.

Problem Areas in Cash Flow Classification

1 Revaluation of Assets

The non-cash aspects were illustrated in Iffy PLC.

2 Translation Adjustments (Overseas Assets and Liabilities)

Accounting for foreign currency assets and liablities are dealt with in Chapter 13. Suffice it to say that revaluations arise on translation and are dealt with in the same way as we treated the premises revaluation in Iffy PLC.

3 Capital Grants

In Chapter 2 we saw that capital grants are often depreciated over ten years. This does not give rise to a funds flow:

	31/12/1990	31/12/1991
Plant at cost	1,000	1,000
Less depreciation	–	–
	1,000	900
Cash	–	60
	1,000	960
Financed by:		
Share capital	600	600
State grant	400	360
	1,000	960

Direct comparison of the two balance sheets suggests a cash inflow from operating activities. The depreciation charge 100 appears to have been used: (a) 40 to repay part of the grant, and (b) 60 to increase liquidity. The correct cash flow from operating activities is 60 (the charge against profits net of the grant).

4 Corporation Tax and Dividend Payments

These were illustrated in Iffy PLC.

5 Undistributed Profits of Related Businesses

These profits increase the carrying value of investments. They do not affect the liquidity of the investor company and must be excluded from the operating activities cash flow even though the investor company's share is included in the group profit and loss from ordinary activities. The Iffy PLC investment in New Ltd was made just before the year end. It represented 40% of their shares. No profit was earned by the investee from the date of the investment up to the year end of Iffy PLC. Had New Ltd earned £100,000 before tax and £65,000 after tax, all of which was retained, Iffy would record the transaction as follows:

1 Bringing £40,000 into profit and loss account as a share of profit of a related business;
2 Increasing the tax provision by £14,000;
3 Disclosing retained earnings of £456,000 (i.e. including the additional £26,000 derived from points one and two above); and
4 Showing the investment at £426,000. None of these adjustments created or consumed cash for Iffy PLC. They would be eliminated in preparing the cash flow statement.

Had New Ltd paid the £65,000 as a dividend Iffy PLC would have taken £26,000 into the cash flow statement as a return on investment and its closing cash would obviously have risen by a similar amount. The investment would be valued at £400,000.

6 Mergers and Acquisitions

FRS 1 requires that the changes that arise as a result of mergers and acquisitions be shown in a note to the cash flow statement. Difficult issues arise with regard to the treatment of consolidation reserve, goodwill, minority interest etc. Such intricacies are best left to accounting professionals.

A HANDBOOK OF PRACTICAL BUSINESS FINANCE

IS AN INCREASE IN CASH AND CASH EQUIVALENTS ALWAYS GOOD?

There are three principal cases in which an increase in cash could conceal a deteriorating financial position. We will examine these using an adjusted balance sheet for Iffy PLC in 1991.

Case 1. The short-term bank borrowings in 1991 are not repayable until six months after the balance sheet date. The summarised cash flow statement would appear as follows:

		£'000
Net cash flow before financing		(280)
Short-term borrowings	950	
Term loan repayment	(200)	750
Increase in cash and cash equivalents		470
Cash and cash equivalents 1 January		(370)
Cash and cash equivalents 31 December		100

The serious decline in liquidity is concealed in financing activities.

Case 2. The short-term bank loans totalled £750,000 of which £430,000 was repayable six months after the balance sheet date while the trade creditors totalled £700,000. The summarised cash flow statement would appear as follows:

		£'000
Net cash flow before financing[1]		(80)
Short-term borrowings	430	
Term loan repayment	(200)	230
Increase in cash and cash equivalents		150
Cash and cash equivalents 1 January		(370)
Cash and cash equivalents 31 December[2]		(220)

[1] Original (£280,000) – extra trade credit £200,000.
[2] Original (£420,000) – reduced loan £200,000.

The serious decline in liquidity is concealed in the trade credit element of operating activities. A return to normal settlement terms might be demanded in 1992 and prove impossible for Iffy PLC to accede to.

Case 3. The short-term bank loans totalled £730,000 of which £430,000 was repayable six months after the balance sheet date. A temporary

112

decline in stocks and debtors enabled Iffy PLC to operate within this level of short-term bank debt. The summarised cash flow statement would appear as follows:

		£'000
Net cash flow before financing[1]		(60)
Short-term borrowings	430	
Term loan repayment	(200)	230
Increase in cash and cash equivalents		170
Cash and cash equivalents 1 January		(370)
Cash and cash equivalents 31 December[2]		(200)

[1] Original (£280,000) – reduced stock and debtors £220,000.
[2] Original (£420,000) – reduced loan £220,000.

The serious decline in liquidity is concealed in the stock and debtor elements of operating activities. A return to normal stocking and customer credit in 1992 could prove impossible for Iffy PLC to fund.

IS A DECLINE IN CASH AND CASH EQUIVALENTS ALWAYS BAD NEWS?

A business in which volume is growing rapidly is likely to experience a decrease in cash before financing activities. Where this deficit is not covered by financing activities the situation can be potentially dangerous. Consider three cases:

- Case 1: the business made a conscious decision to reduce the level of surplus (wasteful?) cash and cash equivalents. The decrease should be a satisfactory development.
- Case 2: the business is planning a share issue or long-term loan which had not been finalised at the balance sheet date. In this case the decrease should not cause concern unless the fund raising initiative collapsed.
- Case 3: the business is unaware of, or prepared to ignore, the principle of using long-term finance to support long-term investment. I generally observe that in such cases things start to go wrong and the decline in confidence results in unbearable pressure from bankers and creditors to restructure the business, often by taking undesirable corrective actions.

Corrective action to protect liquidity

Cash flow statements should be a key element of financial planning. Annual budgets and business plans should be converted into a version three cash flow matrix. If the matrix shows an unacceptable deterioration in liquidity the management have three possible options: (a) arrange a share issue and/or long-term loan: (b) defer part of the long-term investment, or (c) proceed with investment in the face of an undesirable matrix. (This appears to be the approach used by household names such as Saatchi and Saatchi, Brent Walker etc and countless small businesses that fell victim to the liquidator's knife.)

Even when the predicted matrix looks satisfactory a business can find its liquidity deteriorating unacceptably. Major causes of this are: (a) operating losses (they can destroy even the most solid financial structure), and (b) capital cost overruns. Businesses most exposed to these problems are ones that ignore the cash flow matrix rules above. A business with: (a) adequate profit margins, (b) good early warning systems and (c) a management team that is prepared to take sensible, albeit unpalatable decisions in the face of adverse trading conditions will survive and thrive.

It is tragic that the cash flow matrix is not a mandatory part of the disclosure requirements in published accounts. It helps to differentiate between controlled and imprudent business development. The wise business will regard it as a vital part of the short- and medium-term cash planning process.

Chapter 5

Cash Forecasting

This chapter provides a detailed illustration of cash forecasting. To demonstrate it in a reasonably comprehensive way, we will examine the proposals for a new business that Larry Leeds proposes to start in January 1990. We will prepare the figures in detail for one year, but I must stress that if you are a budding entrepreneur you should develop a three-year cash forecast. Failure to do so could leave you unaware of your peak borrowing requirements particularly if you intend to start a seasonal business, a business which takes several years to earn a profit, or a business which will grow very fast in subsequent years.

Sales Forecasts

	Monthly Volumes		Monthly Volumes
January	250	July	2,500
February	500	August	2,750
March	750	September	2,000
April	1,000	October	2,000
May	1,500	November	2,000
June	2,000	December	2,500

Total units in 1990 are 19,750. Unit selling prices are net £20, plus VAT at 17.5% £3 = gross £23.50. Sales in January and February 1991 are forecast at 2000 units each month.

Of each month's sales 60% will be made in the UK. Larry is obliged to charge 17.5% VAT on these items. The balance will be exported. The exports are zero rated. This means that Larry will not charge VAT and will be able to recover it on his inputs.

Purchasing will be arranged so that Larry will have 1.5 months forward sales in stock at each month end, composed of: raw material = 1 month and finished stock = ½ month. Quantities bought will be 1% higher than sales indicate they should be, to allow for wastage and pilferage.

The raw material will cost £6 per unit. The price will fall to £5.20

from 1 April. Suppliers will give one month's credit. VAT will be charged by suppliers at 17.5%.

Larry plans to have a core staff of 13 people. Eight will be involved in production. In a working month (he assumed all months have equal working days) the production staff can make 1,600 units without overtime. Any excess over 1,600 units will be paid at time-and-a-quarter. The production payroll cost without overtime is £6,400 per month or £4 per unit. Each unit produced, in excess of 1,600, will cost £5. Non-production payroll costs will amount to £6,250 per month, and all payroll costs will be paid in the month in which they occur.

The overhead costs are as follows:

Item	Amount	Payable
Power	1,800	Monthly
Light	840	Bi-monthly
Telephone	600	Quarterly
Insurance	10,800	At start of year
Rent	12,000	Quarterly in advance
Rates	7,000	Half-yearly in arrears
Pensions	15% of annual payroll	At end of year
Bank interest (borrowings)	16%	Charged in March & September
Lease charges	3,600	Monthly in advance
Postage and packing	1,200	Monthly %

Jan	Feb	Mar	Apr	May	Jun
2	5	6	8	9	15
Jul	Aug	Sep	Oct	Nov	Dec
12	11	8	8	8	8

Advertising	1,500	Monthly %

Jan	Feb	Mar	Apr	May	Jun
10	10	15	15	10	10
Jul	Aug	Sep	Oct	Nov	Dec
5	5	5	5	5	5

Item	Amount	Payable
Other	900	Equally over year

Customer payments are month of sale 10%, second month 59% and third month 30%. 1% of each month's sales is budgeted to prove irrecoverable. Larry hopes this provision will not be necessary but he is wise to provide for it.

Fixed assets will be bought and paid for in January 1990:

	£
Plant	23,600
Truck	12,000
Car	8,400
	44,000

Larry expects to receive a 30% grant towards the cost of the plant in April.

VAT is paid or recovered quarterly. Material purchases are the only item on which Larry expects to reclaim VAT. This assumption is used to simplify the illustration. In practice VAT paid on other items which add value to goods or services sold to third parties can be offset against that charged to customers. The inclusion of this would make the illustration more complicated and I deemed it undesirable because the amounts involved are trivial and a suitable bookkeeping system ensures they are correctly handled.

Larry and other investors will introduce £40,000 of share capital. The bank will match this with a term loan of £40,000, carrying a 2-year moratorium on capital and interest repayments and overdraft facilities of £30,000, provided that the overdraft is cleared for at least two months during 1990.

The following is Larry's cash forecast based on these data. Where necessary, reference is made in the cash forecast to relevant support schedules.

Monthly Cash Forecast

	Jan	Feb	Mar	Apr	May	June	July	Aug	Sep	Oct	Nov	Dec	Total
Cash in													
Capital	40,000												40,000
Term loan	40,000												40,000
Customers (1)	353	2,820	6,309	9,800	13,642	19,599	26,578	32,206	36,307	30,985	27,918	28,623	236,140
Customers (2)	200	1,600	3,580	5,560	7,740	11,120	15,080	18,840	20,600	17,580	15,840	16,240	133,980
Grant				7,080									7,080
	80,555	4,420	9,889	22,440	21,382	30,719	41,658	51,046	56,907	48,565	43,758	44,863	457,200
Cash out													
Suppliers (3)		8,011	6,230	8,901	10,799	13,885	16,199	14,656	12,342	12,342	13,885	13,885	131,135
VAT (4)		(668)		371			3,361			9,366			12,430
Payroll (5)	12,650	12,650	12,650	12,650	13,400	15,900	17,775	16,525	14,650	14,650	15,900	15,900	175,300
Overhead (6)	14,499	875	972	3,986	783	4,645	3,744	872	846	3,836	696	30,781	66,535
Plant	23,600												23,600
Truck and car	20,400												20,400
Bank interest (7)			243						1,259				1,502
	71,149	20,868	20,095	25,908	24,982	34,430	41,079	32,053	29,097	40,194	30,481	60,566	430,902
Monthly Surplus/deficit	9,404	(16,448)	(10,206)	(3,468)	(3,600)	(3,711)	579	19,993	27,810	8,371	13,277	(15,703)	26,298
Opening cash	–	9,404	(7,044)	(17,250)	(20,718)	(24,318)	(28,029)	(27,450)	(7,457)	20,353	28,724	42,001	–
Closing cash	9,404	(7,044)	(17,250)	(20,718)	(24,318)	(28,029)	(27,450)	(7,457)	20,353	28,724	42,001	26,298	26,298

Support schedules 1 to 7 are provided on subsequent pages.

118

Schedule 1: Sales and Cash Collections (Home)

	Sales incl. VAT	10%	60%	29%	Total Collected
Jan	3,525	353	–	–	353
Feb	7,050	705	2,115	–	2,820
Mar	10,575	1,057	4,230	1,022	6,309
Apr	14,100	1,410	6,345	2,045	9,800
May	21,150	2,115	8,460	3,067	13,642
Jun	28,200	2,820	12,690	4,089	19,599
Jul	35,250	3,525	16,920	6,133	26,578
Aug	38,775	3,878	21,150	8,178	33,206
Sep	28,200	2,820	23,265	10,222	36,307
Oct	28,200	2,820	16,920	11,245	30,985
Nov	28,200	2,820	16,920	8,178	27,918
Dec	35,250	3,525	16,920	8,178	28,623
	278,475	27,848	145,935	62,357	236,140
Jan			21,150	8,178	
Feb			–	10,222	
			167,085	80,757	
	a	b	c	d	e

[a] 60% of 19,750 units at £20 each = £237,000 plus VAT at 17.5% = £278,475.
[b] Verified as 10% of annual gross sales.
[c] Verified as 60% of annual gross sales (January collections included).
[d] Verified as 29% of annual gross sales (January and February collections included).
[e] Verified as follows:

Sales gross		278,475
Less bad debts 1%	2,785	
Less debtors	39,550	42,335
		236,140

Debtors at 31 December: 21,150+8,178+10,222 = 39,550.

A HANDBOOK OF PRACTICAL BUSINESS FINANCE

Schedule 2: Sales and Cash Collections (Export)

	Sales	10%	60%	29%	Total Collected
Jan	2,000	200	–	–	200
Feb	4,000	400	1,200	–	1,600
Mar	6,000	600	2,400	580	3,580
Apr	8,000	800	3,600	1,160	5,560
May	12,000	1,200	4,800	1,740	7,740
Jun	16,000	1,600	7,200	2,320	11,120
Jul	20,000	2,000	9,600	3,480	15,080
Aug	22,000	2,200	12,000	4,640	18,840
Sep	16,000	1,600	13,200	5,800	20,600
Oct	16,000	1,600	9,600	6,380	17,580
Nov	16,000	1,600	9,600	4,640	15,840
Dec	20,000	2,000	9,600	4,640	16,240
	158,000	15,800	82,800	35,380	133,980
Jan			12,000	4,640	
Feb			–	5,800	
			94,800	45,820	
	a	b	c	d	e

[a] 40% of 19,750 units at £20 each = £158,000.
[b] Verified as 10% of annual gross sales.
[c] Verified as 60% of annual gross sales (January collections included).
[d] Verified as 29% of annual gross sales (January and February collections included).
[e] Verified as follows:

Sales gross		158,000
Less bad debts 1%	1,580	
Less debtors	22,440	24,020
		133,980

Debtors at 31 December: 12,000+4,640+5,800 = 22,440.

Schedule 3: Supplier Payments

	Purchase Quantities	Cost per Unit	Purchases Value	Supplier Payment in Arrears
Jan	1,136.25[a]	7.05	8,011	
Feb	883.75[b]	7.05	6,230	8,011
Mar	1,262.50	7.05	8,901	6,230
Apr	1,767.50	6.11	10,799	8,901
May	2,272.50	6.11	13,885	10,799
Jun	2,651.25	6.11	16,199	13,885
Jul	2,398.75	6.11	14,656	16,199
Aug	2,020.00	6.11	12,342	14,656
Sep	2,020.00	6.11	12,342	12,342
Oct	2,272.50	6.11	13,885	12,342
Nov	2,272.50[c]	6.11	13,885	13,885
Dec	2,020.00[d]	6.11	12,342	13,885
	22,977.50[e]		143,477[f]	131,135[f]

[a] Jan 250+Feb 500+50% Mar 375 = 1,125×101%.
[b] 50% Mar 375+50% April 500 = 875×101%
[c] 50% Dec 1,250+50% Jan 1,000 = 2,250×101%.
[d] 50% Jan 1,000+50% Feb 1,000 = 2,000×101%.
[e] This can be verified as follows:
Bought for annual sales	19,750×101% = 19,947.5
Bought for material stock	2,000×101% = 2,020.0
Bought for finished stock	1,000×101% = 1,010.0
	22,977.5

[f] (3,282.5×£7.05)+(19,695×£6.11) = 143,477
Less paid January 1993   12,342
   131,135

Schedule 4: VAT Settlements

	Home Gross Sales	VAT Element 14.89‰	Gross Purchases	VAT Element 14.89‰	Net VAT	Payable
Jan	3,525	525	8,011	1,193	(668)	
Feb	7,050	1,050	6,230	928	122	(668)
Mar	10,575	1,575	8,901	1,326	249	
Apr	14,100	2,100	10,799	1,608	492	371
May	21,150	3,150	13,885	2,068	1,082	
Jun	28,200	4,200	16,199	2,413	1,787	
Jul	35,250	5,250	14,656	2,183	3,067	3,361
Aug	38,775	5,775	12,342	1,838	3,937	
Sep	28,200	4,200	12,342	1,838	2,362	
Oct	28,200	4,200	13,885	2,068	2,132	9,366
Nov	28,200	4,200	13,885	2,068	2,132	
Dec	35,250	5,250	12,342	1,838	3,412	–
	278,475	41,475	143,477	21,369	20,106	12,430
		a		b	c	

VAT due (1,827+1,828+2,925)   7,676

                                                                          20,106

[a] To remove VAT from the home sales and the purchases we use a percentage of 14.89%. This is derived by expressing the VAT 17.5% as a percentage of the gross figure 117.5%. Verified as £278,475 at 14.89%.
[b] Verified as £143,477 at 14.89%.
[c] Verified as £41,475−£21,369 = £20,106.

Note: The VAT liability is calculated quarterly and paid in the following month. Larry will reclaim excess VAT paid at the end of January and receive it in February.

Schedule 5: Payroll

	Total Prod'n	Overtime Prod'n	Paid at Normal	Paid at Overtime	Other	Total Payroll
Jan	500		6,400		6,250	12,650
Feb	625		6,400		6,250	12,650
Mar	875		6,400		6,250	12,650
Apr	1,250		6,400		6,250	12,650
May	1,750	150	6,400	750	6,250	13,400
Jun	2,250	650	6,400	3,250	6,250	15,900
Jul	2,625	1,025	6,400	5,125	6,250	17,775
Aug	2,375	775	6,400	3,875	6,250	16,525
Sep	2,000	400	6,400	2,000	6,250	14,650
Oct	2,000	400	6,400	2,000	6,250	14,650
Nov	2,250	650	6,400	3,250	6,250	15,900
Dec	2,250	650	6,400	3,250	6,250	15,900
	20,750	4,700	76,800	23,500	75,000	175,300
	a	a	b	c		

[a] Verification of production:

Units Normal	Units Overtime	Units Total	For sales	For Fin. stock
16,050	4,700	20,750	19,750	1,000

At full capacity 1,600 units could be produced each month = 19,200 for the year. Due to low initial demand the actual normal time production is:
$$19,200-(1,100+975+725+350) = 16,050.$$
[b] Normal production cost £6,400×12 = £76,800.
[c] Overtime production cost 4,700×£5 = £23,500.
Note: Pension contribution £175,300 at 15% = £26,295.

Schedule 6: General Overheads

	Power	Light	Phone	Insurance	Rent	Rates	Pensions	Leases	Post & Packing	Advertising	Other	Total
Jan	150			10,800	3,000			300	24	150	75	14,499
Feb	150	140						300	60	150	75	875
Mar	150		150					300	72	225	75	972
Apr	150	140			3,000			300	96	225	75	3,986
May	150							300	108	150	75	783
Jun	150	140	150			3,500		300	180	150	75	4,645
Jul	150				3,000			300	144	75	75	3,744
Aug	150	140						300	132	75	75	872
Sep	150		150					300	96	75	75	846
Oct	150	140			3,000			300	96	75	75	3,836
Nov	150							300	96	75	75	696
Dec	150	140	150	–	–	3,500	26,295	300	96	75	75	30,781
	1,800	840	600	10,800	12,000	7,000	26,295	3,600	1,200	1,500	900	66,535

Schedule 7: Bank Interest

		£
(A)	January cash £9,404×10%÷12 =	(78)
	February O/D £7,044×16%÷12 =	94
	March O/D £17,007×16%÷12 =	
	(pre-interest)*	227
		243

* £17,250−£243 = £17,007.

(B)	April O/D £20,718×16%÷12 =	276
	May O/D £24,318×16%÷12 =	324
	June O/D £28,029×16%÷12 =	374
	July O/D £27,450×16%÷12 =	366
	August O/D £7,457×16%÷12 =	99
	September cash £21,612×10%÷12 =	
	(pre-interest)*	(180)
		1,259

* £20,353−£1,259 = £21,612.

(C)	Interest accrued	
	October cash £28,724×10%÷12 =	(239)
	November cash £42,001×10%÷12 =	(350)
	December cash £26,298×10%÷12 =	(219)
		(808)
	Term loan £40,000×16%	6,400

Total cost (A+B+C)	£7,094
Accrued interest £6,400−£808 =	£5,592

Note: Larry used simple interest of 16% on overdrafts and term loans and 10% on surplus cash in computing his provisions and earnings. He assumed that the balance at month-end was a fair representation of the position during the month. In practice, overdraft interest is calculated by banks on a daily basis.

Schedule 8: Profit and Loss Account 1992

	£	£
Sales home[1]	237,000	
export[2]	158,000	395,000
Purchases[3]	122,108	
Less material stocks[4]	10,400	
Materials consumed	111,708	
Production payroll	100,300	
	212,008	
Less finished stocks[5]	9,200	
Cost of sales		202,808
Gross profit		192,192
Operating expenses		
Power	1,800	
Light	840	
Telephone	600	
Insurance	10,800	
Rent and rates	19,000	
Pensions	26,295	
Lease charges	3,600	
Postage and packing	1,200	
Advertising	1,500	
Salaries and wages (non-production)	75,000	
Other	900	
Bad debts[6]	4,365	
Depreciation		
Plant[7]	3,304	
Truck[8]	2,400	
Car[9]	2,100	153,704
Profit before interest and tax		38,488
Term loan interest[14]	6,400	
Net bank interest[14]	694	7,094
Profit before tax		31,394
Corporation tax[10]		7,517
Profit retained		23,877

Schedule 9: Balance Sheet at 31 December 1992

Fixed assets	Cost	Depreciation	Book value
Plant[7]	23,600	4,720	18,880
Truck[8]	12,000	2,400	9,600
Car[9]	8,400	2,100	6,300
	44,000	9,220	34,780

Current assets		
Stocks materials[4]	10,400	
Stocks finished goods[5]	9,200	
Trade debtors[11]	61,990	
Cash	26,298	107,888
		142,668

Payable in under one year		
Suppliers[12]	12,342	
VAT[13]	7,676	
Bank interest[14]	5,592	
Corporation tax[10]	7,517	(33,127)
Net assets		109,541

Financed by:	
Share capital	40,000
Revenue reserve	23,877
	63,877
Government grant[7]	5,664
Bank term loan	40,000
	109,541

Schedule 10: Supporting Notes to Financial Statements

[1] Gross home sales from Schedule 1	278,475
Less VAT	41,475
	237,000
[2] Export sales from Schedule 2	158,000
[3] Gross purchases from Schedule 3	143,477
Less VAT	21,369
	122,108

[4] Material stocks 2,000 items at £5.20 each. It is assumed that stock losses occur prior to issue.
[5] Finished goods stock 1,000 items at £9.20 each. Larry plans to value the finished stock at material cost £5.20 plus 'normal' labour £4.00 = £9.20 per unit.
[6] Bad debts per Schedules 1 and 2 (2,785+1,580) = £4,365.
[7] Plant is depreciated over 5 years straight line:

	Cost	Grant	Net
Plant	23,600	7,080	16,520
Depreciation	4,720	1,416	3,304 (Expense charge)
Balance sheet	18,880	5,664	

[8] The truck is depreciated over 5 years straight line:

	Cost
Truck	12,000
Depreciation	2,400 (Expense charge)
Balance sheet	9,600

[9] The car is depreciated over 4 years straight line:

	Cost
Car	8,400
Depreciation	2,100 (Expense charge)
Balance sheet	6,300

[10] Corporation tax provision:

	£
Profit forecast	31,394
Add depreciation	7,804
	39,198
Less WDA 25%	9,130
Taxable	30,068
Tax at 25%	7,517

Note: The writing down allowance is restricted as follows:

Plant net of grant	16,520
Van	12,000
Car (maximum allowed)	8,000
	36,520
Allowance at 25%	9,130

Larry will be liable to Corporation tax at 25%. This is a preferential rate that applies to profits of under £250,000.

[11] Per Schedules 1 and 2 (39,550+22,440) = £61,990.
[12] Per Schedule 3:
[13] Per Schedule 4: £7,676.
[14] Per Schedule 7: (£6,400−£808) = £5,592.

General Comments on the Data in the Forecast Profit and Loss Account, Balance Sheet and Cash Flow

The forecast profit is based on what Larry believes is a conservative sales target and no production in excess of half the following month's expected demand. This causes poor utilisation of the labour force in early months. Capacity is available to produce significantly more than is required at a production labour cost of £6,400 per month up to end-April. It would be possible to meet the demand in peak months with little overtime by utilising the surplus capacity. Much of the overtime budget of £23,500 could be eliminated in this way – 15% of this sum (£3,525) would not have to be put into the pension fund. If Larry does this, he will have to increase his purchases and supplier payments in the first four months. This would increase the overdraft he needs to above £30,000. Larry feels this would be asking for too much.

The projected profit is a realistic assessment of the worst things that could go wrong. Larry expects to earn a higher profit than this in 1992. In 1993 using similar conservative volume forecasts, Larry anticipates significant profit growth. He intends to expand his production level by recruiting additional staff and acquiring a second machine. A cash forecast (not reproduced here), shows that this can be achieved without further bank loans. This is why Larry intends to retain all the profits earned in 1992.

The cash forecast is very interesting. It reveals the growth in borrowing requirements as sales volume rises and the decline as growth levels off. The rise in sales and the year-end pension contribution cause a significant fall in cash resources in December 1992.

Presenting Cash Forecasts to Financial Institutions in Funding Negotiations

Negotiating bank loans can be a difficult challenge. One major reason is that bankers expect promoters' forecasts to be optimistic. They frequently adjust revenues downwards and costs upwards in assessing loan applications. The unfortunate consequences of this can be two-fold:

1 Projects with great potential, which are conservatively forecast, can sometimes be rejected because the bank adjustments take out the substance rather than over-optimism. Good projects that fail to get off the ground are a tragic waste.
2 Sometimes promoters, anticipating downward adjustments, deliberately place some padding in the forecasts. Tactically, there

is a good deal to be said for this approach. It gets the loan decision based on something similar to the position that is expected. However, bankers frequently review projects previously approved. Unfortunately, they tend to compare actual achievements with the promoters' forecasts, rather than their risk-adjusted versions. This reinforces their view that promoters are always too optimistic.

Qualities of a Good Funding Application

The financial figures should generally cover a period of three years from the start of the loan. The first year should be presented in detail, with monthly (and sometimes even weekly) cash forecasts, and quarterly profit and loss and balance sheet figures.

The figures should be supported by the following data: a detailed description of the business history of the promoter(s); a well argued justification of the size of the market and the share you expect to obtain; and an explanation of the key assumptions implicit in the plan. These include:

Stock holding periods;
Location of key customers;
Cash collection periods:
Location of key suppliers;
Supplier payment periods;
Availability of work force required;
Productivity expectations;
Confidence in fixed asset costs;
Source(s) of capital introduced;
Proposed salary and dividend restrictions; and
Guarantees and security available.

The analysis should appear professional and credible. There is a case for putting in something for the loan analyst to 'discover', so that on the one hand they feel useful and on the other hand realise that the proposal is credible and professional.

Never forget that forecasts are only well conceived paper. A big part of the lending decision is based on belief in the promoter. If a banker likes you, and is confident of your ability to cope with the inevitable business crises, it is possible to obtain loans for moderate projects. If you are disliked or distrusted, you may not be able to finance the best project of the decade.

Larry Leeds made a presentation to his local bank. He was accompanied by a member of the new business section of the Regional Development Agency. The bank authorised overdraft facilities that were sufficient to allow a stock build up that would overcome the mid-year overtime premiums. This was possible because Larry provided a second version of his projections. It was not difficult for him to prepare this. Larry had used a computer spreadsheet and was able to adjust the forecasts quite easily. If you aspire to starting your own business you will need to be able to forecast the cash flow, profit and loss and balance sheet based on your key assumptions. If you can use a computer spreadsheet it simplifies the task.

If you wish to become proficient in this vital task here is a suggestion. You should prepare a revised forecast for Larry Leeds. You may assume that all the projections are correct except that Larry plans to produce 1,600 items each month so as to maximise his production labour utilisation. The finished stocks will become a function of production less sales rather than one-half month of future sales that Larry used in his original forecast. The revised forecast is reproduced in the following schedules so that you can verify your results.

Revised Monthly Cash Forecast

	Jan	Feb	Mar	Apr	May	Jun	July	Aug	Sep	Oct	Nov	Dec	Total
Cash in													
Capital	40,000												40,000
Term loan	40,000												40,000
Customers (1)	353	2,820	6,309	9,800	13,642	19,599	26,578	33,206	36,307	30,985	27,918	28,623	236,140
Customers (2)	200	1,600	3,580	5,560	7,740	11,120	15,080	18,840	20,600	17,580	15,840	16,240	133,980
Grant				7,080									7,080
	80,553	4,420	9,889	22,440	21,382	30,719	41,658	52,046	56,907	48,565	43,758	44,863	457,200
Cash out													
Suppliers (3A)		22,786	11,393	11,393	9,874	9,874	9,874	9,874	9,873	9,873	9,873	13,271	127,958
VAT (4A)		(2,869)	(647)	(122)			5,038			10,814			12,214
Payroll (1A)	12,650	12,650	12,650	12,650	12,650	12,650	12,650	12,650	12,650	12,650	12,650	15,400	154,550
Overhead (2A)	14,499	875	972	3,986	783	4,645	3,744	872	846	3,836	696	27,669	63,423
Plant	23,600												23,600
Truck and car	20,400												20,400
Bank interest			639						1,701				2,340
	71,149	33,442	25,007	27,907	23,307	27,169	31,306	23,396	25,070	37,173	23,219	56,340	404,485
Monthly surplus/(deficit)	9,404	(29,022)	(15,118)	(5,467)	(1,925)	3,550	10,352	28,650	31,837	11,392	20,539	(11,477)	52,715
Opening cash	–	9,404	(19,618)	(34,736)	(40,203)	(42,128)	(38,578)	(28,226)	424	32,261	43,633	64,192	–
Closing cash	9,404	(19,618)	(34,736)	(40,203)	(42,128)	(38,578)	(28,226)	424	32,261	43,653	64,192	52,715	52,715

Support schedules 1A to 8A are provided on subsequent pages.

Schedule 1A: Revised Payroll

	Monthly	Annual
Production wages	6,400	76,800
Other salaries and wages	6,250	75,000
	12,650	151,800
Overtime December[a] 550 at £5		2,750
		154,550
Pension contribution (15%)		23,183

[a] If Larry produces at 1,600 per month, he will have 350 items of finished stock at the end of November. This combined with the planned December production will not be sufficient to meet the expected demand. 550 items will have to be produced at overtime rates.

As a result of the pension adjustment the December and total overheads figures change. The revisions are as follows:

Schedule 2A: Revised General Overheads

	December		Total
Original pensions	26,295	Original	66,535
Revised pensions	23,183		
		Pension	
Change in pensions	3,112	change	3,112
December O/H original	30,781		
		Revised	63,423
December O/H revised	27,669		

Schedule 3A: Purchases and Supplier Payments

	Purchase Quantities	Cost per Unit	Purchases Value	Supplier Payment in Arrears
Jan	3,232[a]	7.05	22,786	
Feb	1,616	7.05	11,393	22,786
Mar	1,616	7.05	11,393	11,393
Apr	1,616	6.11	9,874	11,393
May	1,616	6,11	9,874	9,874
Jun	1,616	6.11	9,874	9,874
Jul	1,616	6.11	9,874	9,874
Aug	1,616	6.11	9,873	9,874
Sep	1,616	6.11	9,873	9,873
Oct	1,616	6.11	9,873	9,873
Nov	2,172[b]	6.11	13,271	9,873
Dec	2,020[c]	6.11	12,342	13,271
	21,968[d]		140,300[e]	127,958[e]

Production units
[a] January and February 1990 3,200 at 101% = 3,232.
[b] December 1990 2,150 items at 101%.
[c] January 1991 2,000 items at 101%.

[d] Annual production 1,600×12 =	19,200
Overtime production December	550
Material stock (year-end)	2,000
	21,750
Add 1% (stock losses)	218
Units to be purchased	21,968

[e] (6,464×£7.05)+(15,504×£6.11) =	140,300
Less paid January 1993	12,342
	127,958
[f] Purchases gross	140,300
Less VAT (15/115)	20,896
Profit and loss charge	119,404

Schedule 4A: VAT Settlements

	Home Gross Sales	VAT Element 14.89%	Gross Purchases	VAT Element 14.89%	Net VAT	Payable
Jan	3,525	525	22,786	3,394	(2,869)	
Feb	7,050	1,050	11,393	1,697	(647)	(2,869)
Mar	10,575	1,575	11,393	1,697	(122)	(647)
Apr	14,100	2,100	9,874	1,471	629	(122)
May	21,150	3,150	9,874	1,470	1,680	
Jun	28,200	4,200	9,874	1,471	2,729	
Jul	35,250	5,250	9,874	1,470	3,780	5,038
Aug	38,775	5,775	9,873	1,471	4,304	
Sep	28,200	4,200	9,873	1,470	2,730	
Oct	28,200	4,200	9,873	1,471	2,729	10,814
Nov	28,200	4,200	13,271	1,976	2,224	
Dec	35,250	5,250	12,342	1,838	3,412	–
	278,475	41,475	140,300	20,896	20,579	12,214
	a		b	c		

VAT due (2,339+1,906+2,924) 8,365

20,579

[a] Verified as £278,475 at 15% of gross revenue.
[b] Verified as £140,300 at 15% of gross cost.
[c] Verified as 41,475−20,896 = £20,579.

Note: The VAT liability is calculated quarterly and paid in the following month. Larry will reclaim excess VAT paid at the end of January, February and March and receive it in February, March and April respectively.

Schedule 5A: Bank Interest

		£
(A)	January cash £9,404×10%÷12 =	(78)
	February O/D £19,618×16%÷12 =	262
	March O/D £34,097×16%÷12 =	455
	(pre-interest)*	——
		638
	* £34,736−£639 = £34,097.	
(B)	April O/D £40,203×16%÷12 =	536
	May O/D £42,128×16%÷12 =	562
	June O/D £38,578×16%÷12 =	514
	July O/D £28,226×16%÷12 =	376
	August cash £424×10%÷12 =	4
	September cash £33,952×10%÷12 =	(283)
	(pre-interest)*	——
		1,701
	* £33,261−£1,701 = £33,962	
(C)	Interest receivable	
	October cash £43,653×10%÷12 =	(364)
	November cash £64,192×10%÷12 =	(535)
	December cash £52,715×10%÷12 =	(439)
		(1,338)
	Term loan £40,000×16%	6,400
	Total cost (A+B+C)	£7,402
	Accrued interest £6,400−£1,338 =	5,062

Note: Larry used simple interest of 16% on overdrafts and term loans and 10% on surplus cash in computing his provisions and earnings. He assumed that the balance at month-end was a fair representation of the position during the month. Overdraft interest is calculated by the banks on a daily basis.

Schedule 6A: Profit and Loss Account

	£	£
Sales home[1]	237,000	
export[1]	158,000	395,000
Purchases[2]	119,404	
Less material stocks[3]	10,400	
Materials consumed	109,004	
Production payroll[4]	79,550	
Cost of sales		188,554
Gross profit		206,446
Operating expenses		
Power	1,800	
Light	840	
Telephone	600	
Insurance	10,800	
Rent and rates	19,000	
Pensions[5]	23,183	
Lease charges	3,600	
Postage and packing	1,200	
Advertising	1,500	
Salaries and wages (non-production)	75,000	
Other	900	
Bad debts[1]	4,365	
Depreciation		
Plant[1]	3,304	
Truck[1]	2,400	
Car[1]	2,100	150,592
Profit before interest and tax		55,854
Term loan interest[1]	6,400	
Net bank interest[6]	1,002	7,402
Profit before tax		48,452
Corporation tax[7]		12,781
Profit retained		35,671

Schedule 7A: Balance Sheet at 31 December 1992

Fixed assets	Cost	Depreciation	Book Value
Plant[1]	23,600	4,720	18,880
Truck[1]	12,000	2,400	9,600
Car[1]	8,400	2,100	6,300
	44,000	9,220	34,780
Current assets			
Stocks materials[3]		10,400	
Trade debtors[1]		61,990	
Cash		52,715	125,105
			159,885
Payable in under one year			
Suppliers[8]		12,342	
VAT[9]		8,365	
Bank interest[6]		5,062	
Corporation tax[7]		11,781	(37,550)
Net assets			122,335
Financed by:			
Share capital			40,000
Revenue reserve			36,671
			76,671
Government grant[7]			5,664
Bank term loan			40,000
			122,335

Schedule 8A: Supporting Notes to Financial Statements

[1] Per original forecast.
[2] Per Schedule 3A.
[3] 2,000 items bought in December at £5.20 (net of VAT).
[4] Per Schedule 1A.
[5] Per Schedule 1A.
[6] Per Schedule 5A.
[7] Corporation tax provision:

	£
Profit forecast	48,452
Add depreciation	7,804
	56,256
Less WDA 25%	9,130
Taxable	47,126
Tax at 27%	12,781

[8] Per Schedule 3A.
[9] Per Schedule 4A.

Control Against Cash Forecasts

Forecasts of cash creation and consumption can prove inaccurate. This arises where key variables are incorrectly predicted. The early identification of such departures is crucial. The most vital elements in the predictions by Larry Leeds are:

1 The ability to achieve the production and sales volumes at the unit prices he predicted.
2 Obtaining the fixed assets at a price within the capital budget and the project grant.
3 Collecting cash from customers at least as quickly as forecast, and paying suppliers at least as slowly as forecast.
4 Non-deviation from the stock holding policy formulated for Larry's business.

If some of these items prove to be wrong (and they invariably do), then it will be necessary to revise the forecasts on a regular basis. If Larry does not do this he will run the risk of exceeding his overdraft limit. Banks expect their customers to provide substantial advance notice when additional funds are required. If they do not get this notice, they charge an interest penalty and 'bounce' cheques. This would be very serious at a time when Larry is trying to establish his reputation with suppliers, customers and the bank. We will see how Larry approaches this in Chapter 9 ('Financial control').

Chapter 6

Ratio Analysis

Ratio analysis is the process by which the financial statements of a business enterprise are tested for stability, profitability and so on. Historic results can be used to measure the effectiveness of the way in which a business has been run in the past. Budgeted future results can be used to test the appropriateness of plans for the ongoing development of the business. The computation of ratios on an historic basis is a passive analysis. Calculating ratios from budgeted figures is constructive. (If the ratio is unsatisfactory it implies a defect in the plan and you may be able to overcome the problem.) Ratio analysis is most frequently carried out on an historic basis. This historic analysis loses some of the major benefits that can be gained by looking into the future. Historic analysis is more often used by writers and teachers. This is because: budgeted figures are not normally published; and key figures are not available because disclosure requirements for published accounts do not apply. For these reasons the illustrations in this chapter are based on historic results.

The following figures have been extracted from the financial statments of a business enterprise for the last two years:

Model Company Ltd Balance Sheet as at 31 December (£'000)

1988		Cost	Aggregate Depreciation	Book Value	1989
	Fixed assets				
440	Land	440	–	440	
752	Buildings	800[1]	64	736	
280	Plant & Machinery	500[1]	170	330	
104	Vehicles	160[1]	88	72	
1,576		1,900	322	1,578	
	Current assets				
700	Stocks				800
1,148	Trade debtors				1,042
93	Prepayments				115
17	Cash				84
1,958					2,041
	Less current liabilities				
	Bank overdraft and term				
186	loan[2]		161		
532	Trade creditors		376		
160	Accruals		150		
40	Other taxes		42		
99	Corporation tax		139		
90	Proposed dividend		120	(988)	
(1,107)					
2,427	Net assets				2,631
	Financed by:		Authorised		
1,700	Ordinary share capital (£1 units)		1,800	1,700	
121	Revenue reserves		–	339	
1,821	Shareholders' funds				2,039
112	Grants[3]				132
388	Term loan[2]				311
106	Deferred tax[7]				149
2,427					2,631

141

Model Company Ltd Profit and Loss Account (£'000)

1988			1989
4,590	Sales		5,000
680	Opening stock	700	
3,600	Cost of production	3,900	
4,280		4,600	
700	Less closing stock	800	
3,580	Cost of sales		3,800
1,010	Gross profit		1,200
(162)	Administration	180	
(436)	Selling and distribution	416	596
412	Profit before interest		604
112	Interest		84
300	Profit before tax		520
(90)	Corporation tax	151	
(15)	Deferred tax[7]	31	182
195	Profit after tax		338
90	Proposed dividend		120
105	Profit retained		218

Note 1: Depreciation

	Cost	Year Purchased	Rate	Annual Depreciation Amount	Years		Aggregate Depreciation
Buildings	800	1986	2%	16	4		64
Plant	400	1986	10%	40	4	160	
	100	1989	10%	10	1	10	170
Vehicles	60	1986	20%	12	4	48	
	100	1988	20%	20	2	40	88

Note 2: Term loan

The company obtained a term loan of £560,000 at 16% on 1 January, 1986. This is repayable by 7 equal annual instalments, starting on 1 January, 1987, of £138,663 each including interest. The breakdown of outstanding balances is:

		31/12/88		*31/12/89*	
		Capital	*Interest*	*Capital*	*Interest*
Instalment due	1/1/89	*66,019*	*72,644*		
	1/1/90	76,582	62,081	*76,582*	*62,081*
	1/1/91	88,835	49,828	88,835	49,828
	1/1/92	103,049	35,614	103,049	35,614
	1/1/93	119,537	19,126	119,537	19,126
		388,003		311,421	

	Average for year	*Year-end*	*Rate %*
Overdraft 1988	£260,000	£120,000	15
1989	£157,000	£84,000	14

Note 3

A grant of 40% was obtained towards the cost of plant and machinery. The grant is depreciated to zero over 10 years.

1988 Extract	Grant 400×40% =		160	
	Less depreciation 3/10		48	112
1989 Extract	Grant 400×40% =		160	
	Less depreciation 4/10		64	
			96	
	Grant 100×40%	40		
	Less depreciation 1/10	4	36	132

Note 4

The company employment averaged 67 people in each year.

Note 5

Cost of Production Analysis

	1988	1989
Materials	2,160	2,262
Labour	1,152	1,287
Manufacturing expenses	288	351
	3,600	3,900

Note 6
Shares in the company have traded on the Unlisted Securities Market within the range £1.50–£1.85 through the last year. The most recent price at which a sizeable number of shares was traded was £1.62.

Note 7
Deferred tax arises because depreciation for tax purposes exceeds that for accounting. The effective corporation rate was 35% in each year.

Assessing Financial Stability

A key measure of financial stability is the degree to which assets are funded by borrowings, as distinct from shareholders' funds. There are a number of ways to assess the proportions.

METHOD 1: DEBT/TOTAL ASSETS RATIO

$$\frac{\text{Total Borrowings}}{\text{Total Assets}} \%$$

The figures for 1989 are:

$$\frac{988+132+311+149}{1578+2041} = 43.7\%$$

By UK standards, Model Company is conservatively borrowed. Many organisations, starved of subscribed capital, use a greater proportion of borrowings. There is a danger point at about 70%. Financial institutions regard a company with a ratio in excess of 70% as over-borrowed. This can result in pressure to dispose of assets to reduce the ratio. Unfortunately, the most disposable assets are usually the ones with the best future profit potential.

Business managers are well advised to hold borrowings below 70%. This avoids outside pressure to dispose of the most attractive liquid assets. As with all ratios it is wise to examine the trend for a number of years. If the ratio had been 25% in 1988, then one might be concerned that similar increases in 1989 and 1990 could push the borrowings too high. I normally use a five-year analysis to assess trends. Only two years are used for Model Company to avoid swamping you with data.

Model Company's ratio in 1988 was:

$$\frac{1107+112+388+106}{1576+1958} = 48.5\%$$

The comparison of 1988 and 1989 results shows that borrowings declined by 4.8 points relative to total assets. Our concern about 1990 is substantially alleviated. Of course, a £2 million asset investment, a month after the balance sheet date, all financed by borrowings, would wreck the picture. We would expect the company and its financiers not to permit such an inordinate change in the financial structure.

METHOD 2: DEBT/SHAREHOLDERS' FUNDS RATIO

$$\frac{\text{Total Borrowings}}{\text{Shareholders' Funds}}$$

The figures for 1989 are:

$$\frac{988+132+311+149}{2039} = 77.5\%$$

This is a different approach to examining the same risk. It shows that borrowings in total are 22.5% lower than owners' funds. This is obviously not too high, as you can see by looking at the relationship between this ratio and the total borrowings/total assets statistic:

		%
Total borrowings	1580 =	43.7
Shareholders' funds	2039 =	56.3
Total assets	3619 =	100.0

Note: 43.7% is 77.5% of 56.3%.

145

The comparable figures for risk maximum to avoid outside influence are total borrowings 70%, shareholders' funds 30% (70% is 233.3% of 30%).

The ratio in 1988 was:

$$\frac{1107+112+388+106}{1821} = 94.1\%$$

We see a reduced dependence on borrowings in 1989.

METHOD 3: MEDIUM AND LONG DEBT/SHAREHOLDERS' FUNDS RATIO

$$\frac{\text{Medium and Long Term Borrowings}}{\text{Shareholders' Funds}}\%$$

The 1989 figure was:

$$\frac{132+311+149}{2039} = 29\%$$

It is normally regarded as bad policy to finance assets with more than £1 of medium- and long-term borrowings per £1 of shareholders' funds. Based on this guideline, the company has a lot of extra borrowing capacity $2039 \times (100\% - 29\%) = 1448$. It has a lot of potential to expand its borrowing base. The 1988 figure is:

$$\frac{112+388+106}{1821} = 33.3\%$$

As expected, the trend discloses a reduced dependence on medium- and long-term borrowings in 1989.

METHOD 4: BANK BORROWINGS/SHAREHOLDERS' FUNDS RATIO

$$\frac{\text{Net Bank Borrowings}}{\text{Shareholders' Funds}}\%$$

The 1989 figure was:

$$\frac{161+311-84}{2039} = 19\%$$

Bankers dislike lending more than £1 per £1 of shareholders' funds (though they sometimes have to do so to support viable, but poorly performing clients). Model Company could borrow up to £1,651 more if it found profitable ways to invest it. I normally advise that a company should restrict net bank borrowings to about 80% of shareholders' funds. This would permit 1,243 of additional bank debt, without breaching the 80% rule. The 1988 figure was:

$$\frac{186+388-17}{1821} = 30.6\%$$

indicating a significant reduction in dependence on bank funding. In analysing the bank borrowing position, some people would ignore the cash in hand. This would increase the ratios to 31.5% in 1988 and 23.1% in 1989, revealing a similar trend.

METHOD 5: CURRENT RATIO

$$\frac{\text{Current Assets}}{\text{Current Liabilities}}$$

1989	1988
$\dfrac{2041}{988} = 2.1$ times	$\dfrac{1958}{1107} = 1.8$ times

Again, we see a stronger financial position in 1989. This ratio measures the surplus or deficit of current assets (which will turn into cash) over amounts due and payable in under one year (which will be paid out in cash). It is a major test of liquidity. It is often suggested the ratio should be 2:1. This is rather superficial, because it fails to recognise the current asset and liability structure of different industries. Consider the following business types:

	Construction or Heavy Engineering	Manufacturing	Wholesale	Retail
Material stock	Very High	Medium	None	None
Work in progress	Very High	Medium	None	None
Finished goods	Low	Medium	High	High
Trade debtors	Medium	High	High	None
Trade creditors	Medium	Medium	High	High
Ratio Range				
High	3.0	2.0	1.5	1.3
Low	2.0	1.5	1.0	1.0

In 1989, Model Company's current ratio exceeds the range for a manufacturing business. The reasons will be examined in the discussion of working capital ratios (Chapter 7).

METHOD 6: LIQUIDITY RATIO (ACID TEST)

$$\frac{\text{Current Assets} - \text{Stocks}}{\text{Payable in Under One Year}}$$

1989
$$\frac{2041-800}{988} = 1.26 \text{ times}$$

1988
$$\frac{1958-700}{1107} = 1.14 \text{ times}$$

The values are sound and are strengthening. The ratio discloses the balance between liquid assets (stocks being excluded) and current liabilities. It is a rather crude instrument since many debtors' accounts would be hard to collect if an urgent need for cash arose, while some stocks could be sold for cash in a crisis. The basic proposition is that what you gain on the swings (cash from stocks) you lose on the roundabouts (less cash from debtors). Large businesses rarely show a ratio greatly in excess of 1 in a manufacturing business or 0.8 in a trading business in Britain. In Method 7 I show how to overcome the defects in this ratio.

METHOD 7: SUBJECTIVE LIQUIDITY RATIO

$$\frac{\text{Personal View of Liquid Value of Current Assets}}{\text{Payable in Under One Year}}$$

I developed this subjective approach to try to overcome some of the defects in the normal liquidity ratio. It involves a judgement about the liquid value of the various assets in different industries.

Let us consider stocks in a variety of businesses:

Business (1) Ethical Pharmaceuticals: A sale is unlikely to stimulate cash business. I would ascribe no value unless capable of being sold back to the supplier. Stock value zero.

Business (2) Partly Completed Houses: Very difficult to liquidate. Other builders would be reluctant to take on unplanned work at short notice except where big profits seem available. Stock value 30%.

Business (3) Fashion Clothing: Unlikely to be realisable after a season ends. Fashions may change before the next season. Stock value starting a season 40%; after season 20%.

148

Business (4) School Outfits: Big discounts may stimulate sales growth coming up to a season. Hard to realise beyond mid-school year. Stock value before school year 70%; near year-end 10%.

Business (5) Perishable Foods: Requires substantial discounts to shift consumer loyalty where supply and demand are well balanced. Stock value 70% of cost, but cash may be slow to realise.

Business (6) High Margin Consumer Products: Items with 25% gross margin may yield about 75% of cost for quick sale. Cash may be hard to realise.

Business (7) Low Margin Consumer Products: Items with 7% gross margin may yield about 60% of cost for quick sale. Cash may be hard to realise.

In our example the realisable value of assets would be arrived at as follows:

Case	Stocks	Debtors*	Cash	Total
1	0	730	84	814
2	240	730	84	1054
3	160-320	730	84	1054 mid-point
4	80-560	730	84	1134 mid-point
5	560	730	84	1374
6	600	730	84	1414
7	480	730	84	1294

*Assuming that the good debtors could be sold to a factoring organisation at 75% of book value (6.5% of debts not accepted by factor).

In computing this subjective liquidity ratio I always seek a ratio in excess of one. If Model Company was involved in ethical pharmaceuticals, the ratio would be too low. If it was involved in any of the other six business types, the ratio would be acceptable.

METHOD 8: INTEREST COVER

$$\frac{\text{Profit Before Interest \& Tax}}{\text{Interest}}$$

1989
$$\frac{604}{84} = 7.2 \text{ times}$$

1988
$$\frac{412}{112} = 3.7 \text{ times}$$

149

This measures the degree of profit being generated for all purposes as compared with the demand for profit to cover interest charges. Bankers tend to require an interest cover of at least three. The logic for this is that £3 profit before interest is needed: £1 to pay the interest cost; £1 to cover taxation and loan repayments; and at least £1 to pay dividends and contribute to expansion.

An excess in one area must cause contraction in another, or the interest cover will fall below three. Reducing interest, tax, dividends or loan repayments would leave more for growth. The higher the cover the greater the potential to finance growth through reinvestment of profits:

Interest Cover Range

	Times Covered					
	2	3	4	5	6	10
PBIT	200	300	400	500	600	1000
Interest	100	100	100	100	100	100
PBT	100	200	300	400	500	900
Taxation (35%)	35	70	105	140	175	315
PAT	65	130	195	260	325	585
Dividend (50%)	32	65	97	130	162	292
Retained	33	65	98	130	163	293

The allocations of PBIT are:

	£	£	£	£	£	£
Interest	1.00	1.00	1.00	1.00	1.00	1.00
Tax	0.35	0.70	1.05	1.40	1.75	3.15
Dividends	0.32	0.65	0.97	1.30	1.62	2.92
Retained	0.33	0.65	0.98	1.30	1.63	2.93
Interest cover	2.00	3.00	4.00	5.00	6.00	10.00

As interest cover improves the proportion of profit available for dividends and reinvestment grows.

150

METHOD 9: REINVESTMENT RATE

$$\frac{\text{Current Year Capital Expenditure}}{\text{Current Year Depreciation}}$$

1989
$$\frac{100}{98} = 1$$

1988
$$\frac{100}{88} = 1.1$$

This ratio discloses the degree to which depreciation charges are sufficient to replace and update fixed assets. At current inflation rates, a business should invest at least 1.5 times its annual depreciation. Model Company may be neglecting modernisation. Substantial outlay is needed, to bring the average to 1.5 times for a 3-year period.

Assessing Profitability

Measuring the adequacy of profits appears straightforward. However, various types of financiers may have different viewpoints (e.g., shareholders probably have a different perspective from bankers who again differ from employees). We will examine a range of ratios in order to correctly assess profitability:

METHOD 1: GROSS PROFIT MARGIN

$$\frac{\text{Gross Profit}}{\text{Sales}}\ \%$$

1989
$$\frac{1200}{5000} = 24\%$$

1988
$$\frac{1010}{4590} = 22\%$$

This shows an improvement in gross profit margin and as such increases the capability of the business to cover its overheads and leave a profit for the shareholders (after tax). Gross margins are similar to product contributions. These are examined in detail in Chapter 11.

This ratio measures the amount left over out of each £1 of sales when the cost of production (or acquisition) has been paid for. The ratio can vary wildly from one business sector to another:

1   Necessities should sell at low margins (often strongly supported by
    government price controls). Luxuries tend to earn greater margins.
    More prosperous customers can choose to accept or reject them.
2   Businesses that are adapting their products in a fast changing
    technology deserve a good gross margin. The cost of new product
    development is high. It must be financed from the gross margin.

Even within a business sector the gross profit margin can be
significantly different:

1   Some products in the range can contribute high margins and others
    lower ones. For example, in the public house trade, beer tends to
    offer lower margins than mixers. Therefore a pub in a working
    class district will be expected to produce a lower gross margin than
    one in the gin and tonic belt.
2   Some products are created within a business and sold to the
    ultimate consumer, while competitors buy-in products in a partly
    manufactured state, leading to big variations in margins.

Some examples of gross profit margins are:

	%
Department stores	44–50
Public houses	35–50
Food retailers	10–35
Pharmacies	15–33
Dairy co-operatives	18–25
Boutiques	40–60
High-technology manufacturing	30–60
Low-technology manufacturing	15–30

METHOD 2: NET PROFIT MARGIN

$$\frac{\text{Profit Before Tax}}{\text{Sales}} \%$$

This ratio shows the amount of profit left out of each £1 of sales. The
profit will be allocated to: provision for taxation; dividends paid and
proposed; and retained to contribute towards expansion.

The ratio can vary significantly between business sectors. Some
businesses require a large asset base to create their sales and profits.

They must obtain a high profit margin. For example, for manufacturing businesses, plant, machinery, material stocks, work in progress and trade debtors are included in their asset base. Some businesses need a smaller asset base. A supermarket would not have most of the above assets in its balance sheet. It consequently needs a small profit margin. The impact of the asset base on the margin required is best measured by return on investment in Method 4 below.

METHOD 3: PROFIT BEFORE INTEREST MARGIN

$$\frac{\text{PBIT}}{\text{Sales}} \%$$

1989
$$\frac{604}{5000} = 12.08\%$$

1988
$$\frac{412}{4590} = 8.98\%$$

Some conservative businesses finance their assets mainly with shareholders' funds. Their interest charge is low. Some aggressive businesses finance their assets mainly with interest bearing debt. Their interest charge is high. Sales and other costs being equal, the conservative business appears more profitable but this is misleading. There is more share capital to be rewarded. Adding back interest and comparing the companies on a profit before interest basis removes the impact of financing styles.

Consider a business, similar in all respects to Model Company, except that it has an additional £300,000 of share capital. It saves £48,000 of interest because of its reduced borrowing. Profit before interest and tax would be £604,000 in both companies. Method 2 suggests the model company is less efficient. Method 3 (above) suggests equality and is a better guide to interfirm performance.

METHOD 4: RETURN ON INVESTMENT

$$\frac{\text{Profit before Interest and Tax}}{\text{Total Assets}} \%$$

1989
$$\frac{604}{3619} = 16.7\%$$

1988
$$\frac{412}{3534} = 11.7\%$$

Return on investment is a key profitability ratio. It shows the profit derived from using assets in a business, regardless of how they are financed. When combined with Methods 5 and 6 it gives a clear insight into the impact of various financing forms on the return to the shareholders. A business should earn a return on investment of at least 12.5%. This provides a base to gear up the return to ordinary shareholders. A difficulty is that assets may be at out of date values.

Assume the market value of land and buildings of Model Company were:

	31/12/89	31/12/88
Land	648	600
Buildings	1080	1000

The ROI is overstated. If these valuations had been included in the profit and loss account and balance sheet, the ratios would change.

Adjusted Profit

		1989		1988
PBIT as reported		604		412
2% of building valuation	22		20	
Depreciation charged	16	6	16	4
Revised PBIT		598		408

The adjusted return on investment would be:

$$\frac{1989}{\frac{598}{1728+402+2041}} = 14.3\% \qquad \frac{1988}{\frac{408}{1600+384+1958}} = 10.4\%$$

Indices of movements in values of land and buildings may be used to restate return on investment where a professional valuation is not undertaken. This adjusted version of return on investment should be used for in-house purposes, even when modern valuations are not being incorporated in the financial statements.

METHOD 5: RETURN ON NET ASSETS

This ratio tests the effect of using interest free borrowings to fund part of the assets. The calculation is:

$$\frac{\text{PBIT}}{\text{Total Assets} - \text{Free Borrowings}}$$

1989	1988
$\dfrac{604}{1578+2041-988+161-132-149}$	$\dfrac{412}{1576+1958-1107+186-112-106}$
$= 24.1\%$	$= 17.2\%$

A significant boost to the owner's return is derived from free borrowings. The 1988 figure is pushed from 11.7% to 17.2% by the £1,139,000 of free borrowings. The 1989 figure rises from 16.7% to 24.1% through the use of £1,108,000 of free borrowings. Management of free funding is very important in creating a good return for the shareholders. The RONA updated valuations are:

1989	1988
$\dfrac{598}{1728+402+2041-1108}$	$\dfrac{408}{1600+384+1958-1139}$
$= 19.5\%$	$= 14.6\%$

METHOD 6: RETURN ON EQUITY PRE-TAX

This ratio measures the return to ordinary shareholders. It is driven by the return on investment and the use of borrowed funds. The use of interest free finance increases the return. The use of interest bearing finance will increase it if the return on net assets exceeds the average cost of interest bearing borrowings. If the return on net assets is below the average cost of interest bearing borrowings the return on equity will be reduced. In such cases the owners would have done better had they financed more of the assets. If the ratio is calculated before tax it will highlight the impact of borrowings on the return. The calculation is:

$$\frac{\text{Profit for Ordinary Shareholders} + \text{Tax Provision}}{\text{Total Assets} - \text{All Liabilities (i.e. Shareholders' Funds)}}$$

$$\begin{array}{cc}
1989 & 1988 \\
\dfrac{520}{2039} = 25.5\% & \dfrac{300}{1821} = 16.5\%
\end{array}$$

The shareholders benefit from the use of interest bearing borrowings. The return on equity in 1989 is excellent by comparison with alternative investments other than high-risk ones. The ROE updated valuations are:

$$\begin{array}{cc}
1989 & 1988 \\
\dfrac{514}{2039+1728-1176} = 19.8\% & \dfrac{296}{1821+1600-1192} = 13.3\%
\end{array}$$

COMPARISON OF RETURNS ACHIEVED PRE- AND POST-BORROWINGS

	Cost-based		Valuation-based	
	1989	1988	1989	1988
ROI (%)	16.7	11.7	14.3	10.4
RONA (%)	24.1	17.2	19.5	14.6
ROE% (pre-tax)	25.5	16.5	19.8	13.3

Two particular features emerge from this table:

1 The return on investment is key to the use of cost effective borrowings. When the ROI is 11.7% the ROE is an unexciting 16.5%. An ROI of 16.7% yields an excellent ROE of 25.5%. Interest rates can have a sizeable impact on the return.
2 The 1988 ROE based on updated values is lower than the return on net assets. This is because the average cost of interest bearing borrowings exceeds the return on net assets. In this case, the company needed lower cost funding or, if this was the maximum sustainable return on net assets, additional shareholders' funds.

We will leave Model Company, temporarily to examine the impact of various ROI percentages on RONA and ROE.

Financing the Asset Structure

Shareholders' funds	400
Free borrowings	300
Interest-bearing Borrowings	300 (cost 15%)
	1,000

ROI, RONA and ROE Computations

ROI	8%	10%	12.5%	14%	16%
(basis)	$\frac{80}{1,000}\%$	$\frac{100}{1,000}\%$	$\frac{125}{1,000}\%$	$\frac{140}{1,000}\%$	$\frac{160}{1,000}\%$
RONA	11.4%	14.3%	17.9%	20%	22.9%
(basis)	$\frac{80}{700}\%$	$\frac{100}{700}\%$	$\frac{125}{700}\%$	$\frac{140}{700}\%$	$\frac{160}{700}\%$
ROE	8.8%	13.8%	20%	23.8%	28.8%
(basis)	$\frac{35}{400}\%$	$\frac{55}{400}\%$	$\frac{80}{400}\%$	$\frac{95}{400}\%$	$\frac{115}{400}\%$

I believe that a business needs a return on equity of at least 20%. This is unlikely to be obtained without a return on investment of 12.5%. Conversely, a high ROI can be geared up to a superb ROE, although this increases the risk (profits before interest could collapse but interest charges would remain).

A HANDBOOK OF PRACTICAL BUSINESS FINANCE

Trends in the Financial Structure

Changes in the financial structure of a business can be difficult to recognise if examining absolute figures. Percentages can be more revealing. Two methods of analysis can be used.

Method 1: Restating the Figures in % Terms

Balance Sheets

	1988%	1989%
Land	12.45	12.16
Buildings	21.28	20.34
Plant and machinery	7.92	9.12
Vehicles	2.94	1.99
Stock	19.81	22.10
Debtors and prepayments	35.12	31.97
Cash	0.48	2.32
Total assets	100.00	100.00
Shareholders' funds	51.53	56.34
Bank borrowings	16.24	13.04
Creditors and accruals	19.58	14.53
Free funding	12.65	16.09
Total funding	100.00	100.00

These figures show the changes in the balance sheet structure. The following comments are appropriate:

1 The composition of the assets discloses:
- Increased plant 1.20%;
- Increased stock 2.29%;
- Increased cash 1.84%; and
- Reduced debtors 3.15%.

2 Movements in financing revealed are:
- Increased owners' funds 4.81%;
- Increased free funds 3.44%;
- Reduced bank debt 3.20%; and
- Reduced creditors 5.05%.

Overall the balance sheet is stronger.

Profit and Loss Account

	1988%		1989%	
Sales		100.00		100.00
Materials	47.06		45.24	
Labour	25.10		25.74	
Manufacturing expenses	6.27		7.02	
Stock change	(0.43)	78.00	(2.00)	76.00
Gross profit		22.00		24.00
Administration	3.52		3.60	
Selling and distribution	9.50	13.02	8.32	11.92
PBIT		8.98		12.08
Interest		2.44		1.68
PBT		6.54		10.40
Tax		2.29		3.64
PAT		4.25		6.76
Dividends		1.96		2.40
Retained profits		2.29		4.36

Features of the Profit and Loss account are:
- Reduced material cost 1.82%;
- Increased selling cost 1.18%;
- Reduced interest cost 0.76%;
- Increased tax provision 1.35%;
- Increased dividends 0.44%; and
- Increased retained profit 2.07%.

Method 2: Indexing Figures from Year to Year

Each 1988 figure is expressed as base 100. The percentage change in the 1989 figures is computed:

Balance Sheet Figures

	1988	1989	Index of Change
Land	440	440	–
Buildings	752	736	−2.13
Plant	280	330	+17.86
Vehicles	104	72	−30.77
Stocks	700	800	+14.29
Debtors	1148	1042	−9.23
Prepayments	93	115	+23.66
Cash	17	84	+394.12
Overdraft and term loans	186	161	−13.44
Creditors and accruals	732	568	−23.99
Proposed dividend	90	120	+33.33
Ordinary share capital	1700	1700	–
Revenue reserves	121	339	+180.17
Grants	112	132	+17.86
Term loan	388	311	+19.85
Taxation	205	288	+40.49

Profit and Loss Account Figures

		1988		1989	Index of Change
Sales		4590		5000	+8.93
Opening stock	680		700		+2.94
Materials	2160		2262		+4.72
Labour	1152		1287		+11.72
Production expense	288		351		+21.88
Closing stock	(700)		(800)		+14.29
Cost of sales		3580		3800	+6.15
Gross profit		1010		1200	+18.81
Administration	162		180		+11.11
Selling and distribution	436		416		−4.59
Interest	112	710	84	680	−25.00
PBT		300		520	+73.33
Taxation	105		182		+73.33
Dividend	90	195	120	302	+33.33
Retained		105		218	+107.62

The key figure in this analysis is the sales growth 8.93%. The following issues should be considered:

a   Relative to the rate of change in sales prices does this statistic imply a growth or decline in volume?

b   If the cost of sales increases (as in this case) by a lower percentage than the sales then the company will expect to improve profits. If costs grow faster than sales serious problems may be arising.

c   Deviations from the movement in sales are:

	Points
Labour costs	+2.79
Production expenses	+12.95
Administration	+2.18
Materials	−4.21
Interest	−33.93

In the balance sheet we find the following major deviations from the sales growth:

	Points
Plant	+8.93
Stocks	+5.36
Prepayments	+14.73
Debtors	−18.16
Creditors	−32.92
Overdrafts	−38.93
Term loans	−28.78

The plant growth pinpoints a decline in utilisation. The stock increase could indicate slow moving lines. The decline in debtors has reduced funding needs significantly which allowed the reduction in creditors and bank borrowings. Will customers continue to settle accounts as quickly? A reversion to the 1988 pattern would reduce cash available to cover overdrafts and creditors. When planning the 1990 budget, this issue will have to be examined.

Productivity Ratios

The two major ratios are sales per employee and profit per employee. Both ratios help to test performance against directly comparable organisations. Problems arise because: (a) a bigger business may be able to utilise its staff more effectively; and (b) most businesses have some diversifications away from their core activity. Such diversifications make interfirm comparison difficult.

Public houses illustrate the problems. Statistics for sales and profits per employee can be affected by:

a   Balance of trade between bar and lounge (prices are higher in lounges and can vary significantly between houses).
b   Balance of sales between pints (lower gross margin line) and mixers for spirits (usually a high margin line).
c   Food sales tend to be more labour intensive than drink sales.
d   Square footage of counter/customer space, e.g. 25% more space may not require a comparable increase in staff.

The ratios for Model Company are:

	1989	1988
Sales per employee	$\dfrac{5,000,000}{67}$ $= £74,627$	$\dfrac{4,590,000}{67}$ $= £68,507$
Profit per employee	$\dfrac{520,000}{67}$ $= £7,761$	$\dfrac{300,000}{67}$ $= £4,478$

These ratios compare favourably with those involved in similar businesses.

Stock Market Ratios

A variety of well publicised ratios can be used to test investment attractiveness. I will examine some basic calculations initially which will help build up to the crucial statistics.

METHOD 1: EARNINGS PER SHARE

This ratio is derived as follows:

$$\frac{\text{Profit Attributable to Ordinary Shareholders}}{\text{Number of Ordinary Shares in Issue}}$$

1989		1988	
$\dfrac{338,000}{1,700,000}$ = 19.88p		$\dfrac{195,000}{1,700,000}$ = 11.47p	

The ratio shows the amount earned in a year on each ordinary share in issue. When looked at over a number of years, EPS is a vital indicator of managerial competence. The key question it raises is how growth compares with alternative investments. A snag is that it is based on historic results. Future prospects are a key influence on a share price. This is why you will frequently see references to prospective EPS in investment commentaries.

METHOD 2: EARNINGS YIELD

$$\frac{\text{Earnings Per Share} \times \text{Nominal Share Price}}{\text{Current Share Price}}\%$$

EPS ignores the market value of a share. The earnings yield, by using the current share price, gives a better indication of the return that is being earned.

For Model Company, the earnings yield is:

$$\frac{19.88p \times £1}{£1.62} = 12.27\%$$

If the company continues to earn the current level of profit for ordinary shareholders, it offers a yield of 12.27%. This yield can be compared with returns from other investments by (a) direct comparison; (b) establishing average yields for industrial sectors; or (c) assessment against the full market. Average yields are readily available from the business pages of national and international newspapers. Intelligent interpretation of average earnings yields can point to the stock market's interpretation of prospects for a business or sector. To illustrate, I have extracted yields at the close of business on Thursday 25 May, 1989 for the following well known businesses:

Earnings Yields

	%
Barclays Bank	19.2
Grand Metropolitan	11.5
Hanson Trust	10.5
Imperial Chemical	10.9
Marks and Spencer	7.0
J. Sainsbury	6.6

Clearly the stock market is very impressed by the growth potential of the last two companies. Investors were prepared to accept the lowest earnings yield in these cases.

METHOD 3: DIVIDEND PER SHARE

$$\frac{\text{Ordinary Dividends Paid and Proposed for the Year}}{\text{Number of Ordinary Shares in Issue}}$$

$$\begin{array}{cc} 1989 & 1988 \\ \dfrac{120}{1700} = 7.06\% & \dfrac{90}{1700} = 5.29\% \end{array}$$

This ratio is of limited benefit unless the shares are trading at par. It helps with the calculation of dividend yield.

METHOD 4: DIVIDEND YIELD

$$\frac{\text{Dividend Per Share} \times \text{Nominal Value Per Share}}{\text{Current Market Price Per Share}}$$

$$\frac{7.06 \times \pounds1}{\pounds1.62}\% = 4.36\%$$

This dividend yield can be compared with similar businesses. Dividend yields for the selected quoted companies on Thursday 25 May, 1989 were:

164

Dividend Yields

	%
Barclays Bank	6.7
Grand Metropolitan	3.7
Hanson Trust	5.6
Imperial Chemical	5.2
Marks and Spencer	4.1
J. Sainsbury	2.9

It is fascinating to contrast these returns with the yields from gilt edged securities. Investors are expecting substantial growth to compensate them for the low current yield.

METHOD 5: DIVIDEND COVER

$$\frac{\text{Profit Attributable to Ordinary Shareholders}}{\text{Ordinary Dividends Paid and Proposed}}$$

1989
$$\frac{338}{120} = 2.82 \text{ times}$$

1988
$$\frac{195}{90} = 2.17 \text{ times}$$

This ratio shows the relationship between profit paid out as dividends and profit retained for growth. As a general rule, companies pay about half the after tax profit to shareholders and retain the rest to finance expansion. Model Company is slightly more biased towards growth. If the historic dividend cover is high a share will be unattractive to investors seeking income. If it is low the share will be unattractive to investors seeking capital appreciation. The converse is also true. Dividend income is exposed to personal tax and, consequently a decision to invest for dividends probably implies a low marginal tax rate, while one to invest for capital appreciation probably implies a high one.

METHOD 6: PRICE EARNINGS RATIO (P/E)

$$\frac{\text{Market Price Per Share}}{\text{Earnings per Share}} = \frac{£1.62}{19.88\text{p}} = 8.15 \text{ times}$$

It can also be expressed as:

$$\frac{100}{\text{Earnings Yield}} = \frac{100}{12.27\%} = 8.15 \text{ times}$$

This signifies that at its current rate of earnings, the company would take 8.15 years to earn its current share price. Of itself this means little. Comparison with other companies in the sector may reveal a deviation. Let us examine some businesses in the drapery and stores sector (as at 26 May, 1989):

Company	P/E
Body Shop International	61.6
Burton Group	8.6
Dunhill Holdings	22.2
Great Universal	15.8
Marks and Spencer	14.2
Next	12.3
Sears	9.6

The stock market is very excited with profit prospects at Body Shop. It is unexcited with Burton Group and Sears.

The price earnings ratio for important quoted enterprises is shown in the *Financial Times* and other relevant newspapers daily. The P/E shown is based on (a) the share price at close of dealing on the previous day and (b) the latest published results from the company.

Where conversion rights attach to shares or loan stock, or options exist, a second version of the price earnings ratio is frequently quoted. This is the fully diluted P/E. To illustrate it we will assume that the bank had a right to convert the term loan of £311,000 into ordinary shares of Model Company at a rate of 1 share for each £1.25 of loan outstanding. Had this option been exercised an additional 248,800 ordinary shares would have been issued and the interest cost would have fallen by £49,760 before tax (or £32,344 after tax at 35%). The fully diluted price earnings ratio is:

$$\frac{(1,700+248.8)\times £1.62}{338+32.344} = 8.52 \text{ times}$$

Investors use P/E ratios to assess buy, hold and sell decisions. This is illustrated using data for Body Shop International. The stock market regards Body Shop as a relatively small company with excellent profit prospects, due to its market niche and expansion potential. Investors may feel this justifies a price earnings ratio of (say) 25. We can make the following statements:

166

a   Last year the earnings per share must have been 9.3p (i.e. share price £5.75/61.6).
b   To justify a share price of £5.75 the stock market will require earnings per share of 23p next year (i.e. £5.75/25).
c   The stock market expects a growth in earnings per share of 150% (i.e. 23p is 250% greater than 9.3p). Our forecast of 23p earnings per share is described as the prospective EPS. The prospective EPS leads us to a prospective price earnings ratio of 25. Investors use deduction (b) to assess buy, sell and hold decisions. A non-shareholder might regard the shares as an attractive buying proposition if he or she felt that the stock market had underestimated the potential growth in earnings per share. An exisiting shareholder would wish to sell shares if he or she believed that the earnings per share would prove to be significantly below 23p.

INSIDER TRADING

This is an appropriate point to mention the thorny issue of insider trading. There is a vital difference in law between a person who invests or divests on the basis of a personal judgement and a person who does so on the basis of facts not available to other investors. A person who uses privileged information to deal in shares is guilty of insider trading. Such a person can be liable to a heavy fine or even a jail sentence. Insider trading arises through the leakage of information about mergers and takeovers. It also arises where dramatic changes in a share price occur prior to the announcement of results, significantly different from market expectations. In such cases the stock market may order an investigation into dealings during a period of unexpected movements in the price of a share.

EXTRAORDINARY ITEMS AND INVESTMENT RATIOS

Sometimes the profit and loss account of a business contains extraordinary items. These items can mask the correct interpretation of how the business has developed and its future prospects. In calculating the following investment ratios, the profit before extraordinary items is used: earnings per share; earnings yield; dividend cover; and price earnings ratio. The calculation of EPS prior to extraordinary items is required by SSAP 3. The other ratios are affected by the EPS. There are sound conceptual arguments in favour of it but like many analysts I have some reservations:

1   It can create an illusion of a well covered dividend, when extraordinary losses have wiped out most or all of the profits of the current year. This results in part or all of the dividend being paid out of previous retained earnings.

167

2 In extreme cases, the extraordinary losses can be greater than the profits earned. The statement that the company has earned profits per share is likely to seriously mislead many shareholders in such cases.
3 It provides an incentive to an unscrupulous management to classify everything conceivable as extraordinary so as to create the illusion that a business is successful.

METHOD 7: ASSET BACKING

$$\frac{\text{Total Assets} - \text{Total Liabilities}}{\begin{array}{c}\text{Number of Ordinary Shares} \\ \text{in Issue}\end{array}} \quad \text{or} \quad \frac{\text{Ordinary Shareholders' Funds}}{\begin{array}{c}\text{Number of Ordinary Shares} \\ \text{in Issue}\end{array}}$$

$$\begin{array}{cc} 1989 & 1988 \\ \dfrac{2039(3619-1580)}{1700} = \pounds 1.20 & \dfrac{1821(3534-1713)}{1700} = \pounds 1.07 \end{array}$$

The shares are currently selling at £1.62. This implies that investors are more concerned with future earnings than asset backing. Some caution is indicated. An unexpected profit set-back would probably see the share price fall towards the asset backing. Investors could incur a sizeable capital loss. An investor assessing a share supported by a high P/E ratio is wise to consider the asset backing as this provides a support level in the event of a profits collapse.

Types of Share Investment Strategy

CATEGORY 1: INVESTING FOR RECOVERY

Shares in this category usually have a strong asset backing (occasionally well in excess of the share price), and a low P/E ratio due to recent losses or indifferent profits. Investments of this type promise substantial growth if profit recovery occurs. If not, the asset backing may underpin the share price unless serious losses are incurred. This type of investment is very attractive where (a) the company is well managed and (b) the industry may have reached the bottom of its cycle.

CATEGORY 2: SHARES IN A HIGH GROWTH COMPANY

The difficulty with this type of investment is that stock market forecasters tend to have excessive expectations for future profit potential. Non-achievement of growth forecasted often results in a collapse in the share price. Such a collapse is sometimes caused by inattention to sound control procedures during a chase for growth. I dislike this type of investment because the downside risk is high. Management frequently have little experience in coping with a crisis. Nevertheless, large capital gains are available to early spotters of potential.

CATEGORY 3: SHARES IN HIGHLY SPECULATIVE BUSINESSES

For example, exploration stocks. Not for widows and orphans. Such shares can yield huge capital gains and losses. My view is that they should be left to the experts. You should not use money you will need later or bank overdraft facilities to finance this type of investment. It is like a big bet on an odds on favourite at a very wet Royal Ascot.

CATEGORY 4: SHARES IN A HIGHLY PROFITABLE COMPANY

Typically, shares in this category have a high price earnings ratio and a share price far in excess of the asset backing. Investments of this type should normally be long term in nature. It is wisest to have a portfolio, so as to reduce the impact of a decline in a particular business sector. Unit trusts are the prudent way to acquire a portfolio, unless the investor has (a) a large investment fund and (b) either considerable time and analytical skills or a highly skilled and reputable adviser.
Final words of advice on this subject are:

1 Non-professionals should always extract the key ratios from the latest financial statements.
2 Never invest on gossip alone. You will lose in the long run.
3 Do not use your holiday money or a bank overdraft. If you do Murphy's Law says that anything that can go wrong will.

In this chapter we examined a number of ratios. Some are crucial performance indicators. It is not always necessary to compute all the ratios but when a key ratio is unstable it becomes necessary to dig deeper. The key ratios for inital diagnosis are:

1   Total debt/total assets;
2   Net bank/shareholders' funds;
3   Interest cover;
4   ROI;
5   ROE; and
6   Gross margin.

Working capital ratios are covered in Chapter 7.

Ratio Analysis Self-study Problem

If you want to obtain maximum benefit from your study of this chapter, you should prepare a ratio analysis based on the financial statements of Swings plc reproduced below. After completion you should identify the messages about the development of the company over the three-year period. My analysis and commentary follow the financial statements.

Swings PLC Profit and Loss Accounts (£'000)

	1989	1990	1991
Sales	193,760	208,676	239,750
Cost of sales[1]	169,122	180,889	201,465
Gross margin	24,638	27,787	38,285
Operating costs[1]	13,452	15,040	16,669
Profit before interest	11,186	12,747	21,616
Interest	1,007	2,243	2,965
Profit before tax	10,179	10,504	18,651
Corporation tax	3,154	4,069	4,973
Profit after tax	7,025	6,435	13,678
Dividends	1,021	1,742	3,484
Retained earnings	6,004	4,693	10,194
[1] Includes depreciation	1,459	1,948	2,137

Swings PLC Balance Sheets (£'000)

	1989	1990	1991
Fixed assets[1]	25,820	56,332	55,972
Current assets			
Stock	16,504	17,702	15,882
Debtors	24,050	35,614	35,798
Cash	8,748	9,382	9,762
	49,302	62,698	61,442
Payable in under one year			
Loans and overdrafts	5,399	31,772	15,544
Trade creditors	21,645	24,357	27,237
Corporation tax	3,154	4,069	4,973
Proposed dividend	792	1,188	2,376
	30,990	61,386	50,130
Net assets	44,132	57,644	67,284
Financed by:			
Share capital[1]	5,633	5,633	5,633
Revenue reserve	22,562	27,255	37,449
Shareholders' funds	28,195	32,888	43,082
Long-term loans	15,937	24,756	24,202
	44,132	57,644	67,284

[1] Nominal value is 10p per share. Latest share price £3.80.

Summarised Ratios

	1989	1990	1991
Debt/assets (%)	62.5	72.4	63.3
Debt/equity (%)	166.4	261.9	172.5
Long debt/equity (%)	56.5	75.3	56.2
Net bank/equity (£)	0.446	1.434	0.696
Current (times)	1.59	1.02	1.23
Liquidity (times)	1.06	0.73	0.91
Interest cover (times)	11.1	5.7	7.3
Reinvestment (times)		15.7	0.83
Gross margin (%)	12.7	13.3	16.0
Pre-tax margin (%)	5.3	5.0	7.8
PBIT margin (%)	5.8	6.1	9.0
ROI (%)	14.9	10.7	18.4
RONA (%)	22.6	14.3	26.1
ROE (pre-tax) (%)	36.1	31.9	43.3
EPS (p)	12.47	11.42	24.28
Dividend yield (%)			1.63
Dividend cover (times)	6.9	3.7	3.9
PE (times)			15.65

STRUCTURAL PERCENTAGES

	1989	1990	1991
Fixed assets	34.4	47.3	47.7
Current assets	65.6	52.7	52.3
	100.0	100.0	100.0
Payable under 1 year	41.3	51.6	42.7
Payable beyond 1 year	21.2	20.8	20.6
Shareholders' funds	37.5	27.6	36.7
	100.0	100.0	100.0

TREND PERCENTAGES

	1989/90	1990/91
Sales	7.70	14.89
Cost of sales	6.96	11.37
Gross margin	12.78	37.78
Overheads	11.80	10.83
Interest	122.74	32.19
Net margin	3.19	77.56
Tax	29.01	22.22
Dividends	70.62	100.00
Fixed assets	125.92	3.09
Stock	7.26	−10.28
Debtors	48.08	0.52
Trade creditors	12.53	11.82
Net bank	299.56	−37.60

Key Features of Swings PLC

The company operates in the food processing sector. Gross margins are tight and overheads are carefully controlled. In November 1990 it acquired a smaller company operating in a higher margin element of the food sector. The controlling shareholders were not able to subscribe to a rights issue and did not want their stake to fall below 50 per cent. As a result, the company was bought for £29m cash. The acquistion had the following major effects:

1 Gearing rose dangerously;
2 Return on investment nose-dived (all assets but only 1.5 months of profit consolidated).

The directors and the company bankers were confident that the projected profitability and positive cash flow would correct these problems in 1991. This proved to be the case and the share price more than doubled during that year. Swings PLC was fortunate. It broke a crucial rule of finance – do not take on too much bank debt – and got away with it. Most similar stories in the last 6 years have had a much less happy ending. The cash flow statement for 1991 shows how the gearing was normalised.

Swings PLC Cash Flow Statement 1991

		£'000
Operating activities [1]		28,269
Servicing of finances [2]		5,261
Cash flow after servicing		23,008
Corporation tax paid [3]		4,069
Cash flow after taxation		18,939
Investing activities [4]		1,777
Cash flow after investing		17,162
Financing activities [5]		–
Net cash flow for year		17,162
Cash and cash equivalents 1 January [6]		(47,146)
Cash and cash equivalents 31 December [6]		(29,984)
[1] Profit before interest and tax		21,616
Add increase in creditors	2,880	
Decrease in stock	1,820	
Depreciation	2,137	6,837
		28,453
Less increase in debtors		184
		28,269
[2] Proposed dividend 1990		1,188
Provisions 1991		3,484
		4,672
Proposed dividend 1991		2,376
Dividends paid		2,296
Interest paid		2,965
		5,261
[3] 1990 provision paid		
[4] Fixed assets 1990		56,332
Less depreciation 1991		2,137
		54,195
Fixed assets 1991		55,972
Net acquisitions		1,777

[5] There were no financing activities during 1991.

[6]	1 Jan	31 Dec	Change
Cash	9,382	9,762	380
Short	(31,772)	(15,544)	16,228
Long	(24,756)	(24,202)	554
	(47,146)	(29,984)	17,162

Part of the long-term loan became repayable in under one year.

173

Chapter 7

Working Capital

In this chapter we examine the working capital structure of a business. The chapter is divided into four sections.

Section 1: The real meaning of working capital. This section explains why funding is required (to finance stocks and debtors less creditors) from the point where goods and services are bought, to collection from customers at or after the goods and services are sold. In particular it focuses on the reasons why funding requirements change as volumes of product or costs rise and fall.

Section 2: Overtrading. This section deals with the situation that arises when a company tries to invest more money in stocks and debtors than its funding permits. It also deals with the causes of the problem and the possible approaches to resolving an overtrading crisis.

Section 3: Working capital ratios. This section describes and illustrates a selection of ratios designed to examine the effectiveness of working capital management in a business.

Section 4: Management of working capital. This section examines effective approaches to management of stocks and debtors. It describes the steps that can be taken to keep down investment in these areas, without damaging sales and profit potential. It also explains how to optimise credit from suppliers of goods and services. The focus is on good management of suppliers, not dirty tricks to slow down payments which, while succeeding for a time, usually turn against the manipulator in the long run.

The Working Capital Cycle

Working capital is probably the least understood area in financial management. The term itself is loosely used. This causes confusion between how much funding is needed and what it is needed for. In order to create real understanding of the concept of working capital, we will first examine the operating cycle of a business (see Fig. 7.1).

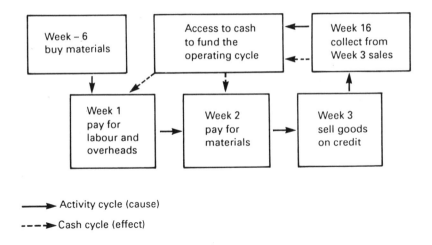

Fig. 7.1 Business Operating Cycle

To show how this operates in a simple business, we will assume the following:

1 The company buys 100 units per week. It starts buying six weeks before production commences.
2 Material costs £10 per unit.
3 Labour costs £5 per unit.
4 Overheads cost £1 per unit.
5 Material suppliers are paid seven weeks after purchase.
6 Customers pay 13 weeks after sale.
7 Sales are 100 units per week at £20 each, starting week 3.
8 There is no inflation.

The working capital required for the operating cycle is:

175

Week	Units Purchased	Unit Cost Purchases	Supplier Payments	Wage and Overhead Payments	Working Capital Invested
−6	100	10			
−5	100	10			
−4	100	10			
−3	100	10			
−2	100	10			
−1	100	10			
1	100	10		600	600
2	100	10	1,000	600	2,200
3	100	10	1,000	600	3,800
4	100	10	1,000	600	5,400
5	100	10	1,000	600	7,000
6	100	10	1,000	600	8,600
7	100	10	1,000	600	10,200
8	100	10	1,000	600	11,800
9	100	10	1,000	600	13,400
10	100	10	1,000	600	15,000
11	100	10	1,000	600	16,600
12	100	10	1,000	600	18,200
13	100	10	1,000	600	19,800
14	100	10	1,000	600	21,400
15	100	10	1,000	600	23,000
			14,000	9,000	

Up to this point the company has recouped no cash from its customers. It has invested £23,000 of finance in the working capital cycle. This investment appears in the balance sheet as follows:

	£
Stock of raw materials (6 weeks at £1,000)	6,000
Stocks of finished goods (2 weeks at £1,600)	3,200
Cost element of debtors' accounts (13 weeks at £1,600)	20,800
Credit from suppliers (7 weeks at £1,000)	(7,000)
Total working capital	23,000
Add profit element in debtors (13 weeks at £400)	5,200
Net current assets (ignoring dividends and bank balances)	28,200

If everything goes according to plan, this company will need access to £23,000 of funds on an ongoing basis, to carry it throught the never-ending cycle from paying suppliers and expenses to collecting from customers. If the company does not have £23,000 of funds, it could be forced into liquidation.

In planning the finances for the business, the owners will need funds for: set-up costs; fixed assets; working capital £23,000; and contingencies. The business could quickly get into difficulties if funds were not adequate to cover the set-up, contingency and fixed asset costs. The result would be to starve the business of finance for the working capital cycle.

Two major complications can increase the working capital requirements – growth in volume and growth in prices.

Growth in volumes

In weeks 3 and 4 the proprietor achieves 120 sales units. He now expects to be able to sell this amount in each subsequent week. He plans to increase his purchasing and production accordingly. The working capital requirement becomes:

Week	Units Purchased	Unit Cost Purchases	Supplier Payments	Wages and Overhead Payments	Working Capital Invested
−6 to 4	1,000	10	3,000	2,400	5,400
5	320[a]	10	1,000	1,200[b]	7,600
6	120	10	1,000	720	9,320
7	120	10	1,000	720	11,040
8	120	10	1,000	720	12,760
9	120	10	1,000	720	14,480
10	120	10	1,000	720	16,200
11	120	10	1,000	720	17,920
12	120	10	3,200[c]	720	21,840
13	120	10	1,200	720	23,760
14	120	10	1,200	720	25,680
15	120	10	1,200	720	27,600
	2,520		16,800	10,800	

[a] He has to make up for a shortfall in purchasing of 10 weeks at 20 per week and supply his new production 120 units.
[b] He has to make up for a shortfall in production of 4 weeks at 20 per week as well as his normal production.
[c] Week 5 purchases at £10 per unit.

The net current assets are now:

	£
Stock of raw materials (6 weeks at £1,200)	7,200
Stocks of finished goods (2 weeks at £1,920)	3,840
Cost element of debtors' accounts (13 weeks at £1,920)	24,960
Credit from suppliers (7 weeks at £1,200)	(8,400)
	27,600
Add profit element in debtors (13 weeks at £480)	6,240
Net current assets (ignoring tax, dividends and bank balances)	33,840

By comparison with the basic example we find that the funds required for working capital finance have grown by £4,600 (£27,600 – £23,000). If the company cannot obtain these extra funds, then it is said to be overtrading.

Overtrading is a condition in which a company has inadequate funds to meet its working capital needs. While overtrading can be caused by other factors, in this case the problem has arisen because the company is trying to sell more than its capital base permits. Too much money is invested in stocks and debtors.

Growth in Prices

In this example, we will assume that after the capital requirements were computed and arranged, an unexpected price increase of £1 per unit of raw materials was imposed by suppliers. The company increased its selling price to £21 each in order to recoup the supplier increase. Apart from these changes, other items, including the sales volume 100 units per week, remained as planned.

The working capital required is now:

Wages	Units Purchased	Unit Cost Purchases	Supplier Payments	Wage and Overhead Payments	Working Capital Invested
−6	100	11			
−5	100	11			
−4	100	11			
−3	100	11			
−2	100	11			
−1	100	11			
1	100	11		600	600
2	100	11	1,100	600	2,300
3	100	11	1,100	600	4,000
4	100	11	1,100	600	5,700
5	100	11	1,100	600	7,400
6	100	11	1,100	600	9,100
7	100	11	1,100	600	10,800
8	100	11	1,100	600	12,500
9	100	11	1,100	600	14,200
10	100	11	1,100	600	15,900
11	100	11	1,100	600	17,600
12	100	11	1,100	600	19,300
13	100	11	1,100	600	21,000
14	100	11	1,100	600	22,700
15	100	11	1,100	600	24,400
			15,400	9,000	

The net current assets are now:

	£
Stock of raw materials (6 weeks at £1,100)	6,600
Stock of finished goods (2 weeks at £1,700)	3,400
Cost of element of debtors' accounts (13 weeks at £1,700)	22,100
Credit from suppliers (7 weeks at £1,100)	(7,700)
Total working capital	24,400
Add profit element in debtors (13 weeks at £400)	5,200
Net current assets (ignoring tax dividends and bank balances)	29,600

In this case additional funding of £1,400 (£24,400−£23,000) is required for working capital. This is a moderate amount unless the company is already overborrowed. We will examine one more illustration and then look at the profit and loss accounts and balance sheets.

179

Growth in Volumes and Prices

In this example we combine the impact of growing volumes and rising prices. Materials cost £11 per unit. The proprietor starts buying 100 units per week, but has to increase purchases because he sells 120 units per week at £21 each.

The working capital required is:

Week	Units Purchased	Unit Cost Purchases	Supplier Payments	Wage and Overhead Payments	Working Capital Invested
−6	100	11			
−5	100	11			
−4	100	11			
−3	100	11			
−2	100	11			
−1	100	11			
1	100	11		600	600
2	100	11	1,100	600	2,300
3	100	11	1,100	600	4,000
4	100	11	1,100	600	5,700
5	320[a]	11	1,100	1,200[b]	8,000
6	120	11	1,100	720	9,820
7	120	11	1,100	720	11,640
8	120	11	1,100	720	13,460
9	120	11	1,100	720	15,280
10	120	11	1,100	720	17,100
11	120	11	1,110	720	18,920
12	120	11	3,520[c]	720	23,160
13	120	11	1,320	720	25,200
14	120	11	1,320	720	27,240
15	120	11	1,320	720	29,280
	2,520		18,480	10,800	

[a] He has to make up for a shortfall in purchasing (10 weeks at 20 per week) as well as buying to fill his new weekly production of 120 units.
[b] He has to make up for a shortfall in production of 4 weeks at 20 per week as well as increasing his weekly production.
[c] Week 5 purchases at £11 each.

The net current assets are now:

	£
Stock of raw materials (6 weeks at £1,320)	7,920
Stock of finished goods (2 weeks at £2,040)	4,080
Cost element of debtors' accounts (13 weeks at £2,040)	26,520
Credit from suppliers (7 weeks at £1,320)	(9,240)
	29,280
Add profit element in debtors (13 weeks at £480)	6,240
	35,520

The funds required for working capital increase by £6,280 (£29,280−£23,000). The company may be exceeding its bank borrowing limit.

The following are the profit and loss accounts and balance sheets after 15 weeks in business, assuming that the company began life with owners' capital of £12,000 and an overdraft limit of £11,000 (total £23,000).

Profit and Loss Accounts and Balance Sheets

	Case			
	1	*2*	*3*	*4*
	Constant Volumes and Prices	*Increased Volumes Constant Prices*	*Constant Volumes Increased Prices*	*Increased Volumes and Prices*
Profit and Loss				
Sales	26,000	31,200	27,300	32,760
Purchases	21,000	25,200	23,100	27,720
Stock materials	6,000	7,200	6,600	7,920
Materials consumed	15,000	18,000	16,500	19,800
Labour and overheads	9,000	10,800	9,000	10,800
	24,000	28,800	25,500	30,600
Stock finished	3,200	3,840	3,400	4,080
Cost of sales	20,800	24,960	22,100	26,520
Profit	5,200	6,240	5,200	6,240

Note: ignoring interest and tax.

181

	Case			
	1	*2*	*3*	*4*
	Constant Volumes and Prices	*Increased Volumes Constant Prices*	*Constant Volumes Increased Prices*	*Increased Volumes and Prices*
Balance Sheets				
Stocks materials	6,000	7,200	6,600	7,920
Stocks finished	3,200	3,840	3,400	4,080
Debtors	26,000	31,200	27,300	32,760
	35,200	42,240	37,300	44,760
Financed by:				
Capital	12,000	12,000	12,000	12,000
Retained profit	5,200	6,240	5,200	6,240
Authorised overdraft	11,000	11,000	11,000	11,000
Excess overdraft	–	4,600	1,400	6,280
Creditors	7,000	8,400	7,700	9,240
	35,200	42,240	37,300	44,760

Overtrading

The following are the major causes of overtrading:

1 Inadequate finance to cover set-up costs and fixed and working capital. This is a big danger for new businesses. They frequently underestimate the amount of funds required for the start-up. I believe this is one of the major reasons why many new businesses fail during infancy. The proprietor has put all his or her personal capital into the business, and borrowed as much as possible from financial institutions. A request for additional loan finance is likely to be refused and failure to recognise the funding required is a serious blemish on a short track record.

2 Operating losses which consume the funds needed to finance the working capital cycle. A loss-making company is poorly placed to raise additional funds from owners or bankers.

3 Growth, not supported by additional funds to cover the extra working capital. The growth can happen in three ways:
   (a) Increase in demand for existing products;
   (b) Introduction of new products which require additional investment in stock and debtors; and

(c) Changes in VAT rates, which increase the cash required to pay suppliers while the cash is still tied up in debtors.
4 Diverting the working capital funds into fixed assets or shares in other businesses. This type of asset expansion should be supported by additional funding rather than misuse of working capital finance.

If the company is starved of funds required for the never-ending working capital cycle and cannot quickly raise additional funds, it will be faced with three unpalatable options.
(a) Reduce the stockholding period. (This could cause a stock-out and result in the loss of profitable sales.)
(b) Increase the pressure on customers to pay. If the demands become unreasonable the customers will take their orders to competitors.
(c) Slow down supplier payments. If this goes too far, they will stop supplies. The production planning process can quickly become unmanageable.

Coping with Overtrading

A company involved in overtrading has some more acceptable options:

1 Get the proprietors to inject more capital (if they have it);
2 Attract a minority shareholder who will invest more capital in the business (and possibly as a result of the improved gearing facilitate additional bank borrowing);
3 Dispose of assets surplus to current requirements; or
4 Assess the working capital and profitability of each product or product group. This examination may result in a decision to discontinue certain products which either make a poor contribution to profits or require too great a working capital investment. Analysis of this type is difficult. It requires a detailed breakdown of stocks, debtors, and creditors over the range of products.

The breakdown can be difficult and time consuming. The work involved is justified if it explains why the working capital investment is unsustainably high. Quite apart from eliminating the potentially disastrous consequences of overtrading, many good companies find that after acquiring poorly managed businesses, they are able to release substantial sums that have been wastefully tied up in the working capital cycle. At the time of writing, many analysts believe this is an important element in the bid for British American Tobacco by the Hoylake consortium.

Working Capital Ratios

There are many ratios designed to measure the level of working capital invested in a business. We will examine certain of the major ones in this section and refer to a variety of others. The illustrations in this chapter are based on the financial statements of Model Company Ltd. as presented in Chapter 6.

Stockholding Ratios

The simplest ratios of stockholding are based on sales. There are five different versions of this ratio in common use:

Method	Description	Calculation	Ratio
1	Days sales in stock	$\dfrac{800}{5,000}$ / 365	58.4 days
2	Weeks sales in stock	$\dfrac{800}{5,000}$ / 52	8.32 weeks
3	Months sales in stock	$\dfrac{800}{5,000}$ / 12	1.92 months
4	Stock/Sales%	$\dfrac{800}{5,000}$ %	16%
5	Stock turns (Sales/Stocks)	$\dfrac{5,000}{800}$	6.25 turns

All these ratios say the same thing in slightly different ways. They are commonly used because many people have neither the time nor enthusiasm to explore in depth. None of them is a good assessment of stockholding because stocks valued at cost are being compared with sales which are, hopefully, at higher prices.

An improvement is to expresss the stocks relative to the cost of sales. Again five methods are in common use as follows:

Method	Description	Calculation	Ratio
6	Days cost of sales in stock	$\dfrac{800}{3,800} / 365$	76.8 days
7	Weeks cost of sales in stock	$\dfrac{800}{3,800} / 52$	10.9 weeks
8	Months cost of sales in stock	$\dfrac{800}{3,800} / 12$	2.53 months
9	Stocks/Cost of sales %	$\dfrac{800}{3,800}\%$	21%
10	Stock turns (Stock/Cost of sales)	$\dfrac{3,800}{800}$	4.75 turns

These ratios are better measures of stockholding and they are frequently used by business managers. The analysis can be further improved. The issues that these ratios conceal are:

1 They fail to recognise that a manufacturing business generally has four types of stock (raw materials, work in progress, finished goods and other); and
2 Stocks can vary enormously during a financial year due to peaks and valleys in supply and demand. Analysis based on year-end figures can be misleading. We will now examine the best ways to evaluate stock holding.

To obtain a detailed analysis of stockholding ratios it is necessary to use management accounts, rather than heavily summarised published accounts. The following additional quarterly information was obtained from the 1989 management accounts of Model Company Ltd.:

	Q1	Q2	Q3	Q4	Year
Opening material stock	250	300	200	150	250
Purchases of materials	478	255	557	1,022	2,312
	728	555	757	1,172	2,562
Closing material stock	300	200	150	300	300
Material consumed	428	355	607	872	2,262
Production labour	280	320	355	332	1,287
Production fuel	30	25	24	26	105
Production maintenance	20	21	30	25	96
Production other	13	15	17	15	60
Opening work in progress	80	85	70	70	80
Closing work in progress	(85)	(70)	(70)	(80)	(80)
Cost of production	766	751	1,033	1,260	3,810
Opening finished stock	270	286	211	153	270
Cost of production	766	751	1,033	1,260	3,810
	1,036	1,037	1,244	1,413	4,080
Closing finished stock	286	212	152	280	280
Cost of sales	750	825	1,092	1,133	3,800
Gross profit	250	275	308	367	1,200
Sales	1,000	1,100	1,400	1,500	5,000

	Q1 Opening	Q2 Opening	Q3 Opening	Q4 Opening	Q4 Closing
Stocks					
Material	250	300	200	150	300
Work in progress	80	85	70	70	80
Finished goods	270	286	211	153	280
Fuel	60	65	70	75	80
Maintenance	40	44	48	52	60
	700	780	599	500	800

We will now examine the stockholding ratios that can be extracted from these detailed figures. Initially we will look at the year end ratios. Subsequently we will examine how the results vary substantially from quarter to quarter.

Method 11

Description	Calculation	Ratio
(a) Days material consumed in material stock	$\frac{300}{2,262} \times 365$	48.4 days
(b) Weeks material consumed in material stock	$\frac{300}{2,262} \times 52$	6.9 weeks
(c) Months material consumed in material stock	$\frac{300}{2,262} \times 12$	1.6 months
(d) Material stock/Material consumed %	$\frac{300}{2,262}$	13.3%%
(e) Material stock turns	$\frac{2,262}{300}$	7.54 turns

Each of these ratios gives a good annualised assessment of the material stockholding. I tend to favour the weeks stocks approach and will concentrate on this from now on. If your company measures stockholding in days, months, percentages, or turns, you will know how to apply this approach to the subsequent illustrations. Before we proceed to the other elements of the total stockholding, let us look at the ratios for material stock on a quarterly basis.

	Q1	Q2	Q3	Q4	Year
Opening					
Material stock	250	300	200	150	250
Material consumed	428	355	607	872	2,262
Weeks stock	7.6[1]	11.0	4.3	2.2	5.7[2]

[1] The calculation of the quarterly figures is based on 13 weeks, e.g. 250/(428/13).
[2] The calculation of the annual figure is based on 52 weeks, e.g. 250/(2262/52).

A new approach has been adopted in calculating these ratios. The material stocks are committed to meet future production requirements. At the start of Q1 the material stocks are adequate to meet the issue requirements for the next 7.6 weeks. This assumes an average weekly issue to production of (428/13) through the first quarter.

From this analysis we see that material stockholding has declined substantially in the third and fourth quarter. The position at the end of the year should be compared against the budgeted issues for the first quarter of 1990.

Method 12

Description	Calculation	Ratio
Weeks cost of sales in finished stock	$\dfrac{270}{3,800 \,/\, 52}$	3.7 weeks

This ratio indicates that the business holds a relatively small finished goods stock. A one-month strike on the production floor could result in a stock-out with potentially serious consequences. However, with the cost of stockholding very high, businesses try to keep finished goods at a low level. The quarterly figures are:

	Q1	Q2	Q3	Q4	Year
Weeks	4.7[1]	4.5	2.5	1.8	3.7

[1] 270 / (750 / 13).

The finished goods stockholding period declines all the way through the year.

Method 13

Description	Calculation	Ratio
Weeks fuel stocks in fuel consumed	$\dfrac{60}{105 \,/\, 52}$	29.7 weeks

Decisions on fuel stockholding are influenced by: (a) predicted price movements (stock high if prices expected to rise and low if expected to fall); and (b) the significance or otherwise of a stock-out due to a supply problem (disastrous for a transport company but not too serious if used to heat a factory).

The quarterly figures are:

	Q1	Q2	Q3	Q4	Year
Weeks	26.0	33.8	37.9	37.5	29.7

In this case we see a build up of stock through Q3 and a small decline thereafter.

Method 14

Description	Calculation	Ratio
Weeks maintenance stock in maintenance cost	$\frac{40}{96/52}$	21.7 weeks

Maintenance stocks can vary enormously in value. Some organisations can buy replacements on demand. Others have to hold specialised parts that might not be required for years. The quarterly maintenance stock analysis is:

	Q1	Q2	Q3	Q4	Year
Weeks	26.0	27.2	20.8	27.0	21.7

In this case the stockholding period does not vary significantly from its high of 27.2 weeks in Q2 to its low of 20.8 weeks in Q3.

Method 15

Description	Calculation	Ratio
Weeks work in progress in cost of production	$\frac{80}{3,810/52}$	1.1 weeks

This ratio suggests the duration of the production cycle. It is a bit misleading. Method 16 is an improved assessment of the work in progress. It assumes that materials are input at the start, while labour and overheads are applied evenly through the process. On this basis the cost of producing goods to an average level in the work in process phase would be computed as follows:

	Q1	Q2	Q3	Q4	Year
Material consumed	428	355	607	872	2,262
Half labour	140	160	178	166	644
Half other (fuel, maintenance, etc.)	31	30	35	33	131
	599	545	820	1,071	3,037

Based on this cost of part production the average production period is:

Method 16

Description	Calculation	Ratio
Weeks work in progress in cost of part production	$\dfrac{80}{3,037 / 52}$	1.37 weeks

Clearly the work in progress can vary from years in major construction activities (building factories, shops, etc) to minutes in uncomplicated and highly automated processes. The quarterly ratios for Method 16 are:

	Q1	Q2	Q3	Q4	Year
Weeks	1.74	2.02	1.11	0.85	1.37

It looks as if the company concentrated on lines with a long production cycle in quarters one and two as compared with quarters three and four.

In summary there are a variety of ways of looking at stockholding. It is wise to be aware of the different approaches. It is important to compare results with the stockholding policy of the company and, where possible, to relate them to competitors.

Debtors Ratios

The simplest form of debtors ratio expresses the results in days, weeks, or months of sales. Following our approach in the stock area we will concentrate on weeks. The Model Company Ltd. debtors ratio at year-end is:

$$\frac{1,042}{5,000 \,/\, 52} = 10.8 \text{ weeks}$$

This preliminary analysis is superficial. Many factors can distort the interpretation. The following are the important issues:

1   Some of the sales may be for cash. They should be excluded in reviewing the average credit period.
2   The turnover figure in accounts does not normally contain VAT. The trade debtors figure does. To make a valid comparison you should either gross up the sales to include VAT or net down the debtors to exclude VAT in computing a sensible ratio.
3   The debtors figure in the balance sheet often includes amounts which relate to staff loans, prepayments etc. These tend to distort a ratio designed to establish the average delay in collecting from customers and should be excluded from the analysis. The notes to the accounts will specify the trade debtors
4   Annual figures can be misleading, where sales revenues fluctuate substantially during a financial year.

The following figures were obtained from the management accounts of Model Company Ltd to assist in calculating the trade debtor ratios:

	Q1	Q2	Q3	Q4	Year
Cash Sales	80	125	70	100	375
Credit Sales	920	975	1,330	1,400	4,625
Total Sales	1,000	1,100	1,400	1,500	5,000
Add VAT (15%)	150	165	210	225	750
Grossed up Sales	1,150	1,265	1,610	1,725	5,750
Trade debtors	590	725	790	1,042	1,042

	Q1	Q2	Q3	Q4	Year
Trade debtor Weeks	7.1[1]	8.2	6.6	8.2	10.0[2]

[1] 590 / (920×117.5% / 13). [2] 1,042 / (4,625×117.5% / 52).

These ratios show a significant movement in the average collection period. The low occurs in Q3. The pattern of sales growth through the year distorts the average in the annual figure and makes it an unreliable measure of credit management. It is wise to assess the average delay period for major customers as well as looking at the overall figures.

The credit period can vary wildly from one type of business to another. Among the notorious slow payers are farmers, chemists, vets, and builders. Among the fastest payers are people to whom a threat to cut off supplies is disturbing (i.e. many retail goods, electricity, telephone, etc.). It is wise to compare your ratios against the credit period that the industry sector offers.

Creditor Ratios

A poor method of creditor assessment, frequently used because no better information is available, is:

Creditors / Average weekly sales

Ideally the ratio should be calculated by taking the amounts due to suppliers for goods and services acquired on credit, and relating this to the average weekly cost of procurement of such goods and services. VAT must be properly treated, either by grossing up procurement costs to match creditors, or by reducing creditors to match the net of VAT procurement cost.

The following information was taken from the management accounts of Model Company Ltd., to assist in computing creditor ratios:

	Q1	Q2	Q3	Q4	Year
Procurement of goods and services on credit (incl. VAT)	930	1,064	1,367	1,499	4,860
Creditors for goods and services (incl. VAT)	360	403	642	376	376
Weeks credit	5.0[1]	4.9	6.1	3.3	4.0

[1] 360 / (930 / 13).

These ratios show that Model Company pays its suppliers reasonably promptly. The Q3 figure appears high, but on investigation, a good explanation was found. During this quarter plant costing £123,000 was bought on credit. It remained unpaid at the end of the quarter and the amount was included in both the procurement and creditor items. This occasional purchase distorted the comparison. The figures were restated as follows:

	Quarter 3
Procurement	1,246
Creditors	519
Weeks credit	5.4

Cash Ratios

Most businesses need to have some cash available at all times. This is caused by petty cash floats and cash receipts not yet lodged.

As a business grows, more cash becomes tied up in this way. This type of cash is treated differently from special funds on short-term deposit, pending the maturity of large bills or funds wastefully left lying in current accounts at banks.

The simplest and mose appropriate method of recognising the cash investment is to take it as a percentage or turns of sales. The Model Company Ltd. figures are:

$$\frac{\text{Cash}}{\text{Sales}} \% \quad \frac{25}{5,000} \% = 0.5\%$$

or

$$\frac{\text{Sales}}{\text{Cash}} \quad \frac{5,000}{25} = 200 \text{ turns}$$

This ratio is normally calculated on an annual basis. A retail business, which earns significant amounts of interest between point of cash sales and payment to suppliers, would compute the ratio more frequently.

The Overall Working Capital Ratio

A widely used ratio of working capital is the percentage that net current assets represent of sales. The ratio for Model Company Ltd. in 1989 is:

$$\frac{\text{Current Assets} - \text{Current Liabilities}}{\text{Sales}} \%$$

$$= \frac{2,041 - 988}{5,000} \%$$

$$= 21.06\%$$

193

This ratio is supposed to reveal the amount of additional funds required to support working capital as sales grow, or capable of being released from working capital as sales decline. It does not do this successfully because not all amounts due and payable in under one year behave in direct proportion to sales (i.e. tax provision, proposed dividend and short-term bank debt).

A better measure is based on the definition of working capital outlined at the start of this chapter. The improved ratio is:

$$\frac{\text{Stock}+\text{Trade Debtors}-\text{Trade Creditors}+\text{Manditory Cash}}{\text{Sales}}\%$$

The 1989 ratio for the Model Company Ltd. is:

$$\frac{800+1,042-376+25}{5,000} = 29.82\%$$

Year-end figures sometimes provide incorrect information on the amount of cash required for the working capital cycle: they should reveal an off season picture of the working capital investment; and they can be further distorted by management decisions to slow down stock purchases and supplier payments and increase customer collection pressure. This is to dress up the balance sheet for publication.

The ratio can be calculated more meaningfullly by averaging the components through the year in three computations:

1 Calculate the average stocks through the year (a simple method is to total the planned stock holding for each of the 12 months and divide by 12): say, £950,000.
2 Calculate the average trade debtors and creditors through the year in the same way; say, trade debtors £1,000,000 and trade creditors £450,000.
3 Assume a constant cash balance (say £25,000) unless the cash sales pattern is subject to huge peaks and valleys.

The working capital ratio based on these averages is:

$$\frac{950+1,000-450+25}{5,000} = 30.5\%$$

We can conclude that if (a) stockholding and (b) average credit given and taken continue at their current durations, then Model Company Ltd. will require an extra £305,000 of working capital finance to support a £1 million sales increase in 1990. A change in stockholding policy, or a decision to give or take more or less credit, would change the amount required. That said, a real growth in sales volume or an inflation-driven price increase will result in the need for additional working capital finance. Note that the £305,000 calculated above greatly exceeds the profit retained in 1989. Model Company will need to arrange additional funds or it runs the risk of overtrading.

Effective Management of Working Capital

Stock in Trade

There is a fine line between carrying too much and too little stock.

PROBLEMS ASSOCIATED WITH UNNECESSARILY HIGH STOCKS

First, too high stocks relative to the level of sales and profits damage return on investment.

	Efficient Ltd.	Less Efficient Ltd.
PBIT	20,000	20,000
Stocks	50,000	100,000
Other assets	100,000	100,000
Total assets	150,000	200,000
ROI	13.3%	10%

Secondly, deteroriation or change in consumer taste can cause stock losses. Thirdly, stockholding costs are high and tend to rise in proportion to sales: fire insurance; clerical costs (recording and control); interest on borrowings to pay suppliers; and space costs (rent, rates etc.).

Finally, if material prices fall, a company will be in a poor position relative to lower stocked competitors.

PROBLEMS ASSOCIATED WITH UNDESIRABLY LOW STOCKS

First, profitable sales may be lost. Our customer, forced to buy from a competitor, may be well treated and not come back to us when our stock shortage is rectified.

Secondly, purchasing costs may rise unduly as a result of emergency

195

buying decisions. A notable example is the high cost 'emergency' airfreight order rather than a timely delivery by road or sea freight.

Thirdly, if the set-up time for a production run is long, then it is more profitable to produce in large batches, e.g.:

a   A company operates a 40 hour week.
b   The direct labour cost per week is £14,000
c   Set-up time is 5 hours for product A or B.
d   The company can produce 10,000 units of product A in 15 hours or 20,000 units of product B in 15 hours.

| | Output Week 1 | | | Output Week 2 | | |
	Units	Total Cost	Unit Cost	Units	Total Cost	Unit Cost
Sharing Facilities						
Product A	10,000	7,000	0.70	10,000	7,000	0.70
Product B	20,000	7,000	0.35	20,000	7,000	0.35
Specialising Facilities						
Product A	23,333	14,000	0.60			
Product B				46,667	14,000	0.30

Using the first week to make only product A we find:

a   Output of this product rises by 3,333 units or 16.66% over the corresponding volume for 2 weeks with shared processing; and
b   The labour cost per unit falls from £0.70 to £0.60 or 14.3%. In the same way output of product B rises by 6,667 units and the unit cost falls from 35p to 30p.

Lastly, if a supplier increases prices it may place the company in a poor position relative to competitors holding high stocks.

THE BASIC PURCHASING/INVENTORY MODEL

This model involves the collection of key data in relation to the product to be purchased, stored and sold. Here is an example:

Description	Data
1 Average expected weekly sales	990 units
2 Standard loss through wastage and pilferage 1% of weekly sales	
3 Delay involved between placing order and receipt of goods	5 weeks
4 Buffer stock to cover against changes in sales demand, standard losses and delivery delays	3 weeks

The following schedule shows the budgeted purchases, stockholding, stock losses and sales:

Week	Opening Start	Order Placed	Delivery	Sales	Stock Losses	Closing Stock	Buffer	Forward Sales
−5	–	8,000	–	–	–	–	–	–
0	–	5,000	8,000	–	–	8,000	3,000	5,000
1	8,000	–	–	990	10	7,000	3,000	4,000
2	7,000	–	–	990	10	6,000	3,000	3,000
3	6,000	–	–	990	10	5,000	3,000	2,000
4	5,000	–	–	990	10	4,000	3,000	1,000
5	4,000	5,000	5,000	990	10	8,000	3,000	5,000
6	8,000	–	–	990	10	7,000	3,000	4,000
7	7,000	–	–	990	10	6,000	3,000	3,000
8	6,000	–	–	990	10	5,000	3,000	2,000
9	5,000	–	–	990	10	4,000	3,000	1,000
10	4,000	5,000	5,000	990	10	8,000	3,000	5,000
11	8,000	–	–	990	10	7,000	3,000	4,000
12	7,000	–	–	990	10	6,000	3,000	3,000
13	6,000	–	–	990	10	5,000	3,000	2,000
14	5,000	–	–	990	10	4,000	3,000	1,000
15	4,000	5,000	5,000	990	10	8,000	3,000	5,000

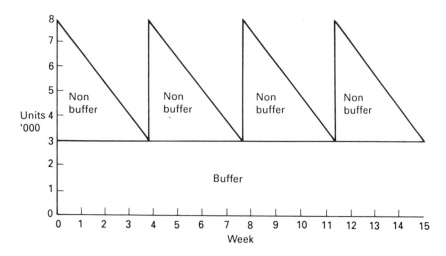

Fig. 7.2   Stockholding

A Problem with the Basic Model (Erratic Sales)

Most organisations experience peaks and valleys in the demand pattern for their products. As a result the purchasing and stockholding pattern is difficult to plan. The model has been adjusted in this second example to reflect the projected forward sales pattern:

Week	Opening Stock	Order Placed	Delivery	Sales	Stock Losses	Closing Stock	Buffer	Forward Sales
−5		7,800[1]						
0		5,200	7,880			7,880	3,180	4,700
1	7,800	–	–	792	8	7,080	3,180	3,900
2	7,080	–	–	891	9	6,180	3,180	3,000
3	6,180	–	–	990	10	5,180	3,180	2,000
4	5,180	–	–	1,089	11	4,080	3,180	900
5	4,080	6,000	5,200	891	9	8,380	3,180	5,200
6	8,380	–	–	1,089	11	7,280	3,180	4,100
7	7,280	–	–	792	8	6,480	3,180	3,300
8	6,480	–	–	1,188	12	5,280	3,180	2,100
9	5,280	–	–	1,287	13	3,980	3,180	800
10	3,980	5,300[2]	6,000	792	8	9,180	3,180	6,000
11	9,180	–	–	1,188	12	7,980	3,180	4,800
12	7,980	–	–	1,089	11	6,880	3,180	3,700
13	6,880	–	–	990	10	5,880	3,180	2,700
14	5,880	–	–	1,287	13	4,580	3,180	1,400
15	4,580	–	5,300	1,386	14	8,480	3,180	5,300
				15,741	159			

Note: buffer computation
15 week purchases   15,741+159 = 15,900
Average weekly   15,900 / 15 = 1,060
Buffer 3 weeks   1,060×3 = 3,180

[1] 5 week sales	5 week stock loss	Buffer	Total
4,653	47	3,180	7,880

[2] Based on continued average weekly sales and stock losses of 1,060 per week, as budget for the next 5 weeks had not yet been prepared.

FLOATING BUFFER STOCKS

Buffer stocks are held as cover against the unexpected. The three major eventualities that can arise are as follows:

1 Sales exceed forecast (you need buffer stock to service ongoing demand).
2 Delivery delays exceed forecast (even if sales are on target you will need a buffer to service demand pending arrival).
3 Stock losses exceed standard.

In order to cope with these possible eventualities the company might set its buffer stocks to cover: demand overrun say 20%; delivery overrun say 2 weeks; and above standard pilferage say 2%. Based on these expectations, the company might set floating buffer stocks. The following table shows the floating buffers to cover against uncertainty:

Week	Opening Stock	Order Placed	Delivery	Sales	Stock Losses	Closing Stock	Buffer	Forward Sales
−5		7,634[1]						
0		5,710[2]	7,634			7,634	2,934	4,700
1	7,634			792	8	6,834	2,934	3,900
2	6,834			891	9	5,934	2,934	3,000
3	5,934			990	10	4,934	2,934	2,000
4	4,934			1,089	11	3,834	2,934	900
5	3,834	6,176[3]	5,710	891	9	8,644	3,444	5,200
6	8,644			1,089	11	7,544	3,444	4,100
7	7,544			792	8	6,744	3,444	3,300
8	6,744			1,188	12	5,544	3,444	2,100
9	5,544			1,287	13	4,244	3,444	800
10	4,244	4,214[4]	6,176	792	8	9,620	3,620	6,000
11	9,620			1,188	12	8,420	3,620	4,800
12	8,420			1,089	11	7,320	3,620	3,700
13	7,320			990	10	6,320	3,620	2,700
14	6,320			1,287	13	5,020	3,620	1,400
15	5,020	5,000 (say)	4,214	1,386	14	7,834	3,134	4,700
16	7,834			1,485	15	6,334	3,134	3,200
17	6,334			792	8	5,534	3,134	2,400
18	5,534			693	7	4,834	3,134	1,700
19	4,834			792	8	4,034	3,134	900
20	4,034		5,000	891	9	8,134		
21				990	10			
22				1,089	11			

	Notes			
	(1)	(2)	(3)	(4)
Order				
Sales next 5 weeks (a)	4,700	5,200	6,000	4,700
Buffer				
Sales overrun 20% ×(a)	940	1,040	1,200	940
Delivery delay				
Sales next 2 weeks	1,900	2,300	2,300	2,100
2% 5 weeks sales	94	104	120	94
Buffer	2,934	3,444	3,620	3,134
Change in buffer (b)	2,934	510	176	(486)
Order placed a+b	7,634	5,710	6,176	4,214

FREQUENCY OF ORDER PLACING

When the cost of placing orders is high, difficult questions arise about order frequency. We will now examine the order placing process for a company with a regular sales pattern and the following data:

Description	Data
Annual sales units	520,000
Budgeted purchase cost per unit	£1
Inventory carrying cost (percentage of average inventory held per annum	25%
Cost per order placed	£300

How often should orders be placed?

Order Frequency Weeks	Orders per Annum	Annual Order Placement Cost	Average Inventory Held (£)	Inventory Holding Cost	Total Stock Costs
1	52	15,600	5,000	1,250	16,850
2	26	7,800	10,000	2,500	10,300
3	17.3	5,200	15,000	3,750	8,950
4	13	3,900	20,000	5,000	8,900
5	10.4	3,120	25,000	6,250	9,370
6	8.7	2,600	30,000	7,500	10,100

We can see from this table that the lowest purchasing cost occurs when orders are based on a four-weekly reorder cycle. The order placing cost is correctly balanced against the cost of stockholding as illustrated in Fig. 7.3.

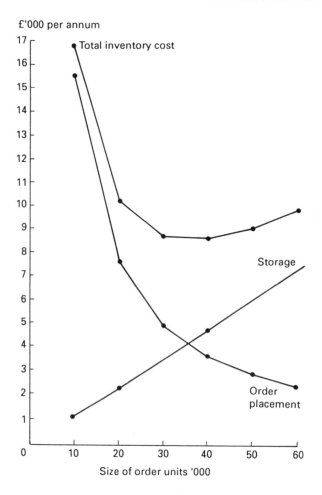

Fig. 7.3 Stockholding Cost

If you want a more scientific measurement of cost effective purchasing, you can use the economic order quantity formula:

$$EOQ = \sqrt{\frac{2\,ap}{s}}$$

where: a = annual sales demand; p = cost of placing an order; and s = storage cost per unit.

$$EOQ = \sqrt{\frac{2 \times 520,000 \times £300}{£0.25}} = 35,326$$

Based on this formula we find that the cost is as follows:

Order Frequency p.a.	Cost per Order	Annual Order Cost	Average Stock Holding	Cost of Holding at 25%	Total Stock Cost
14.72[1]	£300	4,416	£17,663	4,416	£8,832

[1] 520,000÷35,326 = 14.72 orders p.a. or 3.5 week intervals.

The cost saving achieved by EOQ is £68 per annum as compared to the original schedule.

JUST IN TIME

Just in time is an approach to manufacturing developed in Japan. It involves the elimination of buffer stocks and manufacture in small lots. This is contrary to traditional approaches in which the key rules were that long production runs lead to lower unit costs and buffer stocks ensured that direct labour always had a continuous supply of work.

Just in time is very suitable for industries where:

● Large numbers of standardised units are produced;
● Consistent quality is required and the error tolerance is narrow; and
● The manufacturing business can arrange the delivery of components from suppliers very quickly.

It is extensively used in car assembly. Austin Rover claim to have saved £37 million as a result of the introduction of JIT.

The major benefits of just in time production are:

● Problems become highly visible;
● Weaknesses in the production process are more obvious;
● Increased awareness of significant problems. In the early stages of using JIT the problems may occur frequently and rapidly;
● Potential problem identification becomes a management priority. This is a dynamic approach as compared to passive problem solving;
● Since the line must stop to resolve a problem, management and staff learn to cure them quickly;
● Removal of buffer stocks results in reduced incidence of breakage and pilferage during production; and
● The cost of stockholding is reduced. Lower work in progress reduces the interest cost, releases space for other purposes, and reduces the impact of fires and, as a consequence, the cost of insurance.

Trade Debtors

The major issues are:

1 Too high debtor balances unduly fail to improve return on investment.
2 The greater the level of debtors the more exposed a business is to the risk of bad debts.
3 Money unnecessarily tied up in debtors could have been used to reduce bank borrowings and interest thereon. It also damages the net bank/shareholders ratio.

These issues must be weighed against the possible consequences of attempts to speed up debt collection:

1 Depression of demand due to uncompetitive terms of trade.
2 High discounts in order to encourage prompt payment.
3 Heavy expenditure associated with credit control techniques.

THE RULES OF EFFECTIVE CREDIT MANAGMENT

Rule 1

There should be a defined maximum amount of credit for each significant customer. This is the credit limit. It is good practice to ensure that customer orders are charged to the account on a *pro forma* basis before the order is filled. This helps to avoid unauthorised excesses.

Rule 2

Limits should be regularly reviewed to highlight changes in the creditworthiness of each customer.

Rule 3

When customers' purchasing patterns fluctuate wildly from peak to valley, the credit limit should not stay static. The main reason for this is that the size of the customer's net assets is influenced by stocks and debtors thus changing the potential liquidation proceeds. Consider the following example.

Betty Bradford Ltd. has informed us of its planned purchasing pattern. We are its most important supplier:

Quarter	Value of Purchases
1	25,000
2	5,000
3	10,000
4	20,000

Betty normally sells the product about one month after purchase and pays us about two months thereafter. All other features of the business remain fairly constant. Its balance sheets are projected as follows:

Projected Balance Sheets, Betty Bradford Ltd.

	Q1	Q2	Q3	Q4
Fixed assets	38,000	38,000	38,000	38,000
Stocks	8,333	1,667	3,333	6,667
	46,333	39,667	41,333	44,667
Capital	15,000	15,000	15,000	15,000
Bank overdraft				
(secured)	6,333	19,667	16,333	9,667
Creditor	25,000	5,000	10,000	20,000
	46,333	39,667	41,333	44,667

If the company closed down and the liquidation proceeds are fixed assets realising 40% of book value, stocks realising 25% of book value and liquidation costs a preferential £5,000, then our recovery from Betty Bradford Ltd. will be:

	Q1	Q2	Q3	Q4
Cash realised				
Fixed assets	15,200	15,200	15,200	15,200
Stocks	2,083	417	833	1,667
	17,283	15,617	16,033	16,867
Liquidation cost	5,000	5,000	5,000	5,000
	12,283	10,617	11,033	11,867
Less bank recovery	6,333	10,617	11,033	9,667
Proceeds for us	5,950	–	–	2,200
Due to us	25,000	5,000	10,000	20,000
Loss incurred	19,050	5,000	10,000	17,800

A fixed credit limit would not be desirable for this account. If our company was prepared to accept a 50% loss in a closedown, then the limits would be set at: Q1: £9,525; Q2: £2,500; Q3: £5,000; and Q4: £8,900.

Rule 4

A company which sells at a high profit margin is more likely to be prepared to sell goods to customers that are poor credit risks. Contrast the possible impact of a bad debt on suppliers of goods at various profit margins:

	Company				
	A	B	C	D	E
Monthly sales	10,000	10,000	10,000	10,000	10,000
Credit terms	1 month	1 month	1 month	1 month	1 month
Monthly cost of this production	4,000	5,000	7,500	8,000	9,000
True loss for month if account written off	4,000	5,000	7,500	8,000	9,000
Gain if collected	6,000	5,000	2,500	2,000	1,000
Payback (months)	0.7	1	3	4	9
If account closed and balance lost after 6 months successful trade:					
Takings 5 months	50,000	50,000	50,000	50,000	50,000
Costs 6 months	24,000	30,000	45,000	48,000	54,000
Gain (loss)	26,000	20,000	5,000	2,000	(4,000)

The bad debt risk is totally unacceptable for company E, undesirable for companies C and D and may be attractive for companies A and B.

Rule 5

The pareto (80:20) rule applies as reliably to trade debtors as it does to other statistical distributions. If debtors are listed in order of size, then careful attention to the top 20% provides an effective shortcut to risk management. Many companies include a listing of the top 20 debtors in their mangagement accounts in order to highlight their main exposures.

Rule 6

A business should set targets for weekly or monthly cash receipts. The following is an example:

1 Average delay between sales and cash collections four weeks (customers not taking discounts).
2 Customers that buy 40% of each week's sales will take a discount of 1% and settle within 7 days.

Comparison of Target Against Actual Collections

| | | | | Collections | | | |
| | Budget | No | | | | Weekly | Total |
Week	Sales	Discount	Discount	Target	Actual	Variance	Variance
1	36,000	–	7,128[1]	7,128	8,436	1,308	1,308
2	37,000	–	14,454[2]	14,454	15,975	1,521	2,829
3	38,000	–	14,850	14,850	15,684	834	3,663
4	39,000	–	15,246	15,246	14,940	(306)	3,357
5	40,000	21,600	15,642	37,242	40,167	2,925	6,282
6	40,000	22,200	15,840	38,040	39,875	1,835	8,117
7	40,000	22,800	15,840	38,640	36,440	(2,200)	5,917
8	40,000	23,400	15,840	39,240	38,256	(984)	4,933
9	40,000	24,000	15,840	39,840	40,629	789	5,722
10	40,000	24,000	15,840	39,840	37,675	(2,165)	3,557
11	40,000	24,000	15,840	39,840	39,988	148	3,705
12	40,000	24,000	15,840	39,840	40,255	415	4,120
	470,000	186,000	178,200	364,200	368,320	4,120	

[1] Expected collections	Week 1
20% of week 1 sales	7,200
Less 1% discount	72
	7,128
[2]	Week 2
20% of week 1 & 2 sales	14,600
Less 1%	146
	14,454

As compared with the budget, cash collections are running ahead by £4,120. This may not be as good as it sounds. Actual sales may have exceeded target.

A variation of this analysis, that I developed from standard costing principles, revises the target collections on the basis of the actual sales. The second report now presented shows that while performance in cash collections is good, it is not as good as the original table suggests:

	Actual	No		Collections		Variances	
Week	Sales	Discount	Discount	Target	Actual	Week	Total
1	40,000	–	7,920[1]	7,920	8,436	516	516
2	42,000	–	16,236[2]	16,236	15,975	(261)	255
3	36,000	–	15,444	15,444	15,684	240	495
4	38,000	–	14,652	14,652	14,940	288	783
5	42,000	24,000	15,840	39,840	40,167	327	1,110
6	36,000	25,200	15,444	40,644	39,875	(769)	341
7	38,000	21,600	14,652	36,252	36,440	188	529
8	39,750	22,800	15,395	38,195	38,256	61	590
9	39,250	25,200	15,642	40,842	40,629	(213)	377
10	42,750	21,600	16,236	37,836	37,675	(161)	216
11	42,500	22,800	16,879	39,679	39,988	309	525
12	38,750	23,850	16,088	39,938	40,255	317	842
	475,000	187,050	180,428	367,478	368,320	842	

[1] 20% of week 1 sales less 1% discount = 19.8%×40,000 = 7,920.
[2] 20% of weeks 1 & 2 sales less 1% discount (19.8%×82,000) = 16,236 and similarly for following weeks.

Summary of 12 Weeks Cash Collections

Budget collections	364,200
Add volume variance	
367,478−364,200	3,278
	367,478
Actual collections	368,320
Collection efficiency	842

Rule 7

Discounts for prompt payment can be a very expensive way of minimising debtors as the following example shows:

Weekly sales	4,000
Weekly cost of sales	3,000
Weekly gross margin	1,000

Credit terms are 6 weeks or 2% cash discount for 7 day settlement. Annual running expenses excluding discounts £27,000.

		ROI No Discount		ROI Discount
Sales		208,000		208,000
Cost of sales		156,000		156,000
Gross margin		52,000		52,000
Discounts	4,160		–	
Other running exes.	27,000	31,160	27,000	27,000
PBIT		20,840		25,000
Total assets %[1]		180,000		200,000
= ROI		11.58%		12.5%
[1] Debtors		4,000		24,000
Other assets		176,000		176,000
		180,000		200,000

The conclusions from this example are:
- £4,160 is a high annual cost to reduce debtor investment by £20,000. It is 20.8% per annum.
- We obtain a 12.5% ROI without discounts. A 2% discount is counter-productive. ROI becomes 11.58%.
- The maximum discount that could be afforded to advance cash collections by 5 weeks is £2,500 per annum. This is 12.5% per annum or 1.2% for cash in seven days:

		ROI No Discount		ROI Discount
Gross margin		52,000		52,000
Discount	2,500		–	
Other running expenses	27,000	29,500	27,000	27,000
PBIT		22,500		25,000
Total assets		180,000		200,000
= ROI		12.5%		12.5%

Each week the discount on settlement for the previous week is £48.08 or 1.2% (i.e £2,500/52). 1.2%, about the maximum discount that a company can afford, sounds too small to encourage customers to take discounts and settle promptly.

Rule 8

There is a converse to the discount rule. A company should try to charge interest on overdue accounts. This can boost profitability without appearing to charge an unreasonale interest rate. 1.5% per month compounds to 19.56% per annum. Interest charges that result in the loss of profitable business are counter-productive. Interest charges work well when they are standard in a business sector.

Rule 9

A business should prepare an aged debtors list. This involves matching payments and credit notes against the outstanding balance plus sales. It provides a breakdown of the amount due by months. We will examine the detailed ageing of one account and then look at it in the context of an overall aged listing.

The following data were extracted from the debtors ledger balance for client A.

Balance Outstanding Client A 1 January 1990

	£
October net sales	16,325.43
November net sales	18,527.26
December net sales	17,149.88
	52,002.57

During the next three months the following transactions arose:

	Sales	Credit Notes	Cash Collections
January	24,659.44	206.94 (Oct)	16,118.49 (for Oct)
		185.27 (Dec)	
February	15,285.67	1,593.17 (Jan)	16,964.61 (for Dec)
			3,600.00 (for Feb)
March	28,755.83	285.42 (Mar)	23,000.00 (for Jan)
	68,700.94	2,270.80	59,683.10

From this data we prepare an age analysis as follows:

Balance Outstanding	Current Month	Months Due 1	Months Due 2	Months Due 3	Months Due 4
58,749.61	28,470.41	11,685.67	66.27	–	18,527.26

Make Up

	Mar	Feb	Jan	Dec	Nov	Oct
Sales	28,755.83	15,285.67	24,659.44	17,149.88	18,527.26	16,325.43
Credit Notes	285.42	–	1,593.17	185.27	–	206.94
	28,470.41	15,285.67	23,066.27	16,964.61	18,527.26	16,118.49
Cash	–	3,600.00	23,000.00	16,964.61	–	16,118.49
Balance	28,470.41	11,685.67	66.27	–	18,527.26	–

This age analysis pinpoints a problem with the November balance for investigation.

Extract From an Age Analysis

Client	Credit Limit	Balance Outstanding	Current Due	One Month Due	Two Months Due	Three Months Due	Four Months and Over
A	60,000	58,749.61	28,470.41	11,685.67	66.27	–	18,527.26
B	8,000	6,495.26	3,581.53	2,913.73	–	–	–
C	2,000	2,409.67	486.02	430.63	395.77	455.08	642.17
D	500	485.44	245.44	240.00	–	–	–
E	37,500	40,081.63	21,424.40	18,657.23	–	–	–
F	12,500	2,049.43	519.16	–	–	–	1,530.27
G	500	367.25	195.25	172.00	–	–	–
H–Z	19,000	13,214.15	4,086.10	3,193.16	3,047.44	1,643.17	1,244.28
	140,000	123,852.44	59,008.31	37,292.42	3,509.48	2,098.25	21,943.98
% of limit	88.5						
% of total balances			47.6	30.1	2.8	1.7	17.7

Customer	Actions Taken
A	Sales manager to visit.
C	In solicitor's hands (R/D cheque).
E	Special excess to meet seasonal peak purchasing.
F	Representative to meet client.
H–Z	Various recovery actions taken.

This age analysis reveals several key points:

● Overall collections are good;
● Customer A is a serious problem. Action is being taken;
● Customer C is dangerous. Has a stop been placed on further supplies?;
● Customer E must be monitored to ensure that the balance is brought back within the limit; and
● The debtors balances are dominated by two customers: Customer A 47.4%, Customer E 32.4% and all others 20.2%.

The fact that neither of these accounts is trouble free is disturbing. Customer A appears to be in a dangerously powerful position. In addition to financing a debt of this size, we should be concerned about (a) the impact of a large bad debt on a small company profit, (b) over-dependence on A, resulting in demand for large price reductions and (c) continued expansion of the settlement delay period.

Trade Creditors

The rules for management of trade credit are:

1 Do not pay too quickly. It will increase your overdraft interest or reduce your deposit interest; BUT
2 Do not pay too slowly. If suppliers slow down or place a stop on deliveries it can disrupt production and sales. If they instigate recovery action it can harm your business reputation;
3 Seek discounts for prompt payment. A 2% discount for paying one month earlier provides a handsome return;
4 Have several suppliers for each product or service. A strike or other problem at one supplier will not affect continuity or quality of deliveries;
5 Look for adequate credit limits. If seeking extra credit to cover short-term peaks, ensure that it is properly authorised in writing at a sufficiently senior level in the supplier company. If this is not done, the distribution or credit staff in the supplier company might place a stop on deliveries, because they did not know of the additional credit approved; and
6 Prepare an aged schedule of supplier indebtedness. It is very helpful in planning payments and cash forecasting.

Chapter 8

Budgeting

The Purposes of Budgeting

These can be summarised as follows:

1 To prepare a plan of the way that the organisation will develop which is (a) attainable and (b) acceptable to institutions assessing it as a basis for funding.
2 To ensure that the various sections of the organisation are working together. Examples of this would include:
   (a) Purchasing is buying what production requires;
   (b) Production is making what sales expect to sell.
   (c) Sales are only dealing with customers that can be reasonably expected to pay.
   (d) No department is incurring expenditure which the organisation cannot afford to pay for.
3 To anticipate points where the 'resources' of the business are inadequate for its requirements in time to enable extra resources to be brought on stream:
   (a) Making for stock at times when production capacity exceeds market demand in order to be able to fill orders when demand subsequently exceeds supply. The scarce resource in this case would be finished stocks.
   (b) Commissioning the purchase of extra raw materials in time to meet production requirements which will exceed the historic pattern. This is particularly important when suppliers are already producing at full capacity.
   (c) Arranging the recruitment and training of production workers so that the company will be able to produce sufficient quantities for sale when demand increases substantially. The scarce resource is skilled labour and is particularly relevant in businesses where training takes a long time.
   (d) Arranging the purchase of additional space and equipment for production where the existing facilities are inadequate to service future profitable market demands. The scarce resource in this case is fixed assets (owned or rented).

(e) Arranging for additional funds when the company would exceed its spending authority. The scarce resource in this case is cash.

The common feature of all these 'resource' examples is that if a scarcity arose next week it would be exceedingly difficult to fill. You cannot: buy materials from suppliers who don't have them; sell stock you don't have; train workers to a high quality level overnight; or purchase, install and operate machinery instantly. The conclusion from these 'resource' scarcity possibilities is that companies must plan at least six months in advance and in many cases a good deal further ahead.

4   To provide a basis for comparison with actual results. You cannot say whether actual results are good, bad or indifferent unless you have previously defined what you think the results should be.

5   To ensure that priorities are set so as to encourage spending that will be beneficial to the organisation, and discourage spending that will be wasteful.

To satisfy the five purposes a business needs to prepare:

A   *An operating budget*
        Sales
        Costs
        Appropriations
B   *A balance sheet budget*
        Assets
        Liabilities
        Shareholders' funds
C   *A cash budget*
        Customer collections
        Supplier payments
        Payment of expenses
        Loans obtained and repaid
        Asset acquisitions and disposals
        Dividends, taxes, grants etc.

Length of Budget Period

This needs to be:

1   Long enough to identify resources required in time to fill them.
2   Short enough to enable forecasts to be made with a reasonable degree of confidence.

3   Compatible with external reporting obligations.

Most businesses find that a one-year budgetary control cycle, corresponding with their financial year, is most suitable. This can cause some problems in anticipating resource requirements as the following timetable shows. The X Company budgets in November for its financial year January to December:

During Month	Period Planned Ahead (Months)
December	12
January	11
February	10
March	9
April	8
May	7
June	6
July	5
August	4
September	3
October	2
November	1

Clearly, through the second half of the financial year, the company is not looking far enough forward. There are many ways of overcoming this problem. These include first, developing the budget in detail for the financial year, and in outline for one or two years further ahead. Secondly, developing budgets for 12-month periods but in six-monthly cycles. If this is the process, then as well as the budget in November for January/December there would be a budget in May for July/June. When this process is used it pushes the months ahead situation forward as follows:

During Month	Period Planned Ahead (Months)
June	12
July	11
August	10
September	9
October	8
November	7
December	6

You can still use the original budget to control during the July/December period even though the figures may have been changed at the mid year review to reflect current and emerging trends.

The third method is to allow the identification of medium-term resource requirements to become part of the corporate planning process and, finally, to use a three-year capital budgeting cycle to pick up resource requirements.

All of these approaches are used to some degree by organisations committed to quality planning. Which one (or combination) is most suitable for your organisation may have been decided long ago. You should, at least once every five years, examine the planning process. Is it still the most appropriate for the company? If not change it.

Key Elements of a Good Planning Process

The main points here are:

1 The people charged with achievement of income and expenditure budgets must feel stretched to achieve the planned performance, but
2 They must regard the targets as sensible ones, otherwise they may become totally demotivated. Consider the situation where the estimated total market for a product this year is 100,000 units. The market is expected to grow by 10% next year and the company doing the planning currently has a 40% market share. To set a budget of 66,000 units (without concrete marketing plans to secure a 60% market share) would be ludicrous. Sales staff would ignore it. When unfavourable comparisons between budget and actual emerged, they would feel no motivation to try to recover lost ground. They might define satisfactory performance as beating last year's volume by 1 or 2 per cent whereas 20% might have been possible if everyone was committed to trying for a challenging but attainable target.
3 It is best to request the 'experts' in each field to set themselves targets (against an organisation climate that presses people to challenge themselves):
   (a) the specialists should be in possession of greater knowledge of the way the particular area is developing than some non-specialist handing down the budget, and
   (b) most people strive harder to recover lost ground where they set themselves the targets.
4 The sequence of planning must be arranged so that departments that depend on the volume of activities in other areas should have the plans for those areas before they develop their budgets. To illustrate this point, we will examine the relationship between sales, purchasing and production in a company:
   (a) The sales target for Company X is 100,000 units.

(b) The production manager cannot plan what is to be manufactured without knowing the following data: the estimated stock level at the start (5,000 units) and the required stock level (8,000 units) at the end of the budget period; and the expected level of spoilage during production (2,000 units).

On receipt of this data he can compute the production plan as:

	Units
Expected sales	100,000
Spoilage	2,000
Increase in stocks (8,000−5,000)	3,000
Production required	105,000

(c) When the production target has been set he can determine the level of full time and/or overtime hours needed to achieve an output of 103,000 good units and the expected 2,000 spoiled units.

(d) The purchasing manager must wait until the production level 105,000 units is set, and

(e) Combine this knowledge with the raw material stock targets (10,000 units at start of budget period, and 6,000 units at end of period) to compute the purchasing plan as follows:

	Units
Purchased for issue to production	101,000
Plus issues which lower the stock level (10,000−6,000)	4,000
	105,000

The quantitative plan that emerges from this sequential treatment of the sales, production and purchasing is:

		Units
Opening raw materials		10,000
Bought in materials		101,000
		111,000
Held in material stock		6,000
Issues to production		105,000
Opening finished stock		5,000
		110,000
Stock produced		
Less spoiled	2,000	
Closing finished stock	8,000	10,000
For sale		100,000

5   The company must avoid the standard pitfall 'If it is not in the budget, then you cannot do it'. Attractive opportunities, not envisaged at the planning stage, should be capitalised on when they arise. However, in this flexible environment it is essential that, if significant non-budgeted developments are approved (a) they are not allowed to mask the expectation that existing targets must be achieved, and (b) cash is available to fund the expenditure involved rather than trying to divert funds from areas to which they are already committed. Consider the following:

	Original Budget A	New Initiative B	New Real Target A+B
Sales	500	150	650
Running costs	400	100	500
Profit	100	50	150

(a) If sales of 150 from the new initiative are achieved and only 350 on the original product, the original target is met but the result is disastrous.

(b) The company wants sales of 650, it expects to incur 500 of running costs. If only 400 is available to pay these costs, there may be a funding crisis.

6   Another pitfall that can affect budgets is the attitude 'If it is in the budget, you must spend it (you won't get it next year)'. If the time is not right for a particular expenditure, it is essential that managers feel they can postpone it and have it restored at a later date. This is difficult to arrange where budgets tend to be extrapolative. The state system worldwide is frequently caricatured in this.

In summary the key elements of a good budgeting process are:

1   Challenging;
2   Sensible;
3   Committed managers;
4   Departments working together; and
5   Adaptable to changing circumstances.

The Sequence of Budgeting

Define an Appropriate Start Time

Strangely enough the only way to do this satisfactorily is to work back from the date when the budget must be approved. The sequence is broadly as follows:

A   Final approval will come at a board meeting say two weeks before the end of the financial year.
B   Before the budget is presented to the board the operating management team must have time to assess it. You normally need to allow 4–6 weeks for this process. There are hard-nosed negotiations involved in changing unsatisfactory areas.
C   The finance section needs about a week to prepare the overall budgets based on departmental plans.
D   Departments need time to involve staff in budget preparation and to combine the figures from various sections. Since some budgets cannot start until they receive detailed plans for other functions this can take 4–6 weeks.

The time to start the budget can be counted back:

		Longest	*Shortest*
A	After board approval	4 weeks	2 weeks
B	Operating team approval	6 weeks	4 weeks
C	Accounting consolidation	1 week	1 week
D	Detailed departmental budgeting	6 weeks	4 weeks
		17 weeks	11 weeks

If the budget has to be passed through one or more parent company consolidation processes, it will add more time. Extremes would be 4 weeks for inclusion in the European budget and 4 weeks for inclusion in the world budget, resulting in lead times of 25 weeks at longest to 15 weeks at best.

Define the Expected Position at the End of the Current Financial Year

This is necessary for two reasons: (a) if you are using the previous year's financial results as a forecasting base, your starting point can be up to six months out of date; and (b) key data relating to stocks, debtors and creditors will be required.

Define an Acceptable Profit Target

You need a benchmark to compare the proposed budget against. If the proposed budget promises an inadequate ROI it may be necessary to seek amendments. If managers are already committed to unacceptable targets it may be divisive to seek to increase such targets. I believe it is fairer to set out broad parameters initially, debate the parameters with senior staff and, hopefully, have them accepted, and request the development of budgets against the background of the agreed parameters. Setting challenging but reasonable profit targets is difficult. You will need the following information:

1 Three-year historical financial statements and market share and growth statistics.
2 Estimated actual financial statements.
3 Projected movements in size of market, share of market, assets and funding.
4 Products being launched and discontinued.

The following is an illustration of profit target setting:

	Estimated Total Assets At This Year-End	Additional Assets To be Acquired	Deprecia-tion	Estimated Total Assets at End of Budget Year	
Property					
At valuation	990			990	
Depreciation	40	950	-40^2	80	910
Plant					
At cost	270	80^1		350	
Depreciation	90	180	-58^2	148	202
Vehicles					
At cost	90	24^1		114	
Depreciation	60	30	-38^2	98	16
Furniture	50			50	
Depreciation	10	40	-5^2	15	35
		1,200	104	−141	1,163
Stocks		300	113^3		413
Debtors		500	170^3		670
		2,000	387	−141	2,246

Supporting assumptions for this target are as follows:

1 Capital investment programme:
    Plant   £80,000
    Vehicles   £24,000
2 Depreciation rates and amounts:
    Property   4%   40 (990×4%)
    Plant   16 2/3% 58 (350×16 2/3%)
    Vehicles   33 1/3% 38 (114×33 1/3%)
    Furniture   10%   5 (50×10%)
3 (a) Sales of new product £20,000, support assets: stock 12% of sales and debtors 20% of sales.
    (b) Volume of existing products will grow by 20%.
    (c) Cost of materials and production will increase by 8%, affecting stock values. Stocks will also respond to the increased sales volume.

(d)   Selling prices will rise by 5% and will affect debtors. They will also rise in reponse to volume.

Table of Change in Stock and Debtors

	Stock	*Debtors*
In projected balance sheet	*300*	*500*
Volume growth (20% of projection)	60	100
Price growth		
8% of projection+volume increase 360×8%	29	
5% of projection+volume increase		30
New product		
12% sales	24	
20% sales		40
	113	170

The company will have £2,246,000 of total assets. Since it certainly needs a profit before interest of 12.5%, the minimum acceptable profit target would be £281,000 before interest.

While 12.5% is the minimum acceptable ROI target it would be modified in the following cases.

1   The return on investment has averaged 5% in recent years and is expected to be 6% this year. It is probably unrealistic to expect a jump to the minimum economic return in one year. The company might settle for 8% leading to a target of £180,000, but with the expectation that this would move to 10% and 12.5% in the next 2 years.

2   The return on investment has averaged 16% in recent years and is projected to be 17.5% this year. Market conditions are encouraging. We should seek an ROI of at least 18% (even with the new product launch which will be lucky to break even next year). The minimum acceptable profit target is £404,000.

It is important to communicate the volume change and profit expectations to senior management. Try to get their agreement that the target is sensible. If cogent arguments are advanced as to why it is too high, it may be necessary to reduce it, otherwise you will wind up with over-optimistic budgets and a lack of managerial commitment to making them happen. It is hoped this will not happen and the profit target will be acceptable as a framework for the detailed budgets.

Also, let the departments work through the detail of their budgets in sequence and in line with the deadlines.

In preparing the detailed budgets it is important for managers to consider what factors will help and hinder future development. If this is not done, there is a danger that bland assumptions such as 'Since the market has grown by 10% per annum on average over the last 5 years, it will continue to do so and we will maintain our market share.'

The right way to budget is to examine all the factors which will influence the market growth and our share:

A   Projected market total units this year 100,000;
B   Our share was 40% and has grown fairly steadily from 30% 5 years ago; and
C   The market growth averaged 10% over recent years, but is expected to be 8% in the current year.

A quick look at these data suggests: total market next year 108,000, our share 42% and our unit sales 45,360. A more professional analysis might produce the following:

Plus Points	Minus Points
1 An old competitor is getting out of the indstry. He held a 10% share. We should sell an extra 4,536 units. Adjustment 2.	1 An alternative to this product is being introduced. Even though not good it may initially take 5% of the market as customers try it. Adjustment 3.
2 A top class salesman we recruited last year is now well used to his customer portfolio. This should lead to a 2% extra market penetration. Adjustment 4.	2 Our promotional approach will be similar to the current year. A competitor is expected to launch a TV advertising campaign. This may boost his market share by 2% of which we may lose our proportion. Adjustment 5.
3 If recent weakness in sterling continues foreign competitors will have to increase selling prices in Britain by 8%, thus reducing their competitiveness and giving us hope of an extra 5,000 units. Adjustment 6.	3 A new 6-month credit scheme for large customers launched by a competitor is attracting business from other suppliers. It is expected to cost us 4,000 units. Adjustment 7.
4 An improved delivery system which will mean same day supplies rather than next day. This should give us an extra 2% market share. Adjustment 8.	4 Our product is a semi-luxury. The projected market growth may not be achieved due to the impact of mortgage interest rate increases on discretionary spending. This will cost us 840 units. Adjustment 1.

On the basis of this detailed analysis of relative marketing advantages and disadvantages, the projected sales for next year will be as follows:

	Total Market Units	Our Sales Units	Our Market Share %
Projected for this year	100,000	40,000	40.0
Natural growth	10,000	4,000	–
	110,000	44,000	40.0
Impact of our natural trend towards improved market share	–	2,200	2.0
	110,000	46,200	42.0
Impact of declining discretionary incomes[1]	2,000	840	–
	108,000	45,360	42.0
Competitor getting out[2] (108,000×10%×42%)	–	4,536	4.2
	108,000	49,896	46.2
Alternative product taking 5% as curiosity[3] (108,000×5%×46.2%)	–	2,495	2.3
	108,000	47,401	43.9
Extra market penetration as our new sales rep's impact increases[4]	–	2,160	2.0
	108,000	49,561	45.9
New competitor TV advertising[5] (108,000×2%×45.9%)	–	991	0.9
	108,000	48,570	45.0
Currency weakness impact[6]	–	5,000	4.6
	108,000	53,570	49.6
Long-term credit scheme[7]	–	4,000	3.7
	108,000	49,570	45.9
Improved delivery scheme[8]		2,160	2.0
	108,000	51,730	47.9

Based on these data, the marketing people might forecast sales of 51,500 units. They might offer 46,500 units, to allow room for manoeuvre if the organisation is one that always comes back looking for higher sales and reduced costs in the budgeting 'game'.

The vital point about this detailed work is that a difficult to quantify but sensible analysis leads to a budget 6,100 units or 13% higher than a simple extrapolation might imply. In this case it brings good news of the sales potential. How much more important would it be if the minus points were stronger resulting in a target significantly below the straight extrapolation of 45,360 units?

The example shows how using expert knowledge of the marketplace helps to set sensible targets. Before preparing a budget, it is essential to make sure that all factors that may affect the trend have been identified and quantified. Sit down with a blank sheet of paper before getting into detail and ask two questions: (a) what changing factors will affect our sales capability?; and (b) how much will they increase or decrease our selling prospects?

The Purchasing and Production Budget

Some aspects of purchasing and production budgeting are now illustrated:

A Sales target: 100,000 units.
B Opening stock: 5,000 units.
C Closing stock: 8,000 units.
D Products stolen during throughput 2% of annual quantities on production line.
E Products damaged during production but recycled (3% of throughput net of pilferage).
F Products damaged in production and discarded as non recyclable (2.5% of throughput net of pilferage).

The percentages in D, E and F are historic experience. Production management feel they will continue.

The Purchases Budget

	Units	Units
Sales target	100,000	
Add stock increase (8,000–5,000)	3,000	103,000
Gross up to include scrap		
Scrap 105,641×2.5%		
(103,000/97.5%)	105,641	
Scrap 105,641×2.5%		2,641
Gross up to include recycle		
(103,000/97%)	106,186	
Recycle 106,186×3%		3,186
Circulating in production		108,827
Gross up to include pilferage		
(108,827/98%)	111,048	
Pilferage 111,048×2%		2,221
Net issues to production		111,048
Returned to stores		3,186
Issues from stores		107,862

Purchases Cost Budget

1 The current price of materials is £100 per unit;
2 40,000 units will be bought at this price and issued to production before a price increase; and
3 The balance will be bought and issued to production at £105 per unit.

The charge out for issues from stores will be:

	£
40,000 units at £100	4,000,000
67,862 units at £105	7,125,510
	11,125,510

With material stocks valued at £100 and £105, the material cost of sales is:

	£
Opening stock 5,000×£100	500,000
Material issues	11,125,510
	11,625,510
Closing stock 8,000×£105	840,000
Material cost of sales	10,785,510

Direct Labour Budget

We will use the data in the materials budget. We will also assume that the items rejected at quality control have been fully processed, and:

A   A worker takes 20 hours to produce a unit accepted or rejected.

B   Allowing for absenteeism expected to be 5% of normal working hours, each worker will produce for 1,748 hours in the budget year.

C   1,000 is the maximum number of production workers and any extra production will be at overtime (1.5 times basic).

D   Basic rates will average £10,400 per annum.

E   Social security costs employer 9% of basic.

F   Fringe costs (pensions, food subsidies, protective clothing) 15% of basic.

Budget Direct Labour Cost

	£
Items circulating multiplied by hours per item (108,827×20)	2,176,540
Labour hours at basic (1,000×1,748)	1,748,000
Labour hours at 1.5 times	428,540
Production hours at basic	1,748,000
Gross up for public holidays and annual leave (24 days×1,000 staff)	240,000
Normal hours paid	1,988,000
Labour hours at overtime	
428,540 at 1.5 times. Equivalent to 642,810 at normal rate	642,810
Total equivalent hours at normal rate	2,630,810

Hourly rate	£
£10,400 pa/52 weeks/5 days/8 hours =	5.00
Add employment taxes £5×9%	0.45
Fringe costs £5×15%	0.75
Cost per hour	6.20

Budgeted direct labour 2,630,810×£6.20 =	£16,311,022

A standard approach is used to budget for overheads whether they be related to establishment, administration, marketing, production or elsewhere. You start by asking the following questions:

1   What will be the estimated actual cost this year (to bring the fore-casting base up to date)?
2   Will this function be done in the same way next year? This year's cost would be a useless forecasting base if a different quality level was planned:
    ● shift from contracted to own transport
    ● shift from bought-in power to own generator
    ● shift from computer bureau accounting to in-house work etc.
3   Will this function be performed on a similar, greater or lesser scale next year? Some costs rise and fall as volume changes. This can affect the budget size (examined in detail in Chapter 11).
4   When (if at all) will prices change for each unit of service and by how much?
5   Could a similar level of service be obtained at a lower cost?

The three examples that follow show how the answers to these questions help to compute an appropriate budget:

Example 1: Power for Running Production Machines

	£
Estimated actual this year	860,000
Add estimated consumption for two additional machines to meet volume growth (at present tariff rate)	120,000
	980,000
Add 2% inefficiency for existing machines (due to ageing): 860,000×2%	17,200
	997,200
Add impact of price increase 5% expected at month 4	
(a) raising cost to 7% over present year average levels (860,000+17,200)×7%	61,404
(b) additional cost on new machines' power consumption 120,000×7% for 9 months	6,300
Budgeted power cost	1,064,904

There is believed to be no genuine alternative. Question 5 is ignored in this case.

Example 2: Fire Insurance

	£
Estimated actual current year	240,000
Uplift value to be covered by 10% to reflect index of value of industrial buildings	24,000
	264,000
Value of additional building to be covered at premium rate	12,000
Orignal revised budget	276,000
Reduction in premiums arising from installation of fire detection and prevention systems 10% (the finance manager estimates that the capital cost of this system £84,000 is worthwhile).	
Revised budget 276,000×90%	£248,400

Note: Be sure to include maintenance, depreciation, etc. in the fire prevention/ detection budget and the capital cost of £84,000 in the capital and cash budgets.

Example 3: Telephone

	£
Estimated actual current year	525,000
Add 6% (impact of extra staff)	31,500
	556,500
Deduct 10% (new random call monitoring system recently installed)	55,650
	500,850
Add 8% expected average price increase	40,068
	540,918
Reduced to allow for savings from (a) transfer of some long distance calls that must in future use telex, and (b) better night rate utilisation for long distance calls	
Final budget	500,000

Normal Explanations for Shortfall

When the data from Stage 5 have been assembled, they will be put in the detailed operating budget. It is probable that the budgeted operating profit is lower than the target set initially. There are three reasons why this is likely to be so:

1 Experienced managers quickly come to terms with the fact that whatever they offer the organisation will demand more. Managers offer less than they want:
   (a) The sales manager expects to sell 100,000 units. She offers a budget of 91,000. She believes she will be pressed to increase it by 10%, and that if she offered 100,000 a 10% increase would still be demanded. This despite the fact that 100,000 is a challenging target.
   (b) A cost centre manager needs a budget of £200,000. He may ask for £222,222 expecting to be pressured to reduce it by 10%. If he is asked for £200,000, he might only get £180,000.
2 Some managers rebel against the never ending chase for growth. They offer budgets which, even after the padding is removed, leave undemanding targets. The sales manager might offer 85,000 units, expecting a 10% uplift. If she gets away with this, she can make life easier for her staff. She will avoid the overt criticism that unfavourable variances in management accounting reports represent.
3 In developing budgets, many managers slip in new initiatives that they wish to implement. Many of these provide inadequate short-term pay-offs even where the long-term return is attractive. These initiatives come from many sources. Usually some have to be deferred or eliminated. It is dangerous to remove too many. Some new initiatives are necessary to secure the long-term development of the organisation. They are frequently ignored in the chase for profit and leave a business in danger of becoming old fashioned.

We now look at a summarised budget and examine approaches to bridging the gap between it and the profit target of £2 million which the managing director and board are seeking.

Draft Budget

		£
Sales revenue		10,000,000
Materials	5,160,000	
Production labour	1,890,000	
Production overhead	450,000	7,500,000
Administration		518,000
Selling and distribution		344,000
Research and development		238,000
Total cost		8,600,000
Profit		1,400,000

£600,000 additional profit must be found. One popular, but highly dangerous, method of finding it is across the board surgery. This assumes a comparable padding everywhere. A simplistic approach would be to seek a 3.25% increase in sales revenue and a 3.25% reduction in all costs. This would ignore three facts:

1   Some costs will rise if the sales are increased;
2   Some managers budgeted honestly and are being punished for doing so; and
3   Some managers padded their budgets in the expectation of more severe changes and are being rewarded for doing so.

A better approach is to go through all the budgets systematically and try to find the padding. Then to negotiate its removal while leaving the genuine plans untouched. The negotiations must be carefully done and accepted by the budgeters or they will disclaim responsibility for any failure to attain targets in the control phase.

Zero-based Budgeting

In zero-based budgeting a company allows each cost area to plead for positions of importance in the spending power of the organisation. If they come into the rank above the spending limit, the budget will be sanctioned. If they do not, the proposal will be shelved until the next ZBB analysis.

In the following example costs may be incurred at two levels: (a) the minimum viable level; and (b) the quality image level. The company has a spending limit of £1,000,000 for the current year. It is distributing books. The budget bids are:

	Minimum Viable Level	Quality Image Level
Purchase 200,000 paperbacks	500,000	500,000
Post to customers 1st class		200,000
2nd class	150,000	
Take telephone orders		
4 hours a day	8,000	
8 hours a day		15,000
Delivery in boxes		240,000
Delivery in jiffy bags	20,000	
Computerised accounting		95,000
Manual accounting	35,000	
Display in showrooms only	100,000	
and use brochures		150,000
No customer collection service	–	
Full customer collection service		30,000
Premises regularly painted		25,000
Premises tatty	–	
	813,000	1,255,000

The company will make an adequate profit if £1,000,000 is spent. It can offer more than the minimum viable level service in some areas but not all. The judgement of priorities might be as follows:

Cost Head	Rank	Rationale	Item Cost	Total Approved
Paperbacks	1	We cannot function without stocks	500,000	500,000
4 hour order taking	2	We cannot sell without orders	8,000	508,000
2nd class mail	3	Critical to customer supplies	150,000	658,000
Packing in envelopes	4	Critical to customer supplies	20,000	678,000
Showroom display	5	Key to stimulating demand	100,000	778,000
Manual accounting	6	Necessary to ensure adequate control	35,000	813,000
Extra order taking	7	Likely to promote extra business	7,000	820,000
Improved packing	8	Will minimise transit damage and improve reputation with customers	220,000	1,040,000
Promotional brochures	9	Should attract substantial extra profitable business	50,000	1,090,000
Regular painting	10	A tatty premises takes from the business image	25,000	1,115,000
Customer collection service	11	Should improve demand while saving on expensive post and packing	30,000	1,145,000
1st class mail	12	Might speed up deliveries	50,000	1,195,000
Computerised accounting	13	More confidence in record keeping	60,000	1,255,000

The owner might decide to allocate £180,000 to improved packaging and not accept any spending on items 9–13.

By examining the alternatives in decision packages 8 to 13, it might be possible to improve on this. The owner might decide to reduce the quality of improved packing so as to allow some allocation for items 9 and/or 10. To assess this the owner might assess these options:

	£	
(a) Packing cost	130,000	
Promotional brochures	50,000	
Total	180,000	or
Packing costing	180,000	
if the brochure option was favoured then:		
(b) Packing cost	105,000	
Regular painting	25,000	
Total	130,000	or
Packing costing	130,000	

The revised ZBB ranking might now be:

Cost Head	Rank	Rationale	Item Cost	Cumulative Cost
Items 1–7	1	Core service		820,000
Improved packaging (lowest standard)	8	Improve customer service and reduce transit damage	105,000	925,000
Promotional brochures	9	As previously	50,000	975,000
Improved packaging (medium standard)	10	On examination this is deemed more attractive than painting this year	25,000	1,000,000

Cost Reduction

Most organisations have some cost waste. The reasons are usually historical and include:

1 Decisions to spend (often with only marginal benefit), by senior managers to boost their profile of power and influence.
2 Decisions to spend which made very good financial sense at the time. The justification has disappeared in a changing environment. Unfortunately, most businesses have some 'that's the way we always did it' costs.

3   Decisions to provide a standard of service without testing whether customers would be satisfied with a lower-quality, less expensive support.
4   Absence of a climate that deplores waste. This develops over time in organisations that are so profitable that they do not need good cost control, or so unprofitable that the difference to the results from control of spending are insignificant. (This often results in managers trying to crack big and insoluble problems while totally ignoring small and eminently reducible cost waste.)

How can an organisation go about identifying cost reduction opportunities? If cost reduction is sufficiently important it is necessary to identify a manager with the following qualities:

1   Imagination (to conceive of alternative ways of achieving results through lower spending).
2   Analytical skills (to identify the most attractive areas to examine and to quantify accurately the consequences of change).
3   Colleague acceptability (to be able to discuss possibilities with people at all levels in the organisation). The major elements of this are to be: (a) a good listener; (b) not biased in favour of or against specific departments; and (c) perceived to be fair and influential.
4   Power (to ensure that realistic cost reductions are implemented even when strongly opposed by managers of departments who are afraid of adverse effects on their section).

If this sounds like a corporate Clark Kent (Superman), it is. Worse still, getting this person to take the job is difficult: (a) someone else may take over their existing job often for a long period (and might do it better); and (b) it is a sure way to make enemies. You have to break eggs to make the cost reduction omelet. If you have managed to get someone to take the job, they will need a sound methodology. I suggest the following approach.

Step one is to ask each employee to tell you what, in their opinion, is the single biggest cost waste in the company. In doing so, guarantee that the suggestion will not be attributed to the individual. Many ideas will relate to the spending of their immediate bosses or other departments. If this confidentiality is not respected, there is a danger of boss/subordinate or inter-departmental warfare. In examining the data from this fact finding mission, you will tend to find that a range of different views emerge. A large proportion of suggestions will cross departmental boundaries. Do not be worried if some of the ideas are nit-picking or blown out of all proportions. Look for consistency.

Step two is to obtain a detailed breakdown of the cost structure from the annual budget. Armed with this cost structure, the ideas generated at step one, and your own perceptions of cost waste, proceed to slot each cost heading into the cost reduction matrix which I adapted from the Boston Consulting Group Product Portfolio Matrix.

Cost Reduction Matrix

	Perceived Cost Reduction Potential		
Cost Significance	High	Medium	Low
High			
Medium			
Low			

The classification of perceived cost reduction potential into high, medium and low is done as follows: High = saving possible exceeding 10% of budget cost; Medium = saving possible in range 5% to 10% of budget cost; and Low = saving possible less than 5% of budget cost. The size of the possible saving is a subjective opinion formed from the employee ideas and your own judgements.

Overall Cost Significance Table

	£	% of Total Budgeted Cost
Raw material		
Cost of efficient production	714,000	35.70
Pilferage	42,000	2.10
Wastage not recovered	24,000	1.20
	780,000	39.00
Production labour		
Basic pay	320,000	16.00
Overtime on production	90,000	4.50
Rework	30,000	1.50
Employment taxes	44,000	2.20
Pensions	48,000	2.40
Other	28,000	1.40
	560,000	28.00
Production expenses		
Supervision and Q.C.	55,000	2.75
Power	60,000	3.00
Depreciation	16,000	0.80
Rent and rates	18,000	0.90
Maintenance	13,000	0.65
Other	8,000	0.40
	170,000	8.50
Selling and distribution		
Salaries and wages	70,000	3.50
Rent and rates	10,000	0.50
Commission	25,000	1.25
Travel and accommodation	30,000	1.50
Other	5,000	0.25
	140,000	7.00

Overall Cost Significance Table (continued)

	£	% of Total Budgeted Cost
Administration		
Salaries and wages	85,000	4.25
Telephone	20,000	1.00
Rent and rates	18,000	0.90
Light and heat	11,000	0.55
Stationery	9,000	0.45
Audit fee	15,000	0.75
Depreciation	12,000	0.60
Other	10,000	0.50
	180,000	9.00
Research and development		
Salaries and wages	56,000	2.80
Material	24,000	1.20
Other	20,000	1.00
	100,000	5.00
Interest costs		
Long-term loans	40,000	2.00
Short-term loans	5,000	0.25
Leases, etc.	25,000	1.25
	70,000	3.50
Total cost	2,000,000	100.00

Examining the percentages, we find that only two items (cost of efficient production and production labour basic pay) exceed 5% of the total cost structure. This blurs the true position. As a first step to unmasking the real situation we recalculate the cost headings as a percentage of the total cost excluding dominant items: (a) material; (b) cost of efficient production; (c) production basic pay; and (d) departmental salaries and wages.

Cost Significance (Excluding Dominant Items)

	£	% of Remaining Total Cost Budget	
Pilferage	42,000	6.00	M
Wastage	24,000	3.43	
Overtime production	90,000	12.86	H
Overtime rework	30,000	4.29	
Employment taxes	44,000	6.29	M
Pensions	48,000	6.86	M
Other direct labour	28,000	4.00	
Power	60,000	8.57	M
Depreciation	16,000	2.28	
Rent and rates	18,000	2.57	
Maintenance	13,000	1.86	
Other production	8,000	1.14	
Rent and rates (S&D)	10,000	1.43	
Commission	25,000	3.57	
Travel and accommodation	30,000	4.28	
Other (S&D)	5,000	0.71	
Telephone	20,000	2.86	
Rent and rates	18,000	2.57	
Light and heat	11,000	1.57	
Stationery	9,000	1.29	
Audit fees	15,000	2.14	
Depreciation	12,000	1.71	
Other (admin.)	10,000	1.43	
Materials (R&D)	24,000	3.43	
Other (R&D)	20,000	2.86	
Long interest	40,000	5.71	M
Short interest	5,000	0.71	
Leases	25,000	3.58	
	700,000	100.0	

From this analysis, it emerges that overtime production at 12.86% has a high cost significance while pilferage, power, employment taxes, long interest and pensions have medium cost significance. The analysis can be done at a departmental level where appropriate. Combining this objective analysis with informed views about potential savings, we might get:

Potential

	High	Medium	Low
H I G H	Overtime Telephone	Efficient materials Power	Basic pay Supervision & QC Salaries etc. sales Salaries etc. admin. Salaries etc. R&D Interest long loans
M E D	Pilferage Light & heat Unrecovered waste Rework	Travel and accommodation R&D materials Interest/leases	Employment taxes Pensions Commission Rent & rates admin.
L O W	Audit Stationery	Maintenance Other (admin.) Interest short loans	Other production Production Depreciation Production rent & rates Production other Sales rent & rates Sales other Depreciation Other R&D

Cost Reduction Search Strategy

	High	Medium	Low
H I G H	Major search for implementable ideas	Major search for implementable ideas	Hard-nosed, what can we get away with?
M E D	Major search for implementable ideas	Hard-nosed, what can we get away with?	Implement obvious ideas immediately
L O W	Hard-nosed, what can we get away with?	Implement obvious ideas immediately	Implement obvious ideas immediately

To make cost reductions happen, you must:

1 Prove that they will be in the best interest of the organisation. This will be difficult. Many of the people controlling budgets will raise spurious arguments to defend the status quo because they fear change. Concerns that arise in proving it is worthwhile are:
   - You may have to buy fixed assets to save costs.
   - Sometimes employees are so opposed to an idea that even if demonstrably good it may lower morale seriously or in some extreme cases lead to sabotage of the inititative.
   - If it affects third parties, we may be afraid of an unfavourable reaction.
2 Ensure that managers controlling cost areas believe the reductions can be achieved and are committed to making them happen.
3 Provide regular feedback of planned against actual savings in the control reports.
4 Identify some quick wins. Make them happen. Publicise the success. Show the sceptics it works and that they should find savings too.

Many cost reduction ideas involve fixed asset expenditure. These initiatives should be evaluated, using the procedures described in Chapter 12. Examples of this type include mechanised stock control, random telephone monitoring and burglary/fire protection systems.

The final elements of the budgeting process; (a) dividing the budget into accounting periods for use in the control process; (b) converting the budget into cash flows; and (c) the capital budgeting process, are dealt with in other chapters.

Chapter 9

Financial Control

A company that is in control of its finances will consistently know:

1 The reasons for any recent departures from the budget, and the current action being taken to capitalise on favourable and overcome unfavourable developments.
2 The level of sales, costs and profits that are likely to emerge in the financial year, given the actuals achieved to date and the projections for the rest of the year (based on the knowledge of changes experienced and likely to arise, and unbudgeted actions taken or planned in the light of these developments).
3 All significant payments that it will have to make in the next six months and be confident that its cash resources will cover them.

The full management team must be involved in the job of control. If they are, the stakeholders (employees, customers, suppliers, government, etc.) can expect that sensibly formulated plans will be achieved.

We will examine the three key elements of financial control in detail.

Departures from Budget

Knowing They Exist

Quantify the variances. this is quite straightforward and involves computing the actual results and comparing them against the budget. One line from the report might be:

	Budget	Actual	£ Variance	% Variance
Raw materials	650,000	676,000	(26,000)	(4)

The company has overspent £26,000 or 4% on its budget. The £ variance is important to quantify – £26,000 may be regarded as significant in this business. The percentage variance is also worth disclosing. There may be significant potential for corrective action in areas where the overall planned and actual spending is relatively low but the divergence in percentage terms is significant:

	Budget	Actual	£ Variance	% Variance
Power	50,000	62,000	(12,000)	(24)

Comparing these two cost lines we see that if the company regards all variances below £20,000 as insignificant, it might lose sight of the 24% overrun on power costs which may imply poor budgeting and promise significant recovery potential.

The Causes of Variances

The second step in the control process involves trying to establish the reason(s) why the company has incurred a variance. The use of standard costs can be helpful in establishing causes. A standard cost can be defined as the cost of: (1) a defined volume of activity; (2) at a defined level of efficiency; and (3) at a defined cost per unit. This definition helps to identify three kinds of variance: volume, efficiency and price.

We will look behind the budgeted and actual figures for raw materials above and quantify the variances that arise:

		Budget	Actual
Volume produced	A	173,333.33	130,000
Quantity introduced per unit volume	B	3.75	4
Quantity content of volume	A×B	650,000	520,000
Price per unit	C	£1.00	£1.30
Cost content of volume	A×B×C	650,000	676,000

From these background details we can put together an extract from the detailed operating statement as follows:

	£
Standard cost of actual output	
(130,000×3.75 items per unit×£1 per item)	487,500
Add inefficient use of materials	
(130,000 units×0.25 per unit)	32,500
	520,000
Add excess of actual cost over budgeted cost of material issues	
(520,000 unit content by 30p actual cost)	156,000
	676,000

Based on this analysis we see that a direct comparison between budget and actual conceals the fact that significant variances arose. A volume variance was first identified which represents the difference between planned and actual production at standard cost, i.e.:

$$43,333\tfrac{1}{3}\times3.75\times£1 = £162,500$$

This results in the original budget of £650,000 being adjusted to the standard cost of the volume produced:

	£
Original budget	650,000
Less volume variance	162,500
	487,500

Having identified this volume variance we try to ascertain the cause. Was it a deliberate slow down in production to avoid stockpiling in the face of sluggish customer demand? Was it a forced reduction in production because inadequate materials were available, skilled labour hours fell due to absenteeism, or production machine hours fell due to unexpected breakdowns? The answers to these questions will need to be obtained. The variance could be caused by: the

245

marketing/sales department (sluggish sales); the purchasing department (inadequate supplies); the production or personnel department
(inadequate labour hours); or the maintenance department (un-
scheduled maintenance).

Unfortunately one or more of these departments will have to take
the blame. If the volume variance had not been extracted first, then
the poor performance might have been overlooked, as the actual cost
is less than the original budget.

Reponsibility for Variances

On investigation the primary responsibility for the variances may be
identified as:

1   Efficiency is down because each unit of volume required a quantity
    content of 4 as compared to a standard of 3.75.
2   Was this because of poor training of the workforce resulting in
    wasteful quantity inputs? This would be a staff training problem.
    The question would arise whether it is the responsibility of the
    production or personnel department to ensure that production line
    workers have the experience, skill and enthusiasm to work at the
    standard input levels of 3.75 per unit?
3   Or was it the result of poor supervision that allowed sloppy work
    by production staff whose training justifies an expectation of
    standard performance? This would clearly be a production control
    problem.
4   Purchasing will be blamed for the 30% increase in prices relative to
    standard, and will be put under pressure to find ways of
    overcoming the cost overrun already experienced, and to avoid
    similar cost overruns in future.
5   Marketing will be blamed for the 25% production shortfall, if there
    was a management decision to slow down production because of
    sluggish sales.

Revising Expectations for Future Performance

The identification of ongoing consequences of the variances must now
be examined. This is done as follows:

Variance Type	Consequences
1. The standard was set incorrectly. Experience to date this year is a more realistic assessment of the ongoing efficiency.	1. The variance will be defined as uncorrectable. It implies that if no compensating action can be taken: (a) the costs for the rest of the year will exceed plan; (b) the profit for the year will fall short of plan; and (c) we will need more cash to pay for the extra costs.
2. The standard was set correctly but due to inadequate control was not matched by actual performance.	2. The variance will be defined as correctable. It implies that unless compensating action can be located: (a) the cost overrun in this period will affect the expected profit for the year; and (b) We will need more cash to cover the once-off cost overrun.
3. The standard was set correctly. The report is incorrect (i.e. the wrong volume of production or quantity issues recorded).	3. If this is so it may be good news for the company. Some or all of the variance relates to poor transaction recording.
4. The standard was set correctly but a problem arose in spreading it over accounting periods. E.g. a company might (but should not) anticipate a working year of 12 accounting periods each of 20 days duration. In practice it will experience some months where the working days are high (May?) and some where low (December?).	4. The variance in this case is defined as timing. Of itself this is good news because if for example there were only 15 working days in this period then the volume variance will be picked up in later periods when the working days exceed 20.

Whichever is the explanation for the variance, it will be necessary to carry out a detailed examination of the ongoing consequences. They could have a substantial impact on the expected profitability for the year, and the amount of cash required at various times in the year.

The compilation of the estimated actuals should be done some time after the identification of variances. Departmental managers will need time to think about the causes, the suitable corrective actions, and the sometimes insoluble difficulties that uncorrectable variances can cause.

We will now return to the business that Larry Leeds set up in Chapter 5 to illustrate an effective financial control process. We will look at the position after three months of operations. I believe that no business can afford to let three months elapse between budget versus actual comparisons. In practice Larry should have a control report prepared four-weekly or monthly. For purposes of the illustration, given the smallness of his company, we will use quarterly results.

Operating Statement, 3 Months to 31 March 1992

	Budget	Actual	Variance (£)	Variance(%)
Sales volume	1,500	1,600	100(F)	6.7(F)
Sales revenue	30,000	31,000	1,000(F)	3.3(F)
Purchases	38,783	39,167	384(U)	1.0(U)
Less stock	9,600	9,600	–	–
Material consumed	29,183	29,567	384(U)	1.3(U)
Opening fin. stk.	–	–		
Closing fin. stk.	(33,000)	(32,000)	1,000(U)	3.0(U)
Payroll	37,950	39,950	2,000(U)	5.3(U)
Pensions	5,693	5,993	300(U)	5.3(U)
Power	450	400	50(F)	11.1(F)
Light	210	225	15(U)	7.1(U)
Telephone	150	150	–	–
Insurance	2,700	2,700	–	–
Rent and rates	4,750	4,750	–	–
Leases	900	900	–	–
Post and packing	156	180	24(U)	15.4(U)
Advertising	525	750	225(U)	42.9(U)
Other	225	256	31(U)	13.8(U)
Bad debts	332	–	332(F)	100.0(F)
Depreciation	1,951	1,951	–	–
Interest	2,239	2,232	6(F)	0.3(U)
	54,414	58,004	3,590(U)	6.6(U)
Loss	24,414	27,004	2,590(U)	10.6(U)

When Larry first saw these figures he was shocked. He had not realised that the sales in the first quarter were totally inadequate to cover the running costs. He knew the sales were better than budget. He exected a reasonable profit. When he got over the initial panic, he started to examine where things had gone right and wrong and to try and forecast what would happen for the rest of the year.

Balance Sheet as at 31 March 1992

	Budget	*Actual*	*Variance*
Fixed assets			
Cost	44,000	44,000	–
Depreciation	2,305	2,305	–
Book value	41,695	41,695	–
Current assets			
Materials	9,600	9,600	–
Fin. goods	33,000	32,000	1,000(F)
VAT	122	52	70(F)
Insurance	8,100	8,100	–
Grant	7,080	7,080	–
Trade debtors	17,957	15,747	2,210(F)
	75,859	72,579	3,280(F)
Amounts due			
Trade creditors	11,393	11,505	112(F)
Accruals[a]	9,113	9,413	300(F)
Overdraft	34,736	33,634	1,102(U)
	(55,242)	(54,552)	690(U)
Net assets	62,312	59,722	2,590(F)
Financed by:			
Share capital	40,000	40,000	–
Less loss	24,414	27,004	2,590(U)
	15,586	12,996	
Term loan	40,000	40,000	–
Capital grant	6,726	6,726	–
	62,312	59,722	2,590(U)

[a] *Accruals*	*Budget*	*Actual*
Light	70	70
Rates	1,750	1,750
Loan interest	1,600	1,600
Pensions	5,693	5,993
	9,113	9,413

The following are his major conclusions:

1 Larry decided to reduce his selling price to £19 on the UK market. He believes that home sales will exceed his original monthly forecasts by 10% through the remainder of the year. Export sales will be as forecast.

2 Orders for materials have been placed at a rate of 1,632 items per month. This will continue, until such time as Larry finds he is short of stock to feed his revised sales targets.

3 The stock losses have run at 2% of purchases. Larry fears that they will continue at this level.

4 Rework has cost the company £2,000 in the first quarter. With good quality control in place he expects it to cost £1000 in subsequent quarters. Larry did not have an allowance for rework in his original budget.

5 With the exception of interest charges, which will be affected by various changes in cash flows, Larry expects his overheads will closely correspond with budget through the rest of the year.

6 Export customers will continue to settle their accounts on confirmed irrevocable letters of credit – 50% will be received in the month of sale and the balance in the following month. Larry is pleased that this arrangement has left his overdraft position lower than he budgeted at the end of March.

7 On 1 October, 1992 Larry now plans to buy a machine for £12,000 plus 17.5% VAT. This machine will enable him to add 600 units to his output each month with his existing production staff. The machine will have a five-year life and no terminal value.

Based on these forecasts Larry prepared a revised projection of his profits to be earned in 1992.

Revised Forecast Operating Statement

	Year ended 31 December, 1992			
	3 Months Actual	9 Months Estimate	Annual Estimate	Original Budget
Sales volume				
Home	1,000	12,045	13,045	11,850
Export	600	7,300	7,900	7,900
	1,600	19,345	20,945	19,750
Sales revenue	31,000	374,855	405,854[1]	395,000
Opening stock		9,600		
Purchases	39,167	89,105	128,272[3]	119,404
Less stock	(9,600)	(11,440)	(11,440)[3]	(10,400)
Material consumed	29,567	87,265	116,832	109,004
Opening fin. stk.	–	32,000	–	–
Closing fin. stk.	(32,000)	(506)	(506)[3]	–
Payroll	39,950	116,850	156,800[5]	154,550
Pensions	5,993	17,527	23,520[5]	23,183
Power	400	1,350	1,750	1,800
Light	225	630	855	840
Telephone	150	450	600	600
Insurance	2,700	8,100	10,800	10,800
Rent and rates	4,750	14,250	19,000	19,000
Leases	900	2,700	3,600	3,600
Post and packing	180	1,044	1,224	1,200
Advertising	750	975	1,725	1,500
Other	256	675	931	900
Bad debts		2,912	2,912[1]	4,365
Depreciation	1,951	6,453	8,404[6]	7,804
Interest	2,232	4,550	6,782[9]	7,402
	58,004	297,225	355,229	346,548
Profit/(loss)	(27,004)	77,630	50,626	48,452
Corporation tax			12,287[7]	11,781
Retained			38,337	36,671

Note: Support schedules 1–9 follow.

Schedule 1: Sales and Cash Collections Home

	Sales incl. VAT	10%	60%	29%	Total Collected
Actual					
January	2,233	223			223
February	8,930	893	1,340		2,233
March	11,162	1,116	5,358	648	7,122
Revised Budget					
April	14,735	1,474	6,697	2,590	10,761
May	22,102	2,210	8,841	3,237	14,288
June	29,469	2,947	13,261	4,273	20,481
July	36,836	3,684	17,681	6,410	27,775
August	40,520	4,052	22,102	8,546	34,700
September	29,469	2,947	24,312	10,682	37,941
October	29,469	2,947	17,681	11,750	32,378
November	29,469	2,948	17,681	8,546	29,175
December	36,836	3,684	17,682	8,546	29,911
	291,230	29,123	152,636	65,228	246,988[a]
January			22,102	8,546	
February			–	10,682	
			174,438	84,456	

	£
[a] Gross sales (13,045×£19×117.5%)	291,230
Less Bad debt provision 2,912	
Debtors 41,330	44,242
Collected and collectable	246,988

	£
Gross sales	291,230
Less VAT	43,375
	247,855
Exports (Schedule 2)	158,000
Revenue	405,855

Schedule 2: Sales and Cash Collections Export

	Sales	50%[a]	50%[a]	Total Collected
Actual				
January	2,000	1,000	–	1,000
February	4,000	2,000	1,000	3,000
March	6,000	3,000	2,000	5,000
Revised Budget				
April	8,000	4,000	3,000	7,000
May	12,000	6,000	4,000	10,000
June	16,000	8,000	6,000	14,000
July	20,000	10,000	8,000	18,000
August	22,000	11,000	10,000	21,000
September	16,000	8,000	11,000	19,000
October	16,000	8,000	8,000	16,000
November	16,000	8,000	8,000	16,000
December	20,000	10,000	8,000	18,000
	158,000	79,000	69,000	148,000
January			10,000	
			79,000	

[a] 7,900 items will be sold at £20 each. One-half of each month's sales will be paid for within the month of sale. The balance will be collected in the following month. The sales are being made on confirmed irrevocable letters of credit. No bad debts will be incurred. Debtors at 31 December: £10,000.

Schedule 3: Supplier Payments

	Purchase Quantities	Cost Per Unit	Purchases Value	Supplier Payment In Arrears
Jan	3,264[1]	7.05	23,011	
Feb	1,632	7.05	11,506	23,011
Mar	1,632	7.05	11,505	11,506
Apr	1,632	6.11	9,971	11,505
May	1,632	6.11	9,972	9,971
Jun	1,632	6.11	9,971	9,972
Jul	1,632	6.11	9,972	9,971
Aug	1,632	6.11	9,971	9,972
Sep	2,244[2]	6.11	13,711	9,971
Oct	2,244	6.11	13,711	13,711
Nov	2,244	6.11	13,711	13,711
Dec	2,244	6.11	13,711	13,711
	23,664[3]		150,723	137,012

[1] Production January to September 1,600 units per month at 102% = 1,632. Two months stock bought in January.
[2] Production October to January 2,200 units per month at 102% = 2,244.
[3] Bought for Production 9×1,632 = 14,688
Bought for Production 3×2,244 = 6,732
Bought for Stock   1×2,244 = 2,244

                                 23,664

Shrinkage 23,664/1.02 = 23,200

Material stock	March	December	Total
Opening stock		1,600	
Units bought (net)	6,400	16,800	23,200
Units issued	(4,800)	(16,200)	21,000
Closing stock	1,600	2,200	2,200
Unit cost	£6	£5.20	
Stock value	£9,600	£11,440	
Finished stock			
Opening stock		3,200	
Production	4,800	16,200	
Sales	(1,600)	(19,345)	
Closing stock	3,200	55	
Unit cost	£10	£9.20	
Stock value	£32,000	£506	

Schedule 4: VAT Settlements

	Home Gross Sales	VAT Element 14.89%	Gross Purchases	VAT Element 14.89%	Net VAT	Payable
Actual						
Jan	2,233	333	23,011	3,427	(3,094)	
Feb	8,930	1,330	11,506	1,714	(384)	(3,094)
Mar	11,162	1,662	11,505	1,714	(52)	(384)
Revised Budget						
Apr	14,735	2,195	9,971	1,485	710	(52)
May	22,102	3,292	9,972	1,485	1,807	
Jun	29,469	4,389	9,971	1,485	2,904	
Jul	36,836	5,486	9,972	1,485	4,001	5,421
Aug	40,520	6,035	9,971	1,485	4,550	
Sep	29,469	4,389	27,811[1]	4,142	247	
Oct	29,469	4,389	13,711	2,042	2,347	8,798
Nov	29,469	4,389	13,711	2,042	2,347	
Dec	36,836	5,486	13,711	2,042	3,444	–
	291,230	43,375	164,823	24,548	18,827	10,689
VAT due (2,347+2,347+3,444)						8,138
						18,827

[1] Includes £14,100 in respect of additional plant on which 17.5% VAT was charged (net cost £12,000).
Note: The VAT liability is calculated quarterly and paid in the following month. Larry reclaimed excess VAT paid at the end of January, February and March and received it in February, March and April respectively.

Schedule 5: Payroll

	Production	Rework	Other	Total Payroll
Actual				
Jan	6,400	1,000	6,250	13,650
Feb	6,400	500	6,250	13,150
Mar	6,400	500	6,250	13,150
Revised Estimate				
Apr	6,400	333	6,250	12,983
May	6,400	333	6,250	12,983
Jun	6,400	334	6,250	12,984
Jul	6,400	333	6,250	12,983
Aug	6,400	333	6,250	12,983
Sep	6,400	334	6,250	12,984
Oct	6,400	333	6,250	12,983
Nov	6,400	333	6,250	12,983
Dec	6,400	334	6,250	12,984
	76,800	5,000	75,000	156,800

Schedule 6: Depreciation

	£
Original depreciation	7,804
Add new machine 3 months at £2,400 per annum	600
Revised depreciation	8,404

Schedule 7: Corporation Tax

		£
Profit per accounts		50,626
Add depreciation		8,404
		59,030
Less writing down allowances		
original	9,130	
new machine	750	9,880
Taxable profit		49,150
Corporation tax at 25%		12,287

Schedule 8: General Overheads

	Power	Light	Phone	Insur-ance	Rent	Rates	Pensions	Leases	Post & Packing	Adver-tising	Other	Total
Actual												
Jan	150			10,800	3,000				28	375	105	14,758
Feb	130	155							68	150	80	883
Mar	120		150						84	225	71	950
Revised Estimate												
Apr	150	140			3,000			300	96	225	75	3,986
May	150							300	108	150	75	783
Jun	150	140	150			3,500		300	180	150	75	4,645
Jul	150				3,000			300	144	75	75	3,744
Aug	150	140						300	132	75	75	872
Sep	150		150					300	96	75	75	846
Oct	150	140			3,000			300	96	75	75	3,836
Nov	150							300	96	75	75	696
Dec	150	140	150	–	–	3,500	23,520	300	96	75	75	28,006
	1,750	855	600	10,800	12,000	7,000	23,520	3,600	1,224	1,725	931	64,005

Schedule 9: Bank Interest

		£
(A)	January cash (£8,815×10% / 12)	(73)
	February O/D (£19,902×16% / 12)	265
	March O/D (£33,002×16% / 12) (Pre-interest)[1]	440
		632
(B)	April O/D (£37,215×16% / 12)	496
	May O/D (£36,664×16% / 12)	489
	June O/D (£29,784×16% / 12)	397
	July O/D (£16,128×16% / 12)	215
	August cash (£15,745×10% / 12)	(131)
	September cash (£48,885×10% / 12) (Pre-interest)[2]	(407)
		1,059
(C)	Interest receivable	
	October cash (£42,776×10% / 12)	(356)
	November cash (£60,561×10% / 12)	(505)
	December cash (£53,771×10% / 12)	(448)
		(1,309)
	Term loan £40,000×16%	6,400
	Total cost (a+b+c)	6,782
	Accrued interest (6,400−1,309) =	5,091

[1] £33,634−£632 = £33,002.
[2] £47,826+£1,059 = £48,885.
Note: Larry used simple interest of 16% on overdrafts and term loans and 10% on surplus cash in computing his provisions and earnings. He assumed that the balance at the month end, was a fair representation of the position during the month. Overdraft interest is calculated on a daily basis by the banks.

Monthly Cash Forecast

	Jan	Feb	Mar	Apr	May	Jun	Jul	Aug	Sep	Oct	Nov	Dec	Total
Cash in													
Capital	40,000												40,000
Term loan	40,000												40,000
Customers[1]	223	2,233	7,122	10,761	14,288	20,481	27,775	34,700	37,941	32,378	29,175	29,911	246,988
Customers[2]	1,000	3,000	5,000	7,000	10,000	14,000	18,000	21,000	19,000	16,000	16,000	18,000	148,000
Grant				7,080									7,080
	81,223	5,233	12,122	24,841	24,288	34,481	45,775	55,700	56,941	48,378	45,175	47,911	482,068
Cash out													
Suppliers[3]		23,011	11,506	11,505	9,971	9,972	9,971	9,972	9,971	13,711	13,711	13,711	137,012
VAT[4]		(3,094)	(384)	(52)			5,421			8,798			10,689
Payroll[5]	13,650	13,150	13,150	12,983	12,983	12,984	12,983	12,983	12,984	12,983	12,983	12,984	156,800
Overhead[6]	14,758	883	950	3,986	783	4,645	3,744	872	846	3,836	696	28,006	64,005
Plant	23,600									14,100			37,700
Truck and car	20,400												20,400
Bank interest			632						1,059				1,691
	72,408	33,950	25,854	28,422	23,737	27,601	32,119	23,827	24,860	53,428	27,390	54,701	428,297
Monthly surplus/(deficit)	8,815	(28,717)	(13,732)	(3,581)	551	6,880	13,656	31,873	32,081	(5,050)	17,785	(6,790)	53,771
Opening cash	–	8,815	(19,902)	(33,634)	(37,215)	(36,664)	(29,784)	(16,128)	15,745	47,826	42,776	60,561	–
Closing cash	8,815	(19,902)	(33,634)	(37,215)	(36,664)	(29,784)	(16,128)	15,745	47,826	42,776	60,561	53,771	53,771

Forecast Balance Sheet as at 31 December, 1992

	Budget	Revised Estimate	Variance Source	Use
Fixed assets				
Plant	18,880	30,280	600	12,000
Truck	9,600	9,600		
Car	6,300	6,300		
	34,780	46,180		
Current assets				
Stock materials	10,400	11,440		1,040
Stock fin. goods	–	506		506
Trade debtors	61,990	51,331	10,659	
Cash	52,715	53,771		1,056
	125,105	117,048		
Payable in under one year				
Suppliers	12,342	13,711	1,369	
VAT	8,365	8,138		227
Bank interest	5,062	5,091	29	
Corporation tax	11,781	12,287	506	
	(37,550)	(39,227)		
Net assets	122,335	124,001		
Financed by:				
Share capital	40,000	40,000		
Revenue reserve	36,671	38,337	1,666	
	76,671	78,337		
Government grant	5,664	5,664		
Bank term loan	40,000	40,000		
	122,335	122,335	14,829	14,829

Larry was pleased with the revised balance sheet forecast. The picture looked sound. The reduction in export debtors would finance the extra machine and he looked forward to a five-year saving in overtime costs as a result.

Comments on Larry Leeds' Control System

1 The budget against actual comparison was prepared in the first week of April 1992. This allowed Larry to quickly address the major issues facing his business.

2 Informed estimates were used to speed up the reporting process.
3 Larry found the report easy to understand. The first report contained two pages (operating statement at 31 March and balance sheet at 31 March). Larry used this report to revise his estimates for the following nine months. The revised forecast involved a three page report (operating statement for the year to 31 December, 1992, balance sheet at 31 December, 1992 and 9-month forward cash projection). The brevity of the report may not be obvious because of the range of supporting schedules provided.

Flexible Budgeting for Control

If a really good division of costs into fixed and variable components has been developed, it is possible to do a comparison of budget against actual, based on the volume of throughput achieved. This makes the variances more meaningful. The following is an illustration of flexible budgeting. The company expects to achieve an output of somewhere between 90,000 and 110,000 units.

The budgeted cost based on an output of 100,000 units is:

	£
Materials per unit (V)	6.00
Labour per unit (V)	2.50
Overhead per unit (V)	1.50
Overhead per unit (F)	1.98
Total cost	11.98
Unit selling price	15.00
Unit profit	3.02

The actual output was 94,000 units. Comparison between the flexible budget at this level of output and the actual is:

| | Flexible Budget at 94,000 units | | | Actual | |
	Per Unit	Total (£'000)	Per Unit	Total (£'000)	Variance (£'000)
Output		94,000		94,000	
Revenue	15.000	1,410	14.95	1,405.30	−4.70
Materials	6.000	564	5.80	545.20	+18.80
Labour	2.500	235	2.63	247.22	−12.22
Overhead (V)	1.500	141	1.51	141.94	−0.94
Overhead (F)	2.106	198	2.20	206.80	−8.80
Total cost	12.106	1,138	12.14	1,141.16	−3.16
Profit	2.894	272	2.81	264.14	−7.86

This comparison discloses an overall variance of £7,860. It is more revealing than the variance which would have emerged if compared with the target 100,000 units, i.e. £37,860.

The reason for the difference is:

	£
Variance based on budgeted output	37,860
Lost through volume decline	
6,000×£3.02	18,120
	19,740
Fixed costs not recovered	
(6,000×£1.98)	11,880
Actual profit	7,860

Fixed and variable costs will be examined in detail in Chapter 10.

Controlling a Large Product Range

Control tends to be relatively easy when an organisation is providing only one product or service. When a range of items is sold problems can arise:

1   A wide variation can exist in the margins for individual items. The sales revenue can provide a large profit if concentrated into high contribution lines, or a low profit if concentrated into low contribution lines; and
2   A wide variation in the working capital deployed to support individual products exists, resulting in a greater or lesser working capital requirement, depending on the mix of sales.

We will examine a business with three product lines to illustrate the control problems.

Operating Budget, Quarter 1

	Product A		Product B		Product C		Total
Sales volume	100,000		50,000		20,000		
Unit selling price	£1		£2.40		£9		
Sales	100,000		120,000		180,000		400,000
	Per Unit		*Per Unit*		*Per Unit*		
Materials	0.30	30,000	0.70	35,000	2.50	50,000	115,000
Labour	0.25	25,000	0.60	30,000	2.20	44,000	99,000
Variable overhead	0.15	15,000	0.20	10,000	0.30	6,000	31,000
Contribution	0.30	30,000	0.90	45,000	4.00	80,000	155,000
Fixed costs							55,000
Profit							100,000
C/S ratio	30%		37.5%		44.4%		38.8%

For the purposes of this chapter contribution is similar to gross profit and C/S ratio is the contribution as a percentage of sales (i.e. similar to the gross profit margins). A more detailed treatment of contribution is developed in Chapter 11.

Working Capital Budget, Quarter 1

	Stocks/ Material and Labour		Debtors/ Sales %		Working capital/ Sales	
	%	£'000	%	£'000	%	£'000
Product						
A	30	16.5	50	50	66.5	66.5
B	40	26.0	50	60	71.7	86.0
C	50	47.0	50	90	76.1	137.0
Total		89.5		200	72.4	289.5

We will now examine the Quarter 1 results with two different demand patterns and look at the profitability and working capital implications. In each case the sales are £400,000. The profits and working capital required vary significantly:

Case 1: Major Shift Towards Product A

		Product						
		A		B		C		Total
Sales volume		214,000		40,000		10,000		
Unit selling price		£1		£2.40		£9		
Sales		214,000		96,000		90,000		400,000
Materials	0.30	64,200	0.70	28,000	2.50	25,000		117,200
Labour	0.25	53,500	0.60	24,000	2.20	22,000		99,500
Variable O/H	0.15	32,100	0.20	8,000	0.30	3,000		43,100
		149,800		60,000		50,000		259,800
Contribution	0.30	64,200	0.90	36,000	4.00	40,000		140,200
Fixed costs								55,000
Profit								85,200
C/S Ratio %		30		37.5		44.4		35.1

Case 1: Working Capital Actual, Quarter 1

	Stocks/ Material and Labour		Debtors/ Sales %		Working Capital/ Sales	
	%	£'000	%	£'000	%	£'000
Product						
A	30	35.31	50	107	66.5	142.31
B	40	20.80	50	48	71.7	68.80
C	50	23.50	50	45	76.1	68.50
Total		79.61		200	69.9	279.61

In this case even with the unit costs and revenues exactly as planned the profit is down by £14,800 due to the lower weighted average contribution sales ratio.

$$(140,200/400,000)\% = 35.05\%$$

The 3.7% decline causes a profit shortfall of £400,000×3.7% = £14,800.

A lower investment in working capital is required – £279,610 as against £289,500 in the budget. The variation of £9,890 arises because the increased sales of product A require a lower working capital support. The decline is 2.4725% and when multiplied by the sales we get £9,890.

Case 2: Major Shift Towards Product C

		Product						Total
		A		B		C		
Sales volume		34,000		40,000		30,000		
Unit sales price		£1		£2.40		£9		
Sales		34,000		96,000		270,000		400,000
Materials	0.30	10,200	0.70	28,000	2.50	75,000		113,200
Labour	0.25	8,500	0.60	24,000	2.20	66,000		98,500
Variable O/H	0.15	5,100	0.20	8,000	0.30	9,000		22,100
		23,800		60,000		150,000		233,800
Contribution	0.30	10,200		36,000		120,000		166,200
Fixed costs								55,000
Profit								111,200
C/S ratio		30%		37.5%		44.4%		41.6%

Working Capital Actual, Quarter 1

	Stocks/ Material and Labour		Debtors/ Sales %		Working Capital/ Sales	
	%	£'000	%	£'000	%	£'000
Product						
A	30	5.61	50	17	66.5	22.61
B	40	20.80	50	48	71.7	68.80
C	50	70.50	50	135	76.1	205.50
Total		96.61		200	69.9	296.61

In case two, unit costs and selling prices are exactly as planned. The profit is £11,200 better than budget. This is because the weighted average contribution sales ratio has risen to 41.6%. The improved margin gives $2.8\% \times 400,000 = £11,200$ of extra profit. However the company would need to recognise that extra working capital is required. This is £7,410 or 1.8525% of sales.

In practice, you would expect variances to arise relating to product costs and selling prices. Such variances would be extracted before examining the impact of the shift in mix. Note that if product C took a bigger share than 45% of turnover, a profit of £100,000 could be achieved from sales of less than £400,000, while if product A took a bigger share than 25% of turnover, sales could exceed £400,000 and profit still not reach £100,000.

It is possible to control a large range of products using the principles developed above. The calculations can become very cumbersome and the delay in producing the comparison of budget and actual may be more damaging (through slowing down corrective action) than the benefit associated with more detailed control information.

These difficulties can be overcome: (a) By developing a computer model to eliminate the calculations, or (b) By treating products within a narrow band of contribution sales ratios as similar. For example:

Contribution Sales Ratios Range (%)		Simple Average %	Historic[1] Norm
High	Low		
2.5	0.0	1.25	1.4
5.0	2.5	3.75	3.9
7.5	5.0	6.25	6.4
10.0	7.5	8.75	8.5
12.5	10.0	11.25	11.3
15.0	12.5	13.75	13.6
17.5	15.0	16.25	16.1
20.0	17.5	18.75	18.3
25.0	20.0	22.5	21.8
30.0	25.0	27.5	25.9
40.0	30.0	35.0	32.8
50.0	40.0	45.0	43.6

[1] Based on budgeted data for the product groups.

The Qualities of an Effective Financial Control

1 The variance analysis must be prepared regularly. Management accounts should be prepared and interpreted at least quarterly, even in a small firm.

2 The report must be prepared quickly. If something is wrong corrective action must be prompt. The figures should be ready for circulation five days after the end of the accounting period. Slow moving organisations that take a long time to prepare reports miss opportunities to take swift and appropriate corrective actions.

3 It is sometimes necessary to use estimates to produce prompt results. As an example many businesses find that a full count and valuation of stock in trade takes too long, and disrupts production and sales. In these cases the use of book stocks, supported by valid sampling techniques, can overcome the need for lengthy stock count and valuation procedures. Similarly, since many overheads are billed only from time to time, it is necessary to introduce appropriate accruals.

4 The essence of a good comparison of budget against actual is that it is easy to read and that important variances are highlighted.

Two problems arise in trying to meet these criteria. The first is that many reports are too long. Managers find it difficult to identify the critical issues from long reports. Departmental reports can be an effective way of achieving brevity. Consider a company with a large number of products and the following marketing structure:

267

People	Type of Report
Director	Analysis of sales budget against actual by region, followed by a meeting with the area managers to discuss action required.
Regional managers (five regions)	Analysis of sales budget against actual by representative within the region, followed by a meeting with the sales representatives to discuss actions required.
Representatives (60)	Analysis of his or her sales budget against actual by product and customer, to help in preparing for the regional meeting. Analysis of debtor accounts requiring attention
Brand managers (8)	Analysis of brand sales budget against actual by region for discussion with marketing, sales and production.

This outline illustrates how 74 staff could each get an appropriate report. If all 74 staff were given the information relating to each product and customer it is unlikely to be as effective. Reports of this kind are not used often enough.

The second problem is that there is a case for a lot of comparative information. Where the reports are not designed on responsibility lines as outlined above there can be too much data to interpret. The column headings that are sometimes encountered include:

1 Budget this period
2 Actual this period
3 £ variance this period
4 % variance this period
5 Budget year to date
6 Actual year to date
7 £ variance year to date
8 % variance year to date
9 Actual last period
10 Variance against last period
11 Actual this period last year
12 Variance against this period last year

This list is not exhaustive. If 12 items are to be reported you wind up with a page composed of 144 numbers. It becomes difficult to establish which are important and which are not.

We will now examine the reasons people want these column heads included and the possible methods of reducing their number to manageable proportions.

Column Headings	Rationale	Options for Reducing Columns
1–4	These give a full analysis of current perfomance. Item 3 because big % can occur on small items and be controllable, item 4 because big £ variances are always of concern.	The budget, actual and £ variances are derived by addition or subtraction. You only need two of them. The following combinations can be used: (a) budget & £ variance; (b) actual & £ variance. In case (a) actual is omitted; in case (b) the budget is omitted. 3 headings are used.
5–8	The company needs to check year to date results to ensure that recoveries of previous shortfalls are being achieved.	As with the current period, it is necessary to disclose one item from budget and actual. Select the item you used for the period results.
9–10	To keep track of progress since the last period.	This is vital in seasonal businesses. Are these data more or less valuable than items 11 and 12 below? If they are you only need the growth or decline statistic.
11–12	The best measure of progress is often by comparison with last year.	Changes are caused by movements in prices and volumes. The change in volume is the best measure of progress. The percentage change is all you need.

If you examine your columnar requirements carefully, you may be able to keep them to eight or less. This makes the report easier to understand.

A good report is designed to meet the needs of its primary audience, the management team (not group accounting or computer software designers). Complicated terminology, developed by accounting or engineering staff, makes reports difficult to understand and take action on. Report designers frequently overlook the fact that their primary audience may not have the least understanding of complicated terminology. Computer data are often not 'user friendly'.

Often when financial people design control reports they are preoccupied with financial statement data. There are many items which are mainly non-financial in emphasis but are vital for effective financial control. Some of these are:

(a) Planned against actual market share for major products.
(b) Comparison of promotion costs per unit with major competitors.
(c) Comparison of relative quality.
(d) Proportion of trade with major customers against total sales.
(e) Listing of top 10 debtors and creditors.
(f) State of order book.
(g) Planned versus actual scrap and rework
(h) Overtime hours worked as % of normal hours.
(i) Absenteeism statistics.
(j) Spending on capital projects planned versus actual.
(k) Spending to completion on capital projects planned versus estimated actual.

Above all, it is essential that all managers should see the issue of the reports from the management accounting section as the first step in the control process. It helps them to participate in the real financial control activities which start at that stage. Dialogue begins about what has happened and what will happen next. Reports which issue at this stage of the control process often contain revised profit estimates. Such estimates lack the expertise of the budget managers who should know much more about what is going on in their area than the finance people. This knowledge must be harnessed into the control process if it is to operate properly. Sensible revised estimates can only be produced after the management team have carefully examined the causes of current variances, the actions to be taken to overcome unfavourable developments and the implications for future performance in each part of the business.

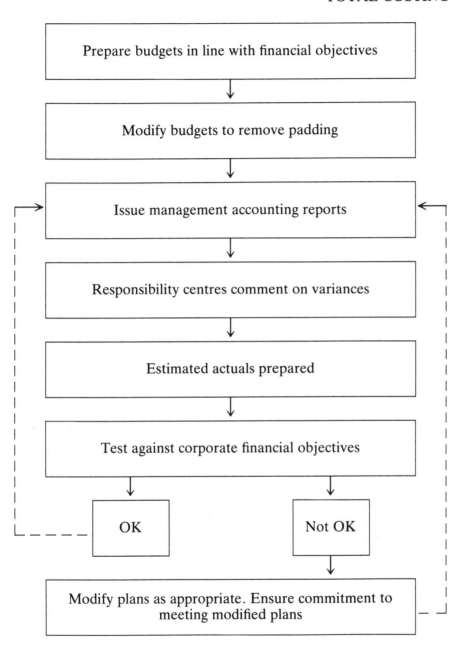

Fig. 9.1 A Model of an Effective Control Process

A company that goes through this cycle at the end of each accounting period can expect its actual results to be at least as good as planned, unless serious unexpected problems arise.

271

Chapter 10

Total Costing

Costing is the process by which the expenses of a business are allocated to the products or services it sells, with a view to establishing how they compare with selling prices available in the market place.

There are two separate approaches to costing: (a) establishing what the actual cost was in the past (called historic cost); and (b) forecasting what the cost will be in the future (called budgeted cost). There are often major differences between the unit cost budgeted and what it proves to be when the historic cost is calculated. The differences are caused by forecasting errors. Incorrect budgeted costs can lead to incorrect management decisions.

Costing is straightforward in a one product business. It can get complicated and subjective where more than one product or service is involved.

Steps in Predetermining Product Costs for One Product

Cost Category and Underlying Data	Cost Calculation	Cost £
Direct materials (excl. VAT)		
Standard unit specifications		
×		
Price per unit	£10	
+	+	
Allowance for spoilage, off cuts and pilferage	10%	11.00
Standard unit labour hours	2	
×	×	
Standard unit rates per hour (including fringe costs)	£3	
+	+	
Allowance for rework, scrap, inefficiency, etc.	6%	6.36
Prime cost		17.36
Budgeted overhead per period	10,000	
/	/	
Units sold in period	5,000	2.00
Total cost		19.36
Selling price available (excl. VAT)		22.50
Profit per unit (13.96% of unit sales price)		3.14

The budgeted profit from sale of 5,000 units is: $5,000 \times 3.14 = £15,700$

We will now look at the results when some of the budgeted costs turn out to be incorrect. There are four cases. In each case only one item turns out to be incorrect.

	Case A Material Cost £12.10 each incl. Waste		Case B Labour Cost £7 each incl. Rework		Case C Overhead cost is £11,000		Case D Sales are 4,000 Units	
	Per Unit	Total	Per Unit	Total	Per Unit	Total	Per Unit	Total
Material	12.10	60,500	11.00	55,000	11.00	55,000	11.00	44,000
Labour	6.36	31,800	7.00	35,000	6.36	31,800	6.36	25,440
Overhead	2.00	10,000	2.00	10,000	2.20	11,000	2.50	10,000
Total cost	20.46	102,300	20.00	100,000	19.56	97,800	19.86	79,440
Sales	22.50	112,500	22.50	112,500	22.50	112,500	22.50	90,000
Profit	2.04	10,200	2.50	12,500	2.94	14,700	2.64	10,560
Profit Margin (%)	9.1		11.1		13.1		11.7	
Change from Budget								
Units		5,000		5,000		5,000		
Unit overruns	×							
Material	£1.10							
Labour			£0.64		×			
Overhead			×		£0.20			
Profit decline		£5,500		£3,200		£1,000		

The decline in profit when volume falls is more complicated. The revised profit is based on the following assumptions: (1) Materials and labour were expended to make 5,000 units. The unsold items remain in stock. The cost structure is:

	Material	Labour
Units produced 5,000 units	55,000	31,800
Less stocks 1,000 units	11,000	6,360
	44,000	25,440

(2) The overhead is £10,000, but the overhead cost per unit rises to £2.50 for the 4,000 items.

Based on these assumptions the profit decline is:

	Per Unit	Total
Profit achieved	2.64	10,560
Add profit that would be achieved if 1,000		
further units sold	5.14	5,140[a]

[a] The full overheads are covered from the 4,000 sold. The extra profit is £22.50−£11.00−£6.36 = £5.14 per unit for the next 1,000 items sold.

Principles of Cost Allocation with Two or More Products

It can be difficult to allocate the costs of a business which has a range of products. Costs can be classified into four types:

1 Costs which can be directly attributed to a product. Obvious examples include:
    (a) raw materials purchased specifically for making that specific product;
    (b) production labour which is specifically traced to that product (job cards);
    (c) power costs, metered as the product is made on a machine; and
    (d) Some carriage costs.
2 Costs which could be directly attributed to specific products, but the cost of measurement exceeds the benefit from its allocation. A supervisor's time could be measured and the cost involved allocated in proportion to time spent. The time involved in recording the activities would be lost for direct supervision. The cost of recording and allocation might exceed the benefit.
3 Costs which can be arbitrarily allocated to products in a sensible way without incurring undue expense. The establishment costs in a finished goods store could easily be allocated in proportion to the estimated space taken up by the finished products held there.
4 Costs which may be almost totally independent of the production and sale of individual product lines, e.g. accounting/bookkeeping/personnel/administration costs.

To compute a product cost it is necessary to classify the costs of the business into the above groups. When this has been done the costs can be attributed to individual products or services. A range of options is available as to how costs should be attributed. These include: actual, arbitrary and scientific.

Cost Attribution Systems

Allocation	*Features*
Direct allocation	Relevant for material, direct labour and some sizeable production costs.
Allocation in proportion to spending planned on dominant costs.	Often suitable where the cost of more 'scientific' methods exceeds the benefits from their use.
Accumulation in an area (often called a cost centre) for transfer to products in proportion to their time in process there. Cost centres may be departments, people or machines.	This approach is used to attribute a wide range of costs in a similar way. The old approach used machine and direct labour hour rates. Modern systems use *cost drivers* and *activity based costing*.

Before attributing costs to products or services we must establish whether they will be incurred if a product or service is not produced. This question relates to the reason(s) why costs behave in the ways that they do. Costs behave in three different ways:

1   Those which rise and fall in direct proportion to output. These costs are called variable costs. Examples are:
    (a)   raw materials. If output declines we will buy less of them or we will carry more in stock. If output increases we will buy more or carry less in stock; and
    (b)   piecework labour, because if they are not making product they are not paid.
    In many text books direct labour is treated as a variable cost. In times of falling demand, this often proves unreliable. Companies cannot afford redundancy costs when reducing staff and fear the cost of recruitment and training when demand picks up.
2   Those which will be incurred on a similar scale regardless of the size of output. These costs are called fixed costs. Examples of fixed costs are:
    (a)   rent & rates based on the occupation of the premises, not the volume of activity taking place there; and
    (b)   administration salaries based on employment costs rather than production activity.
3   Those which are partly fixed and partly variable. These are called semi-fixed, semi-variable, or mixed costs. Examples of semi-variable costs include:
    (a)   machine maintenance which could include an annual overhaul

regardless of ouput (fixed) and a replacement of parts after each 10,000 units (variable),

(b)   a sales incentive scheme based on a flat rate up to a specific level with a % commission for each £ of sales in excess of quota.

Semi-variable Cost Examples

Is distribution cost fixed or variable? We must look at the various components of this cost:

Cost Type	Fixed	Variable (Semi?)
Van driver's wages	/	
Vehicle tax & insurance	/	
Fuel		/
Maintenance of vehicle		/
Depreciation	/	

The semi? is because a tricky issue arises about the cost difference between a fully and partly loaded vehicle. The distribution manager has extracted reliable statistics that provide the following information about a vehicle: (a) weight of product transported when fully laden – 5 tons; (b) fuel cost fully laden 20p; and (c) each 20% reduction in load will result in an 8% decrease in fuel consumption (non-cumulative).

A Weight Carried	B (C+D) Cost per Mile	C Fixed Cost	D Variable Cost	(D/A) Variable Cost per Ton/Mile
5	20.0	12	8.0	1.6
4	18.4	12	6.4	1.6
3	16.8	12	4.8	1.6
2	15.2	12	3.2	1.6
1	13.6	12	1.6	1.6
0	12.0	12		

In this case the cost budget would be developed by classifying: (a) number of miles transported×12p as fixed; and (b) number of miles travelled at each load factor as variable. If the budget is to cover 15,000 miles the forecast is:

(1) Weight Carried	(2) Miles This Load	(2)×12p Fixed Cost	(1)×(2)×1.6p Variable Cost	Total Cost
5	3,000	360	240	600
4.5	4,000	480	288	768
4	5,000	600	320	920
3.5	2,000	240	112	352
3	1,000	120	48	168
		1,800	1,008	2,808

BASE FEE PLUS COMMISSION

(a) Base fee is £15,000 regardless of sales volume.
(b) Each complete 5,000 units sold in excess of quota will attract the following commission: 5% for each complete 5,000 units in excess of 50,000 up to 75,000; and a further 10% for each complete 5,000 units in excess of 75,000.
(c) Each unit is sold for £1.

Total Cost Budget at Various Volumes

Budget Sales	Base Fixed Cost	Low Variable Cost	High Variable Cost	Total Cost
40,000	15,000	–	–	15,000
50,000	15,000	–	–	15,000
55,000	15,000	250	–	15,250
58,000	15,000	250	–	15,250
60,000	15,000	500	–	15,500
65,000	15,000	750	–	15,750
70,000	15,000	1,000	–	16,000
75,000	15,000	1,250	–	16,250
80,000	15,000	1,250	500	16,750
85,000	15,000	1,250	1,000	17,250
90,000	15,000	1,250	1,500	17,750
95,000	15,000	1,250	2,000	18,250
100,000	15,000	1,250	2,500	18,750

Dominant Cost Allocations

To illustrate allocations in proportion to dominant cost, we will examine a business about which the following information has been obtained:

1 A product is made in two sizes. The large version is twice as big as the small one.
2 Material content is in direct proportion to size.
3 Labour content is 25% greater for the large version.
4 Machine running cost is the same for each product.
5 Total direct cost is £250,000 and total overhead to be allocated is £50,000.

We will examine the application of the dominant cost approach in four different business types as follows:

	Case 1 Assembly and Packing Operation		Case 2 Hand Craft		Case 3 Standard Uncomplicated Manufacturing		Case 4 Machine Intensive Process Industry	
	£'000	Direct Cost %	£'000	Direct Cost %	£'000	Direct Cost %	£'000	Direct Cost %
Materials	150	60	55	22	107.5	43	45	18
Labour	55	22	175	70	105	42	25	10
Machine running	45	18	20	8	37.5	15	180	72
Total direct cost	250	100	250	100	250	100	250	100
Overhead	50	20	50	20	50	20	50	20
Total cost	300	120	300	120	300	120	300	120

The dominant cost is obvious in cases 1, 2 and 4, being materials, labour and machine running respectively. In case 3 it is close between material and labour. The combination of material and labour (called prime cost) is a joint dominant cost.

Cost Attribution Methods

To illustrate this we will examine four businesses about which the following information has been obtained.

1 A product is made in two sizes. The large version is twice as big as the small one.
2 Material content is in direct proportion to size.
3 Labour content is 25% greater for the large version.
4 Machine running cost is the same for each product.
5 Total direct cost is £400,000 and total overhead to be allocated is £54,000.

	Case 1 Assembly and Packing Operation	Case 2 Hand Craft	Case 3 Standard Uncomplicated Manufacturing	Case 4 Machine Intensive Industry
Materials	195	90	150	75
Labour	135	270	180	45
Machine running	70	40	70	280
Total direct cost	400	400	400	400
Overhead	54	54	54	54
Total cost	454	454	454	454

Product direct costs based on the data in points one to four above are:

£'000	Case 1 Small	Case 1 Large	Case 2 Small	Case 2 Large	Case 3 Small	Case 3 Large	Case 4 Small	Case 4 Large
Materials	65	130	30	60	50	100	25	50
Labour	60	75	120	150	80	100	20	25
Machine running	35	35	20	20	35	35	140	140
Product direct cost	160	240	170	230	165	235	185	215

OVERHEAD ALLOCATION METHOD 1

Overheads could be spread in proportion to direct materials. One-third of the total material cost applies to the small size which is attributed with one-third of the overhead. The attribution is therefore £18,000. Two-thirds of the overhead or £36,000 is attributed to the large size. Based on this attribution mechanism the combined profit of £66,000 is divided by pack size as follows:

£'000	Case 1		Case 2		Case 3		Case 4	
	Small	Large	Small	Large	Small	Large	Small	Large
Sales revenue	200	320	200	320	200	320	200	320
Product direct cost	160	240	170	230	165	235	185	215
Overhead	18	36	18	36	18	36	18	36
Total cost	178	276	188	266	183	271	193	251
Profit	22	44	12	44	17	49	7	69

OVERHEAD ALLOCATION METHOD 2

Overheads could be spread in proportion to direct labour. Four-ninths of the total labour cost applies to the small size which is attributed with four-ninths of the overhead. The attribution is £24,000. Five-ninths of the overhead or £30,000 is attributed to the large size. Based on this attribution mechanism the combined profit of £66,000 is divided by pack size as follows:

£'000	Case 1		Case 2		Case 3		Case 4	
	Small	Large	Small	Large	Small	Large	Small	Large
Sales revenue	200	320	200	320	200	320	200	320
Product direct cost	160	240	170	230	165	235	185	215
Overhead	24	30	24	30	24	30	24	30
Total cost	184	270	194	260	189	265	209	245
Profit	16	50	6	60	11	55	(9)	75

OVERHEAD ALLOCATION METHOD 3

Overheads could be spread in proportion to machine hours. Fifty per cent of the machine hours are used on each product. Each is attributed with £27,000 of overhead. Based on this attribution mechanism the profit of £66,000 is divided by pack size as follows:

| £'000 | Case 1 | | Case 2 | | Case 3 | | Case 4 | |
	Small	Large	Small	Large	Small	Large	Small	Large
Sales revenue	200	320	200	320	200	320	200	320
Product direct cost	160	240	170	230	165	235	185	215
Overhead	27	27	27	27	27	27	27	27
Total cost	187	267	197	257	192	262	212	242
Profit	13	53	3	63	8	58	(12)	78

OVERHEAD ALLOCATION METHOD 4

Overheads could be spread in proportion to prime cost (combined direct costs are taken as prime cost). The product prime costs are in different proportions in the four industries and the overhead attribution reflects this:

| £'000 | Case 1 | | Case 2 | | Case 3 | | Case 4 | |
	Small	Large	Small	Large	Small	Large	Small	Large
Sales revenue	200.0	320.0	200.00	320.00	200.000	320.000	200.000	320.000
Product direct	160.0	240.0	170.00	230.00	165.000	235.000	185.000	215.000
Overhead[a]	21.6	32.4	22.95	31.05	22.275	31.725	24.975	29.025
Total cost	181.6	272.4	192.95	261.05	187.275	266.725	209.975	244.025
Profit	18.4	47.6	7.05	58.95	12.725	53.275	(9.975)	75.975

[a] The overhead follows the prime cost. Prime cost for the small size is: case 1 40% of total, case 2 42.5%, case 3 41.25% and case 4 46.25%.

The four overhead attribution methods yield different product profits:

	Case 1		Case 2		Case 3		Case 4	
	Small	Large	Small	Large	Small	Large	Small	Large
% Materials	22,000	44,000	12,000	44,000	17,000	49,000	7,000	69,000
% Labour	16,000	50,000	6,000	60,000	11,000	55,000	(9,000)	75,000
%Machining	13,000	53,000	3,000	63,000	8,000	58,000	(12,000)	78,000
%Prime cost	18,400	47,600	7,050	58,950	12,725	53,275	(9,975)	75,975

Which of these profit figures is the most reliable one? In case 1 material is the dominant cost. The percentage of materials is the most logical method. Profits are split £22,000 to the small size and £44,000 to the large size.

In case 2 direct labour is the dominant cost. The percentage of labour is the most logical method. Profits are split £6,000 to the small size and £60,000 to the large size.

In case 4 machine running is the dominant cost. The percentage of machine hours is the most logical method. A loss of £12,000 is incurred by the small size, a profit of £78,000 is earned by the large size. Note that a machine hour rate technique dealt with in the next section of this chapter could be used in this case.

In case 3 no individual cost is dominant. The percentage of prime cost is the most logical method. Profits are split £12,725 to the small size and £53,275 to the large size.

ILLUSTRATION OF MACHINE HOUR RATE COSTING

Steps One to Three

			Allocation of Costs to Machines			
Cost type	Allocation Method	Total Cost	Machine A	Machine B	Machine C	Machine D
Step 1						
Rent & rates	Square footage 4:3:2:1	10,000	4,000	3,000	2,000	1,000
Supervision	Estimated time devoted 1.5:1:1:1.5	18,000	5,400	3,600	3,600	5,400
Machine Insurance	Value of machinery 2.5:1:2.5:1	28,000	10,000	4,000	10,000	4,000
Power	Estimated consumption 3:3:1:4	11,000	3,000	3,000	1,000	4,000
Maintenance	Estimated time devoted 3:2:1:4	24,000	7,200	4,800	2,400	9,600
Total allocated		91,000	29,600	18,400	19,000	24,000
Other costs (in proportion to allocated costs)		39,000	12,686[a]	7,886	8,143	10,285
Total costs		130,000	42,286	26,286	27,143	34,285
Step 2						
Productive hours per period			5,000	4,000	3,000	6,000
Step 3						
Machine hour rate			£8.46	£6.57	£9.05	£5.71

[a] $29,600 \times \dfrac{39}{91} = 12,666$ etc.

Step 4: Illustration of a Job Costing Using These Machines

	£
Direct materials	
1,000 grammes at 50p	500
Direct labour	
240 hours at £3.50 per hour	840
Machine A	
25 hours at £8.46	212
Machine B	
15 hours at £6.57	99
Machine C	
12 hours at £9.05	109
Machine D	
18 hours at £5.71	103
Total cost	1,863

To calculate the selling price, you must specify the profit per labour and machine hour required and apply these rates to the job:

	£	£
Rate per hour required from labour		
£2×240 hours		480.0
Rate per hour required from machines		
A £1.50×25	37.5	
B £1.00×15	15.0	
C £1.50×12	18.0	
D £1.00×18	18.0	88.5
Production cost		1863.0
Price indicated		2,431.5

If quoting for this job, a company would ask this price (more if they thought the customer would accept it). In difficult trading conditions it might quote a lower price to keep the machines working.

Direct labour hour rates are computed in a similar way, the costs being allocated to a person or gang rather than a machine.

Total Cost Absorption: The Snags

In the previous illustrations, we looked at budgeted product cost. Actual results can create two major snags: the costs exceed budget, or volume targets are not achieved. The unit allocation of overhead is wrong and the unit profit is not realised. Conversely, the costs are below budget or volume exceeds budget. The unit allocation of overhead is wrong and the unit profit exceeds the budget. Here are some examples:

	Budget		Actual Case 1		Actual Case 2		Actual Case 3	
	Total	Per Unit	Total	Per Unit	Total	Per Unit	Total	Per Unit
Direct materials	15,000	3	9,000	3	18,000	3	18,000	3.60
Direct labour	10,000	2	6,000	2	12,000	2	12,500	2.50
Prime cost	25,000	5	15,000	5	30,000	5	30,500	6.10
Overheads	5,000	1	5,000	1.67	5,000	0.83	6,000	1.20
Total cost	30,000	6	20,000	6.67	35,000	5.83	36,500	7.30
Sales	40,000	8	24,000	8.00	48,000	8.00	40,000	8.00
Unit Profit		2		1.33		2.17		0.70
		×		×		×		×
Volume		5,000		3,000		6,000		5,000
Total profit		10,000		4,000		13,000		3,500

The budget and actual profit can be reconciled:

	Case 1	Case 2	Case 3
Budgeted profit	10,000	10,000	10,000
Less unit cost overrun			(6,500)
Less volume decline 2,000×£2	(4,000)		
Less overheads not picked up due to unit decline 2,000×£1[1]	(2,000)		
Add volume gain 1,000×£2		2,000	
Add overheads over-allocated 1,000×£1[2]		1,000	
Actual profit	4,000	13,000	3,500

[1] The penalty for underutilised capacity is £0.67 per unit. The profit per unit falls to £1.33.
[2] Improved capacity utilisation reduces the overhead cost to £0.83 per unit and the profit is £2.17 per unit.

The Cost Driven Price Spiral

In case 1 above the decline in volume results in an unacceptable profit. If the owner believes that volume sales will continue at 3,000 units per month for the foreseeable future, he or she might be tempted to increase the selling price to £10 so as to recover the overheads and provide the £10,000 profit required. The new price is calculated as follows:

Calculation of new price in case 1	
Sales volume expected[a]	3,000
Total cost per example	20,000
Profit required	10,000
Revenue required[b]	30,000
Unit selling price required[b/a]	£10

If the owner implements the proposed price increase the volume might fall by a further 20% to 2,400 units. The business would be in a potential price spiral. Falling volumes would result in rising unit overhead costs and higher selling prices until the business priced itself out of existence. This is illustrated using sales volumes of 2,400 and 1,500 as follows:

Calculation of new price 2		
Sales volume expected[a]	2,400	1,500
Variable cost new volume	12,000	7,500
Fixed cost	5,000	5,000
Profit required	10,000	10,000
Revenue required[b]	27,000	22,500
Unit selling price required[b/a]	£11.25	£15

The business is pricing itself into liquidation. A prudent owner should sell at £8 per unit and seek to reduce costs to a level compatible with the future sales expectations. Unfortunately, owners frequently take the view that the volume collapse is temporary and fail to take the necessary cost reduction steps while compounding the problem with inappropriate sales price increases.

To Sell or Not to Sell Unprofitable Products

Discontinuing loss-making products results in the transfer of over-heads to the profitable lines. It can even turn them into loss makers. Where a product or service is unprofitable it is wise to look at the overall profitability with and without it before deciding to discontinue it. The following data were taken from the costing records of a business:

| | Product | | | |
	A	B	C	Total
Unit selling price	£50	£20	£10	
Sales quantity	100	200	400	
	£	£	£	£
Sales revenue	5,000	4,000	4,000	13,000
Direct materials	1,900	1,600	1,700	5,200
Direct labour	2,000	1,200	1,200	4,400
Avoidable overheads[1]	1,000	600	600	2,200
Unavoidable overheads[2]	500	300	300	1,100
Total cost	5,400	3,700	3,800	12,900
Profit/(loss)	(400)	300	200	100

[1] 50% of direct labour.
[2] 25% of direct labour.

The proprietor feels that: (a) the overall profit of £100 is unaccept-able; and (b) that if product A were discontinued the total profit would rise to £500. Do you agree?

The conclusion is faulty. If product A is discontinued, its material, labour and avoidable overhead will no longer be incurred. The product is being allocated £500 of unavoidable cost which will now have to be attributed to products B and C. The results if product A is discontinued will be:

	Product		Total
	B	C	
Unit selling price	£20	£10	
Sales quantity	200	400	
	£	£	£
Sales revenue	4,000	4,000	8,000
Direct materials	1,600	1,700	3,300
Direct labour	1,200	1,200	2,400
Avoidable overheads	600	600	1,200
Unavoidable overheads	550	550	1,100
Total cost	3,950	4,050	8,000
Profit/(loss)	50	(50)	–

The £100 profit has vanished. The question arises . . . should we discontinue product C? If we do, product B will be given a further £550 of unavoidable overhead. It will be a loss maker.

Does this mean that the whole analysis is faulty? No, it shows us that product A is a poor performer. It is making a loss. Since it sells above direct cost, it is recovering some overhead. A range of options is available to try to improve it:

1 Increase the selling price.
2 Increase the volume.
3 Negotiate a lower material cost.
4 Reduce the labour cost (lower overtime, improved efficiency, wage freeze, etc.).
5 Reduce avoidable and unavoidable overheads.

If none of these options is feasible, then the business must search for an alternative product which can cover the product A overheads and yield a profit.

Product A should certainly not be discontinued, unless a replacement product comes on stream, or the situation has deteriorated to a level where the selling price falls below unavoidable cost. When a replacement product is paying the unavoidable costs, it is time to take action on product A. Initially increase the price to make sales profitable and clear the stock. If sales collapse then discontinue it.

A hopeful scenario is:

	\n				

	Product				
	A	B	C	D	Total
Unit selling price	£55	£20	£10	£12	
Sales quantity	40	200	400	320	
Sales revenue	2,200	4,000	4,000	3,840	14,040
Direct materials	760	1,600	1,700	1,260	5,320
Direct labour	800	1,200	1,200	1,400	4,600
Avoidable overheads	400	600	600	700	2,300
Unavoidable overheads	191	287	287	335	1,100
Total cost	2,151	3,687	3,787	3,695	13,320
Profit	49	313	213	145	720

Product A has been increased in price by 10% and declines in volume
by 60%. It is able to generate a profit of 49 after bearing a share of the
unavoidable overheads. The inclusion of product D is vital. Without it,
product A would be loss-making and the overall profit would be lower
as the following three-product profit forecast shows:

	Product			
	A	B	C	Total
Unit selling price	£55	£20	£10	
Sales quantity	40	200	400	
Sales revenue	2,200	4,000	4,000	10,200
Direct materials	760	1,600	1,700	4,060
Direct labour	800	1,200	1,200	3,200
Avoidable overheads	400	600	600	1,600
Unavoidable overheads	275	413	412	1,100
Total cost	2,235	3,813	3,912	9,960
Profit/(loss)	(35)	187	88	240

Activity Based Costing

Traditional cost accounting systems were designed to attribute costs to products or services in a world that was less complicated than it is in the 1990s. Costs were driven by quantities produced or sold or by the passage of time. The significant costs for most businesses were direct material and direct labour. Other costs were insignificant individually and unimportant collectively. Overhead recovery rates based on dominant costs (material, labour or the combination of the two) provided reasonably accurate product costs. Where these proved unreliable the use of machine hour or direct labour hour rates provided relevant information for estimating, tendering and costing.

Such cost attribution systems came into disrepute in the 1980s. There were six major reasons:

1 Some products or services prove more difficult to create than others. General purpose overhead attribution systems tend to flatter the profitability of complex products and punish the ease of creation of straightforward products.

2 Competitors make price reductions that are out of line with the product profitability indications of traditional costing systems. Traditionalists expect the competition to perish on the rock of 'pricing errors'. To their horror they find that the competitors thrive.

3 Price increases are accepted by customers who were expected to complain bitterly.

4 The distinctive competitive edge of many large companies is marketing and branding. They tend to source manufactured components rather than basic raw materials. This type of strategy changed such businesses from being labour intensive to material intensive. Consider the computer hardware industry. Ten years ago direct labour costs were many times greater than they are now. Most components are bought-in! Yet overheads continued to be allocated in proportion to direct labour in many leading computer companies until recently.

5 The 'spreadsheet era' permits the creation of complex allocation models impossible previously.

6 Johnson, H and Kaplan, R (1987, *Relevance Lost: The Evolution of Management Accounting*, Harvard Business School Press) argued that the primary purpose of costing systems used to be to value stocks . . . and that by doing so they fail to assess the profitability of products accurately. Progressive companies have accepted the validity of this argument and have taken steps to measure the costs of products or services more accurately.

Four Steps in Computing Activity Based Costs

Activity based costing was developed to overcome these defects in traditional systems. There are four major steps in the ABC approach:

Step 1

Restructure the cost budgets in terms of services provided rather than by expenditure type. For example, conventional accounting systems frequently aggregate production labour costs as a total amount. An ABC system would redistribute this cost under various headings, e.g. purchasing, set-up, storekeeping, engineering, research, maintenance, packing, quality control and so on.

Step 2

Match the supply of services available with demand. If supply exceeds demand then products that avail of that service should only be allocated that fraction of the cost for which a demand exists. For example, if a machine has annual operating costs of £20,000, a production capability of 10,000 hours and a forecast usage of 4,000 hours, then the products that buy time on the machine should be charged at an hourly rate of £2. The remaining £12,000 of cost represents inefficient utilisation. It should be excluded from the product costs, which would otherwise be uncompetitive. The cost attributed is what it should be, not what it is. The £12,000 cost of underutilisation provides a challenge to the organisation: can they (a) find a way to use the surplus capacity profitably? and, if not, should they (b) lease out the surplus capacity or sell off that service facility and buy it back in as required?

Step 3

Identify the primary determinant of the amount of cost for each particular service. In ABC this is called a cost driver. In some functions the cost driver is easy to identify, e.g. the cost of quality control is determined by the range of products, the volume of each product and quality testing time. In other areas the cost driver can be difficult to determine. An example is building related costs. The best way to handle these is to attribute them to the functions carried out in the building. Space utilised could be the driver but it is frequently worth making judgements about premium and non-premium space and attributing costs in proportion to estimated rentals. This hierarchical attribution makes it easier to deal with onward allocation at step 4.

Step 4

Attribute the cost of providing each function to the products or services that utilise it. The approach involves dividing the budgeted costs of the function (net of underutilised capacity) by the number of units of cost driver planned. As an example we will consider the cost of production set-ups: when a business provides products in a variety of colours, sizes or qualities the inclusion of set-up costs in a generalised overhead recovery rate can lead to incorrect product costs. Long production runs (which involve lower unit set-up costs) are not rewarded for economies of scale. Short production runs are not punished even though the set-up cost per unit produced is above average. This defect can be rectified by computing the cost of a set-up and the number of set-ups involved (the cost driver) in the budget period. The following illustration shows why the use of a *cost driver* (in this case set-up time) is so important in modern industry.

The set-up time for a product has been costed at £200. The product is manufactured in three sizes. The Midi is the most popular size and will be produced in four runs next year. The Mini is less popular, but it will be produced in five runs next year. The Maxi is least popular and will be produced in nine runs next year. Contrast the allocation of set-up costs using traditional and ABC methods:

Traditional Overhead Allocation

	Midi	Mini	Maxi	Total
Volume produced and sold	10,000	1,000	750	
Direct labout budget	100,000	5,000	15,000	120,000
Set-up attributed[1]	3,000	150	450	3,600
Set-up cost per unit	30p	15p	60p	

[1] set-up attributed at 3% of total direct labour.

Traditional Unit Profitability

	Midi	Mini	Maxi
Material	5.00	2.50	10.00
Labour	10.00	5.00	20.00
Overhead (220% of labour)	22.00	11.00	44.00
Total cost	37.00	18.50	74.00
Selling price	40.00	21.00	79.00
Unit profit	3.00	2.50	5.00

The overhead attribution system was 220% of direct labour of which 3% was driven by the cost of a set-up.

Activity Based Allocation

	Midi	Mini	Maxi	Total
Volume produced and sold	10,000	1,000	750	
Set-up times	4	5	9	18
Set-up costs (×£200)	800	1,000	1,800	3,600
Set-up cost per unit	8p	£1	£2.40	

The activity based attribution of set-up costs adds 22p per unit to the profit of Midi and takes 85p and £1.80 from the unit profit of Mini and Maxi respectively. It is easy to believe that if the remaining £260,400 of overheads had been attributed in proportion to relevant cost drivers that the Mini could be proved to be unprofitable. This could lead to a decision to increase the selling price of the Mini significantly.

Important cost drivers that should be considered if a business wishes to attribute costs to products reasonably accurately include:

Cost Driver   **Possible Attribution Proportions**
Material purchasing   Product transactions
Material handling   Product requisitions
Machining   Machine hours
Supervision   Time studies
Quality control   Time studies
Packaging   Packing hours
Shipping   Product specific
Product marketing   Product specific
Interest   Product capital employed
Credit control   Time studies

The important issue is that some costs are not driven by either production or time. Businesses must develop an objective and logical attribution framework. Identification of logical drivers often involves consultation with staff that provide the service. Some cost types are difficult to attribute to specific products or services. Such costs are driven by the entity rather than its products or services. Even in ABC they are often attributed to products using variations on traditional overhead recovery mechanisms. Examples include:

Cost type	Possible Attribution Proportions
Corporate marketing	Budgeted product sales
Research	Budgeted product sales
Personnel	Budgeted head count
Staff training	Budgeted functional usage

Activity Based Costing Illustration

| | £'000 | | | |
	Product A	Product B	Product C	Total
Sales volume	1,000	2,000	1,500	4,500
Sales revenue	10,000	16,000	9,000	35,000
Direct material	3,600	5,000	3,000	11,600
Direct labour	2,500	2,900	2,600	8,000
Total direct	6,100	7,900	5,600	19,600
Material purchasing	20	30	50	100
Material handling	100	340	60	500
Set-up	10	70	20	100
Machining	300	850	250	1,400
Supervision	150	450	200	800
Quality control	50	550	100	700
Packaging	120	440	40	600
Shipping	200	775	125	1,100
Marketing	500	1,840	810	3,150
Interest	250	600	150	1,000
Central costs	300	1,260	540	2,100
Total attributed	2,000	7,205	2,345	11,550
Total cost	8,100	15,105	7,945	31,150
Operating profit (loss)	1,900	895	1,055	3,850
Unutilised capacity				450
Profit before tax				3,400

Product Profitability Labour Based Recovery

	Product A	Product B	Product C	Total
Sales volume	1,000	2,000	1,500	4,500
Sales revenue	10,000	16,000	9,000	35,000
Direct material	3,600	5,000	3,000	11,600
Direct labour	2,500	2,900	2,600	8,000
Overhead recovery (150%)	3,750	4,350	3,900	12,000
Total cost	9,850	12,250	9,500	31,600
Profit before tax	150	3,750	(500)	3,400

Product C which appeared to be loss-making is quite profitable when assessed on ABC lines. Product A is the biggest profit earner (labour-based overhead suggested that it was a small contributor). Product B, the star using traditional costing, earns the smallest profit when activity based costing is used.

Summary of Total Costing Issues

1 The purpose is to compute a cost per unit for comparison with prices available in the market place.
2 Costings produced on the basis of previous performance are usually of little value in decision making. Changes in volume and price make them obsolete.
3 Budgeted costs are only of value when the costs and volumes are reasonably accurately predicted.
4 Costing is easy when one product is produced. When a second and subsequent product(s) is(are) added the overhead must be apportioned. Allocation in proportion to dominant costs is often used. Percentage methods of overhead recovery and machine hour (or direct labour) rate systems can be misleading. Companies that seek accurate insights into product profitability will develop activity based cost systems.
5 Once a suitable overhead attribution system has been developed many companies leave it in place for years. The objectives of the costing system and its ability to meet them should be reviewed regularly.
6 There are many different types of costing systems used in British industry. These include: process costing, joint product costing, by product costing, batch costing, standard costing, etc.

Systems must be finely tuned to meet the specific conditions in the organisation. To do justice to such systems would need a full book in itself. If you wish to examine such systems, I suggest: Horngren, C (1991, *Cost Accounting a Managerial Emphasis*, Prentice-Hall Inc) and Cooper, R and Kaplan, R (1991, *The Design of Cost Management Systems*, Prentice-Hall Inc).

Appendix to Chapter 10

Transfer Pricing

In carrying out a detailed assessment of the effectiveness of financial performance, it is often necessary to introduce transfer costs for products and services. Transfer costs are necessary in four cases:

1   When a business wishes a cost centre to be self sufficient. This involves charging out the cost to user departments that buy their service.
2   When a business wishes to create a profit centre for performance measurement. This involves charging a higher transfer price to departments that buy their service.
3   When a company wishes to create investment centres, often called business units. This involves the allocation of income, expenditure, assets and liabilities to business units to facilitate ROI analysis.
4   Transfer pricing is also necessary when a product or service is partly completed in one group company and transferred to another group company, often overseas, for further processing and/or sale to third parties.

Method 1: Cost Centres

The cost centre method is designed to charge the cost of providing a service to user departments (which benefit from its existence). User departments may or may not have the option of buying from outside suppliers, if they feel that the transfer price is excessive.

Cost centres are frequently used to accumulate the costs of a service department for onward charge to user departments. Examples of cost centres include transport, personnel, maintenance, accounting, training, purchasing, etc. The cost of these functions is treated as an overhead in organisations not using transfer pricing. To achieve a full attribution of the costs of these services to user departments and ultimately products, a transfer pricing system is required.

A TRANSFER PRICING SYSTEM FOR A TRANSPORT DEPARTMENT

The following data have been developed for the transport budget of a medium-sized company. Capacity to transport goods 100,000 miles:
   50% in 10 tonne vehicles used by the Northern Division;
   30% in 6 tonne vehicles used by the Western Division; and
   20% in 4 tonne vehicles used by the Eastern Division.

Transport department costs are budgeted at:

	£
Manager's salary and fringe costs	18,000
Staff salaries wages and fringe costs	96,000
Insurance and tax	10,000
Depreciation	7,600
Fuel	24,000
Maintenance	8,000
Establishment costs[a]	25,000
Personnel and accounting costs[a]	9,000
	197,600

[a] Allocated from central costs of the company.

The chief executive and financial controller have decided to design a transfer pricing system to recover the transport department costs. Assuming that full loads (which all departments aspire to and nearly always achieve) are planned for next year, the charge out could be done by calculating the tonne mile capability and dividing this into the budgeted departmental cost to yield a price per tonne mile. Tonnes shipped are forecast as follows:

Division	Miles	Tonnes Per Mile	Tonne Miles
Northern	50,000	10	500,000
Western	30,000	6	180,000
Eastern	20,000	4	80,000
Tonne miles shipped			760,000

Cost per tonne mile is budgeted at:

$$\frac{197,600}{760,000} = 26p$$

A meeting is convened to introduce the transfer pricing system to the transport manager and the user division managers. On hearing the proposal, the following were some of the printable comments:

1 *Sam Speed (transport manager):* 'Because of late changes in loads

I do not always achieve full shipments. 26p per tonne mile will not recover all my costs which are tightly budgeted. I calculate that if we hit 90% loadings the price should be 29p.'

2 *Norman North (division manager):* 'This proposal is ridiculous. Up to now I have had free transport. Do you expect me to pay £130,000 for what I got for nothing previously? A pal of mine has been pressing me to give him my haulage for 20p per tonne mile. I think I will accept his offer.'

3 *Willie West (division manager):* 'The proposal seems sensible but I reckon these associated overheads are a con job. Why don't you drop out the imaginary(!) £34,000 (establishment, personnel and accounting) and charge out 21p or thereabouts? Norman might accept that rather than going to his pal.'

4 *Eddie East (division manager):* 'Willie's idea is good but it doesn't go all the way. We all know the 10 tonne "gas guzzlers" cause excessive fuel, insurance and maintenance costs. Why not charge Norman 25p and Willie and myself 18p? That should leave everybody happy.'

You would need the wisdom of Solomon to reconcile these comments. If you tried to address these problems and propose a solution, further issues would emerge at the next meeting. Rather than try to solve the problem, we will try to tackle some of the issues.

First, overhead loadings to service departments for onward passage to user departments are an explosive issue. In this example £25,000 of the establishment cost and £9,000 of the personnel and accounting cost is being allocated to the transport department. I believe that if overhead costs must be charged to production or sales departments, it should be done direct rather than through a service department.

Secondly, some departmental costs might be more fairly and accurately recovered by direct charge. In our example each department was using its own size trucks. It would be possible to set up direct charges for: truck staff wages and fringe costs; fuel; insurance and tax; maintenance; and depreciation. This would be time-consuming and expensive but it should avoid arguments.

Finally, a difficulty arises with transfer pricing where poor capacity utilisation is involved. This can be illustrated by doing a revised budget for the transport department assuming that Norman subcontracts his deliveries to his friend:

	£
Manager's salary and fringe costs	18,000
Staff salaries and fring costs	64,000[a]
Insurance and tax	6,000[b]
Depreciation	4,400[b]
Fuel	14,500[b]
Maintenance	4,800[b]
Establishment	25,000
Personnel and accounting	9,000
	145,700
Add 500,000 tonne miles at 20p subcontracted	100,000
	245,700

[a] Staff servicing Northern division redeployed.
[b] Reduced because of disposal of Division North vehicle.

The revised budget highlights two core issues in framing a transfer pricing policy:

1   If Norman subcontracts his deliveries he will save $500,000 \times 6p$ = £30,000. The company will spend £48,100 more than the original budget. What is good for the North Division is bad for the company overall. The proposal fails to achieve 'Goal congruence'.

2   £145,700 must be allocated to the Western and Eastern Divisions. They will be transporting goods for 260,000 tonne miles. The charge out rate rises to $145,700 \div 260,000$ = 56p. The transport division fixed costs of management (£18,000), establishment (£25,000), and personnel/accounting costs (£9,000) may be justifiable when 100,000 tonne miles are available. It cannot be economic to service 34,000 tonne miles with the same fixed cost structure, if the Northern Division opts out.

Possible options include:

1   Impose the proposed system.
2   Modify it by recovering establishment, personnel and accounting costs in a different way.
3   Set up the dedicated vehicles as cost recovery centres, with or without overheads.
4   Charge out at actual rather than budgeted cost as in 3 above.
5   Charge market prices less an appropriate discount. The market price includes a profit element.

6   Scrap the idea. Treat transport as a central overhead which effectively makes it 'free' to user departments.

There is no ideal solution. The company may be forced to impose a solution and place an embargo on individual actions (such as the Northern Division subcontracting its deliveries), if they add to the overall corporate cost.

If the company decides to proceed with transfer pricing it will have to be prepared to impose some potentially unpopular rules. These rules must be designed to forestall actions by divisions which are not congruent with organisational goals. Imposed rules are particularly dangerous in situations where remuneration is affected by divisional performance.

Method 2: Profit Centres

The profit centre approach is designed to earn a profit from charges to user departments and third party customers. User departments may or may not have the option of buying from outside suppliers.

A PROFIT CENTRE TRANSFER PRICING SYSTEM

We will use all the same basic data as in the cost centre illustration. The transport department is required to make a 20% profit from selling its services. If all the transport capacity is used by the operating divisions, it will be necessary to add one quarter to the budget cost to determine the charge out rate:

	Overall Cost £	Tonne Mile Cost p
Budget	197,600	26.0
Mark up 25%	49,400	6.5
Charge out rate	247,000	32.5

Issues that arise using a profit centre approach include:
1   If the managers were dissatisfied with a 26p charge out rate, they will be even less prepared to accept 32.5p.
2   The transport manager will need authority to sell to third parties so as to utilise capacity in slack periods. This can cause the following headaches:

(a) Vehicles not available for divisional deliveries due to previous pledges to third parties:

(b) Additional marketing and servicing costs for third party customers; and

(c) Placing outside customers at the top or bottom of the queue for vehicles can cause serious problems.

3 Outsiders, with low overheads, may offer keener prices. If deliveries are subcontracted to them, is the company prepared to reduce or close down the service department?

The options are similar to those in the cost centre section. The principles of effective transfer pricing are:

1 The system must ensure that no action will be taken that results in an increased cost for the service to the overall company.

2 The issue of under utilised capacity must be addressed if it arises.

3 There is a strong case for using market price as the charge out rate. This forces departments to operate efficiently.

4 Managers must believe the purposes of the system are to help in comparing own supply with subcontract alternatives, and to maximise efficiency.

5 Managers who try to manipulate the system to flatter departmental performance must be stopped.

6 When using a self-sufficient cost centre or a profit centre system, value for money obtained from service departments must be reassessed on a regular basis.

Method 3: Investment Centres

In the profit centre illustration we assumed that a 20% mark up would provide the transport division with an adequate profit. Investment centres measure divisional profitability using ROI. It involves breaking down the company revenue, costs, assets and liabilities to smaller business units. This should motivate divisional managers to seek value for money from the financial structure of the investment centre.

A client of mine operated until about three years ago as a single enterprise. The revenues and costs were each about £300 million and the asset base was £350 million. The company was then divided into seven investment centres. Each unit was structured as an operating subsidiary of the holding company. In spite of the major rows that arose in allocating the revenues, costs, assets and liabilities to business units, the company has operated more successfully in the last three years: sales volume rose more quickly than predicted; costs were more tightly controlled (notably through a reduction in restrictive practices); and the growth in fixed and current assets slowed down.

The major reason for the transformation was that divisional managers felt that they could significantly influence performance in the smaller business units. Previously an apathetic attitude had arisen that to increase sales or reduce costs only created more funds for other managers to waste. I described the purpose of investment centres rather than giving an illustration. This is because the breakdown of revenues, costs, assets and liabilities is a very complicated company-specific issue.

If a company is prepared to fight the inevitable battles involved in creating investment centres it can expect to achieve much improved financial performance. Do not underestimate the trauma of conception and infancy.

International Transfer Pricing

The creation of production units to supply subsidiaries abroad has led to special pricing considerations:

1   The country where profits are taken can have a significant impact on the corporate tax bill. Tax rates vary considerably, even within the European Community. To minimise group tax liabilities organisations are encouraged to sell part-manufactured goods to sister companies in tax havens at low prices. They finish them and sell them to third parties at high prices. Artificial, tax-based, transfer pricing can have the following adverse consequences:
    (a)   Pressure for enormous wage settlements because of the 'paper' profits earned;
    (b)   Inadequate attention to cost control. Cost saving initiatives may seem insignificant relative to profitability; and
    (c)   Expensive litigation where tax authorities/governments feel the transfer pricing system is unfairly designed to dilute their tax collection potential.
2   Subsidiaries, in various countries, bidding against each other for the right to make new corporate products, paying scant attention to the real cost structure involved.
3   The manufacturing unit can lose sight of changing consumer requirements. Organisations must be involved with end-users to sharpen their awareness of product relevance and encourage appropriate new product development.
4   The network of marketing and overhead costs in other countries is often transferred to the production units through complicated cost or profit centre mechanisms. The danger of divisiveness arising

from transfer pricing within a company multiplies, when the costs are transferred from relatively invisible units abroad.

An international transfer pricing policy must be carefully designed to address the needs of various stakeholders: group shareholders; divisional managers and employees; tax authorities in various countries; and suppliers, banks etc.

A detailed illustration is not appropriate because an effective system must be tailored to company needs and the details of such systems are usually closely-guarded secrets.

Chapter 11

Contribution Costing

In Chapter 10 we defined fixed, variable and semi-variable (also called semi-fixed or mixed) costs. These cost types provide the basis for contribution costing developed in this chapter. Initially we will look at contribution costing in a one-product business. Subsequently we will apply it in a multi-product situation. Consider the following data:

1 Over the next year a trading company budgets its material cost at £10 per unit.
2 Other variable costs (per unit £) will be piece work labour 4 and other variable costs 1.
3 Fixed costs total £100,000.
4 Production capacity is 600,000 units.
5 Selling price per unit is £20.

The managing director has asked us to calculate the profit or loss that will be earned if the following units are sold: 10,000, 20,000, 30,000 and 40,000.

Profit and Loss Accounts

Sales volume (units)	10,000	20,000	30,000	40,000
Unit selling price (£)	20	20	20	20
Total sales revenue	200,000	400,000	600,000	800,000
Variable costs				
Material	100,000	200,000	300,000	400,000
Labour	40,000	80,000	120,000	160,000
Other	10,000	20,000	30,000	40,000
	150,000	300,000	450,000	600,000
Contribution	50,000	100,000	150,000	200,000
Fixed cost	100,000	100,000	100,000	100,000
Profit/(loss)	(50,000)	–	50,000	100,000

These results can be obtained more easily using a contribution approach. Contribution is what is left after variable cost has been paid for. In this case the contribution is £5 per unit. Each unit sold will contribute £5 towards the fixed costs – 20,000 units will contribute £100,000 and exactly cover the fixed cost. This is called the break even point. Each additional item beyond the break even sales will contribute £5 profit.

The Contribution Shortcut

Sales volume (units)	10,000	20,000	30,000	40,000
Unit contribution				
Revenue 20				
Variable 15				
Contribution	5	5	5	5
Total contribution	50,000	100,000	150,000	200,000
Fixed cost	100,000	100,000	100,000	100,000
Profit/(loss)	(50,000)	–	50,000	100,000

We can prepare the following contribution and profit forecasts at various volumes:

Units Sold	Contribution Per Unit (£)	Total Contribution	Fixed Cost	Loss	Profit
1	5	5	100,000	99,995	–
2	5	10	100,000	99,990	–
5	5	25	100,000	99,975	–
100	5	500	100,000	99,500	–
1,000	5	5,000	100,000	95,000	–
10,000[a]	5	50,000	100,000	50,000	–
19,999	5	99,995	100,000	5	–
20,000[a]	5	100,000	100,000	–	–
20,001	5	100,005	100,000	–	5
25,000	5	125,000	100,000	–	25,000
35,000	5	175,000	100,000	–	75,000
50,000	5	250,000	100,000	–	150,000

[a] These can be verified against our profit and loss or contribution results previously.

The results can be prepared in a graphical form (see Fig. 11.1). This shows: (a) the loss declining at the rate of £5 per unit as sales volume rises from 1 to 19,999; (b) the total cost equalling the revenue at a volume of 20,000; and (c) the profit growing at the rate of £5 per unit from 20,001 upwards.

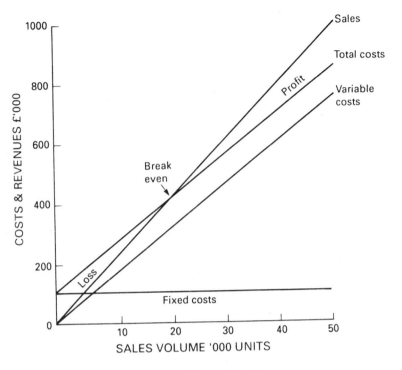

Fig. 11.1 Contribution-based Profit/Loss Graph

This graph shows that where 20,000 units are sold the sales revenue of £400,000 is exactly equal to the sum of the variable costs (£300,000) and the fixed costs (£100,000). When volume of sales rises above 20,000, the revenue exceeds total cost and the profit earned is determined by dropping a line from the sales revenue at any volume to the total cost at that volume, i.e.:

Volume	Revenue	Total Cost	Profit
20,001	400,020	400,015	5
30,000	600,000	550,000	50,000
35,000	700,000	625,000	75,000
40,000	800,000	700,000	100,000
45,000	900,000	775,000	125,000
49,999	999,980	849,985	149,995
50,000	1,000,000	850,000	150,000

When sales volume falls below 20,000 we can determine the loss by dropping a line from the total cost at any volume to the sales revenue at that volume, i.e.:

Sales Volume	Sales Revenue	Total Cost	Loss
5,000	100,000	175,000	75,000
10,000	200,000	250,000	50,000
15,000	300,000	325,000	25,000
19,999	399,980	399,985	5

If the budget is set at 40,000 units, a profit of £100,000 is to be expected. Sales can decline by up to 50% (to 20,000 units) before the company starts to incur a loss. This percentage difference between the budgeted volume and the break even volume is called the margin of safety.

If the budget had been set at 21,000, the margin of safety is only 5% and the business is much more risky.

The Contribution Sales Ratio

To set profit targets for a business we can use a contribution sales ratio. This ratio is developed as follows.

DEFINITION 1: CONTRIBUTION

Contribution is what is left after paying for variable costs:

Units Sold	Sales Revenue[a]	Variable Cost[b]	Contribution[c]
1	20	15	5
2	40	30	10
5	100	75	25
100	2,000	1,500	500
1,000	20,000	15,000	5,000
10,000	200,000	150,000	50,000
20,000	400,000	300,000	100,000

[a] Units sold×£20.
[b] Units sold×£15.
[c] Units sold×£5.

DEFINITION 2: CONTRIBUTION SALES RATIO

The percentage which total contribution is of sales revenue. When selling prices and variable costs are constant, this ratio will be the same at any volume:

Units Sold	Total Contribution	Total Sales Revenue	Contribution Sales Ratio (%)
1	5	20	25
200	1,000	4,000	25
5,000	25,000	100,000	25

This can also be expressed as 1:4. The complementary variable cost/sales ratio is 3:4 or 75%.

Based on this we can develop the formula: C.S. Ratio×(Sales Units×Sales Price Per Unit) = Fixed Cost+Profit. Using this formula we will answer a range of management questions:

1   *What is the break even sales revenue?*
    25%×Sales Revenue (Sales Units×£20) = 100,000+0
    25% of sales = 100,000, so Sales = £400,000.
    Here we are using four known facts to define the volume: (a) selling price £20; (b) variable cost £15; (c) fixed cost £100,000; and (d) profit 0. We need to sell 20,000 units at £20 each to break even. This corresponds with our break even chart.

2   *What will we need to sell to earn a profit of £20,000?*
    25% of sales = £100,000+£20,000,
    or 25% of sales = 120,000, so sales = £480,000.
    This is 24,000 units at £20 each, and this can be verified as follows:

	£
Sales 24,000×£20	480,000
Variable 24,000×£15	360,000
Contribution	120,000
Fixed	100,000
Profit	20,000

3 *What will be the break even sales volume if the material cost rises to £11 (Total variable £16)?*
The contribution sales ratio becomes 20% (£4 contribution from £20 sales), so 20% of sales = £100,000 and sales must be £500,000 or 25,000 units. This is verified as follows:

	£
Sales 25,000×£20	500,000
Variable 25,000×£16	400,000
Contribution and fixed	100,000

4 *Given the rise in variable cost to £16 what will we need to sell to earn a £20,000 profit?*
20% of sales = £100,000+£20,000. Sales must be £600,000 or 30,000 units.

5 *If we increase the selling price to £25 with a £15 variable cost what will be the result if sales are: (a) £100,000; (b) £200,000; (c) £250,000; (d) £300,000; and (e) £500,000?*
The contribution sales ratio is now $\dfrac{£10}{£25}$ % = 40%.

The results are:
(a) 40% of £100,000 = £100,000+P
     P = −£60,000. We lose £60,000.
(b) 40% of £200,000 = £100,000+P
     P = −£20,000. We lose £20,000.
(c) 40% of £250,000 = £100,000+P
     P = 0. We break even.
(d) 40% of £300,000 = £100,000+P
     P = £20,000 profit.
(e) 40% of £500,000 = £100,000+P
     P = £100,000 profit.

We can obtain answers in units by dividing the unit contribution into the fixed cost and profit requirement. Unit answers are less often used for management profit planning purposes than £ answers. I would like you to concentrate on the contribution sales ratio method. However, the five questions are confirmed using the unit contribution approach as follows:

1
$$\frac{\text{Fixed Costs £100,000} + \text{Profit £0}}{\text{Unit Contribution £5}} = 20,000 \text{ units}$$
This requires sales revenue of £400,000.

2
$$\frac{\text{Fixed Costs £100,000} + \text{Profit £20,000}}{\text{Unit Contribution £5}} = 24,000 \text{ units}$$
This requires sales revenue of £480,000.

3
$$\frac{\text{Fixed Costs £100,000} + \text{Profit 0}}{\text{Unit Contribution £4}} = 25,000 \text{ units}$$
This requires sales revenue of £500,000.

4
$$\frac{\text{Fixed Costs £100,000} + \text{Profit £20,000}}{\text{Unit Contribution £4}} = 30,000 \text{ units}$$
This requires sales revenue of £600,000.

5a
$$\frac{\text{Fixed Costs £100,000} - \text{Loss £60,000}}{\text{Unit Contribution £10}} = 4,000 \text{ units}$$
This gives sales revenue of £100,000.

5b
$$\frac{\text{Fixed Costs £100,000} - \text{Loss £20,000}}{\text{Unit Contribution £10}} = 8,000 \text{ units}$$
This gives sales revenue of £200,000.

5c
$$\frac{\text{Fixed costs £100,000}}{\text{Unit Contribution £10}} = 10,000 \text{ units}$$
This gives sales revenue of £250,000.

5d
$$\frac{\text{Fixed Costs £100,000} + \text{Profit £20,000}}{\text{Unit Contribution £10}} = 12,000 \text{ units}$$
This gives sales revenue of £300,000.

5e
$$\frac{\text{Fixed Costs £100,000} + \text{Profit £100,000}}{\text{Unit Contribution £10}} = 20,000 \text{ units}$$
This gives sales revenue of £500,000.

Inclusion of Semi-fixed Costs in One-product Contribution Analysis

The fixed cost of £100,000 is made up of two different components in this illustration: (a) basic fixed costs of £50,000; and (b) additional (rentals of equipment and space) of £50,000 to produce and sell up to 20,000 units and £50,000 for each additional production and sales increment of 20,000 units.

Using our original selling price of £20 and variable cost of £15 we get the following results:

Sales Quantity	Unit Sales Price	Sales Revenue	25% C.S.Ratio	Fixed Cost	Profit/ (Loss)
10,000	20	200,000	50,000	100,000	(50,000)
20,000[a]	20	400,000	100,000	100,000	–
20,000[a]	20	400,000	100,000	150,000	(50,000)
20,001	20	400,020	100,005	150,000	(49,995)
30,000	20	600,000	150,000	150,000	–
40,000[a]	20	800,000	200,000	150,000	50,000
40,000[a]	20	800,000	200,000	200,000	–
40,001	20	800,020	200,005	200,000	5
50,000	20	1,000,000	250,000	200,000	50,000
60,000	20	1,200,000	300,000	200,000	100,000

[a] The result in this case is dependent on whether the fixed cost is structured to meet the higher or lower capacity.

We find that there are three separate break even points as the organisation increases its ability to produce and sell. These occur at 20,000, 30,000 and 40,000 units respectively. The profit and loss situation is best represented in graphic form (see Fig. 11.2).

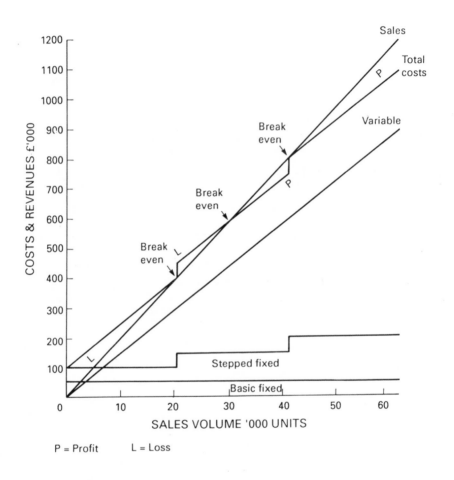

Fig 11.2 Results with Semi-fixed Costs

314

To use the contribution sales ratio in this case we must divide the output into ranges:

	Range 1 0– 20,000	Range 2 20,001– 40,000	Range 3 40,001– 60,000
Fixed cost	100,000	150,000	200,000
C.S. ratio	25%	25%	25%
Break even sales (£)	400,000	600,000	800,000
Break even sales (units)	20,000	30,000	40,000
To earn £20,000 profit the contribution must be (£)	120,000	170,000	220,000
The sales £ must be	480,000	680,000	880,000
The sales quantities are	Out of range	34,000	44,000

Fixed costs grow in steps as volume rises. This type of fixed cost growth structure often occurs. It is related to an organisation's capacity to meet consumer demand. Types of fixed cost that can expand in this way include:

1 *Area costs* (essentially fixed): growing if you need a greater area.
2 *Fixed production costs:* supervision; quality control; production management (assistants!); and machine costs, depreciation, maintenance contracts and insurance.
3 *Administration costs:* additional accounting and personnel staff.
4 *Fixed selling and distribution costs:* warehouse and display space; and transport fixed costs – depreciation (more vehicles), tax and insurance (more vehicles) and more drivers.

Three additional items are now included in the cost and revenue structure to complete the picture:

1 The production capacity is 100,000 units;
2 If sales are to exceed 60,000, the selling price will have to be reduced to £19 per unit; and
3 If production exceeds 50,000, the variable costs will rise to £15.20. This is caused by an 80p reduction in unit material cost and a £1 increase in unit labour cost.

Sales Units	Sales Revenue	25% Contri- bution	24% Contri- bution	20% Contri- bution	Fixed Costs	Profit/ (Loss)
20,000	400,000	100,000			100,000	–
20,001	400,020	100,005			150,000	(49,995)
30,000	600,000	150,000			150,000	–
40,000	800,000	200,000			150,000	50,000
40,001	800,020	200,005			200,000	5
50,000	1,000,000	250,000			200,000	50,000
50,001	1,000,020		240,005		200,000	40,005
60,000	1,200,000		288,000		200,000	88,000
60,001	1,140,019			228,004	250,000	(21,996)
70,000	1,330,000			266,000	250,000	16,000
80,000	1,520,000			304,000	250,000	54,000
80,001	1,520,019			304,004	300,000	4,004
90,000	1,710,000			342,000	300,000	42,000
100,000	1,900,000			380,000	300,000	80,000

This table shows the impact of the cost increase when production exceeds 50,000 units and the price reduction when sales exceed 60,000 units. If we sell 100,000 units the profit will be lower than that obtainable from 60,000 units. We would have to sell 100,000 units at £19.08 to obtain the same profit as we expect to earn if 60,000 units are sold at £20 each. This illustration questions the wisdom of reducing selling price to stimulate demand. £1 of contribution is given away on your existing sales to get extra business. Additional working capital support is also required. The results are now shown in graphic form (see Figs. 11.3–11.5). A division into five segments shows the effect of changes in the cost and revenue structure.

Segment	Unit Volume Scale	Cost/Revenue Scale
1	0– 20,000	0– £400,000
2	20,000– 40,000	£400,000– £800,000
3	40,000– 60,000	£700,000–£1,200,000
4	60,000– 80,000	£1,050,000–£1,600,000
5	80,000–100,000	£1,450,000–£1,900,000

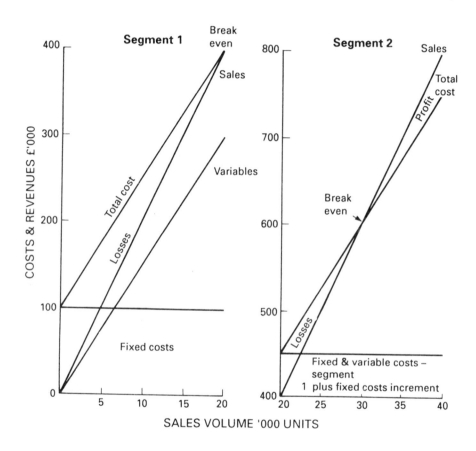

Fig. 11.3   Break Even for Fluctuating Costs and Prices, Segments 1 and 2

317

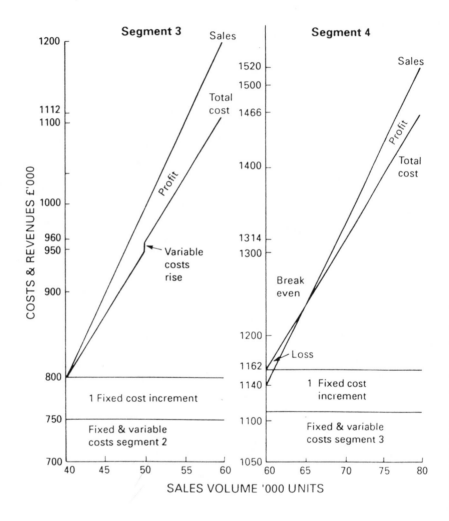

Fig. 11.4 Break Even for Fluctuating Costs and Prices, Segments 3 and 4

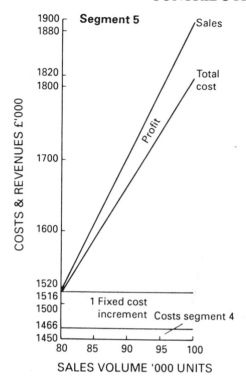

Fig. 11.5 Break Even for Fluctuating Costs and Prices, Segments 4 and 5

Profit Planning: More Than One Product

When a business sells more than one product or the same product in different sizes, it often obtains a higher contribution sales ratio from some lines than others. Margin variations make the setting of profit targets slightly more difficult. We will look at a business which sells 'widgets' in three different sizes. Details of the products are as follows:

	Mini Widget 100 cc	Standard Widget 500 cc	Maxi Widget 1.5 litre
Unit selling price (£)	1.00	4.00	10.00
Unit variable cost (£)	0.60	2.80	8.00
Unit contribution (£)	0.40	1.20	2.00

The fixed costs are £99,000. The proprietor wants to establish the break even sales target.

If he sells only one product, he finds that the break even sales target

319

rises as the pack size increases. This is because the contribution sales ratio falls:

	Mini	Standard	Maxi
C.S. ratio	40%	30%	20%
Break even sales (£)	247,500	330,000	495,000

With a mixture of sales the average contribution ratio will be somewhere between 20% and 40%. He needs to forecast the proportion of sales revenue from each pack size to establish the break even sales. On the basis of recent experience the proprietor forecasts that the mix will be: 50% of turnover Mini widgets; 30% of turnover Standard widgets; and 20% of turnover Maxi widgets.

Based on this forecast he can calculate a weighted average contribution sales ratio. If he assumes sales of £100,000, he can forecast his overall contribution as follows:

	Total	Mini	Standard	Maxi
Sales	100,000	50,000	30,000	20,000
Variable	67,000	= 30,000 (60%) +	21,000 (70%) +	16,000(80%)
Contribution	33,000	= 20,000(40%) +	9,000(30%) +	4,000(20%)

Adding the variable costs for the three sizes he obtains an overall figure of £67,000. This leaves an overall contribution of £33,000 or a weighted average contribution sales ratio of 33%. A turnover of £300,000 is required to break even. This is illustrated in Fig. 11.6.

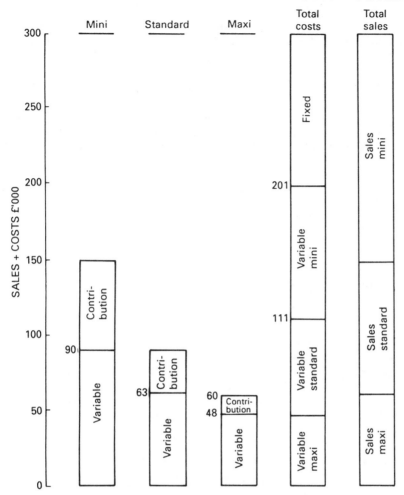

Fig. 11.6 Widget Break Even

This does not mean that a fixed overhead allocation in proportion to sales revenue will leave each product at break even. The following product profits and losses would result from such a fixed cost apportionment:

	Mini	*Standard*	*Maxi*	*Total*
Sales	150,000	90,000	60,000	300,000
Variables	90,000	63,000	48,000	201,000
Contribution	60,000	27,000	12,000	99,000
Fixed cost allocation	49,500	29,700	19,800	99,000
Profit/(loss)	10,500	(2,700)	(7,800)	–

321

Nor does it mean that overheads are allocated in proportion to variable costs. This would give the following product profits and losses:

	Mini	Standard	Maxi	Total
Contribution as above	60,000	27,000	12,000	99,000
Fixed cost allocation[a]	44,328	31,030	23,642	99,000
Profit/(loss)	15,672	(4,030)	(11,642)	–

[a] The fixed cost recovery rate is $99,000 \div 201,000 = 49.25\%$. Mini: £90,000×49.25% = £44,328. Standard: £63,000×49.25% = £31,030. Maxi: £48,000×49.25% = £23,642.

The correct recovery of fixed costs will be based on product contributions as follows:

	Mini	Standard	Maxi	Total
Contribution as above	60,000	27,000	12,000	99,000
Overhead recovery rate	60,000	27,000	12,000	99,000
	–	–	–	–

Weighted Average Contribution Sales Ratios (a short cut)

There is a simple mathematical approach to determining the weighted average contribution sales ratio. It involves looking at the impact of each product on the business as follows:

	Product C.S.Ratio (A)	Proportion of Total Sales (B)	Contribution to Total Business (A × B)
Mini	40%	50%	20%
Standard	30%	30%	9%
Maxi	20%	20%	4%
Weighted average contribution			33%

When he heard the break even sales were £300,000 the owner asked a number of questions: the first was 'I want a profit of £33,000. What will I have to sell?' The answer is £400,000. This is derived from the formula we learned earlier: 33% sales = £99,000+£33,000. So sales must be 132,000×(100/33) = £400,000. This can be proved by a product profit and loss account:

	Mini		Standard		Maxi		Total
Sales	200,000		120,000		80,000		400,000
Contribution	80,000	+	36,000	+	16,000	=	132,000
Fixed							99,000
Profit							33,000

The next question was 'If 10% of turnover shifts from the Mini to the Maxi widget (a) what will be my break even sales and (b) what will I have to sell to earn £25,000 profit?' The shift from high contribution Mini to lower contribution Maxi will reduce the weighted average contribution as follows:

	Product Contribution Sales Ratio (A)	Proportion of Total Sales (B)	Contribution to Total Business (A × B)
Mini	40%	40%	16%
Standard	30%	30%	9%
Maxi	20%	30%	6%
			31%

The break even is derived from the formula: 31% sales = 99,000, so sales must be £319,354.83. This can be proved as follows:

	Mini		Standard		Maxi		Total
Sales	127,741.93		95,806.45		95,806.45		319,354.83
Contribution	51,096.78	+	28,741.93	+	19,161.29	=	99,000.00
Fixed							99,000.00
Break even							–

These exact figures cannot be achieved at the planned selling prices. The answer to the nearest pack sizes is:

	Mini		Standard		Maxi	Total
Sales	127,742.00		95,808.00		95,810.00	319,360.00
Contribution	51,096.80	+	28,742.40	+	19,162.00	99,001.20

To earn a profit of £25,000 he must sell: 31% of sales = £99,000+ £25,000 so sales = £400,000. This is proved as follows:

	Mini	Standard	Maxi	Total
Sales	160,000	120,000	120,000	400,000
Contribution	64,000	36,000	24,000	124,000
Fixed				99,000
Profit				25,000

In answering question one we found that sales of £400,000 would provide a profit of £33,000. This falls to £25,000 as demand shifts from the Mini to the Maxi widget. The weighted average contribution sales ratio has dropped from 33% to 31%. This shows that targets based on a predetermined mix need to be adjusted if the actual mix is different. The owner would need to sell £425,806 to clear £33,000 from the new mix.

Next, the owner remembered seeing that the Standard and Maxi widget incurred losses if fixed costs were allocated in proportion to revenue. He asks: 'What would happen to break even if the selling prices of the Standard and Maxi widget were increased to £4.50 and £11.50 respectively?' We will assume the mix of turnover remains as originally planned. The mix of demand might change in practice. Percentage results will be awkward so we will express the contribution sales ratios in fractions. The new weighted average contribution sales ratio is:

	C.S.Ratio (A)	Mix (B)	Contribution (A×B)
Mini	4/10	5/10	2/10
Standard	17/45[a]	3/10	51/450
Maxi	35/115[b]	2/10	7/115
Weighted average			1936.5/5175

	(a)	(b)
[a,b]Unit Sales Price	4.50	11.50
Unit Variable	2.80	8.00
Unit Contribution	1.70	3.50
C.S.Ratio	17/45	35/115

The break even sales target becomes: 1936.5/5175% of sales = £99,000. Sales must be approximately £264,562. This can be verified from a product profit and loss:

	Mini	Standard	Maxi	Total
Sales	132,281	79,369	52,912	264,562
Contribution	52,912 +	29,984 +	16,104 =	99,000
Fixed				99,000
				–

Finally, the purchasing manager has heard that a 10% increase in the cost of materials is to be made by suppliers. This is the only variable expense in the business. The owner wishes the sales target required to (a) break even and (b) earn a profit of £19,350 if price increases take place. The revised contribution sales ratio becomes:

	Mini	Standard	Maxi
Unit sales price (£)	1.00	4.00	10.00
New unit variable costs (£)	0.66	3.08	8.80
New unit contributions (£)	0.34	0.92	1.20
New product C.S.ratio (%)	34	23	12

The weighted average contribution sales ratio becomes:

	C.S.Ratio (A)	Mix (B)	Contribution (A×B)
Mini	34%	50%	17.0%
Standard	23%	30%	6.9%
Maxi	12%	20%	2.4%
			26.3%

The break even becomes: 26.3% of sales = £99,000 and sales must be £376,426. The profit and loss account becomes:

	Mini	Standard	Maxi	Total
Sales	188,213	112,928	75,285	376,426
Contribution	63,992	25,973	9,035	99,000
Fixed				99,000
				–

To earn a profit of £19,350 the sales target is: 26.3% of sales = £99,000 + £19,350. Sales must be £450,000 leading to this profit and loss account:

	Mini	Standard	Maxi	Total
Sales	225,000	135,000	90,000	450,000
Contribution	76,500	31,050	10,800	118,350
Fixed				99,000
Profit				19,350

As some organisations plan and control operations in quantities we will now re-answer the four questions assuming that the forecast sales mix is in quantities not £. This will result in a different weighted average contribution sales ratio and change the sales targets. To compute the weighted average contribution we will assume that 1,000 widgets are sold:

	Mini	Standard	Maxi	Total
Packs sold	500	300	200	1,000
Sales revenue	500	1,200	2,000	3,700
Contribution	200	360	400	960

The weighted average CS ratio 960/3700 = 25.94594%. This is very much lower than the average with the original mix. With a low proportion of sales (13.5% approx.) being derived from the high contribution Mini widget the margins are as follows:

	C.S. Ratio (A)	Mix (B)	Total (A×B)
Mini	40%	13.51351%	5.40541%
Standard	30%	32.43243%	9.72972%
Maxi	20%	54.05405%	10.81081%
			25.94594%

To earn a profit of £33,000 (Q1) we need sales of: 25.94594% of sales = £99,000 + £33,000. Sales must be £508,750. This is proved as follows:

	Mini	Standard	Maxi	Total
Packs sold	68,750	41,250	27,500	137,500
Sales revenue	68,750	165,000	275,000	508,750
Contribution	27,500	49,500	55,000	132,000
Fixed				99,000
Profit				33,000

The pack sales targets are obtained as follows: if 1,000 packs yield £3,700 revenue, then the average pack will yield £3.70. £508,750/£3.70 = 137,500 total pack sales.

The shift in demand from Mini to Maxi (Q2) will reduce the contribution sales ratio still further:

	Mini	Standard	Maxi	Total
Packs sold	400	300	300	1,000
Sales revenue	400	1,200	3,000	4,600
Contribution	160	360	600	1,120

C.S. ratio 24.34782%: Q2(a) break even sales £406,607; and Q2(b) sales to earn £25,000 profit = £509,286. The profit and loss account to give a profit of £25,000 is derived from the pack sales £509,285.84/ £4.60. Average pack sales yield = 110,714 packs:

	Mini	Standard	Maxi	Total
Pack sales	44,286	33,214	33,214	110,714
Sales revenue	44,286	132,856	332,140	509,282
Contribution	17,715	39,857	66,428	124,000
Fixed				99,000
Profit				25,000

The increase in selling price (Q3) raised the contribution margin on (a) Standard (b) Maxi and (c) weighted average. The new weighted average is:

	Mini	Standard	Maxi	Total
Pack sales	500	300	200	1,000
Sales revenue	500	1,350	2,300	4,150
Contribution	200	510	700	1,410

1410 ÷ 4150% = £99,000. The break even sales target is £291,383. The profit and loss budget becomes:

	Mini	Standard	Maxi	Total
Pack sales	35,106	21,064	14,043	70,213
Sales revenue	35,106	94,788	161,489	291,383
Contribution	14,042	35,808	49,150	99,000
Fixed				99,000
				—

The increase in variable costs (Q4) results in a contribution from 1,000 packs of:

	Mini	Standard	Maxi	Total
Packs	500	300	200	1,000
Sales revenue	500	1,200	2,000	3,700
CS ratio %	34	23	12	
Contribution	170	276	240	686

686÷3,700% of sales = £99,000. The break even sales must be £533,965. 686÷3,700% of sales = £118,350. To earn a profit of £19,350 we must sell £638,331.

Contrast of Sales Targets

			Money Mix	Product Mix
(1)		To earn £33,000 profit	400,000	508,750
(2)	(a)	To break even with sales 40:30:30:	319,355	406,607
	(b)	To earn £25,000 profit with sales 40:30:30:	400,000	509,286
(3)		To break even at higher selling prices	264,562	291,383
(4)	(a)	To break even at higher variable costs	376,426	533,965
	(b)	To earn £19,350 profit at higher variable costs	450,000	638,331

Dealing with a Large Range of Products

The following details relate to a range of 20 products:

Product	Unit Selling Price	Unit Variable Cost	CS Ratio	% of Total Sales	% Input to Weighted Contribution
1	5.00	4.00	20%	2.5	0.50
2	5.00	4.50	10%	3.5	0.35
3	5.00	3.60	28%	6.0	1.68
4	9.00	6.30	30%	7.5	2.25
5	9.00	7.20	20%	6.5	1.30
6	9.00	7.65	15%	5.0	0.75
7	12.00	10.80	10%	1.5	0.15
8	12.00	10.08	16%	5.0	0.80
9	15.00	9.00	40%	3.0	1.20
10	18.00	13.50	25%	4.0	1.00
11	20.00	17.00	15%	6.0	0.90
12	25.00	24.00	4%	8.0	0.32
13	32.00	28.16	12%	4.0	0.48
14	40.00	32.80	18%	3.5	0.63
15	50.00	39.00	22%	2.5	0.55
16	60.00	47.40	21%	4.0	0.84
17	80.00	71.20	11%	10.0	1.10
18	100.00	86.00	14%	8.5	1.19
19	120.00	109.20	9%	6.0	0.54
20	250.00	217.50	13%	3.0	0.39
				100.0	16.92

If the fixed costs are £33,840, the break even sales target is £200,000. 16.92% of sales = £33,840.

This could have been approximated by combining products with similar contribution sales ratios:

Range	Product	CS Ratio	Sales %	Simple Average	Simple Weighting
1	9	40	3.0	70%/2 = 35%	
	4	30	7.5	35%×10.5% =	3.675
		70	10.5		
2	3	28	6.0		
	10	25	4.0		
	15	22	2.5		
	16	21	4.0	136%/6 = 22.7	
	1	20	2.5	22.7×25.5% =	5.780
	5	20	6.5		
		136	25.5		
3	14	18	3.5		
	8	16	5.0		
	6	15	5.0		
	11	15	6.0		
	18	14	8.5		
	20	13	3.0	134%/10 = 13.4%	
	13	12	4.0	13.4%×50% =	6.700
	17	11	10.0		
	2	10	3.5		
	7	10	1.5		
		134	50.0		
4	19	9	6.0	13%/2 = 6.5%	
	12	4	8.0	6.5%×14%	0.910
		13	14.0		17.065

A contribution sales ratio based on the simple average for each product group gives a break even sales figure of £198,301. This underestimated the target by 0.85% – an insignificant error. A retailing organisation, selling thousands of products at varying contribution margins, would have to accept an error of this magnitude unless a computer programme had been developed to reduce the calculations involved to manageable proportions.

Limiting Factors

The contribution sales ratio can sometimes encourage a business to adopt an inappropriate marketing strategy. The ratio can be adapted to reflect the limiting factor, so as to overcome this defect. The limiting factor can be a shortage of:

1 Customer demand:
2 Supply of raw material;
3 Skilled labour;
4 Production machinery/space; or
5 Working capital finance.

We will now examine a business that sells four products:

	Product			
	1	2	3	4
	£	£	£	£
Unit selling price	1.00	2.00	5.00	10.00
Unit material	0.60	0.50	3.75	4.50
Unit labour	0.10	1.00	0.25	4.00
Unit contribution	0.30	0.50	1.00	1.50
Production hours	2	3	4	3.6
Working capital/ sales %	40	20	25	10

If the limiting factor is customer demand of £100,000 then sales staff should try to encourage customers towards product one because it maximises contribution:

	Product			
	1	2	3	4
Sales	100,000	100,000	100,000	100,000
Contribution (CS ratio)	30	25	20	15
Contribution	30,000	25,000	20,000	15,000
Promotional sequence	(a)	(b)	(c)	(d)

If the same material is used in all four products and only £47,250 of this material is expected to be available, then sales staff should try to

332

encourage customers towards product 2 because it maximises contribution:

	Product			
	1	*2*	*3*	*4*
Material	47,250	47,250	47,250	47,250
Contribution/ material ratio[1] (%)	50	100	26.7	33.3
Contribution	23,625	**47,250**	12,600	15,750
Promotional sequence	(b)	(a)	(d)	(c)

If the same production staff make all four products and only £19,500 of work can be produced, then sales staff should try to encourage customers towards product 3 because it maximises contribution:

	Product			
	1	*2*	*3*	*4*
Skilled labour	19,500	19,500	19,500	19,500
Contribution/ labour ratio[2] (%)	300	50	400	37.5
Contribution	58,500	9,750	**78,000**	7,313
Promotional sequence	(b)	(c)	(a)	(d)

If the four products are made on the same machine and 120,000 machine hours are available, then sales staff should try to encourage customers towards product 4 because it maximises contribution:

	Product			
	1	*2*	*3*	*4*
Production hours	120,000	120,000	120,000	120,000
Contribution per hour[3]	15p	16.7p	25p	41.7p
Contribution	18,000	20,000	30,000	**50,000**
Promotional sequence	(d)	(c)	(b)	(a)

If only £25,000 of working capital finance is available, then sales staff should try to encourage customers towards product 4 because it maximises contribution:

	Product			
	1	2	3	4
Working capital	25,000	25,000	25,000	25,000
Contribution per £ capital[4]	75%	125%	80%	150%
Contribution	18,750	31,250	20,000	**37,500**
Promotional sequence	(d)	(b)	(c)	(a)

The highlighted product maximises contribution in each limiting factor situation. The promotional sequence is indicated by the letters (a) = best to (d) = worst.

You will find that the display strategy in good retailers follows the principles outlined above. High contribution lines are given a lot of display space. Low contribution lines get little display space. Items in short supply also get little display space.

NOTES TO LIMITING FACTORS' TABLES

Material Supplies – Note 1

Unit contribution	£0.30	£0.50	£1	£1.50
Unit material	£0.60	£0.50	£3.75	£4.50
Contribution per £ materials	50%	100%	26.7%	33.3%

Skilled Workers – Note 2

Unit contribution	£0.30	£0.50	£1	£1.50
Unit labour	£0.10	£1.00	£0.25	£4.00
Contribution per £ labour	300%	50%	400%	37.5%

Production Hours – Note 3

Unit contribution	£0.30	£0.50	£1	£1.50
Hours per unit	2	3	4	3.6
Contribution per hour	15p	16.7p	25p	41.7p

334

Working Capital – Note 4

Unit contribution	£0.30	£0.50	£1	£1.50
Working capital per unit	£1×40%	£2×20%	£5×25%	£10×10%
Contribution per £ working capital	0.75	1.25	0.80	1.50

In spite of the implications of maximising contribution per £ of limiting factor a prudent business will try to sell a variety of products. If only one line is sold, a collapse in selling prices or an increase in variable costs could reduce earnings drastically. A portfolio of products offers protection against this danger. Secondly, customers get annoyed if a full range of products is not available. Finally, customers who intend to buy low contribution items often also make impulse purchases of high margin items. This is particularly important in retailing.

Operating Leverage

The final issue to be examined in this chapter is operating leverage. This is the ratio of contribution to profit. The ratio is 2:1 in company A and 7:1 in company B below:

	Budget Company A	Budget Company B
Sales	100,000	100,000
Variable costs	80,000	20,000
Contribution	20,000	80,000
Fixed costs	10,000	70,000
Profit	10,000	10,000

Company A is variable cost intensive (80% of sales). Company B is not (20% of sales). The impact of a 25% decline in sales is:

	Actual Company A	Actual Company B
Sales	75,000	75,000
Variable costs	60,000	15,000
Contribution	15,000	60,000
Fixed costs	10,000	70,000
Profit/(loss)	5,000	(10,000)

A recession would result in a substantial loss in company B. A profit would still be earned in company A, albeit halved. If the owners could arrange their support costs as either variable or fixed, it is clear that they should try to make as many as possible variable when the future demand is not promising.

Consider the impact of a 20% increase in sales budget:

	Actual Company A	Actual Company B
Sales	120,000	120,000
Variable	96,000	24,000
Contribution	24,000	96,000
Fixed	10,000	70,000
Profit	14,000	26,000

Company B will obtain a £16,000 increase in profits. Company A will get a £4,000 increase. If the owners could decide to arrange their support costs as either variable or fixed, it is clear that they should try to make as many as possible fixed when the future demand is promising. The results are affected by the operating leverage. The effect of leverage is that any percentage change in sales revenue will result in a change in profit of that percentage change in sales revenue, multiplied by operating leverage. Our example companies show that this is true:

	Change in Sales (%)	Operating Leverage	Change in Profit %	£	Budget Profit	Actual Profit
Lovely actual A	+20	2:1	+40	+4,000	10,000	14,000
Lovely actual B	+20	8:1	+160	+16,000	10,000	26,000
Gloomy actual A	−25	2:1	−50	−5,000	10,000	5,000
Gloomy actual B	−25	8:1	−200	−20,000	10,000	−10,000

This will be true for as long as the percentage change is measured against the original budget. If somewhat later when company B was achieving £120,000 of sales we were asked what would be the impact of a further 10% increase in sales, the answer would be a 37% profit increase. The operating leverage has become 96:26.

Can you use this knowledge to best capitalise on predicted market trends? Possibly! If the outlook for sales growth is promising it may be desirable to try to convert some of the variable costs into fixed in order to capitalise on the operating leverage effect and to avoid being ripped off by vendors in a sellers' market.

Variable costs that may be convertible include:

1 Manufacture of components previously bought in;
2 Transfer of piece-work operatives onto the payroll;
3 Cancellation of distribution contracts and replacement with own fleet; and
4 Creation of a maintenance function instead of using contract maintenance, etc

If the outlook is for a sustained decline in sales volume, it may be attractive to try to convert some fixed costs into variable, thereby reducing the operating leverage and capitalising on discounts offered by suppliers in a buyers' market. Fixed costs that might be convertible into variable include:

1 Subcontracting previous staff jobs. Many British businesses have placed their product distribution on contract during this decade.
2 Specialising in marketing, while allowing other businesses to manufacture your products. This is a feature of the corporate strategy of many large companies. It is particularly interesting in industries where a high quality 'just in time' system has developed.
3 Shifting from interest-bearing borrowings towards a higher equity base. This makes the payout a function of performance rather than

contractual obligation. The impact of such a refinancing proposal on company B is illustrated as follows:

(a) The fixed costs include interest on a £100,000 loan at 16% per annum;
(b) This is to be replaced with £100,000 of new equity;
(c) Company B, which currently has an equity base of £100,000, normally pays out half of its profit to shareholders by way of dividend; and
(d) Corporation tax is ignored.

	Pre-issue	Post-issue	Pre-issue 25% Decline	Post-issue 25% Decline
Sales	100,000	100,000	75,000	75,000
Variable	20,000	20,000	15,000	15,000
Contribution	80,000	80,000	60,000	60,000
Fixed	70,000	54,000	70,000	54,000
Profit/(loss)	10,000	26,000	(10,000)	6,000
Dividend	5,000	13,000	–	3,000
Retained	5,000	13,000	(10,000)	3,000

If volume declines this small company incurs a serious loss without the refinancing. The additional equity injection leaves company B in a better position. A small profit is earned and a tiny dividend can be paid.

As a second illustration we will assume that company A expects sales to double next year. It will need to raise £40,000 to finance additional assets as the sales increase. It can obtain this by way of loan costing 16%, or equity. Assuming a 50% dividend cover, and ignoring corporation tax which way should company A fund its expansion?

	Budget Company A	Budget Including New Debt	Budget Including New Equity
Sales	100,000	200,000	200,000
Variable	80,000	160,000	160,000
Contribution	20,000	40,000	40,000
Fixed	10,000	16,400	10,000
Profit	10,000	24,600	30,000
Dividend	5,000[a]	12,300[b]	15,000[c]
Retained	5,000	12,300	15,000

[a] 5% on the existing capital base £100,000.
[b] 12.3% on the existing capital base £100,000.
[c] 10.7% on the enlarged capital base £140,000.

If volumes remain high and the company is not overborrowed, the use of debt will be more attractive to shareholders.

These examples achieve two objectives:

1 They illustrate how new finance can change the operating leverage of a business beneficially (more debt as sales rise and less debt as sales fall); and

2 They show how new equity issues are not always in the best interests of shareholders. In company B it would be wisest to sell shares if the collapse in demand is foreseen. In company A additional debt is preferable unless the business is already overborrowed.

Chapter 12

Capital Investment Decisions

This chapter deals with the methodology for assessing capital investment proposals. The chapter is divided into five main sections:

1 Shows how to test the adequacy of returns based on cash forecasts.
2 Examines errors and risks associated with such cash forecasts.
3 Examines a straightforward approach to assessing the cost of capital in project appraisal.
4 Looks at the types of barriers that can be used to stop projects being undertaken which:
  (a) Do not promise an adequate return;
  (b) Are being commissioned without passing through the test and approval phase;
  (c) Although promising a good return, cannot be undertaken because all available funds have been committed to better projects.
5 Summarises the major rules involved in a good capital project appraisal policy.

Evaluating Capital Projects

The following data have been projected for a capital investment that is currently being evaluated by the Model Company:

1 *Capital cost:* New plant and machinery £400,000.
2 *Expected operating life:* 4 years.
3 *Forecast sales quantities and prices.*

Year	Units	Per Unit
1	1,000	£300
2	1,600	£300
3	2,500	£250
4	1,500	£250

The capacity of the machine is 3,000 units per annum.

4   Forecast operating costs (£'000)

Year	Materials	Labour	Other	Total
1	60	40	50	150
2	96	64	60	220
3	150	100	80	330
4	90	60	50	200

Should the company approve the proposal? The funding will require a return in excess of 15%. We will ignore corporation tax initially. Five major project evaluation techniques are applied to the proposal.

Method 1: Return on Investment

Forecast Profit and Loss Accounts (£'000)

	Years 1	2	3	4	Total
Sales	300	480	625	375	1,780
Materials	60	96	150	90	396
Labour	40	64	100	60	264
Other	50	60	80	50	240
Depreciation	100	100	100	100	400
Cost excluding interest	250	320	430	300	1,300
Profit before interest	50	160	195	75	480
Annual return on investment (£400,000)	12.5%	40%	48.75%	18.75%	

It is sometimes argued that the return should be based on the average investment (£200,000 in this case). This would result in a doubling of all the above ratios, e.g. 25% in year 1 etc.

Averaging can also be applied to the cash returns. Average return on investment is:

$$\frac{480}{400}\% = 120\% \text{ over 4 years} = 30\% \text{ per annum}$$

341

This could also be commmpared with the average amount at risk (£200,000) to give 60%.

Average return on investment is often taken as an indicator of good projects. It suffers from two serious problems. These problems are such that it should only be used to eliminate proposals that do not merit more detailed investigation. The problems are, first, that where profits emerge unevenly, it takes no account of the fact that early profits are more valuable than later ones. Early profits should provide additional income, through reinvestment. Contrast these two projects:

Year		A	B	Change in Profit if B Preferred
		£'000		
0	Total investment	300	300	
1	Profit before interest	80	140	+60
2	Profit before interest	90	110	+20
3	Profit before interest	110	90	−20
4	Profit before interest	140	80	−60
	Average annual profit	105	105	
	Average annual return on investment	8.75%	8.75%	

Project B is clearly better but return on investment does not recognise this fact.

The second problem with ROI is that it is very difficult to decide between projects with different lives. Consider these two examples:

Year		C £'000	D £'000	Change in Profit if Project C Preferred
0	Total investment	400	400	
1	Profit before interest	50	20	+30
2	Profit before interest	55	50	+5
3	Profit before interest	75	75	−
4	Profit before interest	−	47	−47
	Average annual profit	60	48	
	Average return on investment	15%	12%	

Which is better, 15% for 3 years or 12% for 4 years? Return on investment will not tell you. It all depends on what return can be obtained by reinvesting the early surpluses.

These illustrations point to the need for a more searching test of the timing of funds flows in capital investment appraisal. Conventional return on investment analysis cannot handle timing properly.

Method 2: Payback

Payback examines the flows of cash associated with the project. For the rest of this chapter we will use the convention year 0 to denote the time at which funds will start moving in or out of the business. We will assume that all cash flows occur at year-end in assessing the project. The payback in its simplest form is as follows:

Year			£'000
0	Capital investment		−400
1	Sales	300	
	Cash costs	−150	150
	Balance outstanding		−250
2	Sales	480	
	Cash costs	−220	260
			10

Before the end of year two, the net cash created more than repays the initial finance raised. The project has a payback of under two years. Note that since depreciation is not a cash cost it is excluded from the analysis.

Unfortunately the true payback is a bit more complicated. The company will have to pay interest at 15% per annum on the funds raised to acquire the plant. To simplify the illustration we will assume that the sales and cash costs are incurred at year-end. This is consistent with a conservative approach to project evaluation. The corrected payback is:

Year		£
0	Capital investment	−400,000
1	Add interest	60,000
		−460,000
	Deduct net cash proceeds	150,000
		−310,000
2	Add interest	46,500
		−356,500
	Deduct net cash proceeds	260,000
		−96,500
3	Add interest	14,475
		−110,975

In year 3 the forecast cash flow is £295,000. This exceeds the £110,975 not yet recovered. The payback is under 3 years. If we assume an equal monthly cash flow through year 3, then the payback is 2 years and 4 months approximately, including interest. The financing cost is not usually included in the payback evaluation. It can be handled more satisfactorily by methods 3 and 4 which we will examine later.

Payback also has defects as a capital investment appraisal tool. These are illustrated in two further investment opportunities:

		Project	
		E	F
Year		£	£
0	Total investment	20,000	20,000
1	Cash flow	3,000	10,000
2	Cash flow	7,000	7,000
3	Cash flow	10,000	3,000
4	Cash flow	15,000	1,000

The payback on both investments is three years. Project F is substantially worse than Project E. Consider the flows of cash within the payback period:

1 The extra £7,000 of cash provided by Project F in year 1 is more attractive than the comparable amount in year 3 from Project E. This is not recognised by payback.
2 Beyond the payback period Project E provides a £15,000 cash flow. Project F provides only £1,000. This is not recognised by payback. In fact, Project E is quite a good investment. Project F should not be considered. It provides a very poor return.

Payback is a good screening tool. It eliminates projects that depend too much on long-term cash flows. This is desirable in cases of products, services and markets that can change rapidly. It is fair to say that many bad projects undertaken during the years 1950–1975 would have been avoided had payback been used. At that time payback had been dismissed by many accounting experts as too unsophisticated. A good rule of thumb is that projects (other than long-term infra-structure development) should not be undertaken if the payback period is longer than four years. Many businesses that created capacity based on forecasts of long-term sales growth still regret that they ignored payback. A classic example is Burmah Oil. It commissioned giant tankers in the expectation of ever-increasing oil consumption. It did not materialise.

THE TIMING ASPECT OF CAPITAL EXPENDITURE CASH FLOWS

The key element in my crictism of both return on investment and payback is their inability to adequately reflect the timing of cash flows in their analytical framework. To assess timing we must apply the principles of compounding and discounting. A short reminder of some mathematics lessons at school is a good starting point.

At school we learned mathematical formulae, about compounding discounting and annuities. We frequently apply these formulae, even though the underlying logic is often long forgotten.

Formula 1: Compound Interest

$$A = P \times (1.0R)^n$$

where A = future amount, P = principal, R = rate of interest and n = number of years. Based on this formula if you invest £100 for three years at 10% per annum and we assume (a) no withdrawals of capital or interest and (b) no withholding taxes, you can expect to recover £133.10. This is confirmed by the following table:

Year		£
1	Sum invested	100.00
	Interest earned	10.00
2	Balance forward	110.00
	Interest earned	11.00
3	Balance forward	121.00
	Interest earned	12.10
	Total recovered	133.10

Formula 2: Discounting (stage 1)

Divide both sides of an equation by an equal amount and you obtain another valid equation:

$$\frac{A}{(1.0R)^n} = \frac{P \times (1.0R)^n}{(1.0R)^n}$$

Formula 3: Discounting (stage 2)

Cancel the similar values in the denominator and numerator of the right hand side to obtain another valid equation:

$$\frac{A}{(1.0R)^n} = P$$

To verify this we will pose the following question. How much would you be prepared to pay now in exchange for a guarantee of £133.10 in three years' time assuming no withholding tax? Using formula three the answer is £100. This is computed as follows: $P = £100 = £133.10/(1.1)^3$. It can be proved as follows:

Year		£
3	Amount recovered	133.10
	Year 3 interest	12.10
2	Net investment	121.00
	Year 2 interest	11.00
1	Net investment	110.00
	Year 1 interest	10.00
Maximum outlay		100.00

Formula 4: Discounting Annuities

This formula helps us to assess the maximum amount we would be prepared to pay for a constant future cash return. For example, I am promised £100 per annum for three years, starting one year from now. Assuming that I require a return of 15% per annum, how much should I be prepared to pay now? The answer is:

Year			
1	*2*	*3*	*Total*
$\frac{£100}{(1.15)}$	$\frac{£100}{(1.15)^2}$	$\frac{£100}{(1.15)^3}$	
= £86.96	= £75.61	= £65.75	£228.32

This can be verified in present or future value terms as follows:

Year		Present Value	Year		Future Value
3	Lump sum	100.00	0	Deposit	228.32
	Interest	13.04		Interest	34.25
		86.96			262.57
2	Lump sum	100.00		Receipt	100.00
		186.96			162.57
	Interest	24.39		Interest	24.39
		162.57			186.96
1	Lump sum	100.00		Receipt	100.00
		262.57			86.96
	Interest	34.25		Interest	13.04
0	PV	228.32		FV	100.00

We will now use formula one (compounding) to assess the Model Company project. We will make the following assumptions:

1 The project will obtain £400,000 from the treasurer of the company.
2 Any cash created by the project will be repaid at year-end. On receipt the treasurer will split the proceeds into capital and interest elements.
3 If the project is viable the sum repaid (net of interest) should exceed £400,000.

The following table shows the compound and discount rates to apply to a single sum and an annuity in computing the present and future value at an interest rate of 14%:

CAPITAL INVESTMENT DECISIONS

Years	PV £1	PV £1 Annuity	FV £1	FV £1 Annuity
1	0.8772	0.8772	1.1400	1.1400
2	0.7695	1.6467	1.2996	2.4396
3	0.6750	2.3216	1.4815	3.9211
4	0.5921	2.9137	1.6890	5.6101
5	0.5194	3.4331	1.9254	7.5355
6	0.4556	3.8887	2.1950	9.7305
7	0.3996	4.2883	2.5023	12.2328
8	0.3506	4.6389	2.8526	15.0853
9	0.3075	4.9464	3.2519	18.3373
10	0.2697	5.2161	3.7072	22.0445
11	0.2366	5.4527	4.2262	26.2707
12	0.2076	5.6603	4.8179	31.0887
13	0.1821	5.8424	5.4924	36.5811
14	0.1597	6.0021	6.2613	42.8424
15	0.1401	6.1422	7.1379	49.9804
16	0.1229	6.2651	8.1372	58.1176
17	0.1078	6.3729	9.2765	67.3941
18	0.0946	6.4674	10.5752	77.9692
19	0.0829	6.5504	12.0557	90.0249
20	0.0728	6.6231	13.7435	103.7684
21	0.0638	6.6870	15.6676	119.4360
22	0.0560	6.7429	17.8610	137.2970
23	0.0491	6.7921	20.3616	157.6586
24	0.0431	6.8351	23.2122	180.8708
25	0.0378	6.8729	26.4619	207.3327

The two most interesting points from these tables are: (a) the huge penalty involved in waiting 25 years to recover cash (96p in £1), and (b) the realisation that £1 per annum saved and earning interest at 14% per annum compounds to £207 over 25 years (before tax).

Method 3: Future Value

Year		£
0	Treasurer's advance	400,000
1	add interest (15%)	60,000
		460,000
	Project cash flow	150,000
	Net treasury advance	310,000
2	Add interest (15%)	46,500
		356,500
	Project cash flow	260,000
	Net treasury advance	96,500
3	Add interest (15%)	14,475
		110,975
	Project cash flow	295,000
	Net treasury surplus	+184,025
4	Add interest (15%)	27,604[a]
		+211,629
	Project cash flow	175,000
	Future project surplus	+386,629

[a] The Treasurer will be able to use the surplus funds of £184,025 to replace borrowings that would otherwise be needed. It is fitting that the Project should be given credit for this saving. If the cash generated lives up to the forecasts this will be an excellent investment.

350

The future value method copes well with the timing of cash flows as we can see by contrasting Projects A and B using an interest rate of 14%:

Future Values, Projects A and B

Year		Project A	Project B
0	Treasurer's advance	300,000	300,000
1	Add interest (14%)	42,000	42,000
		342,000	342,000
	Project cash flow	80,000	140,000
	Net treasury advance	262,000	202,000
2	Add interest (14%)	36,680	28,280
		298,680	230,280
	Project cash flow	90,000	110,000
	Net treasury advance	208,680	120,280
3	Add interest (14%)	29,215	16,839
		237,895	137,119
	Project cash flow	110,000	90,000
	Net treasury advance	127,895	47,119
4	Add interest (14%)	17,906	6,597
		145,801	53,716
	Project cash flow	140,000	80,000
	Project (deficit) surplus	(5,801)	26,284

In this illustration we see how the early return of higher amounts to the treasurer, even though followed by lower amounts later, results in Project B creating a surplus, whereas Project A is in deficit. Using future value analysis Project B would be accepted (unless a third more profitable alternative were available). Project A would be rejected.

Future value analysis overcomes timing differences in comparing projects. It is seldom used in industry, because it is bad for contrasting projects with different lives or capital costs.

A HANDBOOK OF PRACTICAL BUSINESS FINANCE

Method 4: Net Present Value

The most popular technique for project valuation is net present value analysis. It involves bringing future cash flows back to what the corporate treasurer would be prepared to pay for them now. This is called the present value. The treasurer will use Formula 3 to assess the discounted value of the future cash flows. These discounted cash flows are compared with the capital cost of the project. If they exceed the capital cost, then the project is attractive.

We will return to our Model Company project to see how this method works. The corporate treasurer would require repayment of £400,000 net of interest from the Model project:

Year	Net Inflow	Discount Factor Formula 3 (15%)	Net Present Value
1	150,000	$1/(1.15)$	130,435
2	260,000	$1/(1.15)^2$	196,597
3	295,000	$1/(1.15)^3$	193,967
4	175,000	$1/(1.15)^4$	100,057
Present value of discounted cash flows			621,056
Less capital cost			400,000
Net present value			221,056

Since the NPV is positive (£221,056) it is more than capable of repaying the loan. The project is profitable. This result can be reconciled with the future value we obtained in Method 3, as follows:

$$\frac{\text{Future value}}{\text{Discount factor}} \quad \frac{386,629}{(1.15)^4} = £221.056.$$

In order to simplify the calculations it is easy to compute discount tables. Most modern calculators have a constant divisor built into their program. This can be used to obtain the present value of £1 using the following steps:

1 Enter 1
2 Enter divide by 1.15 (the rate of interest)
3 Press equals (value obtained 0.8695652 1 year)
4 Press equals (value obtained 0.7561436 2 years)
5 Press equals (value obtained 0.6575161 3 years)
6 Press equals (value obtained 0.5717531 4 years)

Discount factors for subsequent years are obtained by continuing to press equals. Using this table corrected to five decimal places we can calculate the net present value more easily as:

Year	Net Cash Flow	Discount Factor	Net Present Value
0	−400,000		
1	+150,000	0.86956	130,434.00
2	+260,000	0.75614	196,596.40
3	+295,000	0.65752	193,968.40
4	+175,000	0.57175	100,056.25
			621,055.05
Deduct capital investment			400,000.00
Net present value			221,055.05

To help you understand net present value we will now assess Projects A and B, assuming an interest rate of 14% (in £'000):

	Project A			Project B		
Year	Cash	Discount	NPV	Cash	Discount	NPV
0	−300	1	−300.000	−300	1	−300.000
1	+80	0.87719	70.175	+140	0.87719	122.807
2	+90	0.76947	69.252	+110	0.76947	84.642
3	+110	0.67497	74.247	+90	0.67497	60.747
4	+140	0.59208	82.891	+80	0.59208	47.366
Net present value			(3.435)			15.562

These results are again verifiable against the future values (i.e. £5,801 ×0.59208 = £3,435. £26,284×0.59208 = £15,562).

Method 5: Internal Rate of Return

Another approach to project evaluation is to establish the internal rate of return. This concept, frequently referred to as IRR, is the maximum funding cost which the corporate treasurer could afford to charge and still recover the funds advanced to the project, after taking interest out of the future cash flows. Consider the following simple example. A company has proposed an investment of £50,000 which will provide an annuity cash return of £34,321 for two years. The company accepts all projects with a positive net present value at 15%. It also requires the IRR to be reported in the appraisal process. Because of the annuity cash return the IRR is easy to calculate:

The steps are as follows. First, divide the annuity into the capital cost (£50,000/£34,321 = 1.4568) and then prepare or look up an annuity table for two years. The relevant table can be prepared as follows:

%	PV £1 (Year 1)	PV £1 (Year 2)	PV £1 (2 Years)
20	0.83333	0.69444	1.52778
22	0.81967	0.67186	1.49153
24	0.80645	0.65036	**1.45682**
26	0.79365	0.62988	1.42353
28	0.78125	0.61035	1.39160
30	0.76923	0.59172	1.36095

Next locate the value 1.4568 in the table (highlighted for convenience). It is 24%. The treasurer could afford to charge 24% and still recover the full capital sum advanced. This can be verified as follows:

Year	Loan From Treasurer	Interest at 24%	Due to Treasurer	Repaid	Loan
0	50,000	12,000	62,000	34,321	27,679
1	27,679	6,643	34,322	34,321	–

This process will not work when the cash flow from operations is uneven. If this project promised cash returns of £20,000 in year 1 and £52,000 in year 2, the computation of the IRR is more difficult. It can be approximated using the following steps:

1 Average cash flow (50,000 + 20,000) ÷ 2 = £35,000.
2 Evaluate annuity factor £50,000 ÷ £35,000 = 1.42857.
3 Locate a factor above this from present value of annuity tables, i.e. 26%:

23%	24%	25%	26%
1.47399	1.45682	1.44	1.42353

4 Find the NPV at this discount rate:

Year	Cash Flow	Factor 26%	NPV
0	−50,000	1.00000	−50,000
1	+20,000	0.79365	+15,873
2	+52,000	0.62988	+32,754
			−1,373

5 Find the NPV at a lower discount rate (say 20%):

Year	Cash Flow	Factor 20%	NPV
0	−50,000	1.00000	−50,000
1	+20,000	0.83333	+16,667
2	+52,000	0.69444	+36,111
			+2,778

6 Interpolate to find the change effected:

Discount Rate		NPV
	26%	−1,373
	20%	+2,778
Movement	6%	4,151 (2,778+1,373)

If the movement was completely linear the correct discount to bring a break even NPV would be

$$20\% + [6\% \times \frac{2,778}{4,151}] = 24.015\%$$

This is very close to the correct IRR. If you needed to calculate the IRR more accurately you could use a computer spread sheet. The program to assess the project IRR using Lotus 123 incorporates the following steps:

1 Enter initial flow   −50,000 (cell D3)
2 Enter year 1 flow   20,000 (cell D4)
3 Enter year 2 flow   52,000 (cell D5)
4 Enter trial rate   20% (cell E3)
5 Enter @IRR (E3, D3..D5) (cell F3)

If you did this correctly cell F3 should now display 0.23923. This is an IRR of 23.923%. We can verify this as follows:

Year	Cash Flow	Factor 23.923%	NPV
0	−50,000	1.	−50,000.00
1	+20,000	0.8069527	+16,139.05
2	+52,000	0.6511726	+33,860.98
			+0.03

Lotus 123 can also be used to calculate the NPV. You will need to add two additional items into your Spread sheet:

Step 6   Enter interest rate 15% (cell E4); and
Step 7   Enter @NPV (E4, D4..D5) + D3 (cell F4).

Cell F4 should now be displaying £6,710.775. This is the NPV. Note how a slightly different logic is used. If we had not added +D3 at the end of cell F4 we would have obtained the gross present value (i.e. ignoring the capital cost). This brief lesson in computer programming will save you a lot of long sums, when you are evaluating a complicated project.

The internal rate of return on our basic illustration is 38.8767%. This was computed on Lotus 123 using the steps outlined, with five years of cash flows. The following table proves the result:

Year	Cash Flow	Discount 38.8767%	NPV
0	−400,000	1	−400,000.00
1	+150,000	0.7200631	108,009.46
2	+260,000	0.5184909	134,807.63
3	+295,000	0.3733462	110,137.12
4	+175,000	0.2688328	47,045.74
			−0.05

Using Lotus 123 to calculate the NPV for our Model Company project, I obtained an NPV of £221,056.20.

Coping with Errors and Uncertainty in Our Project

The project might obtain approval on the basis of this evaluation. If the project were approved, many risks and forecasting errors could adversely affect the NPV. The major risks and errors to consider include: (1) Does the project require debtor and stock finance? (2) Will the company have to pay tax on the project profits? (3) Are there errors in operating cash flow forecasts? If so, which are the most and least critical forecasts?

We will examine these questions in two stages: (a) the impact of a specific answer to the first two questions which involve errors in the original project evaluation; and (b) the relative importance of possible errors in the forecast cash flows.

Investment in Stocks and Debtors

This is an area that is frequently overlooked or underestimated in project evaluation. It should not be. It increases the initial funding required. Even if the company can recover the working capital when the project ends, the application of discount rates lowers the net present value quite dramatically.

To illustrate the impact of working capital, we will use the data in our Model Company illustration and assume that (a) stocks will represent 25% of next year's material and labour cost and (b) debtors will represent 20% of next year's sales (this means that no cash will be collected from customers for 2.4 months after the sales commence in year 1 and collections will continue for 2.4 months after sales cease at the end of year 4). The effect of this is approximated by assuming a

357

cash outflow at the start of each year to reflect the strain on cash resources imposed by allowing credit to customers. The third assumption is (c) that funds invested in working capital will be recovered at the end of the project.

The project cash flows can now be revised as follows:

		Year			
	0	1	2	3	4
Materials and labour		100,000	160,000	250,000	150,000
Total stocks	25,000	40,000	62,500	37,500	
Incremental stocks	−25,000	−15,000	−22,500	+25,000	+37,500
Sales		300,000	480,000	625,000	375,000
Debtors	60,000	96,000	125,000	75,000	
Incremental debtors	−60,000	−36,000	−29,000	+50,000	+75,000

The project analysis would now be revised:

	Original Cash Flow	Stocks	Debtors	New Net Cash Flow	Discount 15%	Net Present Value
0	−400,000	−25,000	−60,000	−485,000		
1	+150,000	−15,000	−36,000	+99,000	0.86956	86,086
2	+260,000	−22,500	−29,000	+208,500	0.75614	157,655
3	+295,000	+25,000	+50,000	+370,000	0.65752	243,282
4	+175,000	+37,500	+75,000	+287,500	0.57175	164,378
	480,000	−	−	+480,000		651,401
Less initial investment						485,000
Revised present value						166,401

The working capital adjustment reduced the NPV by £54,655 as compared with the original forecast. In addition, it reveals the need for £85,000 of additional finance. If this was ignored the company might overstretch their borrowing facilities.

If you wanted to make this analysis more accurate, you could build up and recover the working capital investment on a monthly basis. The change in funding required and NPV would not be significant. The calculations involved are quite complex.

The Impact of Taxation on the Project

Corporation tax can significantly reduce the NPV of a project. It is foolish to ignore it, even when tax depreciation benefits the organisation early in the project.

To adjust our project for corporation tax we will use the following additional information:

1 The corporation tax rate is 33%.
2 A writing down allowance of 25% for corporation tax purposes is available on the plant, if it is acquired. This allowance is calculated in the same way as reducing balance depreciation (i.e. allowance is based on the remaining undepreciated value).
3 In law, corporation tax is payable nine months after the end of the accounting period in which a profit is earned. We will treat it as payable one year in arrears. This simplifies the calculations and is consistent with our treatment of cash flows occurring at year-end.
4 The company will depreciate the plant over four years on a straight line basis for accounting purposes. This assumes no proceeds will be realised on disposal. This assumption gives rise to a balancing allowance for corporation tax purposes.

Computation of Corporation Tax Liabilities (£'000)

Year	Pre-tax Profit	Add Depreciation	Deduct WDA[a]	Taxable Profit	Tax at 33%
1	50	100	−100.00	50.00	16.500
2	160	100	−75.00	185.00	61.050
3	195	100	−56.25	238.75	78.788
4	75	100	−168.75	6.25	2.062
	480	400	−400.00	480.00	158.400

[a] Cost of plant   400,000
    WDA at 25%   100,000

    Written down value   300,000
    WDA at 25%   75,000

    Written down value   225,000
    WDA at 25%   56,250

    Written down value   168,750
    Disposal proceeds   0

    Balancing allowance   168,750

A HANDBOOK OF PRACTICAL BUSINESS FINANCE

Over the life of the plant, the company expects to obtain a tax deduction for the loss of value of £400,000 it will experience. In this case the deductibility occurs more slowly for corporation tax than it does for accounting purposes. A deferred tax situation will arise. This would not affect the project evaluation, which is done on a cash basis.

The NPV of the Model Project After Tax

Year	Previous Cash Flow	Corporation Tax	Net Flow	Discount 15%	NPV
0	−485,000		−485,000		
1	+99,000		+99,000	0.86957	86,087
2	+208,500	−16,500	+192,000	0.75614	145,179
3	+370,000	−61,050	+308,950	0.65752	203,141
4	+287,500	−78,787	+208,713	0.57175	119,332
5		−2,063	−2,063	0.49718	−1,026
	+480,000	−158,400	+321,600		552,713
Less capital cost					485,000
Net present value					67,713

The NPV declines by £98,688 (as compared with the previous result) when corporation tax is deducted.

Impact on Future Financial Statements

We will now forecast the profit and loss account and balance sheet of the project for four years. This part of the process is often ignored. I strongly recommend it: it helps to check the accuracy of project cash flows; and it is wise to assess the impact of the project on future profitability, borrowings and interest cover.

Project Profit and Loss Accounts

Year	1	2	3	4	Total
Sales	300,000	480,000	625,000	375,000	1,780,000
Cash costs	150,000	220,000	330,000	200,000	900,000
Depreciation	100,000	100,000	100,000	100,000	400,000
	250,000	320,000	430,000	300,000	1,300,000
Profit before tax	50,000	160,000	195,000	75,000	480,000
Corporation tax	−16,500	−61,050	−78,788	−2,062	−158,400
Deferred tax[a]	0	8,250	14,438	−22,688	0
Profit after tax	33,500	107,200	130,650	50,250	321,600
Cumulative profit	33,500	140,700	271,350	321,600	

[a] Deferred tax arises because accounting depreciation exceeds writing down allowances:

Year	2	3	4
Depreciation	100,000	100,000	100,000
WDA	75,000	56,250	168,750
Deferrable	25,000	43,750	(68,750)
Deferred (33%)	8,250	14,438	(22,688)

A HANDBOOK OF PRACTICAL BUSINESS FINANCE

Project Balance Sheets

Year	0	1	2	3	4
Plant at cost	400,000	400,000	400,000	400,000	400,000
Less depreciation	–	100,000	200,000	300,000	400,000
	400,000	300,000	200,000	100,000	–
Stocks	25,000	40,000	62,500	37,500	–
Debtors	60,000	96,000	125,000	75,000	–
Deferred tax			8,250	22,688	
Surplus repaid[a]				114,950	323,662
	485,000	436,000	395,750	350,138	323,662
Borrowed funds[a]	485,000	386,000	194,000		
Corporation tax		16,500	61,050	78,788	2,062
Cumulative profit		33,500	140,700	271,350	321,600
	485,000	436,000	395,750	350,138	323,662

[a]

Year	Loan	Change Stock	Change Debtors	Operating Cash Flow	Corporation Tax	Loan
1	485,000	15,000	36,000	(150,000)	–	386,000
2	386,000	22,500	29,000	(260,000)	16,500	194,000
3	194,000	(25,000)	(50,000)	(295,000)	61,050	(114,950)
4	(114,950)	(37,500)	(75,000)	(175,000)	78,788	(323,662)

The Impact of Errors in Other Forecasts

In order to understand the impact of errors on other forecasts we will now calculate the change in present value that would arise if each individual forecast worsened by 10%. We hold the other variables constant so as to test the sensitivity of each individual forecast. The interesting principle of relevant cash flows is illustrated in this analysis. We measure the incremental change in NPV, rather than recomputing all the cash flows. This will make the examples easy to follow while providing accurate conclusions about the change in NPV.

Example 1: Sales Prices Fall 10%

Year	Reduced Operating Cash Flow	Reduced Debtors	Corp. Tax	Incremental Net Cash Flow	Discount Factor	NPV
0		6,000		6,000		
1	−30,000	3,600		−26,400	0.86956	−22,956
2	−48,000	2,900	9,900	−35,200	0.75614	−26,616
3	−62,500	−5,000	15,840	−51,660	0.65752	−33,967
4	−37,500	−7,500	20,625	−24,375	0.57175	−13,936
5			12,375	12,375	0.49718	6,153
	−178,000	0	58,740	−119,260		−91,322
Less initial saving						6,000
Decline in present value						85,322

To prove that incremental analysis yields a correct answer we will re-evaluate the NPV of the full project, using sales prices reduced by 10%:

				£'000					
Year	Fixed Asset	Revised Sales	Costs	Stock	Revised Debtors	Revised Corp.Tax	Net Flow	15% Factor	NPV
0	−400			−25.0	−54.0		−479.0		
1		270.0	−150	−15.0	−32.4		72.6	0.86956	63,130
2		432.0	−220	−22.5	−26.1	−6.6	156.8	0.75614	118,563
3		562.5	−330	25.0	45.0	−45.2	257.3	0.65752	169,174
4		337.5	−200	37.5	67.5	−58.2	184.3	0.57175	105,396
5						10.3	10.3	0.49718	5,127
	−400	1,602.0	−900	−	−	−99.7	202.3		461,390
Initial cost									479,000
Net present value									−17,610
Initial NPV									67,713
NPV relevant flows only									−85,323

The difference is due to rounding.

Example 2: Sales Volume Falls – 10%

Year	Reduced Sales	Material & Labour	Reduced Stocks	Reduced Debtors	Corp. Tax	Cash Flow	Discount Factor	NPV
0			2,500	6,000		8,500		
1	−30,000	10,000	1,500	3,600		−14,900	0.86956	−12,956
2	−48,000	16,000	2,250	2,900	6,600	−20,250	0.75614	−15,312
3	−62,500	25,000	−2,500	−5,000	10,560	−34,440	0.65752	−22,645
4	−37,500	15,000	−3,750	−7,500	12,375	−21,375	0.57175	−12,221
5					7,425	7,425	0.49718	3,692
	−178,000	+66,000	−	−	36,960	−75,040		−59,442
Less initial saving								8,500
NPV relevant flows only								50,942

Example 3: Operating Costs Rise 10%

Year	Extra Production Costs	Fixed Costs	Extra Stocks	Corp. Tax	Cash Flow	Discount Factor	NPV
0			−2,500		−2,500		
1	−10,000	−5,000	−1,500		−16,500	0.86956	−14,348
2	−16,000	−6,000	−2,250	4,950	−19,300	0.75614	−12,854
3	−25,000	−8,000	2,500	7,260	−23,240	0.65752	−15,281
4	−15,000	−5,000	3,750	10,890	−5,360	0.57175	−3,065
5				6,600	6,600	0.49718	3,281
	−66,000	−24,000	−	29,700	−60,300		−42,267
Less initial saving							2,500
NPV relevant flows only							39,767

Example 4: Increase in Plant Cost 10%

Year	Extra Capital Cost	Corp. Tax	Net Cash Flow	Discount Factor	NPV
0	−40,000		−40,000		
2		3,300	3,300	0.75614	2,495
3		2,475	2,475	0.65752	1,627
4		1,856	1,856	0.57175	1,061
5		5,569	5,569	0.49718	2,769
	−40,000	13,200	−26,800		7,952

Less extra outlay	−40,000
NPV relevant flows only	32,048

Example 5: Funding Cost Plus 10%

Year	Original Cash Flow	Corporation Tax	Net Flow	Discount 16.5%	NPV
0	−485,000		−485,000		
1	99,000		99,000	0.85837	84,979
2	208,500	−16,500	192,000	0.73680	141,466
3	370,000	−61,050	308,950	0.63244	195,392
4	287,500	−78,788	208,712	0.54287	113,303
5		−2,062	−2,062	0.46598	−961
	480,000	−158,400	321,600		534,179

Less capital cost	485,000
Net present value	49,179
Original NPV	67,713
Change in NPV	18,534

Example 6: Working Capital Plus 10%

Year	Extra Stocks	Extra Debtors	Extra Net Cash Flow	Discount Factor	NPV
0	−2,500	−6,000	−8,500		−8,500
1	−1,500	−3,600	−5,100	0.86956	−4,435
2	−2,250	−2,900	−5,150	0.75614	−3,894
3	2,500	5,000	7,500	0.65752	4,931
4	3,750	7,500	11,250	0.57175	6,432
	−	−	−		−5,466

Table of Relative Risks for Model Project Forecasts

The original NPV (after inclusion of working capital and corporation tax) was £67,713. The following table shows the relative importance of the various project forecasts:

Variable Adjusted	NPV Change	% of Base NPV	% Total Changes	Rank
Sales price	−85,322	126.0	36.8	1
Sales volume	−50,492	74.6	21.8	2
Operating costs	−39,767	58.7	17.2	3
Plant cost	−32,048	47.3	13.8	4
Funding cost	−18,534	27.4	8.0	5
Working capital	−5,466	8.1	2.4	6
	−231,629		100.0	

This table shows us that the project is disturbingly sensitive to a fall in selling price. The margin of error, which is dangerously small, can be calculated as follows:

Sales price (10%×£67,713/£85,322) = 7.9%.

The margin of error for the other variables is:

Sales volume 14.4% (£10%×£67,713/£50,492)
Operating costs 17.0% (10%×£67,713/£39,767)
Plant cost 21.1% (10%×£67,713/£32,048)
Working capital 123.9% (10%×£67,713/£5,466)
Financing cost 39%. The margin for error on financing costs is based on the variation between 15% and the project IRR. This was calculated by computer at 20.896%:

Year	Net Cash Flow	Discount 20.896%	NPV
0	−485,000		
1	99,000	0.82716	81,889
2	192,000	0.68419	131,364
3	308,950	0.56593	174,844
4	208,713	0.46811	97,701
5	−2,063	0.38720	−798
	321,600		485,000

This exactly covers the capital cost as you would expect.

Cost of Capital for Project Evaluation

This is one of the most controversial areas in accounting. I will treat it in a straightforward and pragmatic way. If you wish to obtain a detailed understanding of the problems involved, then I recommend *Financial management and policy* by James C. Van Horne, published by Prentice-Hall International (ISBN 0-13-316811-5).

For a practical approach I suggest the following methodology:

1 Assess the amount of funds available to finance capital investments (the capital budget).
2 Assess the proportion of these funds that will be raised from shareholders and from interest-bearing loans.
3 Establish the return(s) required by the funds' providers.
4 Calculate the weighted average cost of capital from the data assembled at steps 1 to 3 above.
5 Discount all proposed investments at the weighted average cost of capital. Accept projects that provide a positive NPV and reject ones that do not.
6 Keep a running total of the balance of available funds that has not been committed to projects.
7 Where projects proposed exceed funds available, use a profitability index to indicate the best opportunities.

Two issues in this series of steps need to be explained.

A HANDBOOK OF PRACTICAL BUSINESS FINANCE

Weighted Average Cost of Capital

The computation is illustrated using two situations:

Situation 1

Type	Funds to be Raised £'000	Proportion of Total %	Return Required £'000	Weighted Average Cost of Capital %
Bank	800	40	80.4 (10.05%)	4.02
Owners	1,200	60	240.0 (20.00%)	12.00
Total	2,000	100	320.4	16.02

The interest rate on bank loans is 15%. Interest is allowable as a deduction for corporation tax purposes. Allowing for this the after tax cost is $15\% \times (1-0.33) = 10.05\%$ i.e. net of tax cost. The return required by owners is 20%. This return is a function of expectations of shareholders for growth in dividend income and share price appreciation. It will be higher than 20% in a fast growing or high risk enterprise and lower than 20% in a stable but low growth business. The weighted average cost of capital combines the high cost equity with the lower cost debt to yield an overall figure of 16.02% (say 16%).

Situation 2

Type	Funds to be Raised £'000	Proportion of Total %	Return Required £'000	Weighted Average Cost of Capital %
Bank	1,000	50	107.2 (10.72%)	5.36
Owners	1,000	50	220.0 (22.00%)	11.00
Total	2,000	100	327.2	16.36

In this case I used an interest rate of 16% (10.72% after tax), because of the higher gearing. The increased risk increases the return that the owners require to 22%. The assessment of the average cost of bank funds is more complicated, when borrowings are drawn from a variety of sources at different rates. Averaging is done as above. Here is an example:

Source	Amount £'000	Mix %	Service cost %	Service cost £'000	Weighted Average %
Sterling	5,000	50	10	500	5.0
ECU	2,500	25	8	200	2.0
Hire purchase	1,500	15	24	360	3.6
Leasing	1,000	10	20	200	2.0
	10,000			1,260	12.6

The return required by shareholders is influenced by a range of items: the industry sector (risk profile); dividend growth expectations; share price appreciation expectations; marketability or non-marketability of shares; magnitude of gearing, etc. For practical purposes I suggest the following values:

	High Risk	Medium Risk	Low Risk
Quoted company	25%	20%	17%
Unquoted company	28%	23%	20%

Profitability Index

Growth PLC is considering some capital investment proposals. It has £4.5 million to spend:

	£'000		
Proposal	Capital Cost	NPV	Profitability Index
1	2,000	1,000	.5 (NPV/cap cost)
2	1,500	900	.6
3	1,800	990	.55
4	2,500	1,200	.48
5	1,000	800	.8
6	200	180	.9

At first glance proposals 1 and 4 appear to offer the biggest return and should be accepted (using all the available funds). A closer inspection reveals that an NPV of £2,870,000 is available from the other four projects. The profitability index steers us to the best portfolio.

369

Proposal	Capital Cost	Unused Balance	NPV	Cumulative NPV	Profitability Index
6	200	4,300	180	180	.9
5	1,000	3,300	800	980	.8
2	1,500	1,800	900	1,880	.6
3	1,800	–	990	2,870	.55

Accept/Reject Criteria in Project Evaluation

Every business should develop criteria upon which projects are accepted and rejected. It is difficult to generalise about such criteria. The major problem is that projects have very different characteristics and risk profiles. The following guidelines should help you to formulate your accept/reject criteria:

Project Type	Maximum Risk Profile	Payback Period
1 Replacement of out of date assets	Medium	5 years
2 Project associated with value engineering or cost reduction	High	2 years
3 Project associated with infrastructure development	Low	10+ years
4 Project to acquire long-term secure returns (e.g. an assurance company seeking a long-term return to underpin bonuses)	Low	10+ years
5 Discretionary projects of a social or cultural nature	Not for commercial return	–

Setting payback limits can help to avoid time-consuming studies of unattractive projects. If passing the payback test, more detailed discounted cash flow techniques should be applied. This chapter stresses the application of discounting based on the cost of capital. In general, projects which fail to produce a positive present value should be rejected. An exception arises when the ability to remain in business depends on modernising the asset base. In such cases a capital investment might be undertaken, even though the NPV is negative. The impact of approving the project on future profit and loss accounts, balance sheets and key ratios should be computed. This is done by preparing the project financial statements and combining them with the figures previously developed for corporate planning purposes.

Summary and Methodology of High-quality Project Evaluation

In this chapter we examined the range of financial evaluation techniques that can be applied to capital investment proposals: return on investment, payback, net present value and internal rate of return.

We saw that ROI and payback help us to quickly identify projects too risky to warrant the deeper investigation involved in discounted cash flow techniques. We concluded that you cannot get right answers from any of the techniques where the cash flow forecasts are wrong (e.g. tax ignored). We looked at how to quantify the relative importance of each variable in the forecast cash flows. We also examined a pragmatic approach to assessing the cost of capital. We saw how a profitability index helps to identify the most suitable investments in a capital rationing situation.

Ten Strong Statements on Capital Investment

1   Always define the maximum amount you are prepared to spend on capital projects. This element of capital project evaluation is necessary to avoid overtrading.
2   Avoid assumptions that historic data can be extrapolated indefinitely into the future. Remember my comments on the Burmah Oil tanker fleet.
3   Never spend money on capital investments that is needed for, and committed to, other organisational uses.
4   Have clearly defined payback and NPV criteria against which projects will be accepted or rejected. These norms vary from business to business. They are related to changes in production technology and consumer taste. Criteria should be regularly reviewed as conditions change.
5   Don't waste a lot of time on complicated cost of capital calculations. Pragmatic discount rates are the sensible approach for most UK businesses.
6   Avoid funding capital investments from short-term sources. Remember our conclusions from the funds flow matrix in Chapter 4.
7   When computing project cash flows, remember to charge an appropriate amount for R&D. The best projects are ones that provide margins adequate to cover the cost of a search for even better ones.

8   Think long and hard before investing in a project which adds more than 25% to sales, assets or staff. If it goes sour it could seriously damage the business. The Saatchi and Saatchi consultancy division is a recent example.

9   Remember the mnemonic GIGO (Garbage In Garbage Out). Time spent on improving the accuracy of cash forecasts is the secret of winning in the capital investment race.

10 Carefully consider the impact of major new investments on the overhead structure of the business. An investment that imposes a small additional strain on the establishment should not significantly affect the fixed costs. A major new investment will cause extra fixed costs, unless the business is operating below its establishment cost capacity.

Chapter 13

Foreign Currency Transactions

Most companies are involved in some foreign currency transactions. These transactions give rise to a variety of additional risks and rewards. In this chapter we examine how Mundi Ltd manages the financial aspects of its foreign currency transactions. The content is divided into four sections:

- Types of transactions
- Recording transactions
- Commercial risks
- Exchange risks and rewards

Types of Transactions

Mundi Ltd is involved in the following types of foreign currency transactions. It:

1   Sells goods priced in foreign currencies;
2   Collects from customers in foreign currencies;
3   Purchases goods priced in foreign currencies;
4   Pays suppliers in foreign currencies;
5   Owns assets abroad, denominated in foreign currencies;
6   Borrows money in a foreign currency;
7   Tenders for contracts in foreign currencies; and
8   Has a wholly-owned subsidiary in America, which keeps its accounts in US dollars.

In all these cases Mundi Ltd must record the transactions correctly, decided how to treat them in its £ sterling financial statements, and take steps to minimise the impact of unfavourable changes in exchange rates.

Recording Transactions

The eight types of foreign currency transaction can be divided into four groups for accounting purposes.

1 Those which are really sterling transactions, but are initially priced in a foreign currency. These include purchases and sales of the parent company, payments to suppliers and receipts from customers.
2 Those which create an ongoing foreign currency exposure. These include owning assets and having borrowings abroad.
3 Those involving investment in subsidiaries and related companies that maintain their accounts in foreign currencies.
4 Those which may or may not create a foreign currency exposure. Tendering is the source of this uncertainty.

The rules for recording transactions are that group one transactions must be converted into sterling when the transaction takes place. Group two transactions are also converted into sterling when the transaction takes place. They create assets or liabilities and give rise to subsequent exchange gains or losses. The assets or liabilities must be revalued for inclusion in the sterling balance sheet at the rate of exchange ruling on that date.

Group three transactions are left in the currency of the subsidiary or related company. They are converted into sterling for inclusion in the next balance sheet and revalued in subsequent balance sheets.

Groups four transactions are ignored until they crystallise. This does not mean that Mundi Ltd should not take steps to eliminate the potential exchange risk.

Recording Group One Transactions

The recording is straightforward. Consider the following transactions of Mundi Ltd:

A On 9 August, 1989 Mundi Ltd sold goods to an American customer for £100,000 cash. The best exchange rate quotation from three London banks was £ = $1.609–1.630. This was accepted. How should the transaction be recorded? The rule is that banks buy high (right-hand quote) and sell low (left-hand quote). The bank will buy the dollars. They will credit our account with £61,349.69 (i.e. $100,000/1.63). This will be recorded as a sale and cash receipt.
B On 9 August, 1989 Mundi Ltd bought goods from a German supplier for DM240,000 cash. The best exchange rate quotation

374

was £ = DM3.0529–3.0964 which was accepted. How should the transaction be recorded? The bank sells DM low (left-hand quote). They will charge Mundi Ltd £78,613.78 (i.e. DM240,000/ 3.0529). This will be recorded as a purchase and cash payment.

Recording Group Two Transactions

The sales described in group one would create an asset and assume a group two dimension if they were made on credit. The purchases described in group one would create a liability and assume a group two dimension if they were made on credit.

EXAMPLE 1

We will assume that the sale by Mundi Ltd for $100,000 is to be paid for on 9 November, 1989. The sale and debtor will be recorded at £61,349.69 as previously. The proceeds at settlement are uncertain at this stage. We will assume two possible exchange rates at 9 November to show how the customer settlement is handled. The bank buys the dollars high.

	Case 1	Case 2
£ =	$1.409–1.430	$1.809–1.830
Proceeds	£69,930.07	£54,644.81
Debtor balance	£61,349.69	£61,349.69
Exchange gain	£8,580.38	
Exchange loss		£(6,704,88)

In case 1 sterling is weak and Mundi Ltd earns an extra profit. In case 2 sterling is strong. Mundi Ltd loses money between sale and settlement. Should Mundi Ltd risk a possible elimination of its profit on the transaction between sale and settlement? The gambler will take the risk. Sterling might weaken and result in a currency gain. Mundi Ltd is not prepared to take the risk. We will see how it protects itself later.

A further complication can arise. Mundi Ltd prepares its balance sheet as at 31 October, 1989. The US debtor appears in the books at £61,349.69. This amount is unlikely to be correct for balance sheet purposes. We will assume two rates of exchange at 31 October:

	Case 1	Case 2
£ =	$1.389–1.410	$1.829–1.850
Correct balance	£70,921.99	£54,054.05
Recorded balance	£61,349.69	£61,349.69
Exchange gain	£9,572.30	
Exchange loss		£(7,295.64)

The trade debtor amount will be adjusted in the balance sheet to £70,921.99 and an exchange gain of £9,572.30 will be added to the profit in case one. The trade debtor amount will be adjusted to £54,054.05 and an exchange loss of £7,295.64 will be charged against profits in case two.

The final settlement may be known when the balance sheet is being prepared. Any further exchange movement is ignored unless a significant loss is involved. A second adjustment is required at settlement:

	Case 1	Case 2
£ =	$1.409–1.430	$1.809–1.830
Proceeds	£69,930.07	£54,644.81
Debtor balance	£70,921.99	£54,054.05
Exchange gain		£590.76
Exchange loss	£(991.92)	

The proceeds (£69.930.07 or £54,644.81) are received. The profit and loss account will be charged with a loss of £991.92 in case one or credited with a gain of £590.76 in case two.

EXAMPLE 2

If the purchases from Germany are to be paid for on 9 November, 1989 the situation can be summarised assuming the following exchange rates:

	Case 1	Case 2
31 October £ =	DM2.8529–2.8964	DM3.2529–3.2964
9 November £ =	DM2.9029–2.9464	DM3.2029–3.2429

	Case 1 £	Case 2 £
Purchase/creditor	78,613.78	78,613.78
Gain/(loss)	(5,511.15)	4,833.46
31 October creditor	84,124.93	73,780.32
Gain/(loss)	1,448.99	(1,151.77)
Settlement	82,675.94	74,932.09

In case one the cost £78,613.78 is recorded as a purchase and creditor in August. The creditor is increased to £84,124.93 at 31 October and an exchange loss of £5,511.15 is charged against profits. Part of the loss £1,448.99 is recovered at settlement and increases the November profit.

In case two the cost £78,613.78 is recorded as a purchase and creditor in August. The creditor is reduced to £73,780.32 at 31 October and an exchange gain (£4,833.46) is credited to profits. Part of the gain (£1,151.77) is lost back at settlement and reduces the November profit. Should Mundi Ltd risk a possible increase in cost, due to a weakness in sterling between purchase and settlement? The gambler will take the risk. Sterling might weaken and result in a currency gain. Mundi is not prepared to take the risk. We will see how it protects itself later.

Once the German stock has been purchased and converted to sterling at 9 August, future stock valuation is based on this price. If Mundi Ltd bought a fixed asset priced in a foreign currency, it would convert it to a sterling value at acquisition and use this value for depreciation and balance sheet purposes.

EXAMPLE 3: FOREIGN CURRENCY BORROWING/REPAYMENTS

Foreign currency borrowing can be very attractive. The interest rates on borrowing in major foreign currencies are currently lower than on sterling loans. Mundi Ltd borrowed $600,000 on 9 August at 7% per annum. The loan is repayable in five equal annual instalments of capital and interest. This is how the transaction is recorded:

A HANDBOOK OF PRACTICAL BUSINESS FINANCE

$ Cash Flows

Year	Opening Loan	Interest at 7%	Total Repaid	Capital Repaid	Closing Loan
1	600,000	42,000	146,334	104,334	495,666
2	495,666	34,697	146,334	111,637	384,029
3	384,029	26,882	146,334	119,452	264,577
4	264,577	18,520	146,334	127,814	136,763
5	136,763	9,573	146,336	136,763	–
		131,672	731,672	600,000	

Sterling Equivalent (Exchange Rate 9 August 1.63)

Year	Opening Loan	Interest at 7%	Total Repaid	Capital Repaid	Closing Loan
1	368,098	25,767	89,775	64,008	304,090
2	304,090	21,286	89,775	68,489	235,601
3	235,601	16,492	89,775	73,283	162,318
4	162,318	11,362	89,775	78,413	83,905
5	83,905	5,873	89,778	83,905	–
		80,780	448,878	368,098	

The interest cost is £80,780. This is £87,226 lower than a UK loan at 14%, with the same repayment terms and period, would cost. The potential saving appears attractive. But there is a serious snag. Mundi Ltd will have to buy dollars to make the capital and interest repayments. The cost of the dollars will rise if sterling weakens. We will examine three cases:

	Case 1 $1.20 = £	Case 2 $1.30 = £	Case 3 $1.40 = £
Annual repayment[a]	121,945	112,565	104,524
Total repaid[b]	609,725	562,825	522,620

[a] Mundi Ltd must buy $146,334 at £ = $1.20, $1.30 and $1.40 respectively.
[b] Assumes a constant, but weaker sterling through the five-year period (i.e. £121,945× 5 = £609,725 etc.).

The repayments on a sterling loan at 14% would be £107,221 per annum. If the exchange rate averages less than £ = $1.365 the 'cheap'

378

US loan will prove to be a Greek (!) gift. Mundi Ltd would not take this risk. It has better exchange risk management techniques. Nevertheless, if sterling remains stable or strengthens the interest and cash flow savings will be significant.

Recording Group Three Transactions

The day-to-day financial records of overseas subsidiaries and related companies are usually maintained in their local currencies. The UK parent will not need to record such transactions except for planning, control and consolidation purposes. Many UK companies use pre-determined exchange rates for planning and control purposes and do not adjust to actual rates unless the predetermined rate has been seriously misjudged. The reason for this is that the rules for conversion of foreign currency assets, liabilities and equity are focused on annual performance. These rules are defined in SSAP 20 and can be summarised as follows:

ACCOUNTING FOR FOREIGN CURRENCY SUBSIDIARIES

The financial statements of overseas subsidiaries can be maintained in two different ways. First, the books and accounts may be maintained in sterling. Under this method each transaction is converted to sterling at the rate ruling at the time.

SSAP 20 defines the circumstances in which this form of accounting is appropriate: 'The affairs of the foreign enterprise must be so closely interlinked with those of the investing company that its results may be regarded as being more dependent on the economic environment of the investment company's currency than their own reporting currency. In such cases the consolidation should be prepared as if all transactions had been entered into by the investing company itself in its own currency (sterling).'

This method of accounting is called the temporal rate method. The rare occasions in which it is appropriate are defined in paragraphs 2,3 and 4 of SSAP 20.

Secondly, the books and accounts may be maintained in a foreign currency. The conversion of such figures into £ for consolidation recognises that the investment is made in the net worth rather than the individual assets and liabilities. Amounts in the balance sheet (other than net worth) should be converted to £ at the exchange rate ruling on the balance sheet date. Amounts in the profit and loss account should be converted at the average rate ruling throughout the financial year or at the closing rate for the financial year.

Using either version of the second method, exchange gains and losses can be divided into trading (dealt with in the profit and loss

379

account) and non-trading (carried directly to reserves). This contrasts with the temporal rate method where all exchange gains and losses are dealt with through the profit and loss account.

The closing rate method is more important than the temporal rate method. It is used in all the illustrations in this chapter. The same dollar profit and loss account and balance sheet is used to illustrate the translation process as sterling weakens and strengthens.

The financial result of SubMundi Inc, a US subsidiary of Mundi Ltd, have been received for inclusion in group accounts. The translation process is shown in the following illustrations:

Illustration 1: £ Strengthening   Profit and Loss Translation

Exchange Rates			Last Year	This Year
Average	£ =		$1.50	$1.70
Closing	£ =		$1.60	$1.80

$1989	£1989 Closing	Average		$1990	£1990 Closing	Average
980,000	612,500	653,333	Sales	1,152,000	640,000	677,647
735,000	459,375	490,000	Cost of sales	864,000	480,000	508,235
245,000	153,125	163,333	Gross profit	288,000	160,000	169,412
186,000	116,250	124,000	Other expense	198,000	110,000	116,471
59,000	36,875	39,333	Profit pre tax	90,000	50,000	52,941
23,600	14,750	14,750	Tax	36,000	20,000	20,000
35,400	22,125	24,583	Profit post tax	54,000	30,000	32,941
32,000	20,000	20,000	Proposed dividend	32,000	17,778	17,778
3,400	2,125	4,583	Profit retained	22,000	12,222	15,163

Sterling strengthened through 1989 and 1990. If the exchange rate had remained at £ = $1.60 at the end of 1990 the sales of $1,152,000 would have translated into £720,000 and the retained profits into £13,750. As sterling strengthens the buying power of the translated dollar sales decline to £640,000 on average and £576,000 at closing rate. Similarly the sterling buying power of the dollar profit retained declines to £15,163 on average and £12,222 at closing rate. Mundi Ltd would have preferred a constant exchange rate or a weakness in sterling (to increase the UK buying power of its dollar earnings).

Even using average rate translation, the tax liability and the proposed dividend must be translated at the closing rate. They are monetary liabilities driven by balance sheet translation rules. Both average and closing rate translations are shown in this example. In subsequent illustrations only the closing rate conversion is shown (the vast majority of businesses use it for translation).

Illustration 1: £ Strengthening   Balance Sheet Translation

Exchange Rates Closing			1989	1990		
			£ = $1.60	$1.80		
$1989	*£1989*				*$1990*	*£1990*
324,000	202,500	Fixed assets			288,000	160,000
300,000	187,500	Current assets			360,000	200,000
		Payable in under one year				
160,000	100,000	Creditors			144,000	80,000
5,000	3,125	Bank loans			10,600	5,889
23,600	14,750	Tax provision			36,000	20,000
32,000	20,000	Proposed dividends			32,000	17,778
(220,600)	(137,875)				(222,600)	(123,667)
403,400	252,125	Net assets			425,400	236,333
Financed by:						
400,000	285,714	Share capital[1]			400,000	285,714
3,400	2,125	Revenue reserve[2]			25,400	14,347
–	(35,714)	Exchange losses[3]			–	(63,728)[4]
403,400	252,125				425,400	236,333

Closing rate conversion must be used. Each component of the net assets is translated at the closing rate of £ = $1.60 in 1989 and £ = $1.80 in 1990.
[1] The capital was introduced at start up. This was in 1988 when the exchange rate stood at £ = $1.40. The share capital will always be translated at this rate thereafter.
[2] These are the closing rate profits retained. Average rate translation would have increased the revenue reserve and the translation loss by £5,399 (1989 £2,458).

	1989	1990
	£	£
Opening net assets	285,714[a]	252,125[c]
Closing net assets	250,000[b]	224,111[d]
[3] Exchange loss year	35,714	28,014
Opening loss		35,714
[4] Exchange loss cumulative		63,728

[a] $400,000/1.4 = £285,714.   [b] $400,000/1.6 = £250,000.
[c] $403,400/1.6 = £252,125.   [d] $403,400/1.8 = £224,111.

Sterling strengthened dramatically in this example. It had the following serious consequences for Mundi Ltd:

1 Sales, profits, assets and liabilities of SubMundi Inc translated into a lower sterling value than if the exchange rate stayed constant.
2 The starting capital (invested in weakening dollar net assets) resulted in translation losses.

If the exchange rate was £ = \$1.60 at the end of 1990 the translated value of the dollar net assets would have been £265,875 (\$425,400/1.6). Strength of sterling in illustration reduced their value on translation by £53,175. The balance sheet using an exchange rate of £ = \$1.60 would have been:

Revised Balance Sheet Translation

Closing Exchange Rate £ = \$1.60 1990

\$1989	£1989		\$1990	£1990
403,400	252,125	Net assets	425,400	265,875

Financed by:

400,000	320,000	Share capital[1]	400,000	320,000
3,400	2,125	Revenue reserve[2]	25,400	15,875
–	(70,000)	Exchange losses[3]	–	(70,000)[4]
403,400	252,125		425,400	265,875

[1] As per illustration 1.

[2] Profit 1989 (at £ = \$1.60)	2,125
Profit 1990 (at £ = \$1.60)	13,750
	15,875

	1989	1990
	£	£
Opening net assets	320,000[a]	252,125[c]
Closing net assets	250,000[b]	252,125[d]
[3] Exchange loss year	70,000	–
Opening loss		70,000
[4] Exchange loss cumulative		70,000

[a] \$400,000/1.25 = £320,000.   [b] \$400,000/1.6 = £250,000.
[c] \$403,400/1.6 = £252,125.   [d] \$403,400/1.6 = £252,125.

Mundi Ltd recognised the risk of losses that could occur if sterling strengthened. In the last section of this chapter we will see how they reduce the translation risk.

We will now examine how sterling weakness affects the translation of dollar results.

Illustration 2: £ Weakening   Profit and Loss Translation

Exchange Rates Closing			1989 $£ = \$1.20$	1990 $\$1.00$		
$1989	*£1989*				*$1990*	*$1990*
980,000	816,667	Sales			1,152,000	1,152,000
735,000	612,500	Cost of sales			864,000	864,000
245,000	204,167	Gross profit			288,000	288,000
186,000	155,000	Other expenses			198,000	198,000
59,000	49,167	Profit pre tax			90,000	90,000
23,600	19,667	Tax			36,000	36,000
35,400	29,500	Profit after tax			54,000	54,000
32,000	26,667	Proposed dividend			32,000	32,000
3,400	2,833	Profit retained			22,000	22,000

If the exchange rate remained at £ = $1.40 at the end of 1990 translation of the sales and retained profits would have been £822,857 and £15,714 respectively. Mundi Ltd gained from weakness of sterling.

Illustration 2: £ Weakening   Balance Sheet Translation

Exchange Rates Closing			1989	1990		
			£ = $1.20	$1.00		
$1989	*£1989*				*$1990*	*£1990*
324,000	270,000	Fixed assets			288,000	288,000
300,000	250,000	Current assets			360,000	360,000
		Payable in under one year				
160,000	133,333	Creditors			144,000	144,000
5,000	4,167	Bank loans			10,600	10,600
23,600	19,667	Tax provision			36,000	36,000
32,000	26,666	Proposed dividends			32,000	32,000
(220,600)	(183,833)				(222,600)	(222,600)
403,400	336,167	Net assets			425,400	425,400
Financed by:						
400,000	285,714	Share capital[1]			400,000	285,714
3,400	2,833	Revenue reserve			25,400	24,833
–	47,620	Exchange gain[2]			–	114,853[3]
403,400	336,167				425,400	424,400

If the exchange rate was £ = $1.40 at the end of 1990 the net assets would have translated to £303,857. Weakness of sterling increased the buying power of the dollar assets on translation.

[1] The capital was introduced when the exchange rate stood at £ = $1.40. The share capital will always be translated at this rate thereafter.

	1989	1990
	£	£
Opening net assets	285,714[a]	336,167[c]
Closing net assets	333,334[b]	403,400[d]
[2] Exchange gain year	47,620	67,233
Opening gain		47,620
[3] Exchange gain cumulative		114,853

[a] $400,000/1.4 = £285,714.   [b] $400,000/1.2 = £333,334.
[c] $403,400/1.2 = £336,167.   [d] $403,400/1.0 = £403,400.

There are three major issues involved in the translation of SubMundi Inc. First, the assets and liabilities are converted at the rate ruling on the balance sheet date. If the exchange rate remained at £ = $1.40 the net assets would have translated to £303,857. A translation loss of

£67,524 occurs as sterling strengthens to £ = $1.80. A translation gain of £121,543 occurs as sterling weakens to £ = $1.

Second, the retained profit is translated as the sum of the closing rate dollar figures for the two years since SubMundi Inc was formed. If the exchange rate remained at £ = $1.40 the retained profits would have translated into £18,143. A translation loss of £3,796 occurs as sterling strengthens to £ = $1.80. A translation gain of £6,690 occurs as sterling weakens to £ = $1.

The final feature is that these losses and gains are included in the shareholders' funds as follows:

	Strong	Weak
Net asset translation	67,524	121,543
Retained profits	3,796	6,690
Per shareholders' funds	63,728	114,853

Commercial Risks

The risks involved in foreign currency transaction can be substantial. The area of export selling is most exposed. Assessment of credit risk can be more complicated and acquiring and interpreting credit checks and references presents problems. The prudent vendor will try to eliminate the risk through one of the following: credit insurance; debt factoring; confirmed irrevocable letters of credit; cash on delivery; or sight drafts. Also, delays in delivery and damage in transit are more likely than with home sales.

Exchange Risks and Rewards

Some businesses ignore exchange risk. They argue that, over a long period, profits and losses on exchange tend to cancel out. Many businesses cannot risk exposure to exchange losses. They could result in loss of confidence by financial institutions, suppliers and customers and shareholders.

The prudent business will seek ways of protecting itself against exchange risks. Management of a business may be able to plead innocence where a company fails for other unforeseen reasons. If the failure is due to currency speculation, which is not the core business, stakeholders are likely to be unforgiving. To protect against the risk of exchange losses a business will have to be prepared to sacrifice the chance of exchange profits. A range of protection options is available:

1   Forward exchange purchase contracts.
2   Forward exchange sale contracts.
3   Incompany risk matching.
4   Foreign currency option contracts.
5   Interest rate swaps.
6   Borrowing in stable currencies.

We will look at how Mundi Ltd uses these techniques to reduce its foreign exchange exposures.

Forward Exchange Purchase Contracts

Mundi Ltd bought goods costing DM240,000, on 9 August, 1989 payable in 3 months' time. One way of eliminating the exchange risk would be to buy the German currency now, open a German deposit account and lodge the Marks to it. A simpler method would be to arrange a forward exchange purchase contract. In theory this uses a UK bank in the creation of a German deposit account. This is how it works.

The bank quoted a three-month forward rate of £ = DM2.9856–3.0282. If Mundi Ltd accepts this quote it will commit itself to buy the funds required for settlement for 240,000/2.9856 = £80,385.85. This is £1,772.07 dearer than the spot exchange rate would have cost. The extra cost arises because interest rates are much lower in Germany than the UK. In theory this suggests that sterling will weaken, otherwise German investors would deposit all their savings in Britain. German interest rates would rise to stem the outflow and British interest rates would fall to reduce the inflow.

This is how the bank was able to quote £ = DM2.9856–3.0282. If Mundi Ltd accepts the quote the bank will:

FOREIGN CURRENCY TRANSACTIONS

	£
(1) Borrow £77,643.23 for 3 months to finance an immediate purchase of DM237,037[a]	77,643.23
(2) Pay interest on the loan at 14.125% per annum for 3 months £77,643.23×3.53125%	2,741.78
Charge Mundi Ltd	80,385.00
(3) Deposit the Marks at 5% per annum	237,037
This will earn DM237,037×1.25%	2,963
	240,000

(4) The loan will be repaid using the cash to be received from Mundi Ltd in three months. The quote was expressed as DM 240,000/80,385 = DM2.9856.

[a] The amount to be deposited is 240,000/101.25% = 237,037. To finance this deposit the bank would have to borrow 237,037/3.0529 = £77,643.23. The cost of the contract is based on the interest rate differential. If Mundi Ltd had bought the Marks on 9 September it would have cost £78,613.78 (240,000/3.0529). The three-month settlement delay increases the cost (ignoring the opportunity cost of late settlement). The fact that German interest rates are lower than UK rates causes the increase. The Mark is said to be at a premium against sterling.

Forward Exchange Sale Contracts

To illustrate the forward exchange contract I will assume that Mundi Ltd sold goods for DM240,000 on 9 August, 1989, payable in three months. The bank were asked to offer protection against the potential exchange risk. This is how they computed the quotation:

		DM
(1)	The bank would borrow DM237,037 for 3 months	237,037
(2)	Pay interest at 5% per annum on the DM loan 237,037×5% for 3 months.	2,963
		240,000

		£
(3)	Convert the proceeds to £ DM237,037 / 3.0964	76,552.45
(4)	Deposit them in London	
(5)	Earn interest on the deposit £76,552.46×14.125% for 3 months.	2,703.26
	Promise Mundi Ltd	79,255.71
(5)	The bank will repay the DM borrowing with the customer cash collection	

The customer rate was calculated at DM240,000 / 79,255.71 = DM3.0282. Mundi Ltd would only collect £77,509.37 if it could sell the Marks on the spot market. It gains £1,746.34 (ignoring the earning potential of an earlier settlement) from the interest rate differential. The £ is said to be at a discount against the Mark.

Incompany Risk Matching

If Mundi Ltd did expect to have simultaneous receipts and payments in Marks it would be foolish to take on the cost of buying and selling forward. No exchange risk is involved. Similarly the bank that enters a forward exchange purchase contract will seek a matching sale contract with a different customer. This will save it from having to create loan and deposit accounts. To remove all exchange risk the bank will seek to arrange contracts that expire at the same time. If a bank has too many requests for one type of contract it will seek to discourage demand by quoting unattractive rates (like a bookmaker lowering the price of a heavily-backed horse). For this reason a wise company will seek quotes from about three banks before entering a forward exchange contract. A further method of incompany risk matching is called 'leading and lagging'. If Mundi Ltd expected to receive DM400,000 on 1 December, 1989 it could delay settlement of its DM240,000 until that date ('lag') and sell the net exposure DM160,000 forward. If Mundi Ltd expected to receive DM400,000 on 1 November it could speed up the settlement of its DM240,000 until that date ('lead') and sell the net exposure DM160,000 forward.

FOREIGN CURRENCY TRANSACTIONS

In the first section we saw how a US$ loan at 7% could become very expensive. Mundi Ltd could eliminate the exchange risk if it was confident of generating sales revenue of US$146,334 per annum for 5 years. Mundi Ltd could use this cash flow to repay the capital and interest.

Foreign Currency Option Contracts

A company tendering for contracts in a foreign currency is in an unclear exchange risk situation. If the tender succeeds it is exposed. If the tender fails it is not.

Foreign currency option contracts have been developed to cover such unclear situations. The option provides the right (but not the obligation) to buy or sell a foreign currency, at a defined price, on or before a specified date.

ILLUSTRATION OF A PUT (SELL) OPTION CONTRACT

Mundi Ltd tendered for a contract that would create net cash of US$15 million if successful. The exchange rate at the time was £ = US$1.50. The company was concerned about the possible combination of a successful tender and a weakening dollar. The bank quoted for a put option as follows: exercise price £ = US$1.50 and cost of contract = £300,000 (3% of £10 million). Mundi Ltd accepted the quotation. Four things can occur which will result in a profit or loss. First, say the tender is unsuccessful and the dollar strengthens to £ = US$1.40. To exercise the option, the company would have to buy dollars on the spot market. The option is rejected:

	£
Cost of currency purchase $15 million/1.4	10,714.285
Option premium	300,000
Cost of exercising option	11,014,285
Proceeds from exercise of option	10,000,000
Loss from option exercise	1,014,285

The company can restrict its loss to £300,000 by not exercising the option.

Secondly, say the tender is successful and the dollar strengthens to £ = US$1.40. The company rejects the option because:

	£
Proceeds of sale in market $15 million/1.4	10,714,285
Less option premium	300,000
Net received	10,414,285
Proceeds from exercise of option	10,000,000
Extra profit from non-exercise	414,285
There is a break even position at £ = US$1.4563.	
Proceeds of sale in market $15 million/1.4563	10,300,000
Less option premium	300,000
Proceeds from exercise of option	10,000,000

If the dollar is stronger than £ = $1.4563 Mundi Ltd will gain by not exercising the option. If the dollar is weaker than £ = $1.4563 the option should be exercised. This will restrict the loss to £300,000 (the option premium).

Thirdly, suppose the tender is unsuccessful and the dollar weakens to £ = US$1.60. Even though the tender is unsuccessful the company will benefit by exercising the option:

	£
It buys $15,000,000 spot £ = $1.60	9,375,000
It exercises the option and collects	10,000,000
Gross profit from option exercise	625,000
Option premium	300,000
Net profit from option exercise	325,000

Exercising the option is beneficial if the dollar weakens beyond $1.50. At this exchange rate the holder loses £300,000. The loss declines as the dollar weakens towards the break even point £ = US$1.5464. A profit is earned if the weakness is greater.

Finally, say the tender is successful and the dollar weakens to £ = US$1.60. The option is exercised because:

	£
Sale in market would realise	9,375,000
Option exercise realises	10,000,000
Gross loss avoided	625,000
Option premium	300,000
Net loss avoided	925,000

Exercising the option restricts the loss to £300,000. Non-exercise would result in a loss of £925,000.

Interest Rate Swaps

An interest rate swap is not a true currency exposure instrument. It is dealt with in this section because it usually involves foreign currency borrowing or depositing. The swap mechanism is similar to an option contract. Loans are frequently made at variable interest rates. Such loans involve the risk of interest rate increases as well as exchange fluctuations. It is possible to protect against interest rate increases using a swap. The bank locates another customer that wishes to protect itself against a decline in interest rates and the exposures are matched.

For example, Mundi Ltd borrowed US$10 million. The interest rate is variable and the company wishes to protect itself against a rate increase. Other Inc. has a deposit of US$10 million on which the interest rate is also variable and it wishes to protect itself against a rate decline. A bank offers a forward rate agreement to Mundi Ltd at 10% and to Other Inc. at 8%. Actual rates are:

Quarter	Loans	Deposits
1	11%	9%
2	13%	11%
3	10.5%	8.5%
4	8%	6%

In quarter 1, Mundi Ltd incurs excess interest of US$25,000 ($1,000,000×1% for 3 months). It recovers the $25,000 excess from the bank and achieves its target cost. Other Inc. earns excess interest of US$25,000. It pays the bank the $25,000 excess and it also achieves its target return.

In quarter 4, Mundi Ltd pays the bank the $50,000 it saved in interest. Other Inc. recovers $50,000 it failed to earn. Both companies are charged a fee for the exposure matching.

Financing Overseas Subsidiaries

In the second part of this chapter we saw how the sterling performance of SubMundi Inc was affected by exchange rates. Had Mundi Ltd used $ bank loans to defray part of the set-up cost the scale of potential exchange losses could have been minimised. This is because the bank debt will be translated at the closing rate.

Introducing $200,000 of 8% loan in place of a similar amount of capital at formation would change the results as follows:

Illustration 3: Strengthening   Profit and Loss Translation

Exchange Rates			1989 £ = $1.60	1990 $1.80		
$1989	*£1989*				*$1990*	*£1990*
980,000	612,500	Sales			1,152,000	640,000
735,000	459,375	Cost of sales			864,000	480,000
245,000	153,125	Gross profit			288,000	160,000
186,000	116,250	Operating cost			198,000	110,000
59,000	36,875	PBIT			90,000	50,000
16,000	10,000	Interest			16,000	8,889
43,000	26,875	PBT			74,000	41,111
17,200	10,750	Tax provision			29,600	16,444
25,800	16,125	Profit after tax			44,400	24,667
16,000	10,000	Proposed dividend			16,000	8,889
9,800	6,125	Profit retained			28,400	15,778

Profit retained and loss items are the same as illustration 1 except:

1   the $200,000 loan created an interest cost of $16,000;
2   the tax provision (tax rate 40%) was reduced by $6,400 as a result of the tax deductable interest cost;
3   the same dividend, 8 cents per share, was paid on the 200,000 share capital base.

Illustration 1: £ Strengthening   Balance Sheet Translation

Exchange Rates			1989	1990		
			£ = $1.60	$1.80		
$1989	*£1989*				*$1990*	*£1990*
324,000	202,500	Fixed assets			288,000	160,000
300,000	187,500	Current assets			360,000	200,000
		Payable in under one year				
160,000	100,000	Creditors			144,000	80,000
21,000	13,125	Bank loan[1]			20,200	11,222
17,200	10,750	Tax provision			29,600	16,444
16,000	10,000	Proposed dividend			16,000	8,889
(214,200)	(133,875)				(209,800)	(116,555)
409,800	256,125	Net assets			438,200	243,445
Financed by:						
200,000	142,857	Share capital[2]			200,000	142,857
9,800	6,125	Revenue reserve			38,200	21,903
–	(17,857)	Exchange losses[3]			–	(32,426)[4]
209,800	131,125	Net worth			238,200	132,334
200,000	125,000	Long-term debt			200,000	111,111
409,800	256,125				438,200	243,445

[1] Loan 1989 (from illustration 1)	5,000
Add interest 1989	16,000
Revised loan 1989	21,000
Loan 1990 (from illustration 1)	10,600
Add interest 2 years	32,000
	42,600

Less reduced dividend paid	16,000	
Less reduced tax paid	6,400	22,400
Revised loan 1990		20,200

[2] The share capital was introduced at £ = $1.40.

	1989	1990
	£	£
Opening net assets	142,857[a]	131,125[c]
Closing net assets	125,000[b]	116,556[d]
[3] Exchange loss year	17,857	14,569
Opening loss		17,857
[4] Exchange loss cumulative		32,426

[a] $200,000/1.4 = £142,857.   [b] $200,000/1.6 = £125,000.
[c] $209,800/1.6 = £131,125.   [d] $209,800/1.8 = £116,556.

Contrasting the exchange losses:

	Illustration 1	Illustration 3
1989	35,714	63,728
This year	17,857	32,426

The equity declines in value as the £ strengthens. The use of a $200,000 loan reduces the translation loss. Had SubMundi Inc been financed totally by loans and repatriated all surpluses no exchange loss would have been suffered.

Illustration 4: Weakening   Profit and Loss Translation

Exchange Rates			1989 £ = $1.20	1990 $1.00		
$1989	*£1989*				*$1990*	*£1990*
980,000	816,667	Sales			1,152,000	1,152,000
735,000	612,500	Cost of sales			864,000	864,000
245,000	204,167	Gross profit			288,000	288,000
186,000	155,000	Operating cost			198,000	198,000
59,000	49,167				90,000	90,000
16,000	13,334	Interest			16,000	16,000
43,000	35,833	Profit pre tax			74,000	74,000
17,200	14,333	Tax			29,600	29,600
25,800	21,500	Profit after tax			44,400	44,400
16,000	13,333	Proposed dividend			16,000	16,000
9,800	8,167	Profit retained			28,400	28,400

Interest, tax and dividend as per illustration 3.

Illustration 4: £ Weakening   Balance Sheet Translation

Exchange Rates			1989	1990		
			£ = $1.20	$1.00		
$1989	*£1989*				*$1990*	*£1990*
324,000	270,000	Fixed assets			288,000	288,000
300,000	250,000	Current assets			360,000	360,000
		Payable in under one year				
160,000	133,333	Creditors			144,000	144,000
21,000	17,500	Bank loans			20,200	20,200
17,200	14,333	Tax provision			29,600	29,600
16,000	13,334	Proposed dividends			16,000	16,000
(214,200)	(178,500)				(209,800)	(209,800)
409,800	341,500	Net assets			438,200	438,200
Financed By:						
200,000	142,856	Share capital			200,000	142,856
9,800	8,167	Revenue reserve			38,200	36,567
–	23,810	Exchange gain[1]			–	58,777[2]
209,800	174,833	Net worth			238,200	238,200
200,000	166,667	Long-term debt			200,000	200,000
409,800	341,500				438,200	438,200

	1989	1990
	£	£
Opening net assets	142,857[a]	174,833[c]
Closing net assets	166,667[b]	209,800[d]
[1] Exchange gain year	23,810	34,967
Opening gain		23,810
[2] Exchange gain cumulative		58,777

[a] $200,000/1.4 = £142,857.   [b] $200,000/1.2 = £166,667.
[c] $209,800/1.2 = £174,833.   [d] $209,800/1.0 = £209,800.

Summary of Translation Issues

1   The closing rate method is nearly always used in the balance sheet.
2   There is a choice of profit and loss translation methods. Once a method has been selected it must be applied consistently.

3   A strengthening £ results in exchange losses on translation of overseas assets. These losses will be abated in so far as foreign currency loans are used to finance the net assets.

4   A weakening £ results in exchange gains. The use of foreign currency loans to fund the net assets dilutes the gain.

5   Where an overseas company invests in sterling assets points three and four operate in reverse. Losses occur on translation if sterling weakens and gains if it strengthens.

6   Rates of exchange can vary unpredictably. A passive approach to translation risk management is to assume that gains and losses will cancel out over a long period. This is a dangerous assumption. The prudent organisation will seek to minimise the risk of translation losses. This can be done by using local currency borrowings to finance part of the asset base. Total elimination of translation exposure can be achieved by using all local currency borrowings and supporting them by a parent company guarantee to protect the lenders. In such a case the UK parent will be indifferent to exchange rate fluctuations.

Mundi Ltd decided that the risk of translation losses was too significant to leave exposed. It was satisfied that the size of US$ cash inflows would underpin repayment obligations on a high level of $ borrowings. On formation SubMundi Inc was financed a follows:

	$
Share capital	40,000
8% fixed interest loan	360,000
	400,000

A parent company guarantee was used to support the high gearing. The translated results as sterling strengthened over the next two years were:

Illustration 5: Strengthening   Profit and Loss Translation

Exchange Rates	1989	1990
Closing	£ = $1.60	$2.00
Average	£ = $1.50	$1.80

$1989	£1989 Closing	£1989 Average		$1990	£1990 Closing	£1990 Average
980,000	612,500	653,333	Sales	1,152,000	576,000	640,000
735,000	459,375	490,000	Cost of sales	864,000	432,000	480,000
245,000	153,125	163,333	Gross profit	288,000	144,000	160,000
186,000	116,250	124,000	Operating cost	198,000	99,000	110,000
59,000	36,875	39,333	PBIT	90,000	45,000	50,000
28,800	18,000	19,200	Interest	28,800	14,400	16,000
30,200	18,875	20,133	Profit before tax	61,200	30,600	34,000
12,080	7,550	7,550	Tax provision	24,480	12,240	12,240
18,120	11,325	12,583	Profit before tax	36,720	18,360	21,760
3,200	2,000	2,000	Proposed dividend	3,200	1,600	1,600
14,920	9,325	10,583	Profit retained	33,520	16,760	20,160

The change in financial structure affects the profit and loss account as follows:

1   Interest on the $360,000 loan cost $28,800.
2   The tax provision fell by $11,520 (40% of the interest charge).
3   The dividend of 8 cents applied to only 40,000 shares.

Illustration 5: £ Strengthening   Balance Sheet Translation

Exchange Rates Closing			1989 £ = $1.60	1990 $2.00		
$1989	£1989				$1990	£1990
324,000	202,500	Fixed assets			288,000	144,000
300,000	187,500	Current assets			360,000	180,000
		Payable in under one year				
160,000	100,000	Creditors			144,000	72,000
33,800	21,125	Bank loans[1]			27,880	13,940
12,080	7,550	Tax provision			24,480	12,240
3,200	2,000	Proposed dividend			3,200	1,600
(209,080)	(130,675)				(199,560)	(99,780)
414,920	259,325	Net assets			448,440	224,220
Financed by:						
40,000	28,571	Share capital[2]			40,000	28,571
14,920	9,325	Revenue reserve			48,440	26,085
–	(3,571)	Exchange loss[3]			–	(10,436)[4]
54,920	34,325	Net worth			88,440	44,220
360,000	225,000	Long-term debt			360,000	180,000
414,920	259,325				448,440	224,220

[1] Bank loan 1989 (per illustration 1)   5,000
Add interest 1989   28,800

Revised loan 1989   33,800

Bank loan 1990 (per illustration 1)   10,600
Add interest 2 years   57,600

  68,200
Reduced dividend paid   28,800
Reduced tax paid   11,520   40,320

Revised loan 1989   27,880

[2] The share capital was introduced at £ = $1.40.

	1989 £	1990 £
Opening net assets	28,571[a]	34,325[c]
Closing net assets	25,000[b]	27,460[d]
[3] Exchange loss year	3,571	6,865
Opening loss		3,571
[4] Exchange loss cumulative		10,436

[a] $40,000/1.4 = £28,571.
[c] $54,920/1.6 = £34,325.
[b] $40,000/1.6 = £25,000.
[d] $54,920/2 = £27,460.

398

FOREIGN CURRENCY TRANSACTIONS

The effect of this high geared structure is to reduce the potential exchange loss to £10,436 even if sterling strengthens to £ = $2 by the end of 1990. If Mundi Ltd had used $400,000 of share capital it would have experienced a translation loss of £136,641. The treasury manager was awarded a handsome bonus for saving the group £126,205.

Illustration 6: £ Strengthening

Exchange Rates	Start–1988	End–1988	End–1989
Closing £ = $	1.25	1.60	2.00
Average		1.50	1.80

Profit and Loss Translation

$ 1988	£ 1988 Closing	£ 1988 Average		$ 1989	£ 1989 Closing	£ 1989 Average
980,000	612,500	653,333	Sales	1,152,000	576,000	640,000
735,000	459,375	490,000	Cost of sales	864,000	432,000	480,000
245,000	153,125	163,333	Gross profit	288,000	144,000	160,000
150,000	93,750	100,000	Operating cost	162,000	81,000	90,000
36,000	22,500	24,000	Depreciation	36,000	18,000	20,000
28,800	18,000	19,200	Interest	28,800	14,400	16,000
214,800	134,250	143,200	Total expense	226,800	113,400	126,000
30,200	18,875	20,133	Profit pre-tax	61,200	30,600	34,000
12,080	7,550	7,550	Tax provision	24,480	12,240	12,240
18,120	11,325	12,583	Profit after tax	36,720	18,360	21,760
1,920	1,200	1,200	Proposed dividend	1,920	960	960
16,200	10,125	11,383	Profit retained	34,800	17,400	20,800

The $360,000 loan was at 8% per annum. The interest cost is $28,800. The tax liability declined by 40% of the interest cost i.e. $11,520. The replacement of share capital with loan finance resulted in a reduction in the proposed dividend. The payout is 4.8% on the $40,000 share capital. Average rate translation is also shown in this illustration.

A HANDBOOK OF PRACTICAL BUSINESS FINANCE

Illustration 6: £ Strengthening

Exchange Rates	Start–1988	End–1988	End–1989
Closing £ = $	1.25	1.60	2.00
Average		1.50	1.80

Balance Sheet Translation

$ 1988	£ 1988		$ 1989	£ 1989
360,000	225,000	Fixed assets at cost	360,000	180,000
36,000	22,500	Aggregate depreciation	72,000	36,000
324,000	202,500	Book value	288,000	144,000
		Current assets		
120,000	75,000	Stock	140,000	70,000
159,000	99,375	Debtors	226,000	113,000
(12,800)	(8,000)	Cash[1]	(12,600)	(6,300)
266,200	166,375		353,400	176,700
		Current liabilities		
160,000	100,000	Creditors	164,000	82,000
12,080	7,550	Tax provision	24,480	12,240
1,920	1,200	Proposed dividend	1,920	960
(174,000)	(108,750)		(190,400)	(95,200)
416,200	260,125	Net assets	451,000	225,500

Financed by:

40,000	32,000	Share capital[2]	40,000	32,000
16,200	10,125	Revenue reserve	51,000	27,525
–	(7,000)	Exchange loss[3]	–	(14,025)[4]
56,200	35,125	Net worth	91,000	45,500
360,000	225,000	Long-term debt	360,000	180,000
416,200	260,125		451,000	225,500

[1] Original cash last year		16,000
Less interest last year		(28,800)
Revised cash last year		(12,800)
Original cash this year		16,200
Less interest 2 years		57,600
		(41,400)
Reduced dividend paid	17,280	
Reduced tax paid	11,520	28,800
Revised cash this year		(12,600)

[2] The share capital was introduced at £ = $1.25.
Decline in value of net worth: £
£ start last year 40,000/1.25   =   32,000
£ end last year 40,000/1.6   =   25,000

[3] Exchange loss   7,000
£ start this year 56,200/1.6   =   35,125
£ end this year 56,200/2   =   28,100   7,025

[4] Cumulative exchange loss   14,025

The effect of this high geared structure is to reduce the potential exchange loss to £14,025 even if sterling strengthens to £ = $2 by the end of 1989. Mundi Ltd decided this was the optimum structure for SubMundi Inc. even though it involved a very high gearing.

Chapter 14

Mergers and Acquisitions

The advent of the Single European Act is likely to increase the already hectic pace of takeover activity. This chapter focuses on four topics:

1 Why companies seek merger and acquisition opportunities.
2 Valuation of businesses in takeover negotiations.
3 Preparation of consolidated accounts subsequent to mergers and acquisitions.
   - Definition of a merger
   - Accounting for mergers
   - Definition of an acquisition
   - Accounting for acquisitions.
4 Special considerations in mergers and acquisitions.

Reasons for Takeover Activity

The Purchaser Perspective

The major objective of the purchaser in merger activities is to create wealth for the shareholders. This can be achieved in a variety of ways:

A Increasing earnings per share. The EPS drives the price earnings ratio. It in turn drives the share price which is the key barometer of shareholder wealth. A takeover which will increase the ongoing EPS expectation is intrinsically attractive.

B Reducing the risk profile of the business should earn it a higher P/E ratio. A classic example is the tobacco industry. The consistent decline in consumption of tobacco products has led to the classification of the industry as high risk, in spite of the large positive cash flows it creates. Major diversification by Imperial Tobacco and BATS, over the last twenty-five years were designed to increase their P/E ratios by persuading investors that the acquisitions should be valued at a higher number of years of future profits.

C Takeover of businesses on a lower P/E ratio, where the stock-market values the earnings acquired at the purchaser's P/E. Williams Holdings has used this strategy to build a huge group over the last six years.

Consider the following example:

	Company A	Company B
Projected EPS	20p	10p
Share price	£4	£1.2
P/E	20	12
Shares in issue £m	20	40

If company A offered 14m of its share in exchange for the 40m shares of company B and the offer was accepted the impact on its share price could be as follows:

Projected combined earnings (£4+£4)	£8m
Shares in issue (20m+14m)	34
Projected EPS	23.53p
Post-merger P/E	20
Post-merger share price	£4.71

The bid should be attractive to company B shareholders. The whole company was valued at £48m. It is now worth £66m (14m shares at £4.71 each). The takeover may be in the same business or a totally different field.

D Research worldwide tends to suggest that the bigger the market share a business has the greater will be its ROI. This is mainly caused by synergy (combining production, marketing, administration, research etc., making mergers of competitors potentially attractive to both parties).

E A longer-term way of increasing wealth is to acquire a business with underexploited assets. The introduction of sophisticated management techniques offers the promise of increased sales, reduced costs, and release of underutilised assets. This has been a cornerstone of the BTR takeover strategy.

F Many recent takeover bids have been inspired by the belief that the value of the parts is greater than the stock-market capitalisation of the whole. A classic example is the Hoylake consortium bid for British American Tobacco.
   The objective was believed to be:
   (a) To finance the acquisition mainly through 'junk bonds' (they had not yet been totally discredited);

(b) To sell off all the non-tobacco subsidiaries and use the proceeds to repay the borrowings; and

(c) To wind up with a major tobacco business which cost relatively little.

On 26 September 1989 BAT announced its own demerger proposals. These involved stock-market flotations of the Argos retailing subsidiary and the Wiggins Teape Appleton pulp and paper division. BAT would issue free shares in the divisions to be quoted. Shareholders would wind up with holdings in three companies if the proposal succeeded. Sir James Goldsmith, on behalf of Hoylake voted in favour of the proposals. The free shares were issued and are now separately quoted. It will remain a classic example of the value of the parts exceeding the whole.

A second reason for takeover activity is to improve the stability of the business. Major elements of this strategy include:

G   A company that is overborrowed may choose to buy one that is cash rich. Some companies have acquired investment trusts (typically valued at less than their asset backing, and then liquidated them to release cash in this way).

H   A company that depends heavily on a key supplier may choose to acquire it to assure quality, quantity and price of key materials.

I   Equally a company that depends heavily on one customer may choose to acquire it to assure continuity of sales.

J   A company that lacks key management skills may acquire a company that has the required skills (management buy in). British Aerospace bought a property company during 1989 with a major purpose of acquiring its managerial skills.

K   Eliminate overdependence on one product. This is like the tobacco example at point B above. However the thrust of the diversification strategy is the increased stability of a portfolio rather than an immediate increase in shareholder wealth.

L   Buying established businesses tends to be less risky than developing new products from start up. This is associated with point K above.

M   As we saw in Chapter 7 a business that is growing rapidly is likely to be heavily cash negative. Acquisition of a cash rich company in exchange for shares can help to solve a potential overtrading crisis. Amstrad is an excellent recent example.

A buyer wants to make a takeover at as low a price as possible. A seller will strive to obtain the best possible exit price for its shareholders. Vendors can often get the initial bid improved by emphasising the reasons why the purchaser needs the takeover more than the seller. The negotiations involve a search for a price acceptable to both parties. The arrival of a counterbid can lead to an auction. In such cases the vendor is likely to obtain an attractive price. Management of an organisation, faced with an unwanted takeover bid, may try to attract a counterbid from a more acceptable source (a 'white knight'). Sometimes the white knight is not as acceptable in retrospect as was thought at the time.

Reasons a Business is For Sale

There are seven main reasons why a business may be for sale:

1 Wish to link up with state of the art production, product development or marketing skills;
2 Own inability to capitalise on excellent products due to under-capitalisation or lack of managerial skills;
3 Owner management wish to retire and have no family successors prepared or competent to run the business;
4 Perhaps it is obvious but some offers are so good that the recipient company simply cashes in;
5 The management may have harvested the business for some years by failing to replace obsolete equipment or invest in new product development;
6 Overvalued assets, notably stock and debtors; and
7 Understated libilities.

1–4 offer promising bid potential. 5–8 suggest difficult problems ahead if a bid succeeds.

Raising the Price

There are four major factors that vendors must take into account in valuing their business during takeover negotiations:

1 The stock market value of control, if it is quoted. This is not just a simple matter of multiplying the number of shares in issue by the current share price. Factors that need to be considered include:
   (a) Share prices tend to reflect the value of small parcels of equity. Companies that try to acquire large blocks of shares generally have to pay a substantial premium over the pre-bid share price.
   (b) Some quoted shares trade at a discount on their real value. Large blocks of shares may be held for long-term strategic purposes. The supply of shares for sale may be small. You might expect these conditions to artificially boost the share

price because demand exceeds supply. Investors usually avoid such shares because of concern about marketability.

2 The asset value of the business. This is not quite as straightforward as it seems. If no takeover is in prospect, a business may avoid the trouble and expense of revaluing appreciating assets. In defending a takeover bid a company will fight to ensure that the value of properties, brand names etc., are included in the bid price.

3 The dividend income of the shareholders. This is particularly important where (1) the vendor tends to pay out a higher proportion of profits as dividends than a potential purchaser, or (2) where prospects for the business as a separate entity promise substantial dividend growth.

4 Qualitative factors not adequately reflected in the share price, assets and dividends. These include:

(a) The capability of management and their preparedness to work for the new business combination;

(b) The position of the product portfolio (stage in life cycle, quality relative to competitors, and market potential for products in development); and

(c) The value to the purchaser of synergistic opportunities. A vendor will argue that these benefits cannot be availed of by the purchaser unless a takeover is agreed. They will want part of the benefit included in the business valuation.

Vendors will use these factors in defending the bid. They will also try to cast doubt about aspects of the potential purchaser's management, products, markets and financial situation. This defensive tactic peaked with the attack on each other's products and past performance when Hanson were bidding for Imperial Tobacco. Bidders, defenders and their financial advisers have been forced to behave in a more civilised way since then.

Valuation Methods

This section deals with the valuation of takeover candidates. The example assumes that: the suitor is acceptable; fair values for assets have been agreed between the parties before the valuation commences; and the takeover consideration will be a share exchange. Other forms of consideration are discussed later.

Relevant Data Vendor and Purchaser

	Seller Plc	Buyer Plc
Ordinary shares in issue (millions)	6	20
Earnings per share (pence)	12.5	20
Dividend per share (pence)	6.7	8
Asset backing per share (£)	1.5	1.2
Latest share price (£)	1.25	3

BUYER PLC: PROPOSAL 1

Based on this data Buyer Plc asserts that Seller Plc is worth £7.5m (6 million shares at £1.25).
    The following formula can be used to quantify the share exchange appropriate to this and other valuation methods:

$$\text{Vendor contribution to merged group} \times \frac{\text{Purchaser shares in issue}}{\text{Purchaser contribution to merged group}}$$

Buyer Plc would issue shares in proportion to the stock market values contributed by both parties. Adapting the formula, we can calculate the shares to be issued as follows:

$$7.5^1 \times \frac{20^2}{60^3} = 2.5 \text{ million shares}$$

[1] Vendor capitalisation contributed.
[2] Purchaser shares in issue.
[3] Purchaser capitalisation contributed.

Buyer Plc would offer 10 new shares for each 24 Seller Plc shares. We can verify the accuracy of the formula in the following way:

Combined capitalisation 60+7.5	(A)	67.5m
Shares now in issue 20+2.5	(B)	22.5m
Value per share A/B	(C)	£3
Seller Plc value 2.5 million×(C)		£7.5m

SELLER PLC:COUNTERPROPOSAL 1

The directors of Seller Plc will certainly regard the initial offer as unacceptable. Their starting position could be that the share exchange should be based on relative net assets contributed to the new group. Adapting the formula the share exchange would be:

407

$$9^1 \times \frac{20^2}{24^3} = 7.5 \text{ million shares}$$

[1] Vendor assets contributed
[2] Purchaser shares in issue.
[3] Purchaser assets contributed.

Buyer Plc would have to offer five new shares for each four Seller Plc shares. 27.5 million shares would now be in issue with a combined asset backing of £33 million. The group asset backing is £1.20 per share. This leaves Seller Plc shareholders in the same net asset position as before the merger.

Neither of these valuation methods is ideal. As you might expect in a preliminary skirmish Buyer Plc is offering too little and Seller Plc is asking too much. If a merger is to be consummated a compromise is required.

BUYER PLC: PROPOSAL 2

Buyer Plc proposes a share exchange based on the proportion of earnings contributed by each company. The share exchange is:

$$6 \text{ million} \times 12.5\text{p}^1 \times \frac{20 \text{ million}^2}{20 \text{ million} \times 20\text{p}^3} = 3.75 \text{ million shares}$$

[1] Vendor earnings contributed.
[2] Purchaser shares in issue.
[3] Purchaser earnings contributed.

Buyer Plc would offer 15 new shares for 24 Seller Plc shares.

SELLER PLC: COUNTERPROPOSAL 2

The directors of Buyer Plc are pleased with the improved offer. They intend to improve it. They suggest the exchange should be based on the projected dividend payouts of both parties. The share exchange becomes:

$$6 \text{ million} \times 6.7\text{p}^1 \times \frac{20 \text{ million}^2}{20 \text{ million} \times 8\text{p}^3} = 5 \text{ million shares}$$

[1] Vendor dividend payout.
[2] Purchaser shares in issue.
[3] Purchaser dividend payout.

Buyer Plc wold offer five new shares for each six Seller Plc shares.

Shareholders in both organisations will have differing views about the relative importance of assets, earnings, dividends and share prices. To sell the proposal to their shareholders, the management of both companies will have to be able to persuade them that individual's priorities are catered for.

Buyer Plc announced that the maximum value they would place on Seller Plc was £12m. We will now examine the impact of a share exchange based on this valuation on the shareholders in both companies.

A Share Exchange Consideration

Based on the valuation of £12m and the current Buyer Plc share price of £3, the consideration would be an exchange of 2 Buyer Plc shares for each 3 Seller Plc shares. The forecast results of the business combination are as follows:

Ordinary shares in issue	(£1 nominal)	A	24m
Combined earnings[1]		B	£5.4m
Earnings per share	B/A	C	22.5p
Dividend cover[2]		D	2.5 times
Forecast dividend	B/D	E	£2.16m
Dividend per share	E/A		9p
Price earnings ratio[3]		F	15
Forecast share price	C×F		£3.375
Group assets[4]		G	£32.88m
Asset backing per share	G/A		£1.37

[1] The effect of synergy.
[2] Maintaining the Buyer Plc cover.
[3] Anticipating a favourable stock market reaction to the merger proposal.

[4]	£m	£m	£m
Combined assets at merger			33.0000
Extra earnings (5.4−4.75)		0.6500	
Less tax 33%	0.2145		
Increased dividend	0.5600	0.7745	0.1245
			32.8755

409

A HANDBOOK OF PRACTICAL BUSINESS FINANCE

Should a Holder of 1,000 Seller Plc Shares Accept?

	Pre-Merger £	Post-Merger £	% Change
Market value of investment	1,250	2,251[1]	+80
Earnings expected	125	150[2]	+20
Dividends expected	67	60[3]	−10
Asset backing expected	1,500	914[4]	−39

[1] 667×£3.375.
[2] 667×22.5p.
[3] 667×9p.
[4] 667×£1.37.

Buyer Plc shareholders are being offered a substantial increase in earnings and capitalisation. If they accept they will receive a lower dividend income and have a lower asset backing.

Should a Holder of 1,000 Buyer Plc Shares Accept?

	Pre-Merger £	Post-Merger £	% Change
Market value of investment	3,000	3,375	+12.5
Earnings expected	200	225	+12.5
Dividends expected	80	90	+12.5
Asset backing expected	1,200	1,370	+14.2

Buyer Plc shareholders are being offered a strengthening of all their statistics. They may feel that too much of the share price appreciation is being given to Seller Plc shareholders. The directors might consider an adaptation of the offer to overcome some of the complaints that could be expressed by both sides. The adaptation might involve a loan stock component. A tentative alernative was now proposed by Buyer Plc.

A Share and Loan Stock Consideration

Buyer Plc proposes an exchange of one new share plus 50p of 10% loan stock for each two Seller Plc shares. Forecast results for the business combination might be as follows:

Ordinary shares in issue	(£1 nominal)	A	23M
Combined earnings[1]		B	£5.30M
Earnings per share	B/A	C	23p
Dividend cover		D	2.5
Forecast dividend	B/D	E	£2.12M
Divided per share	E/A		9.2p
Price earnings ratio		F	15
Forecast share price	C×F		£3.465
Group assets[2]		G	£31.53M
Asset backing per share	G/A		£1.37

	£M	£M
[1] Forecast earnings previous		5.4000
Loan stock interest		
3 million×50p×10%	0.1500	
Tax on loan stock interest		
£150,000@33%	0.0495	0.1005
Revised earnings		5.2955
[2] Combined assets		33.0000
Less loan stock		1.5000
		31.5000
Increased earnings	0.5455	
Increased dividend	0.5210	0.0245
		31.4755

Should a Holder of 1,000 Seller Plc Shares Accept?

	Pre-Merger £	Post-Merger £	% Change
Market value of investment	1,250	2,148[1]	+72
Earnings expected	125	165[2]	+32
Dividends and interest	67	96[3]	+43
Asset backing	1,500	1,185[4]	−21

[1] (500×£3.465)+(500×£0.83).
[2] (500×23.1p)+(500×10%).
[3] (500×9.2p)+(500×10%)
[4] (500×£1.37)+(500×£1).

The loan stock is redeemable in five years. It is likely to have a market value of about 83p due to the low interest coupon. This alternative is more attractive to Seller Plc shareholders who are concerned about income and asset backing. They must concede some capital appreciation potential to improve these elements.

Should a Holder of 1,000 Buyer Plc Shares Accept?

	Pre-Merger £	Post-Merger £	% Change
Market value of investment	3,000	3,465	+15.5
Earnings expected	200	230	+15.0
Dividends expected	80	92	+15.0
Asset backing	1,200	1,370	+14.2

Buyer Plc shareholders obtain a slight improvement in all their returns, in the short term, as compared to the share exchange. In the medium term, if profit growth exceeds the cost of servicing the loan stock, the gearing will prove beneficial, provided the P/E does not fall to reflect the increased risk.

A Cash Consideration

Instead of, or as well as, the previous options, Buyer Plc might offer £9.6 million cash or £1.60 per share. Buyer Plc would probably create 3.2m new shares and arrange a rights issue or placing to avoid diluting the asset base of the group.

SHOULD A HOLDER OF 1,000 SELLER PLC SHARES ACCEPT?

A shareholder who accepts this offer will receive £1,600 in cash. This is 28% more than the pre-merger value of their holding. At current interest rates a deposit of this sum will increase their income to say £192. This is more than would be earned from either of the other options. The snag is that they would now be invested in non-appreciating assets. Shareholders who accept the cash offer will: have an alternative investment in mind; wish to become more liquid; or regard an ongoing investment in the group as unattractive.

SHOULD A HOLDER OF 1,000 BUYER PLC SHARES ACCEPT?

The ongoing returns to Buyer Plc shareholders will be similar to those outlined in the share exchange proposal. The exact figures will depend on the price at which the shares are sold.

Post-takeover Consolidations

A business combination may be defined as a merger or an acquisition, depending on the circumstances.

Definition of a Merger

The definition of a merger in SSAP 23 (*Accounting for Acquisitions and Mergers*) can be summarised a follows:

1   The combination of businesses arises from an offer open to all equity and voting shares not already held by the offerer.
2   The offerer has secured, as a result of the offer, at least 90% of the shares and voting rights of the offeree.
3   Immediately prior to the offer, the offerer did not hold 20% or more of the shares or voting rights of the offeree.
4   At least 90% of the purchase consideration, including that given for shares held prior to the offer, is in the form of equity capital.

Where there is more than one class of equity in the offeree, these tests should be applied to each class of equity separately. Based on this definition, the cash offer in our takeover example is not eligible for merger accounting. The share exchange offer would be if: it was open to all vendor shareholders; at least 90% accepted the offer; and Buyer Plc did not hold 20% of the vendor shares prior to making the offer.

A share and loan stock offer could be eligible, if the three conditions applied and at least 90% of the consideration was in the form of shares. This is not the case in our illustration.

Accounting for Mergers

The key rules of merger accounting are as follows:

1   It is not necessary to adjust the carrying value of assets and liabilities to fair value. Appropriate adjustments to achieve uniformity of accounting policies are required.
2   In the group profit and loss account for the period in which the merger took place, the profits or losses of subsidiaries, brought in for the first time, are included whether derived before or after the merger.
3   Distributable profits of the subsidiary prior to the merger can be paid out as group dividends.
4   Differences between the carrying value of the investment (normally the nominal value of the shares issued as consideration) and the nominal value of the shares acquired are treated as a reserve arising on consolidation.

A HANDBOOK OF PRACTICAL BUSINESS FINANCE

APPLICATIONS OF MERGER RULES

We will use the offer of two Buyer Plc shares for each three Seller Plc shares to illustrate merger accounting. The financial statements for the parent, subsidiary and group for the year ending after the merger are as follows:

Balance Sheets (£'000)

	Buyer	Seller	Group
Tangible fixed assets	19,600	3,500	23,100
Investment in subsidiary (Rule 4)	4,000	–	–
	23,600	3,500	23,100
Current assets			
Stocks	6,800	3,600	10,400
Debtors	8,400	4,800	13,200
Parent current account	–	300	–
Cash	1,500	200	1,700
	16,700	8,900	25,300
Current liabilities			
Short term loans	3,100	–	3,100
Creditors	4,000	2,500	6,500
Subsidiary current account	300	–	–
Proposed dividend	2,320	–	2,320
	(9,720)	(2,500)	(11,920)
Net assets	30,580	9,900	36,480
Financed by:			
Share capital	24,000	6,000	24,000
Revenue reserves (Rule 3)	6,580	3,900	10,480
Consolidation reserve (Rule 4)	–	–	2,000[a]
	30,580	9,900	36,480

[a] Purchase consideration (net of goodwill)		9,000
Less reserves at acquisition	3,000	
Investment at par	4,000	7,000
Consolidation reserve		2,000

414

Profit and Loss Accounts (£'000)

	Buyer	Seller	Group
Profit after tax	4,900	900	5,800
Proposed dividend	2,320	–	2,320
	2,580	900	3,480

The reconciliation (in £'000) with the company accounts is:

	Buyer	Seller
Net assets pre-merger year	24,000	9,000
Shares issued as consideration	4,000	
Profits in merger year	2,580	900
Shareholders' funds	30,580	9,900

Note that the above accounts correspond with the data used in the valuation examples earlier in the chapter (also in £'000):

		Buyer	Seller
(1)	Share capital before merger (a)	20,000	6,000
(2)	Asset backing (b)	£1.20	£1.50
(3)	Net assets before merger (a)×(b)	24,000	9,000

If, to ensure uniformity of accounting policies, the value of the Seller Plc assets had to be reduced by £500,000, Rule 1 would also have to be applied. This amount would be deducted from the consolidation reserve and the fixed asset value. The balance sheet total would now be £35.98m.

If the consideration for the merger had been 7 million shares, the summarised results would be:

	Buyer	Seller	Group
Net assets excluding investment	26,580	9,900	36,480
Investment in subsidiary (Rule 4)	7,000	–	–
Net assets	33,580	9,900	36,480
Financed by:			
Share capital	27,000	6,000	27,000
Revenue reserve	6,580	3,900	10,480
Consolidation reserve (Rule 1)	–	–	(1,000)[b]
	33,580	9,900	36,480
[b] Purchase consideration			
(net of goodwill)		9,000	
Less reserves at acquisition	3,000		
Investment at par	7,000	10,000	
Consolidation reserve		(1,000)	

The availability of reserves against which negative consolidation adjustments can be charged is a very important issue in some mergers. If the Buyer Plc share price collapsed to 50p during the merger negotiations they might have to increase the exchange to 18m. The necessary consolidation adjustment (12m) would eliminate all the group reserves. Buyer Plc should withdraw from the merger negotiations.

Definition of an Acquisition

In any case where a takeover does not meet all the conditions for merger accounting, acquisition accounting must be used.

Accounting for Acquisitions

The key rules in ED 53 are summarised as follows:

1 The fair value of the purchase consideration determines the cost of the acquisition to the acquiring entity.
2 The fair value of the identifiable net assets acquired will be used as the carrying amounts for the newly acquired assets and liabilities in consolidated financial statements.
3 The difference between the fair value of the purchase consideration and the sum of the value of the identifiable net assets is goodwill.

416

4 The investment is replaced by the fair value of the identifiable net assets acquired and the goodwill in the group accounts.
5 The profits of the company being acquired should only be brought into the group accounts from the date of acquisition.

APPLICATION OF ACQUISITION RULES

In order to compare merger and acquisition accounting we will make the following (not all very likely) assumptions:

1 Prior to the offer, Buyer Plc had acquired a 25% stake in the company in exchange for 800,000 ordinary shares. This made the takeover an acquisition.
2 The market value of Buyer Plc shares at the time of both share exchanges was £3.
3 All profits in the first year of consolidation occurred post-acquisition.
4 The group provided for the same total dividend pay out.

Balance Sheet Extract £'000

	Buyer	Group
Goodwill (Rule 3)[1]		3,000
Investment[2]	12,900	
Net assets[3]	26,580	36,480
	39,480	39,480
Financed by:		
Share capital	24,000	24,000
Share premium (Rule 1)	8,000	8,000
Revenue reserve[4]	7,480	7,480
	39,480	39,480

Profit and Loss Account Extract £'000

	Buyer	Seller	Group
Profit after tax (Rule 2)	4,900	900	5,800
Proposed dividend	2,320	–	2,320
	2,580	900	3,480
Reserves at acquisition	4,000	3,000	4,000
	6,580	3,900	7,480

			£'000
[1] Purchase consideration			12,000
Fair value of assets acquired			9,000
Goodwill			3,000
[2] Fair value of consideration			12,000
Post acquisition profit			900
Investment in seller plc			12,900
[3] Net assets (Buyer at acquisition)			24,000
Post acquisition (Buyer)		2,580	
Post acquisition (Seller)		900	3,480
Fair value of assets acquired (Rule 1)			9,000
			36,480

[4] Pre acquisition profits of the subsidiary are not available for distribution.

The significant differences between the two types of accounting are:

Profits Available for Distribution

	£'000	£'000	£'000
Merger	10,480		
Acquisition		7,480	
Difference			3,000
Represented by:			
Share premium			8,000
Consolidation reserve			(2,000)
Goodwill			(3,000)
			3,000

The Seller Plc net assets may need to be adjusted: (a) to reflect under or over valuation, and (b) to harmonise accounting policies. An adjustment that led to a fair value of the net assets acquired increasing by £500,000 would reduce the goodwill to £2.5M. An adjustment that led to a fair value of the net assets acquired declining by £800,000 would increase the goodwill to £3.8M.

Purchased goodwill would have to be eliminated over its useful life, in line with ED 47 as explained in Chapter 2.

In the illustrations of merger and acquisition accounting I showed the balance sheets and profit and loss accounts of Buyer and Seller as well as the group figures. This was so that you could see how the group figures were derived. The published accounts of the group would not disclose the figures for the components. Note that SSAP 14 requires that, in respect of all material acquisitions during a year, the consolidated financial statements should contain sufficient information about the results of subsidiaries acquired to enable shareholders to appreciate the effect on the consolidated results.

Special Considerations in Takeovers

1   Investment in businesses listed on the Stock Exchange can be affected by two very important rules:
    (a)   When another business acquires a 30% or greater stake in a company, the buyer is obliged to bid for the remaining equity.
    (b)   The bidder is obliged to offer the highest price paid for any shares acquired in the last six months to all vendor shareholders.
2   The holder of 90% of the shares in a subsidiary may be in a position to acquire compulsorily the remaining shares. The Companies Act 1985 rules that this can only be done within the six months following the offer becoming unconditional.
3   The acquiring company is faced with some major risks in undertaking a takeover:
    (a)   The cost (money and management time) can be very high. If the bid succeeds management neglect of normal tasks can result in serious disimprovement in performance. If the bid fails there will be a large expenditure on merchant banking advice, accounting assessments and communications with shareholders. These will have to be charged against the existing business and will reduce the profitability and financial stability.
    (b)   The valuation of assets being acquired may not be prudent: additional depreciation may be required when accounting policies are harmonised for consolidation; proper deductions

may not have been made to reflect the realisable value of slow moving stock; and bad debt provisions may prove to be inadequate.

(c) Customers and staff of the company being acquired may be less than happy with the new proprietors. This can result in lost sales, poor productivity and resignations by key staff. Service contracts provide some protection against the problems caused by resignations.

(d) Liabilities may be understated.

(e) In a takeover attempt which is bitterly opposed the vendor company management may introduce a 'poison pill'. Techniques include: automatic transfer of attractive assets to third parties; creation of unacceptable levels of debt that are automatically taken up if the bid succeeds; retirement of key managers (with ridiculous 'golden handshakes') etc.

Most of these concerns can be handled in an agreed bid:

1 Warranties can be obtained relating to realisable values of assets;
2 The buyer may choose not to take on the liabilities or obtain an indemnity against undisclosed items;
3 Part of the consideration can be deferred and made contingent on a defined level of future profit;
4 Indemnity can be requested to protect against 'poison pills'; and
5 Study of accounting policies and recalculation of depreciation provisions can be undertaken, etc.

In a contested bid they are very dificult to manage.

In spite of the issues of concern a takeover is often the most efficient way to expand or diversify a business. There are five basic categories of takeover:

1 Purchase of businesses that are supplying similar products or services in the same market (e.g. the merger of two UK newspapers). The impact of scale and experience in the business sector limits the risk in this type of takeover.
2 Purchase of businesses that are supplying similar products or services in other markets (e.g. the acquisition of a UK newspaper by an Australian one). Scale benefits and sectoral experience limit the risk.
3 Purchase of businesses in the same sector that supply substantially different products or services to different customers (e.g. a merger between a property developer and a building products manufacturer). The risk is greater because key managers in both companies may have little experience of success factors in the other part of the business sector.

4 Purchase of a key supplier or customer. This type of takeover can be very attractive. Knowledge and experience in the business sector reduces the risk. It suffers from one major drawback: the lead time from buying or creating products or services for sale to collection from third party customers lengthens. Substantial extra working capital is required.

5 Conglomerate diversification. For example, purchase of a clothing retailer by a computer manufacturer. Where an acquisition involves a totally different technology and customer base the risk increases dramatically. Such diversification was very popular in the 1980s. The companies involved and the stock market seemed to forget the huge catalogue of disasters in the history book. Of course, the exception proves the rule. I feel it is right to single out Hanson group as particularly successful at conglomerate diversification over the years. I hope it keeps fine for them and the others who seem to have the formula right.

Successful takeover activity requires a high level of professionalism. A company must: (a) assess the potential of a large range of candidates correctly. The number of assessments that turn into bids is usually small, and (b) be prepared to back down if the price becomes unrealistic. Megalomania has resulted in many acquisitions at ridiculous prices. Defining your maximum price and sticking to it is a rare and precious skill.

If you go down the takeover trail the short-term cost can be very high. In the longer term the payoff (for an excellent management team) can be attractive growth in earnings and share price.

Chapter 15
Any Other Business

You are nearing the end of a long but I hope valuable agenda. It is my final duty as chairman of the board to discuss any other business and to summarise our meeting. Four topic areas need to be discussed under any other business.

Corporation Tax

The legal minimisation of taxation liabilities is a highly specialised area. Financial directors of most businesses find it impossible to keep up to date with changes in tax legislation. They are prepared to pay significant fees to have the financial structure regularly examined for tax minimisation opportunities, and to ensure that any possible tax advantages or disadvantages associated with capital investment proposals, leasing, mergers and acquisitions etc. will be optimised.

The alternative is to permit tax planning to form part of the external audit. This can best be described as imprudent. The tax consultant is focused on what is the liability rather than what it might have been if the business had been structured for greater tax efficiency. Also, it is easier to design a tax efficient structure in advance than to restructure at a later date. The cost of quality tax planning is high but it can have a significant impact on shareholder wealth. The wise business will be prepared to pay the price.

Group Accounts

Section 150(1) of the Companies Act 1948 requires the presentation of group accounts to members of a holding company. The only exception is in section 150(2), where the holding company is at the end of its financial year the wholly-owned subsidiary of another body corporate incorporated in Great Britain. The preparation of group accounts involves the adding together of the financial results for the parent company and the subsidiaries. The rules of consolidation are explained in SSAP 14. These can be summarised as follows:

1   Transactions between group companies are excluded. Only sales, costs, assets and liabilities that relate to third party transactions are included. Items that need to be adjusted include:
    (a)   Supply of goods or services to other subsidiary companies;
    (b)   Purchase of goods or services from other subsidiary companies;
    (c)   Amounts owed to or from other subsidiary companies; and
    (d)   Inter-subsidiary service charges and dividends.
2   Profits legitimately recognised in the accounts of individual subsidiaries, but which have not been realised on sale to third parties must be eliminated. Stock value must be reduced to recognise: the lower profit by increasing the cost of sales in the profit and loss account; and the cost (or net realisable value, if lower) to the group in the balance sheet.
3   The cost of the acquisition (stated in the investing company balance sheet) must be eliminated against the shareholders' funds of the subsidiary in which the investment is made. This was dealt with in Chapter 14 (accounting for mergers and acquisitions).
4   Where the subsidiary is not wholly owned:
    (a)   The full assets and liabilities, after adjusting for items 1 to 3 above, will be aggregated in the group balance sheet and the minority interest in the net assets recognisd as a long-term debt; and
    (b)   The full sales, costs and profits, after adjusting for items 1 to 3 above, will be aggregated in the group profit and loss account and the minority interest in the profit after tax and dividends must be added to the long-term debt in the group balance sheet.
5   Accounts for individual group companies may use accounting policies different from the group. The accounts must be adjusted to ensure uniformity of accounting policies in the group accounts.
6   Wherever practicable the financial satements of all subsidiaries should be prepared to the same accounting date and for identical accounting periods as the holding company.

A 60% investment in Baba Ltd was acquired by Dada Plc one year ago for £870,000. The revenue reserves of Baba Ltd were £500,000 at that date. The following balance sheets and profit and loss accounts show how these rules are applied in acquisition accounting:

Balance Sheets (£'000)

	Dada Plc	Baba Ltd	Group
Tangible fixed assets			
Cost	5,000	1,000	6,000
Aggregate depreciation[1]	2,000	300	2,400
	3,000	700	3,600
Investment in Baba Ltd[2]	870		
Current assets			
Stock[3]	1,800	700	2,585
Debtors	2,500	800	3,300
Loan to parent[4]		300	
Cash	800	100	900
	5,100	1,900	6,785
Payable in under one year			
Bank overdrafts	300	600	900
Trade creditors	1,200	400	1,600
Loan from Baba Ltd[4]	200	–	–
	(1,700)	(1,000)	(2,500)
Net assets	7,270	1,600	7,885
Financed by:			
Share capital[6]	5,000	1,000	5,000
Revenue reserve[5,6]	2,270	600	2,285
Minority interest[6]	–	–	600
	7,270	1,600	7,885

Note: The various footnotes are covered in the following discussion.

Baba Ltd sent goods costing £75,000 to Papa Plc. It charged £100,000. The goods have not been received or included in the accounts of Papa Plc. The fixed assets of both companies are two years old. Depreciation is 20% straight line in Papa Plc and the group. Baba Ltd charges 15% straight line.

Note 1: The aggregate depreciation of Baba Ltd must be increased

424

by £100,000. One-half of this relates to last year and must be charged against the pre-acquisition profits. The balance relates to this year.

Note 2: The investment in Baba Ltd is eliminated as follows:

	Papa Plc.	Minority	Total
Share capital	600	400	1,000
Revenue reserve	300	200	500
Depreciation adjusted	(30)	(20)	(50)
Eliminated	870		
Credited to minority		580[6]	1,450

Note 3: The goods sold by Baba Ltd must be taken into stock in Papa Plc. The cost is determined by dividing the sale into two parts:

£'000	Inter Group	Minority	Total
Sale	60	40	100
Unrealised profit	15	–	15[4]
Stock Papa Plc	45	40	85[4]

Note 4: The intercompany accounts are adjusted as follows:

£'000	Papa Plc	Baba Ltd
Per company accounts	200	300
Add stock[3]	85	
Less unrealised profit	–	15
Cancelled creditor	285	
Cancelled debtor		285

Note 5: The group revenue reserve is:

£'000	Group	Papa Plc		Baba Ltd.
Per company accounts		2,270		600
Les pre-acquisiition		–		500
		2,270		100
Less depreciation			50	
unrealised profit		–	15[3]	65
		2,270		35
Minority		–		20
Balance sheet	2,285	2,270		15

The minority shareholders are interested in 40% of the profits of Baba Ltd. Since they sold 40% of the stock to Papa Plc at the full price their claim is £40,000 from Baba Ltd. Because Papa Plc increased the depreciation charge of Baba Ltd by £50,000 the claim on the group is £20,000.

Note 6: The minority interest is:

	£'000
At acquisition	580[2]
Post-acquisition	20[7]
	600

Note 7:

£'000		Group	Minority
Profit as per Baba Ltd	100		
Less depreciation adjustment	50		
	50		
Allocated to minority 40%	(20)		20
Less unrealised stock[3]	(15)	15	

426

Profit and Loss Account £'000

	Papa Plc	Baba Ltd	Group
Sales	10,000	3,000	12,900
Opening stock	1,600	500	2,100
Purchases	7,100[a]	2,000	9,000[7]
	8,700	2,500	11,100
Closing stock	1,900[a]	700	2,585[3]
Cost of sales	6,800	1,800	8,515
Gross margin	3,200	1,200	4,385
Administration	800	470	1,270
Selling and distribution	750	426	1,176
Depreciation	1,000	150	1,200
	2,550	1,046	3,646
Profit before tax	650	154	739
Corporation tax	228	54	282
Profit after tax	422	100	457
Minority	–	–	20
Retained	422	100	437
Opening reserve	1,848	–	1,848
Closing reserve	2,270	100	2,285

[a] The purchases and closing stock of Papa Plc are adjusted to reflect the full cost of the goods in transit from Baba Ltd in its own profit and loss account.
[7] The intercompany purchase/sale of £100,000 is not a third party transaction. It is eliminated from the group purchases and sales. The valuation of stock in transit at £85,000 excludes the inter-group profit other than the minority share. The group gross margin is therefore £15,000 less than the sum of the individual companies.

Finance Leases

A finance lease is one in which the user of a leased asset bears substantially all of the risks and rewards consistent with ownership. It should be presumed that this is the case, when at the inception of the lease, the present value of the minimum lease payments, including any

427

initial payment, amounts to substantially all (normally 90% or more) of the fair value of the leased asset. The present value should be calculated by using the interest rate implicit in the lease. The methodology for calculating present value is described in Chapter 12.

When a finance lease is commenced, the lessee (user of the asset) records the item, both as an asset (which will be depreciated in line with normal accounting policy) and as a liability (broken into current and non-current components). This treatment, introduced in August 1984, is interesting. The lessor is the legal owner of the asset. The asset is not recorded in the lessor's balance sheet, because what is really owned is a stream of future payments from the lessee. The lessee is not the owner. The leased item is nevertheless recorded as a leased fixed asset.

Whether the lease proves profitable or not, the lessee will have the use of a depreciating asset, with an ongoing earnings potential and obligations to repay instalments to the lessor which are very similar to those arising under a term loan or hire purchase agreement. There are two major reasons for this treatment:

1 The balance sheets of financial institutions were becoming silly. They showed many tangible fixed assets suited to lessees' needs rather than banks' needs. SSAP 21 is designed to reflect their 'true' asset, a stream of future cash in the lessor's balance sheet.
2 The balance sheets of lessees did not reveal the scale of future repayment obligations, implicit in their finance leases. This was off-balance sheet finance. SSAP 21 was the first step by the Accounting Standards Committee to try to cope with the problem.

The following tables show how the balance sheet of a company using a financial lease compares with that of a term borrower. The data for the tables is as follows:

A Alpha Ltd wishes to acquire a machine which will cost £1 million.
B Alpha is quoted £437,977 per annum for three years repayable in arrears. It can be arranged as a term loan or a finance lease. An interest rate of 15% is involved in both quotations.
C The machine will have a three-year operating life. It is expected to have a disposal value of £1.
D A profit before interest and depreciation of £700,000 is expected to be earned from using the machine.
E Corporation tax is ignored.

Schedule of Lease Repayments

Year	Loan	Interest	Repaid	Loan	Current	Non
1	1,000,000	150,000	−437,977	712,023	331,174	380,849
2	712,023	106,803	−437,977	380,849	380,849	−
3	380,849	57,127	−437,976	−	−	

Lessee Balance Sheet (Extract)

Year	0	1	2	3
Machine	1,000,000	1,000,000	1,000,000	1,000,000
Depreciation	−	333,333	666,666	999,999
Book value	1,000,000	666,667	333,334	1
Cash[1]	−	262,023	524,046	786,070
	1,000,000	928,690	857,380	786,071
Financed by:				
Retained profit[2]	−	216,667	476,531	786,071
Lease current	287,977	331,174	380,849	−
Lease non-current	712,023	380,849	−	−
	1,000,000	928,690	857,380	786,071

[1] Cash Balances

	Y1	Y2	Y3
Opening cash	−	262,023	524,046
Profit	700,000	700,000	700,000
	700,000	962,023	1,224,046
Repayment	437,977	437,977	437,976
Closing cash	262,023	524,046	786,070

[2] Retained Profit

	Y1	Y2	Y3
Pre-interest and depreciation	700,000	700,000	700,000
Less depreciation	(333,333)	(333,333)	(333,333)
finance charge	(150,000)	(106,803)	(57,127)
Profit year	216,667	259,864	309,540
Cumulative	216,667	476,531	786,071

429

The figures would be exactly the same if the asset was being acquired with term loan finance, except for the labelling of the debt. Prior to SSAP 21 the asset and the underlying borrowings would not have been included in the balance sheet. The figures would have been produced as follows:

Lessee Balance Sheet (Extract)

	Y0	Y1	Y2	Y3
Cash[1]	–	262,023	524,046	786,070
Financed by: Retained profit[1]	–	262,023	524,046	786,070

[1] The cash flows are the same as the retained profits. This is because the lease repayments are treated as a running expense, instead of the depreciation and interest charges that cause them.

This results in an earlier recognition of profit:

	Y1	Y2	Y3	Total
Lease depreciation	333,333	333,333	333,333	999,999
Lease interest	150,000	106,803	57,127	313,930
	483,333	440,136	390,460	1,313,929
Lease repayment	437,977	437,977	437,976	1,313,930
Change in charges	45,356	2,159	(47,516)	(1)
SSAP 21 profit	216,667	259,864	309,540	786,071
Pre-SSAP 21 profit	262,023	262,023	262,024	786,070
Cumulative profit	262,023	524,046	786,070	

If the company was liable to corporation tax at 35% on its profit the figures would have to be revised as follows:

Term Borrower Balance Sheet (Extract)

	0	1	2	3
Machine	1,000,000	1,000,000	1,000,000	1,000,000
Depreciation	–	333,333	666,666	999,999
Book value	1,000,000	666,667	333,334	1
Deferred tax		29,167	80,209	
Cash[1]	–	262,023	419,046	539,076
	1,000,000	957,857	832,589	539,077
Financed by:				
Retained profit[2]	–	140,834	309,746	510,946
Corporation tax[3]		105,000	141,994	28,131
Debt current	287,977	331,174	380,849	–
Debt non-current	712,023	380,849	–	–
	1,000,000	957,857	832,589	539,077

Cash Balances	Y1	Y2	Y3
Opening cash	–	262,023	419,046
Profit	700,000	700,000	700,000
	700,000	962,023	1,119,046
Corporation tax		(105,000)	(141,994)
Repayment	(437,977)	(437,977)	(437,976)
Closing cash	262,023	419,046	539,076

[2] *Retained Profit*	Y1	Y2	Y3
Pre interest and depreciation	700,000	700,000	700,000
Less depreciation	(333,333)	(333,333)	(333,333)
Interest	(150,000)	(106,803)	(57,127)
Pre tax profit	216,667	259,864	309,540
Corporation tax[3]	(105,000)	(141,994)	(28,131)
Deferred tax	29,167	51,042	(80,209)
Profit year	140,834	168,912	201,200
Cumulative	140,834	309,746	510,946

[3] *Corporation Tax*	Y1	Y2	Y3
Pre tax profit	216,667	259,864	309,540
Add depreciation	333,333	333,333	333,333
	550,000	593,197	642,873
Less writing down allowance[a]	250,000	187,500	562,500
Taxable profit	300,000	405,697	80,373
Corporation tax (35%)	105,000	141,994	28,131

431

ᵃ Writing Down Allowance	Y1	Y2	Y3
Cost/balance forward	1,000,000	750,000	562,500
Balancing allowance			562,500
WDA (25%)	250,000	187,500	
Balance forward	750,000	562,500	

⁴ Deferred Tax	Y1	Y2	Y3
Depreciation	333,333	333,333	333,333
WDA	250,000	187,500	
Balancing Allowance	–	–	562,499
Deferrable	83,333	145,833	(229,166)
Deferred at 35%	29,167	51,042	(80,209)
Deferred tax balance	29,167	80,209	–

The figures would be slightly different if the asset was being acquired under a finance lease, complying with SSAP 21:

SSAP 21 Lessee Balance Sheet (Extract)

	Y0	Y1	Y2	Y3
Machine	1,000,000	1,000,000	1,000,000	1,000,000
Depreciation	–	333,333	666,666	999,999
Book value	1,000,000	666,667	333,334	1
Deferred tax⁴		15,875	16,630	–
Cash¹	–	262,023	432,338	602,654
	1,000,000	944,565	782,302	602,655
Financed by:				
Retained profit²	–	140,834	309,745	510,947
Corporation tax⁴	–	91,708	91,708	91,708
Debt current	287,977	331,174	380,849	–
Debt non-current	712,023	380,849	–	–
	1,000,000	944,565	782,302	602,655

¹ Cash Balances	Y1	Y2	Y3
Opening cash	–	262,023	432,338
Profit	700,000	700,000	700,000
	700,000	962,023	1,132,338
Corporation tax Repayment	(437,977)	(91,708) (437,977)	(91,708) (437,976)
Closing cash	262,023	432,338	602,654

432

[a] *Retained Profit*	*Y1*	*Y2*	*Y3*
Pre-interest and			
depreciation	700,000	700,000	700,000
Less depreciation	(333,333)	(333,333)	(333,333)
Finance charge	(150,000)	(106,803)	(57,127)
Pre-tax profit	216,667	259,864	309,540
Corporation tax[3]	(91,708)	(91,708)	(91,708)
Deferred tax[4]	15,875	755	(16,630)
Profit year	140,834	168,911	201,202
Cumulative	140,834	309,745	510,947

[3] *Corporation Tax*	*Y1*	*Y2*	*Y3*
Pre-tax profit	216,667	259,864	309,540
Add finance charge	150,000	106,803	57,127
Depreciation	333,333	333,333	333,333
	700,000	700,000	700,000
Lease instalment	437,977	437,977	437,976
Taxable profit	262,023	262,023	262,024
Corporation tax (35%)	91,708	91,708	91,708

Leasing is treated as follows for corporation tax purposes: The depreciation and finance charge are disallowed in the lessee's tax computation. The lease payments are deducted in calculating the tax liability. The lessor is allowed the writing down allowances as a tax deduction and is charged to tax on the lease instalments. These rules are a continuation of the tax treatment that applied to leases prior to SSAP 21.

[4] *Deferred Tax*	*Y1*	*Y2*	*Y3*
Finance charge	150,000	106,803	57,127
Depreciation	333,333	333,333	333,333
	483,333	440,136	390,460
Lease instalment	437,977	437,977	437,976
Deferrable	45,356	2,159	(47,516)
Deferred tax (35%)	15,875	755	(16,630)
Deferred tax balance	15,875	16,630	–

The cost of lease instalments, having been allowed as a deduction for corporation tax and being the same in total as the depreciation and finance charges, gives rise to a deferred tax adjustment to eliminate timing differences.

A Different Treatment for Operating Leases

An operating lease is one which does not transfer substantially all the risks and rewards of ownership of an asset to the lessee. If it is clear that, after netting out the finance charge, less than 90% of the capital cost is repaid through the life of the lease, then it is an operating lease. Operating leases are treated as follows: the asset remains in the

433

balance sheet of the lessor and is not included in the balance sheet of the lessee. The lease instalments are taxable in the hands of the lessor and allowed as a deductible expense in computing the tax liability of the lessee.

Because of this treatment, future repayment obligations could be concealed by using an operating lease. SSAP 21 makes certain this will not happen. The user of an asset under an operating lease is required to disclose:

1 The operating lease rentals in its profit and loss account.
2 In the notes attached to the balance sheet the payments that it is committed to make in future years, analysed between those in which the commitment expires within that year, in the second to fifth years inclusive and over five years from the balance sheet date. An intelligent examination of the notes to the balance sheet will enable a reader to understand the scale of operating lease activities and the ongoing repayment obligations involved. A simple example of an operating lease is a five year lease on an aeroplane: (a) the lessee could expect to pay far less than 90% of the capital cost over the lease period. The life of an aircraft is perhaps 20 years; and (b) the lessor takes most of the risks and rewards consistent with ownership, by having to locate a lessee or purchaser for the asset on expiry of the operating lease.

The last item on the agenda is to summarise the meeting. I have decided to do this by tracing our way through the life of a business. I will trace your way through it as if it was a person. There are five stages.

The Life of a Business

Business Infancy

It is a frightening fact that the majority of new businesses in the UK die in infancy. Some of the reasons for the mortality have a strong financial dimension:
1 The promoter starts business life with too little capital.
2 The first year sales forecast is too optimistic: product returns and rejects; slow to get widespread customer acceptance.
3 Necessary tangible fixed assets are overlooked.
4 Running expenses are underestimated: spoilage, rework etc.; costs the promoter overlooked.
5 High financing costs. It is unfortunately true that to borrow money is much cheaper and easier for a large and stable business than a

fledgling. Not alone are interest rates higher (understandable because the risk is usually greater), but also some of the cheapest sources are closed to the infant. The most expensive legitimate sources include: hire purchase; leasing; factoring debts; bill and invoice discounting; instalment payment schemes (e.g. insurance); and bridging loans. The most economic sources include:

(a) Authorised supplier credit. It is well worth the promoter's time to negotiate good supplier credit terms as John Bermingham did in Chapter 2;

(b) Customer deposits and cash with order or on delivery sales. The business that can get these starts life with a decided edge; and

(c) Additional equity capital. Most new business promoters want to own 100% of their fast growing infant. This is fine if it can be properly controlled, like any child. For many infant businesses the right thing to do is to give away a sizeable stake in the company before conception or early in life. There are five major sources:

   (i) An active partner. Ideally with different skills and experience from the promoter.

   (ii) A sleeping partner. Ideally with strong skills in areas where the promoter is deficient,

   (iii) A venture capital injection. It is difficult to attract venture capital before startup even in state of the art technology. The more mundane business must wait until a track record is established. The major advantages are opening doors to cheap sources of finance, strong board representation, and conservation of cash. The investor is seeking capital appreciation not dividends.

   (iv) Business Expansion Scheme Equity. The advantages are similar to venture capital. The BES may give the promoter more freedom than a venture capitalist, and

   (v) Equity investment by a key supplier or customer. They know the industry well and often provide specialised help at little or no cost.

I strongly recommend that the infant business adopt one of these equity sources. It will enable the business to grow more rapidly. Growth leads to sturdy adulthood and an opportunity to buy back the equity.

6 Failure to provide funds to meet the working capital needs of a fast growth business. Much was said about overtrading in Chapter 7. The partnership (point five) can provide the funds for expansion.

7 The business can't afford professional managers. The owner puts urgent priorities on the long finger. Financial priorities include: preparation of management accounts; review and revision of cash

forecasts; managing suppliers and bankers; and identifying and claiming grant aid. The partnership can overcome this problem by ensuring that there are two senior staff to perform key tasks.

Childhood

If and when the infant survives to school days it will have to learn to cope with a whole new set of problems.

1 Only one string to it bow (product). Any business that is totally dependent on one product line is likely to be pressured to diversify and spread the risk.
2 But the child has not been able to save the money it will need for product or market diversification.
3 The promoter has been too busy surviving to keep up to date with industry technology and changing customer needs.
4 The child has grown big enough to be a thorn in the side of important competitors. They use price wars, extended credit and other dirty tricks to spank it.
5 A local financial engineer wants to play with the toys and mounts an unwanted takeover bid. The child neglects the business while protecting itself.
6 A major customer knows that the child is terribly dependent on its orders. It demands large discounts and overextended credit.
7 The business has grown to a size where to manage all the priorities is becoming too much for the child (ambitions to be world champion in five different sports). The wise promoter will bring in the gang (professional managers). The trouble is that they want to play different games and he won't let them. If they are good they leave and play elsewhere. If they are not good they stay and keep the company stuck in a groove.
8 The Revenue Commissioners realise that the child is 'rich'. They take away 33% of its new toys each year. The 'selfish' child wants these toys to play expansion, research and other games.

The child is so depressed by this treadmill that it wished it just went to school and played like most of the other kids. The analogy I used is sadly true for most youthful businesses. A minority manage to break through the clouds to a high flying and enjoyable teenage. How do they do it? The answer is two words: Planning and people. It sounds simple and obvious and it is.

Managers can be classified into firefighters and planners. The firefighters spend all their time trying to combat the latest problems (some trivial). The planners try to anticipate problems before they occur and take steps to avoid them.

PLANNING

Many of the problems that people experience through their lives can be traced back to their formative years. It is the same with young businesses. Top quality planning from the outset can help to overcome many of the childhood problems we outlined above. The following are some of the key elements.

The business should plan from the beginning to create substantial retained earnings. These are needed to:

(a)   Finance the cost of the search for new products or services;

(b)   Contribute towards funding the introduction of a suitable product or service when it is located;

(c)   Strengthen the equity base in case an unwanted takeover bid has to be defended;

(d)   Fight a price or discount war mounted by a large competitor; and

(e)   Permit the recruitment of managers for marketing, finance and other functions when required.

The promoter must plan for sufficient time to identify problems and find ways of avoiding them rather than waiting until they occur and winding up in a crisis treadmill. This is easier to say than do. The natural instinct of the child (promoter) is to defend itself against the current crisis and put planning for tomorrow on the long finger. It requires a very special kind of experience and dedication to ensure that high quality planning is not sacrificed on the altar of firefighting.

PEOPLE

Friends have a very important role in shaping a child in its formative years. The sensible child recognises that many things occur in business which are difficult to handle due to lack of previous experience. One way of coping effectively with this is to identify a mentor who is available to advise the business when important issues arise. The mentor is often a person related to the promoter who is prepared to spend time exploring issues and providing second opinions. The effective mentor has three vital qualities: a wide knowledge of business issues; a network of people who can be tapped for specialised advice on key matters at little or no cost; and financial independence which will allow him or her to advise the business without charging a lot for the service.

Such people are difficult to find. One must be located and cultivated. If a suitable mentor is not available within the family the promoter can use a suitable sleeping partner, venture capitalist or other investor but they usually expect to be well paid.

If the planning and people issues are properly managed the business can look forward to an enjoyable childhood. Issues that the mentor can provide important help with include capital project appraisal, corporation tax management, stock market flotation, and market and product diversification.

The Teens

It may take less than 13 years for a business to reach its teens. This period usually involves an introduction to courtship. The wise promoter will be anxious to avoid the danger of an undesirable marriage (merger). The promoter usually uses a merchant bank to advise on a suitable partner. Many of the important issues in planning a suitable marriage were explained in Chapter 14. If the discussions and negotiations lead to a merger or acquisition, family financial reporting (group accounts) will have arrived. A brief summary of the important issues involved in group accounting was presented under Group Accounts in this chapter.

Adulthood

The business is now mature. A new set of responsibilities are in place. As a parent it must protect its children (the employees and shareholders). Many of the risks that were taken as a child are no longer acceptable. Strangely many adult businesses make decisions which are inconsistent with responsible parenthood. These include leveraged buyouts, speculation in currency, commodity and interest rate futures, conglomerate diversification, and financial engineering.

The responsible parent needs to put two vital control mechanisms in place:

1　Excellent control systems to ensure that managers cannot commit the organisation to major initiatives which could endanger its very survival if they go wrong. These would involve a limitation on authority to undertake capital investment, foreign currency transactions, tax-based leasing etc. without approval from the board of directors.
2　A board of directors with the skills, experience and authority to stop decisions being made which could put the business at risk. They must be prepared to stop proposals by senior executives where necessary.

Old Age

An objective of a business should be to never reach old age. The characteristics to be avoided if the secret of eternal youth is to be found and applied are:

438

1   An ageing management team, set in its ways and resistant to change.
2   A portfolio of products that have passed the peak of their lifecycle.
3   Plant and machinery that is not capable of competing with the most modern competitor equipment.
4   Overdependence on reputation and lack of attention to quality of product or service.
5   A bureaucratic corporate climate that discourages entrepreneurial flair and over-rewards safe behaviour.

The key ways of overcoming the malaise of corporate old age are:

1   A planned approach to management succession. This involves retraining, recruitment, promotions etc.
2   A target to replace at least 10% in value of group sales with new products or services each year.
3   Adherence to the guideline in Chapter 6 that the expenditure on tangible fixed assets should average at least one-and-a-half times the depreciation charge.
4   A constant updating of key staff through contact with customers, competitors, development agencies etc.
5   A rewards system (salaries, profit sharing, share options, fringe benefits and so on) that recognises the contribution of the old stagers whose key role is often defensive and the 'young bloods' whose creative and entrepreneurial spirit will maintain the pace of modernisation if constructively controlled.

Summary of the Meeting

1   All my staff must fully understand the financial consequences of the business decisions in which they are involved.
2   It is unlikely that you will remember all the applications we encountered during this meeting.
3   So I exhort you to keep the minutes in your office and refer to them when important financial decisions are on the agenda for future management or board meetings.
4   Don't forget that, no matter how carefully you studied the minutes, the pressures of business life will allow key issues to slip into oblivion unless you find time to practise applying them.
5   The world is changing rapidly. Major changes in accounting and finance will undoubtedly take place in this decade. To keep up with the pace of change you need to:
● Read the business page of a quality newspaper every day;

- Keep wide awake for new financial issues mentioned by accountants, bankers etc. at board meetings; and
- Never be afraid to ask questions about things you don't understand. Your colleagues probably don't understand them either!

Good luck in applying the things you learned in this book.

Ray Fitzgerald
June 1992

Index

441